IMAGINARY CITIES

Darran Anderson

Influx Press, London

Published by Influx Press

Office 3A, Mill Co. Project

Unit 3, Gaunson House

Markfield Road, London, N15 4QQ

www.influxpress.com

First published 2015.

Printed and bound in the UK by Clays Ltd.,
St Ives plc.

ISBN: 978-0992765590

To Christiana, Caspian and the future.

Contents

The Turk 441

Flotsam and Jetsam 545

IMAGINARY CITIES

Darran Anderson

Cities, like dreams, are made of desires and fears, even if the thread of their discourse is secret, their rules are absurd, their perspectives deceitful, and everything conceals something else.

— Italo Calvino, *Invisible Cities*

The Men of a Million Lies, or How We Imagine the World

Plato's Cinema

Before there were films, there was cinema; the flickering shadow play of fire and motion on limestone cave walls. We might assume the paintings the more bohemian troglodytes smudged with charcoal and ochre were simply representational, charting exaggerated auroch kills. What then of the oldest symbol archaeologists have found? A simple red disc carbon-dated to 40, 800 years ago, in the depths of Cueva de El Castillo, Cantabria. Was it the infernal crucible of our sun? It was logical for the life-giving ball of magnetic fields and plasma to be worshipped, before mankind's act of folly and vanity in creating gods in its simian image. In the thousands of years to follow, the descendants of the cave-artists would depict on stone, clay, bone, bamboo, wood, papyrus, wax, fabric, slate, paper and pixels, everything that existed beneath that sun; what is and, most crucially for our purposes here, what might be.

Consider, however, that red disc as something else entirely. We view the existence of everything bound by relativity. There is no escape from context. The eye, and its position, is the fulcrum on which the entire visible universe pivots. When the artist ventured into the caverns to leave a circular mark on eternity, he or she may well have been painting the singularity that is the pupil of a human eye. Interpretation is everything. Perhaps in the half-light, the artists, as much pattern-seeking mammals as we are, painted not simply what they'd seen but what they'd hallucinated or dreamt, in some kind of desperate prophecy or ceremonial magic. Humanity has always looked for the dubious reassurance of auguries and, through wishful thinking and pareidolia, has continually found threats of danger and promises of treasure. Might we have envisaged then what was to come? A floating city on a shimmering horizon. Minarets in frost. A Neolithic painter dreaming of skyscrapers.

Darkness is misconceived as nothingness; rather it is a state of 'intrinsic light', within which a great deal of visual information may be discerned; a catalyst for the unintentional creative process known as 'prisoner's cinema'[1]. 'If you want to know how much darkness there is around you, you must sharpen your eyes, peering at the faint lights in the distance.'[2] Whether hallucinations in the dark are a source of torment or liberation, or both, is down to the viewer. Banished to the bowels of the

---

1   *Hallucinations*, Oliver Sacks, Pg. 33-34

2   From Italo Calvino's *Invisible Cities*, a book by a literary master to which this book is a diminished non-fiction mirror.

Earth, Milton's fallen archangel Lucifer declares, 'The mind is its own place, and in itself / Can make a heaven of hell, a hell of heaven.'[3] It can walk through walls or be imprisoned by the sky.

3   *Paradise Lost*, lines 254-255

The Deceptions of Memory

In 1296, the middle-aged Marco Polo found himself inconveniently in prison. He had been captured in the Eastern Mediterranean at the helm of a Venetian galley by rival sailors from the Most Serene Republic of Genoa. Given that the two republics were locked in the War of Saint Sabas, this was inopportune, especially given he had a siege catapult onboard. Polo's fortunes improved however when he discovered his cellmate was a writer, Rustichello of Pisa, who was an enthusiastic listener to Polo's tall-tales of voyages in the mysterious Orient. This was good luck as it made Polo's fame. It was bad luck for the very same reason.

Initially written as a guide for budding merchants, the asides and tangents that made up the quartet of books 'Description of the World' were fascinating yet scarcely believable. They quickly became immensely popular yet they earned Polo the cruel nickname 'Il Millione' ('the man of a million lies'). It was doubted by some that he'd even travelled at all except around his own vast imagination[45].

The accounts did however contain many genuine discoveries alongside exaggerations, half-truths and myths ('How the Prayer

4   A mirror text to Polo's is Xavier Maiestre's *Journey Across My Room*, in which a prison cell is transformed into vast expanses. In a world of far more deceptive untruths, there are few historical figures as 'unjustly mocked' as Polo, as Baudelaire put it in *On Wine and Hashish*.

5   Another theory places Polo in Persia for years borrowing tales from travelling merchants, as suggested Pg. 6 *Marco Polo's Le Devisement Du Monde: Narrative Voice, Language and Diversity* by Simon Gaunt

of the One-Eyed Cobbler Caused the Mountain to Move'[6] for example) mixed together without differentiation. We can now pour scorn on his claims of desert Sirens, colossal elephant-eating birds, idolatrous sorcerers who could control sandstorms, or witnessing Noah's Ark perched on a snow-bound mountaintop. At the time, these were scarcely more unbelievable than his claims of stones that ignite, paper currency, seeing the highest mountains in the world or visiting golden cities draped with the finest silks. In an age when travel took months, even years, myths abounded in the land between cities. The further away, the wilder the myths, and Polo had traversed the known world[7].

Polo's travelogue notes many curious cities on his winding road (Baudas, Samarcan, Caracoron) culminating in the opulent palaces of the Chinese Mongol Emperor Kublai Khan, at whose court he was guest for seventeen years. The explorer's recollections range from the mercantile (lists of industries and natural resources) to the fanciful; cities where the inhabitants are perpetually drunk, where men eat birds and ride around on stags, where marriages are arranged between ghosts, and the lord in his marble palace drinks wine from levitating goblets. Often Polo would add boasts, 'no one could imagine finer' recurs, and even suggest he was holding back for fear of arousing incredulity in the readers ('I will relate none of this in this book of ours; people would be amazed if they heard it, but it would serve no good purpose') which only served to further his ridicule.

6   *The Travels of Marco Polo*, translated by L. F. Benedetto, Pg. 30

7   Or at least that which was known to Western chroniclers.

Beyond their narrow confines, the world was more extraordinary than his sceptics could imagine. Raised in the seemingly-impossible floating city of Venice, a maze of canals and alleys built on stilts in a lagoon, Marco Polo had no such limitations. Imaginary cities posed no threat to a man who was born in one.

When a book leaves the protective custody of its creator, it is rightly at the mercy of its readers but also, if prominent enough, at the hands of those who have not read it. In the age before the printing press, Polo's tales spread largely through word of mouth, with cumulative error compounded by jealousies and speculations. The stories, already partially there, metamorphosed further into myth. To accuse Polo of inventing fictions is to assume that perception and memory are not partially fictional to begin with. 'I will have spent my life trying to understand the function of remembering,' the narrator in Chris Marker's *Sans Soleil* acknowledges, 'which is not the opposite of forgetting, but rather its lining. We do not remember. We rewrite memory much as history is rewritten.' Fragments of the real are retained, though they evolve with time to fit the wisdom or fallacy of hindsight and are juxtaposed with memories of dreams and thoughts and memories of memories. We are unreliable narrators even to ourselves.

Nostalgia is not what it used to be. In Terence Davies' *The Long Day Closes*, the director remembers a blissful, family tableau at Christmas, where an old streetlamp and snow appear within the living room. It did not strictly happen and yet there is no lie involved[8]. This streetlight occurs again and again, through the back of the wardrobe and into Narnia, the glow of light through Victorian London fog in Holmes and Jekyll, the impossible co-existence of night and day in Magritte's *The Empire of Lights* series[9]. By its ethereal light, things we think we know appear to change.

All great imaginary cities merge the matter-of-fact with the surreal. They are adrift in the skies but are, at least momentarily, anchored[10]. In the Chinese epic *Dream of the Red Chamber*, Cao Xueqin wrote 'Truth becomes fiction when the fiction's true / Real becomes not-real where the unreal's real.'[11]

It appears as an engraving on an arch leading to the Land of Illusion, but the traffic is not one-way. The state of ambiguity between real and unreal is still one we broach with a degree of hostility. Yet the border is a disputed one. Consider the way cities brand themselves; how the fictions of Meyrink, Kafka and Hašek were moulded by the versions of Prague they lived in and how that same city is now moulded by their fiction. Consider how, upon visiting, the mind turns to murderers haunting bridges[12]

8   *The Shape of Time: Remarks on the History of Things* by George Kubler shows us that time is much more complex and relativist than our linear way of thinking permits.

9   Bill Gold's iconic poster for *The Exorcist* was inspired too by the series.

10   See the legend of Clonmacnoise monastery when an otherworldly ship suddenly appeared and caught its anchor on an altar rail (as adapted in Seamus Heaney's *Lightenings*).

11   *The Dream of the Red Chamber: An Allegory of Love,* Jeannie Jinsheng Yi, cited Pg. 19

12   Scenes from Dostoevsky's *Crime and Punishment*, which in turn echo Gogol's earlier character Ivan Yakovlevich throwing The Nose from a bridge into the Neva.

in St. Petersburg, diabolical cats walking upright through Moscow[13], a Museum of Innocence[14] in Istanbul, Martian invaders stalking the streets of Woking[15] and any number of such tales.

On Bloomsday, Dublin celebrates its fictional recreation in a text dedicated to the day and the city in which Joyce had first courted his wife. City begets text begets city. Despite writing in continental exile for years, Joyce claimed 'I want to give a picture of Dublin so complete that if the city one day suddenly disappeared from the earth it could be reconstructed out of my book.'[16]

Perhaps it could be but it would be as much Joyce as Dublin. Joyce's father once remarked of his son, 'If that fellow was dropped in the middle of the Sahara, he'd sit, be-God, and make a map of it.'[17] The mapmaker would be partial myth-maker. Would such a place, with its semi-fictional characters, selective editing and bias of perspective(s) be accurate, a deception or simply how we subjectively inhabit all our cities? The truth is refracted through many prisms and our reflections are as true and as distorted as a hall of mirrors. All cities are subject to the Rashomon effect. Even the assumption that cities are simply settings falls short when considering architecture as narrative[18]

---

13   Bulgakov's *The Master and Margarita*, a street-sign warning for which now adorns Patriarch Ponds, Moscow.

14   This actual museum was created in Istanbul at the time of its fictional counterpart, both by Orhan Pamuk.

15   H.G. Wells' *The War of the Worlds*.

16   Cited in *Ulysses* by James Joyce, Jeri Johnson, Oxford World Classics

17   *Vico and Joyce*, Donald Phillip Verene, Pg. 84

18   Stories and interpretations often differ, hence the periodic clashes at shared holy sites in Jerusalem.

— the Avenue of Sphinxes at Luxor, the Churning of the Sea of Milk at Angkor Wat, Trajan's Column in Rome. In Victor Hugo's Notre Dame de Paris, Frollo claims the book will kill the building, 'Small things overcome great ones'[19]; an intriguing idea but one disproved by the fact that all cities can, and should, be read.

It would be foolish to deny the value of lying. Marco Polo was always destined to be accused because it's what the audience was prepared for. When faced with the blank space on the map, we turn to the fantastical. Consider not simply the sea serpents and 'here be dragons' on archaic maps but the casts of extraterrestrials with which we have populated distant planets in our age of reason. The creator of arguably the earliest surviving science fiction text (*True History*), Lucian of Samosata justified the honesty of dishonesty, a quality he shared with Polo (with a nod to Epimenides[20]), 'Many others, with the same intent, have written about imaginary travels and journeys of theirs, telling of huge beasts, cruel men and strange ways of living [. . .] my lying is far more honest than theirs, for though I tell the truth in nothing else, I shall at least be truthful in saying that I am a liar.'[21]

19   Pg. 146

20   The Cretan Epimenides stated, 'All Cretans are liars' and created the paradox that bears his name.

21   Lucien 2007, Pg. 4 as cited in Pg. 18 of *Travellers' Tales of Wonder: Chatwin, Naipaul, Sebald* by Simon Cooke

Cartography and the Canvas of White Spaces

Faced with vast swathes of land that revealed the extent of their ignorance, the powerful in Europe sought to fictitiously colonise areas they could not reach. It was an attempt at control and reassurance. Centuries before installing favourable dictators in client states, they did so with imaginary characters, one of whom would be name-checked by Polo. In 1165, the Byzantine Emperor Manuel I Komnenos received a letter purporting to be from the hitherto unknown court of one Presbyter Johannes, the self-anointed 'Lord of Lords'. It boasted of a kingdom to 'surpass all under heaven', which 'extends beyond India [. . .] towards the sunrise over the wastes, and it trends toward deserted Babylon near the Tower of Babel.'[22]

It boasted of housing a menagerie of creatures both scarcely-believable (elephants, rhinoceros etc.) and mythological ('griffins . . . men with horns . . . men with eyes before and behind, centaurs, fauns, satyrs . . . cyclopses'). The scribe spoke of the lands of the known world and how apocalyptic misfortunes would befall them. In Biblical fashion, revelations of utopias were defined by contrast with dystopias, 'Our land streams with honey and is overflowing with milk. In one region grows no poisonous herd, nor does a querulous frog ever quack in it; no scorpion exists, nor does the serpent glide amongst the grass, nor can any poisonous animals exist in it or injure anyone' (the aforementioned cyclopses and griffins presumably being

22   *Inventing the Enemy,* Umberto Eco, cited Pg. 159

tame). Yet, even in this early example, it is clear that utopias and dystopias are intertwined, 'With us, no one lies, for he who speaks a lie is thenceforth regarded as dead — he is no more thought of or honoured by us. No vice is tolerated by us.' We might consider the practicalities of a world where no lie is permitted or the possibility of pleasure in a world without vice (bar cannibalism oddly) and how such a heaven, or any heaven for that matter, could function in any way other than as a tyranny.

The standard life-giving rivers, boundless jewels and protective amulets follow, though there are intriguing flights of fancy in fire-dwelling, silk-spinning salamanders, a river of vanishing stones and an ocean of sand in which fish thrive. The central palace itself is the stuff of wonders or gaudy baroque horror: crystal windows, golden tables, ivory columns and twin golden-apple glitter-balls. Knights joust indoors, sliding on splayed panicking horses along floors of polished onyx. If the inhabitants are not sufficiently awed or cowed into obedience, there is a prototype telescreen at hand: 'Before our palace stands a mirror . . . guarded day and night by three thousand men. We look therein and behold all that is taking place in every province and region subject to our sceptre.' Such was the attraction of this innovation that it aided the rise of what became known as 'speculum literature', the surveillance and indexing of every aspect of life. To survey was to master.

At its most attractive, this desire to explore and to chart evolved into the fashion for *wunderkammer* or 'cabinets of curiosities'; deliberately eclectic assemblage of curios, from embalmed extinct birds to the tusks of narwhals. Many of these were inventions, whether explicitly — proto-surreal paintings by Bosch or Arcimbaldo for example, or deceptively — a desiccated dragon claw or the last bottled breath of Caesar. John Tradescant's Musaeum Tradescantium contained a mermaid's claw and a tree-grown goose. On occasion, they would report tantalising magical powers. In the case of the Cathay Chan mentioned in John de Mandeville's travels, there is both, with minstrels 'in divers' instruments . . . lions, leopards and other diverse beasts . . . and enchanters, that . . . make to come in the air . . . the sun and the moon to every man's sight.'[23]

These forgeries, tall-tales and wild (tree-grown) goose chases belong to a bygone age but *wunderkammers* eventually evolved into the museums of today (with a curious tangent in the travelling circus freak-show). The original intention of cabinets of curiosities was not simply to showcase oddities but to propagandise the vastness and diversity of the colonial realm and reinforce dominion[24]. It was also subconsciously an admission of the insecurity of the rulers in question. To chart and to collect is to attempt to control and to control is to doubt and fear.

The objects displayed in *wunderkammers* came with a smuggled form of revenge. Where they stood apart from or in opposition to conventional thinking, questions inevitably arose.

---

23   *The Travels of Sir John Mandeville*, Pg. 155

24   The African masks, Egyptian obelisks and Oriental carvings, and the journeys, crimes and intrigues that brought them to our capitals indicate the imperial motivation was slow to dissipate.

Where these threatened the carefully-assembled hierarchies of the court and the heavens, they were damned as heresies, but investigations and collections went on in private. Enquiring minds, rather than vainglorious emperors, began assembling their own wunderkammers and through their studies they began to notice not just the differences in these strange fossilised creatures and elements but their similarities. Magic gave way to science, alchemy to chemistry, divine design to natural selection. The world could no longer be contained in cabinets.

Faust the Imperial Architect

Cities where the Enlightenment flourished were portrayed by reactionaries as places of sinister black magic. Edinburgh became known for body-snatchers and split personalities, as if warning that this is where free enquiry leads. It was likewise no accident that the fictional city of Wüttemberg (part Cambridge, part Stuttgart) in Marlowe's *Doctor Faustus* is a university town[25]. Learning, in an age where it was the light to theocratic darkness, was to be feared and reviled because it threatened vested interests. Steam propulsion and the telegraph soon meant information could no longer be contained as it once was in fiefdoms, either regal or papal. If there was a Faustian moment, it was when these advances were applied to the conquering of land and peoples. Imperial urban planners attempted to recreate their capitals in lands ill-suited topographically and sociologically. Traces of these experiments can be seen in mouldering buildings from Cuba to Congo to Viet Nam, and in the recycled names of homesick settlers from New York[26] to New Zealand[27].

---

25   Though Marlowe had a much more subversive attitude towards the devil and those who make deals with him.

26   Before being named after the soon-to-be-deposed English King James II, New York bore the names New Angoulême, Rio de San Antonio and New Amsterdam.Manhattan survives from its original Algonquian inhabitants. All were futures not taken.

27   Dunedin comes from the bastardised Gaelic (meaning 'hill fort') name of the city that evolved into Edinburgh. Replicas can be found from Canada to Zimbabwe to Australia.

The waves rolled back. It was part of the fetishism of being a young European noble to undertake the Grand Tour through the remnants of Mediterranean antiquity. They would return with relics, new-found learning and the occasional exotic disease. They would also, in moods of quixotic nostalgia, attempt to recreate what they'd seen[28]. Orientalist follies began to be built not only in the secluded grounds (the Chinese pavilion at *l'isle-adam*) or private rooms of landed gentry (the Arab Hall of Leighton House and Chinese palace at Oranienbaum for example) but as birthday-cake phantasias on the promenades of the capitals and seaside resorts. When the faux-Moorish Morozov Mansion[29] was unveiled, the millionaire owner's mother turned to him in despair, 'Until now only I have known how much of a fool you are. Now the whole of Moscow will too.'[30]

At their best, the appropriations and approximations of other cultures gave birth to intriguingly mutated structures as in the flaring dragon-finned, and sadly unbuilt, temples of Hugo 'Fidus' Höppener, which look as if they could wrench their bones free of the streets, rise up and incinerate their surroundings. Gazebos and verandas appeared as fragments of the Tropics in countries scoured by Atlantic winds, rain, and quiet desperation. Bastardised Arabian and Asian

---

28   Or didn't see, as Kircher's alien obelisk depictions of the Pyramids of Giza
        attest, from *Sphinx Mystagoga* (1676).

29   Designed by Victor Mazyrin.

30   The house briefly became a base for anarchists and artists of Proletkult after the
        Revolution before their dissolution by the Bolsheviks (as covered in *Architecture
        and Revolution* ,edited by Neil Leach, Pg. 26 onwards).

facades, drained of context and meaning (or rather imbued with new unintended ones), were grafted onto existing structures. A fine example of the territorialising tendency was the Victorian adventure novel. 'I absolutely refuse to leave . . . ' Conan Doyle wrote in *The Lost World*, 'until we . . . are able to take back with us something in the nature of a chart.'[31]

Phileas Fogg's 80-day venture around the world may have begun as a bet in the Reform Club but it was also a ritualistic exercise in summarising the globe, bankrolled by Barings. There was always a sense of geographical and metaphysical conquering to even the most frivolous of japes. Phileas Fogg circumnavigates the globe so that London could symbolically possess it.

31   Pg. 95

The Dialectics of Inspiration

For all the deformities and thefts, creativity is fuelled by cultures clashing and creating hybrids that appear new, often by accident. It's a question of taste whether the result is an inauthentic grotesque or a Palladian masterpiece (the best are often both)[32]. Authenticity is in the eye of the beholder and it inevitably shifts and evolves according to perspective. We think of the ancient civilisations as starting points, yet the Parthenon mimicked that which came long before (the Temple of Hatshepsut predates it by a thousand years). Even the architectural fashion of kitsch is ancient, with the Romans importing mock pyramids after the conquest of Egypt.[33]

It need not be a judgement to state that artists are thieves, or as Gaudí more eloquently put it, 'Man does not create, he discovers.'[34] Culture is an echo chamber and even the most original of thinkers are prone, consciously or subconsciously, to kleptomania. This is not a problem except to the pedantic, the insecure and the territorial. It is simply a question of absorption. 'Gaudí's version of art nouveau was highly inclusive, even cannibalistic,' Charles Jencks wrote, 'it swallowed Moorish elements . . . Gothic motifs . . . it borrowed nature's plants and animals . . . early Cubist advertisements. There wasn't a

---

32   What native cultures think of appropriations is rarely recorded but worth uncovering.

33   The Pyramid of Cestius stands in Rome to this day.

34   Casanelles 1967, Pg. 13

communicational mode Gaudí didn't use at least once.'[35]   The results are unlike almost any other architect even though the ingredients are available to all. Any sins are absolved by quality. It's Gaudí's imagination but what, we might ask, risking an unweaving of the rainbow[36], was that imagination constructed from?

To the sweltering imperial clerk or soldier, it seems a comfort to inhabit something resembling home. These buildings began akin to the forts of frontiers people in the Americas and South Africa, where a pretence of the lifestyles of old could be maintained in alien surroundings. Outposts in the homelands of others, they would soon fall prey to an encroaching siege mentality. The urge for a refuge in the supposed wilds came long before homesteaders. The fabled medieval African empire of Prester John is a reassuringly Christian arcadia, both familiar and different. It was closer however to those French colonial posters of Indochine; the glorious stone somnambulists of Bayon luring the adventurous and credulous to slow death by malaria and paperwork in a pestilential heat. Prester John, his cities and his empire were, of course, fabrications; created perhaps by a listless travelling salesman, a Silk Route bandit, a hermit fantasist or a Byzantine courtier requiring a distraction for some indiscretion. Myths however are magnetic and gradually Prester John began to assimilate aspects of other stories. He became a descendant of one of the Three Magi, the vanquisher

---

35   *What is Post Modernism?*, Charles Jencks, Pg. 98

36   Keats' dinner party remark on the 28th December 1817 regarding Newton's discoveries.

of the giants Gog and Magog, the seducer of Amazons. Some truth seeped dangerously into the narrative. Crusaders in the Middle East heard reports that the grandson of Prester John had amassed forces and was advancing from the East to help them defeat the Saracens. In reality, the army that was galloping their way was Genghis Khan's 'devil's horsemen'[37]. It was into such a milieu of mistruths and wild speculations that Polo's tales were borne. He was accordingly laughed at and mocked, except by those who knew that empires follow explorers; those who dreamed of storming those oriental cities, imaginary or otherwise.

37   James Chambers, 2003

In Morphia Veritas

Five hundred years after they were written, Marco Polo's accounts of his time at the summer residence of Kublai Khan found their way indirectly to the poet Samuel Taylor Coleridge through their inclusion in the book *Purchas's Pilgrimage*. 'In Xamdu did Cublai Can build a stately palace . . . ' went the passage, 'a sumptuous house of pleasure, which may be removed from place to place.'[38] Having read the sequence whilst convalescing on an Exmoor farm and 'in consequence of a slight indisposition'[39], Coleridge administered himself with enough laudanum (a potent cocktail of opium and alcohol) to fall into a three-hour sleep, or a state of hypnagogia, in which he dreamt of witnessing first-hand the palace at Xanadu. Coleridge awoke with an entire epic poem formed in his mind. He would title it *Kubla Khan Or, A Vision in a Dream*.

Kubla Khan is often called a work of visionary poetry without much consideration of why. Most begin and end with the premise of an opiated decadent voyaging through time and space. The poem is not however hallucinatory in a lysergic sense. Instead, it glides in a blissful then darkening swoop, 'through caverns measureless to man / Down to a sunless sea'[40], as if a camera rising and falling. This is cinema before the camera was invented.

38   *The Road to Xanadu: A Study in the Ways of the Imagination,*
        John Livingstone Lowes, Pg. 326

39   *The Collected Works of Samuel Taylor Coleridge,* Pg. 511

40   *The Collected Works of Samuel Taylor Coleridge,* Pg. 513

It is no accident that the poem coincides with the first golden age of manned flight. Coleridge was in impressionable adolescence when the Montgolfier brothers initiated a craze for hot air balloon flights, which Coleridge later called 'an image of human longing and inspiration, both uplifting and terrifying'[41]. It was a description that matched his drug use. For all the intent of surveying the golden city and 'stately pleasure-dome' of Khan, there is remarkably little description in Coleridge's verse. As befits a poem written in essentially a heroin stupor, it is lucid in the sense of lucid-dreaming rather than clarity. The poet's view drifts off from the city to the surroundings. It becomes a poem of absence as much as presence. We never find out what pleasures took place in its halls or who the monarch of the title was or the woman who haunts the moonlit chasm or her demon lover. When it returns to the city, it is with the intimation of ruin; 'The shadow of the dome of pleasure / Floated midway on the waves; / Where was heard the mingled measure / From the fountain and the caves.'

All cities are built with their ruins in mind, even if only subconsciously; what one failed postcard painter and mass-murderer, of whom more hereafter, called *Ruinenwert* ('ruin value'[42]). The hidden momentary pleasures of life taking place in monuments built ultimately for oblivion.

Transcribing the lines whilst fresh in his memory, Coleridge received a visit from an unwelcome guest referred to only as

41   *The Age of Wonder*, cited Pg. 161

42   *The Ghosts of Berlin: Confronting German History in the Urban Landscape*,
          Brian Ladd, Pg. 141

'a person on business from Porlock'[43] who kept him for over an hour. When Coleridge returned to the poem, he found the three hundred verses he'd envisaged 'had passed away like the images on the surface of a stream into which a stone has been cast.' They would never return. He morosely added 'A Fragment' to its title. It is tantalising to consider where the poem might have gone. Yet *Kubla Khan* is stronger for its fleeting brevity, its glimpses. It enchants as the mysterious oriental castle on the Walsperger map[44] does, lying beyond man-eating giants, the island of Sweden, the land where no-one dies and a Nile with its source in the mountains of the moon. The demonisation (literally in some cases) of the Person from Porlock is unfair; Coleridge was always destined for a come-down. It nevertheless intrigues to note, as Borges did[45], how the original pleasure-dome built by Kublai Khan had similar origins to the poem written about it. In *The Compendium of Chronicles* by Rashid al-Din Tabib, it is claimed 'to the east of Shang-tu, Kubla-Khan built a palace, according to a plan he had seen in a dream and kept in his memory.'

Dream becomes real becomes dream.

43   Cited on Pg. 22 of *The Book of Interruptions*, David Hillman

44   *Mapping Our World: Terra Incognita to Australia*, Pg. 51

45   *The Dream of Coleridge: Selected Nonfictions*, Pg. 369

Here be Cities

'Seen in a dream and kept in his memory' is a useful addendum to what survives of our early maps of the earth's surface, where astral projection seems more of a contributing factor than geographical measurements. The edges of the Babylonian *Imago Mundi* map fade into obscurity with notes on lands that even birds and sunlight cannot reach. Most early cartographers did not concede so easily or poetically to mystery. In the absence of evidence, they turned to invention. The traditional 'here be dragons' became a menagerie of creatures collected in bestiaries. Some were real, some were fake. Rhinos and elephants were filed alongside griffins and manticores, at times grappling within historiated initials on medieval illuminations. It was only a matter of time before these creatures assumed human form. In various manuscripts, the Ethiopian Blemmyes[46] were shown to be headless, naked, good-humoured cannibals, wearing smiling faces on their chests. In Homer's *Odyssey*, the hero and his shipmates are lucky to escape the city of Telepylos, home of the man-eating Laestrygonians. Even in the 20th Century, such fantasies appeared in print, as in Andrew Lang's *The Disentanglers*, where the man-eating Berbalangs can teleport as points of red flame.[47]

A process of othering was prevalent throughout, as it is still. Darkest Africa, and other climes, was cast in the shadow of those

---

46   A once-real Nubian tribe.

47   Pg. 231-232

who charted it from a distance. The inhabitants were required to be savages so that the outsiders might well, by contrast, appear civilised, not least to themselves. The slaughter of natives was pre-emptively and retrospectively justified by accounts of pagan savagery (the horrors of Aztec human sacrifice in Charles Derennes Guna's *Les Conquerants d'Idoles* for example). To paint them as subhuman caricatures was to absolve the conquerors of their future sins against them. You can, after all, only murder what is human. By the time Theorodor de Brys engraved his visions of the New World, he included so many imagined wonders and brutalities that the very real massacres of natives were treated as fictional horrors. Even in our age, sympathetic revisionist stories almost always feature a colonial redemptive figure, from *Dances with Wolves* to the Space Pocahontas of *Avatar*. Native ways are mastered and surpassed; their plight is shrunk and commodified into pleasing coming of age tales for the errant youths of their oppressors.

'We carry with us the wonders, we seek without us,' Thomas Browne wrote; 'There is all Africa, and her prodigies in us . . . '[48] There are many sides to such a claim. In one sense, it is a testament to the value and depth of the roaming imagination; Comte de Lautréamont, for example, having incandescent dying visions of antichrists and oceans[49] in a decaying Paris under siege. The problem comes in whether such a view comes as questions or imposing answers. There is not a great leap

48   *Religio Medici* (1642) Section 15

49   *Les Chants De Maladoror*

from zeal of the mapmakers to Manifest Destiny, as embodied in Judge Holden's creed in Cormac McCarthy's *Blood Meridian*, 'Whatever in creation exists without my knowledge exists without my consent.'[50]

The sleep of reason breeds monsters, Goya wisely put it[51], and the view from 'civilisation' towards the colonies often had a nightmarish aspect, both in infinitesimal detail (De Quincey in junk-sickness having visions of endless labyrinthine Eastern temples) and claustrophobic constriction (the penny dreadful fixation with the Black Hole of Calcutta). This says much more about the viewer than the viewed, the insatiable need of the disordered mind to impose total order. It also revealed the real source of their angst; the squirming orientalist mass De Quincey hallucinated was in fact the bustling Oxford Street in which he lost his love Ann forever, via the prism of Piranesi's engravings. The Black Hole of Calcutta was somewhere in the hovels of London. Travelling on a railway arch above London, Gustave Doré looked down[52] on the backyards of the terraces and sketched them carrying on in circles forever like Dante's *Inferno*.

50   Pg. 209

51   Etching number 43 from *Los Caprichos* series (circa 1798)

52   'Over London-by Rail' (1872)

Dentata

Having deemed those outside the Occident as 'other', scribes fixated on theological points as to whether dog-headed cynocephalus or, for that matter, black people had souls. What they were actually doing was offering a glimpse into their own minds. When they wrote of fierce yet pliant Amazons for example, in Ancient Greek papyri or early modern science-fiction, the authors were essentially revealing their own fears, fantasies and prejudices. The titillating dread of matriarchal dominance appears throughout time, from myths of *vagina dentata* to the vandalising of fertility carvings like the sheela na gigs in Ireland. A recurring trope has been for a male traveller to chance upon a city run exclusively by women. Tales like Anna Adolph's *Arqtiq*, where telepathically-encouraged equality reigns in a crystal city under the polar ice are relatively few, given the magnetism of anxiety has a stronger pull than hope.

Most visions are either forebodingly dystopian or fantastically impractical. Almost all speak of the projection of neurosis and guilty conscience. In *Tarzan and the Ant Men*, the explorers chance upon the city of Alali built around an ominous amphitheatre and stone corrals for male slaves. This proved to be the template for a great many 1950s pulp novels and films in which a hapless XY-chromosomed astronaut lands on a strange planet to be worshipped and then tormented, physically, sexually or otherwise, by societies of females (an update of the explorer as visiting god/sacrificial victim trope). It was the stuff of male terror and fantasy, two sides of the same coin.

'Ashair is a forbidden city. No stranger who enters . . . may leave alive' warns *Tarzan and the Forbidden City*, 'What becomes of him here — whether he be destroyed immediately or permitted to live for whatever useful purpose he may serve — rests wholly with the discretion of the Queen. Your capture will be reported to her; when it suits her convenience, your fate will be decided.' The threat is presented as a delicious one to secretly wantonly-submissive alpha males.

Other accounts are less simple-minded. While *The Amazonian Republic, Recently Discovered in the Interior of Peru* (1842) by Timothy Savage portrays an inferior female version of Washington DC in the jungle, Walter Besant's *The Revolt of Man* (1882) inverts society through the 'Great Transition' to depict civilisation run with males in subservience. Aiming to warn against the rise of feminism, it is a nevertheless a satirical book that is wise almost despite itself, pointing out the injustices and imbalances of actual society in reversal: 'Oh, Professor! when I think of the men working at their looms from morning until night, cooking the dinners and looking after the children, while the women sit about the village pump or in their clubs, to talk unmeaning politics . . .'[53] before reaffirming patriarchal order through a rebellion of the aristocratic and the testicular; 'They were marching, heads erect and flashing eyes; the look of submission gone — forever. Yes; these men might be shot down,

53   Pg. 23

but they could never be reduced to their old condition'[54].

Accounts of matriarchal cities by female authors are characteristically complex. Charlotte Perkins Gilman's *Herland* presents a splendid subtopia that is nevertheless circumspect and patronising: 'Jeff drew a long breath.' I wouldn't have believed a collection of houses could look so lovely,' he said.

'They've got architects and landscape gardeners in plenty, that's sure,' agreed Terry [. . .]

'This is no savage country, my friend. But no men? Boys, it behooves us to go forward most politely.'[55]

Such aspiring mediocrity is absent in Elizabeth Burgoyne Corbett's *New Amazonia: A Foretaste of the Future*, where a future Ireland is populated by excess English females, who have fed on canine life-force which causes them to live longer and grow humongous. Mary E. Bradley Lane's *Mizora* is situated within a Hollow Earth, a common Victorian subgenre that suggested the polar regions somehow concealed entrances to a tropical inner planet. Here amidst buildings of onyx, marble and gold, the Aryan female population has risen up against other races and the now-extinct male population. Through parthenogenic reproduction, Mizora has flourished; there are street-lights, aeroplanes, proto-telephones ('the power to annihilate space as an impediment to conversation'[56]), synthetic meat and electrically-controlled weather. The streets are swept mechanically while carriages of

54   Pg. 319

55   Pg. 15

56   Pg. 77

glass manoeuvre at high speed. Redemption would be godless.

'Prayer will never produce an improved air-ship. We must dig into science for it. Our ancestors did not pray for us to become a race of symmetrically-shaped and universally healthy people, and expect that to effect a result. They went to work on scientific principles to root out disease and crime and want and wretchedness, and every degrading and retarding influence.'[57]

Architecture features in these tales of subjugation and liberation partly because it is intrinsically there in social relationships. Nowhere is the wedding of house and wife (or consort and harem) more evident than in Margaret Atwood's *The Handmaid's Tale*:

'I wait, for the household to assemble. Household: that is what we are. The Commander is the head of the household. The house is what he holds. To have and to hold, till death do us part.

The hold of a ship. Hollow.'[58]

Here we have the dehumanising architecture of imprisonment, with its echoes of the blueprints of slaves laid in holds below decks as human cargo[59]. Atwood's vision of a future of female serfs and religious autocrats is chilling because for all its surreality, we recognise it.

Dystopias are rarely sudden but incremental, even if the

57   Pg. 121

58   Pg. 91

59   A manuscript marked 'Stowage of the British Slave Ship Brookes', 1790 shows
          tiers of slaves packed into horrendously cramped conditions

proceeding collapse appears so: 'That was when they suspended the Constitution. They said it would be temporary. There wasn't even any rioting in the streets . . . There wasn't even an enemy you could put your finger on.'[60]

Neither do they come out of the blue: 'As we know from the study of history, no new system can impose itself upon a previous one without incorporating many of the elements to be found in the latter, as witness the pagan elements in Medieval Christianity and the evolution of the Russian 'KGB' from the Czarist secret service that preceded it.'[61]

Again and again, the dystopia defines itself in terms of the architecture of space and time: 'What I need is perspective. The illusion of depth, created by a frame, the arrangement of shapes on a flat surface. Perspective is necessary. Otherwise there are only two dimensions. Otherwise you live with your face squashed up against a wall, everything a huge foreground, of details, close-ups, hairs, the weave of the bed-sheet, the molecules of the face. Your own skin like a map, a diagram of futility, criss-crossed with tiny roads that lead nowhere.'[62] Yet, for all its theocratic darkness, it is a story that is left open to the possibility of change given that it is told post-regime. Even dystopias pass. Time is the final dictator.

In response to the supposedly benevolent but imprisoning chivalric roles set out for women, Christine de Pizan went beyond

---

60   Pg. 183

61   Atwood's accompanying 'Historical Notes'.

62   Pg. 153

the reactive with *The Book of the City of Ladies*. To subvert the gilded prisons of cloisters and ivory towers, de Pizan assembled a cast of extraordinary females from history and legend (Sappho, Isis, Agrippina etc.) and has them build a city by and for themselves, a city which, demonstrating that modernism and post-modernism has always been with us, is the book they feature in. It is also a call to arms to build the just city in real life; 'Most excellent, revered, and honoured princesses . . . and, indeed, all women who have loved and do love and will love virtue and morality, as well as all who have died or who are now living or who are to come, rejoice and exult in our new City which, thanks to God, is already formed and almost finished and populated.'[63]

You will not find the city on any map but it gives justification to Oscar Wilde's assertion that 'A map of the world that does not include Utopia is not worth even glancing at, for it leaves out the one country at which Humanity is always landing. And when Humanity lands there, it looks out, and, seeing a better country, sets sail. Progress is the realisation of Utopias.'[64] The journey and the direction, rather than the destination, are key.

Atwood has suggested that utopias become dystopias in how they deal with those who don't fit into the plans. It is also a question of who defines progress. Hausmann demolishing old Paris or Robert Moses bringing expressways into New York could be creative or destructive depending on the point of view.

---

63   Part Two, section 69.1

64   From Wilde's *The Soul of Man under Socialism*, cited in *The Literary Utopias of Cultural Communities, 1790-1910*, edited by Marguérite Corporaal, Evert Jan van Leeuwen.

Were the boy gang tormenting 'Old Misery' in Graham Greene's *The Destructors* simply harbingers of necessary change? Might we see, as Kirill Eskov has in *The Last Ringbearer*, the Fellowship of the Ring as saboteurs of essential progress, a ragged luddite band of aristocrats, lunkheaded peasants and reactionary priests preventing the vital industrialisation of Mordor?

Robinsonade

The traditional place to find utopia was via the pretence of newly-discovered islands. The earth is now surveyed by orbiting satellites but was once, not long ago, largely uncharted. The ignorance, and the possibilities therein, was vast. It was a matter of time before the islands encountered by Odysseus, St Brendan, and Militrisa and Gvidon became politicised but there's always been a combination of practicality and wonder present. A child — and most children are architects — dreams of building anew like the *Swiss Family Robinson*. This blissful isolated reverie is shattered by the horror of discovering footprints on an otherwise deserted island[65].

Ghost islands have long haunted imaginations. In *Inventing the Enemy*[66], Umberto Eco astutely pointed out that the fascination was not so much with imaginary islands as with lost ones. Until the mastery of longitude, which eluded sailors for millennia, there was always the tantalising prospect of finding a paradise island and being unable to return to it. This chimes with the devastatingly sweet melancholy we often feel towards the past; tangibly close yet perpetually out of reach. The price of the future is that you leave the past, never to return. The utopias we encounter on these imaginary island cities are thus ones that could have been; maps of forfeited pasts, just as much as potential futures.

---

65   Defoe's *Robinson Crusoe*, as cited on Pg. 2, *Nabobs: Empire and Identity in Eighteenth-Century Britain* by Tillman W. Nechtman

66   Pg. 192-193

One of the attractions of the utopian island city is that there need be no excess or dissent. Assuming there's a navy patrolling the waters to keep the unwelcome at bay, the planner would be able to exert tyrannical control, and even keep reality temporarily at bay. To the ominously-ordered mind of the pedant, the urge to decide on everything is too much to resist. The all-too human complexities and difficulties would be forced to yield. Caliban would be 'civilised', banished or perish.

Though his planned city was landlocked, Plato wrote the blueprint for these models in *The Republic*, via his semi-imaginary tutor Socrates. What Plato was building was a gilded prison; many would follow. His city is the people (they share the same word, *polis*). Famously the philosopher sought to exile the poets, or artists. This was partly because poets in those days had a tendency to wield a satirical edge and also because poetry, like all the great things in life, is a supremely useless activity in a strictly-utilitarian sense. Poets were egotistical and corrupted the youth (a crime for which tellingly Socrates would die). By doing so, Plato was attempting the impossibility of banishing the contrary and the conscience from his realm.

The Republic could only work if Plato was satisfied with tomb-building. Paradoxically, this demonstrated a profound and wilful misrepresentation, on his part, of what a city is.

'When Plato turned his back on the disorder and confusion of Athens,' Mumford noted, 'to rearrange the social functions of the city on an obsolete primitive pattern, he also turned his back, unfortunately, on the essential life of the city itself, with its power to crossbreed, to intermingle, to reconcile opposites, to create new syntheses, to elicit new purposes not predetermined by the petrified structure itself . . . what he did not suspect apparently was that this geometric heaven might, in terms of man's suppressed potentialities, turn out to be a living hell.'[67]

It would be limited to the number of people who could be commanded by a solitary voice[68]. This voice was the aristocrat who baulks at the melting pot of the metropolis, the esteemed hermit who recoils from the footprints of others.

The Republic would reinforce the appeal of an ideal city, a city that would dispose of unideal inhabitants. We can locate this tendency easily in speculative fiction. In Alexander Moszkowski's city of Baleuta, poets are likened to terrorists by the philosopher ruling class. Their leader is arrested and exiled to a convict island (always the mirror of utopian islands) and his verse is incinerated. In Greg Bear's *Strength of Stones*, living mechanical cities lurch across the surface of the Abrahamic planet God-Does-Battle. These crystal-domed cities, with names like Thule, Mandala, Resurrection and Fraternity, are programmed to wrench out heretics and unbelievers but they are too exacting and humanity too flawed. The population goes into precipitous decline and the cities stagnate. Outsiders come scavenging in their debris-strewn wake. Others actively rail against cities that have rejected them with Oedipal scorn.

In *Judge Dredd*, mutants were banished to the radioactive

67   *The City in History,* Mumford, Pg. 186

68   Cited in Pg. 53, *Aristotle's Criticism of Plato's Republic,* Robert Mayhew

Cursed Earth wilderness between the American Mega Cities; twice-victims of the militarist societies that spawned them[69]. The fantasies are by no means confined to comic books and sci-fi pulp. Every society in the process of dysfunction slips into the scurrilous refuge of purity, othering, blood-letting.

Plato is to blame then. Except these are superficial readings of *The Republic*. Plato frames the story as a dialogue between Socrates and a group of diminutive thinkers. It is multi-layered slippery discussion. Socrates places philosophers with uncharacteristic egotism as the leaders of the Republic whilst elsewhere suggesting that his wisdom is inherently imperfect[70]. Even more tellingly, he accedes to the multiplicity of the city by claiming it is there, rather than in an individual man, that they should seek justice. He warns continually against rule by military, oligarchy, sectarian demagogues and above all the tyranny of a singular power. We can never dispel the layers of awareness and satire at work. The hint is in the attendant 'Allegory of the Cave', which strongly suggests that nothing is as it seems to the senses. Lastly, the setting of the tale must be considered. Socrates has been coerced into Cephalus' house and spends time confirming his hosts' prejudices amidst simmering hostility and pitfalls. He leads them through loaded questions, building this state up from scratch, adding people and layers beginning from a single naked figure. He relates his tale in

69   In later years, this exile has been reversed with numerous effects, both predictable and unforeseen.

70   Plato's account in *Apology* is not quite the 'I know only one thing for sure: that I know nothing' admission frequently quoted.

the manner of one of the exiled poets (he was a troublemaker like they), full of slights, hints and tricks, it is a meta account delivered by an unreliable narrator; not primarily an attempt to instruct but rather an attempt to escape, both the building and the confines of the reader's interpretation.

The city of Athens revenged itself on Socrates, for whom there was no escape except by his own hand. His descendant in utopian speculation Thomas More would not be afforded that gesture of free will. Between ecclesiastical manoeuvres and self-flagellation, More studied Plato's accounts and came up with his own similarly shape-shifting account called, to give it its full Latin title, 'A truly golden little book, no less beneficial than entertaining, of a republic's best state and of the new island Utopia'. As with Plato, one-dimensional readings are to be discouraged. Utopia means 'No place'. The traveller to the crescent shaped island off the coast of South America, Raphael Hythlodaeus, is noted as a 'dispenser of nonsense or windbag'[71]. The capital of the man-made island Amaurot is seated directly at its centre, walled and behind a thorn-filled ditch. The natives speak their own language, a likelihood ignored by most speculators, which adds a further level of mistrust to the account[72]. Life is good in Utopia. Private ownership is abolished. The houses are well-built and sheltered from the weather (no mean feat in More's day). Citizens compete with each other

71   Cited Pg. 11, *Urban Utopias: The Built and Social Architectures of Alternative Settlements*, Malcolm Miles.

72   Translation is treason as the saying goes, though treason is not necessarily a negative thing.

by growing elaborate gardens. Work is limited to six hours a day and eight hours sleep is encouraged. War and lawyers are forbidden. No-one starves or works like a beast. 'What justice is there in this: that a nobleman, a goldsmith, a banker, or any other man, that either does nothing at all, or, at best, is employed in things that are of no use to the public, should live in great luxury and splendour upon what is so ill acquired.'[73] Everyone will have what they need.

Yet there is something about the tone that suggests, as his forefather Plato suggested before him, all is not what it appears. Each trait, followed to its logical conclusion, speaks of potential tyrannies. Citizens wear comfortable clothes but they are essentially unchanging uniforms. Syphogrants are employed to monitor how people spend their leisure time. Idleness is disapproved of, as are 'foolish and mischievous games'[74]. Leaving appointed cities will result in punishment, up to being forced into slavery. 'There are no taverns, no ale-houses . . . nor any other occasions of corrupting each other, of getting into corners, or forming themselves into parties; all men live in full view.'[75]

It is not entirely known, perhaps even by More himself, just how sincere his Utopia was (a reason for its continuing intriguing appeal). This inconclusive thought experiment is fittingly open-ended, given that cities are never entirely finished, knowable

---

73   Pg. 100

74   Pg. 52

75   Pg. 63

or singular. In Lafferty's *Past Master*, More is snatched by time travellers and taken to the perfect but stilted city Cosmopolis (near the chaotic but free slums, the Cathead and the Barrio) on the planet Astrobe. His claims that his manuscript was a satire seem unconvincing. They make him president for his sins.

For all his undoubted intelligence, it was extremely perilous for More, under the watchful eye of an erratic, vainglorious and occasionally murderous king, to be espousing things such as communism, no matter how tongue in cheek or experimental. For some time, More walked a curious path, much like his book, as if trying to stay within the eye of a tornado. Faced with a regent not known for subtlety or complexity of thought, Thomas More's head soon gazed sightless onto the Thames from London Bridge, before his daughter stole it away in a red leather bag. The Tudor Golden Age continued without his visions.

Where the Wild Things Are

Centuries later when Joseph Conrad came to write his evisceration of genocidal colonial savagery *Heart of Darkness*, he pointedly began it not on the Congo where he had sailed and witnessed grave horrors but on the Thames. Explorers precede invaders. Henry Morton Stanley was funded by King Leopold to claim the Congo for Belgium, to locate resources like ivory and rubber, and ominously check for weaknesses amidst the native populations. Beating and shackling locals at the neck, he was nicknamed *bula matadi*[76], or 'breakstones'. On one occasion, a member of his party, the whiskey heir Jameson, was said to have bought an eleven-year-old girl for six handkerchiefs and had her butchered by cannibals while he sketched the grotesque scene.

Differences in technology proved crucial to the initial take-over of the region making the invaders appear like formidable magicians; using batteries to have an iron grip, threatening to ignite villages with magnifying glasses, firing blanks to suggest immunity to bullets[77]. Leopold's plans to institute free cities under a puppet regime soon gave way to mass murder, torture and slavery. In *Heart of Darkness*, Marlowe sailed upstream to locate the megalomaniac Kurtz. In reality he was called Captain Léon Rom. He found him living near Stanley Falls, with the heads of twenty one women and children decorating his flower-

---

76   *The Afro-Modernist Epic and Literary History*, Kathy Lou Schultz, Pg. 40

77   *King Leopold's Ghost*, Adam Hothschild, Pg. 145-146

bed. Leopold's imagined free city on the Congo went unbuilt though rubber-production soared. It did not need to be built. It already existed. Its name is Brussels, one of many cities of imperial glory.

The poet Cavafy didn't just imply that we needed the 'other' in his poem 'Waiting for the Barbarians' but that they were already here, in the citadel, in the Green Zone, within the civilised. Few barbarian excesses, though they were fixated upon, could compete with what industrialisation was capable of in terms of scale and impact.

In *Gulliver's Travels*, Swift turns the gaze back on civilisation in words voiced by the king of Brobdingnag: 'He was perfectly astonished with the historical account gave him of our affairs during the last century; protesting "it was only a heap of conspiracies, rebellions, murders, massacres, revolutions, banishments, the very worst effects that avarice, faction, hypocrisy, perfidiousness, cruelty, rage, madness, hatred, envy, lust, malice, and ambition, could produce . . . I cannot but conclude the bulk of your natives to be the most pernicious race of little odious vermin that nature ever suffered to crawl upon the surface of the earth."'[78]

Yet the guilt absolved and the 'savage' continued to be used as the cracked mirror for the civilised, whether he or she was portrayed as noble, in the vein of Rousseau, or animalistic. The age of empire was able to absorb the horrors of the Crimean War with chivalrous verse recounting suicidal cavalry charges

[78]   Pg. 173

against artillery batteries[79]; what it struggled with were the revelations of the Méduse or Franklin's doomed expedition in the Northwest Passage, in which their esteemed contemporaries devoured each other's flesh. The latter were witnessed by Inuits who tried to help the doomed lead-poisoned madmen of the lost ships HMS Terror and Erebus. The uneasy question raised was not 'Where are the barbarians?' but 'Who?'

'Man has gone out to explore other worlds and other civilisations,' Stanislaw Lem wrote in *Solaris*, 'without having explored his own labyrinth of dark passages and secret chambers, and without finding what lies behind doorways that he himself has sealed.'[80]

79   Tennyson's 'The Charge of the Light Brigade.'

80   Pg. 165

No North, No South, No East, No West

The maps remain though the figures are long gone. Depictions of the world have always been influenced by loyalties to the local and the ideological. The translation of the three dimensional earth into a two-dimensional form is inevitably warped but inaccuracies are exacerbated by the biases of cartographers, who have traditionally placed their countries of origin near the centre. We rarely consciously noticed that our maps at school were aligned to a seemingly arbitrary point; the Greenwich Meridian line of a now-lost empire. It needn't have been this way and isn't elsewhere.

There have been other cartographies. The north-orientation of the earth on maps was not a natural or inevitable decision but one deliberately chosen (partly due to navigating via the North Star) and one that, in case of the traditional Mercator map stretches and shrinks particular landmasses. Before this, maps faced towards the rising sun (hence the word 'orientate'). Simply turning the map upside down is as accurate and more revelatory than the version we'd become accustomed to; obscure regions become prominent and the prominent obscure.

Medieval Christian maps placed Jerusalem at the centre — the *axis mundi*[81]. The Beatine maps centred according to an axis of the Mediterranean, the Nile, and the Don. The United Nations azimuthal equidistant projection centres on the

---

81   Anti-semites to the core, Nazi cartographers intended to both resurrect and usurp this with the mythical Thule at the crux.

North Pole. Buckminster Fuller's *Dymaxion* is a 'deck plan of the six and one half sextillion tons Spaceship Earth'[82] which returns obliquely to the earliest Homeric maps of a vast island surrounded by sea. There are any number of other possibilities from the ornate beauty of Nasuh the Swordsman's maps and Abraham Cresques' *Catalan Atlas* to the city maps of Braun and Hogenberg's *Civitates Orbis Terrarum* and Cahill's modernist octahedral 'Butterfly Map'. Such are our prejudices that when the 'Blue Marble' photograph was taken, from Apollo 17, it was flipped by NASA to place Antarctica at the bottom.

Similarly, the very idea of uncovering the white blanks on the map is largely a fiction. The vast majority of these areas were already populated and already mapped whether in maps, songlines or local folklore. The actual uninhabited discoveries in the great age of exploration amount to the Antarctic wastes and a litany of tiny remote islands amounting to barely the size of Britain and populated today by fewer people than Dublin. Likewise, our maps can tell us stories of political machinations and subterfuge; all those straight lines and right angles cutting across tribal lands, mountain ranges, rivers, drafted by autocrats and bureaucrats in drawing rooms, decisions which haunt us to this day. Given how much identity is tied in with nationalism, it is worthwhile but troubling to consider how borders have shifted and countries have been born and have died. Where are the patriots now of Dahomey, Later Baekje, the Khanate of Kazan, Free Ilocos, the Zaporizhian Host, Tutul-Xiu, Kara

82   Cited on Pg. 221, *Great Maps*, Jerry Brotton

Koyunlu, the Republics of Sonora and Ezo and the Bavarian Soviet Republic? Which states today will evolve or disintegrate? And what new countries are to come? We may be forced to notice the earth abruptly shifting beneath us but we cannot seem to accept the slow continental creep that render our affairs absurdly transitory.

Borges, a secular patron saint of maps as well as books, provided an allegory in 'On Exactitude in Science'. In the short but vast piece, he describes an empire which commissioned a map of itself so detailed and authoritative that it entirely covered the land it represented; 'In the Deserts of the West, still today, there are Tattered Ruins of that Map, inhabited by Animals and Beggars.' Borges knew that the map, even though it was accurate, was a creation. So too was the empire beneath it. 'It is the real, and not the map,' Baudrillard wrote in *Simulations*, 'whose vestiges persist here and there in the deserts that are no longer those of the Empire, but ours. The desert of the real itself.'[83]

Viewed under a microscope, the ragged remnants of the map might reveal other maps; of the cosmos and the synaptic circuitry of emperors, writers, artists, cartographers, mystics, vandals, saints and other lunatics. The map may not be the territory but the relationship between the map and the mapmaker is a symbiotic one. Each defines the other.

'The world described in Genesis, created by mysterious cosmic forces, was a volatile and dangerous place,' Myron Krueger

83   Pg. 1

wrote, 'It moulded human life through incomprehensible caprice. Natural beneficence tempered by natural disaster defined reality. For centuries, the goal of human effort was to tap Nature's terrible power. Our success has been so complete, that a new world has emerged. Created by human ingenuity, it is an artificial reality.'[84]

When Rome imagined itself into becoming the centre of the world it did so from the centre of a web: 'if we were to make a symbolic map of the Roman world, its most conspicuous feature would be a centralised network of roads.'[85] What marked out its successful advances also marked out the paths its downfall would take when power began to slip away, the retreats straggling armies and invaders would take and a gleaming target right there at the hub of the map. The centre moved elsewhere and has been moving since, even when the architects of civilisations try to turn it into stone.

'The city is a fact in nature, like a cave, a run of mackerel or an ant-heap,' Louis Mumford wrote in *The Culture of Cities*, 'But it is also a conscious work of art, and it holds within its communal framework many simpler and more personal forms of art. Mind takes form in the city; and in turn, urban forms condition mind.'[86]

These states are reciprocal. In *Moby Dick*, Queequeg has a map of the earth and the heavens tattooed onto his flesh. It anchors

84   *Artificial Reality*, Pg. xi

85   *Meaning in Western Architecture*, Christian Noburg-Schulz, Pg. 84

86   Cited in Pg. 29, *Architettura Della Città*, Aldo Rossi

him and it anchors the universe but mapping is an impossible task. Everything is continually changing and any such map will appear true only for a brief window of time and space. When Heraclitus wrote 'you can't step in the same river twice'[87], he meant not only that the river would have changed, but that you would have too. A history then of ever-changing cities, whether real or unreal, must also be a history of the imagination. Melville had a point when he wrote, 'It is not down in any map; true places never are'[88], but likewise imaginary places are never entirely unrealised. We can find them all around us.

87   Quoted Pg. 1, *Platonic Conversations*, Mary Margaret McCabe

88   *Moby Dick*, Pg. 57

The Tower

Before we proceed, spare a thought for the cities which we will never know, the cities of which no accounts survive, where no ruins have been found. 'Nothing has really happened,' wrote Virginia Woolf, 'until it has been recorded.'[1] This is true only to a point, for the soil contains secrets and what is true now may one day vanish from record. Consider the cities that will be built when we have turned to dust and are long forgotten. All cities contain their own eventual ruins. So too do lives. And in the long scheme of things, ruins are the best we can hope for. They are traces at least, marks on oblivion. We may not be able to defeat death but we can hope temporarily to elude the second death, the one that erases evidence that we ever really existed to begin with. This urge is one of the fundamental drives of art. It is, in part, why we build.

---

1   Cited Pg. 2, Nigel Nicholson, 2000

Let us return to the people who assembled the first cities, who challenged the gods by defiling heaven's unobscured view of the plains. Contrary to the fantasies of megalomaniacs, there never was nor can there be a year zero. Cities were placed to benefit from the natural environment. A city built on a river for trade follows the contours and dictates of water. The cycle of rain seeping through soil and rising from the ocean plays a part in its construction. A city built on a hill for defence will be subject to the lay of the land, to prevailing winds and erosion, to the lifespan of volcanoes and earthquakes, to the availability of stone and wood and so on. The curious town of Taghaza, which Ibn Battuta encountered on his travels in West Africa, was made entirely from rock salt, given that was the one natural resource they had access to; there 'he had the curious experience of sleeping in a house and praying in a mosque made entirely of salt blocks.'[2]

2   *The Adventures of Ibn Battuta, a Muslim Traveler of the Fourteenth Century,*
        Ross E. Dunn, Pg. 297

The Sun King

All cities are affected by the strength and motion of sunlight. 'What slice of the sun does your building have?'[3] Louis Kahn asked, a question considered by every right-thinking architect, whether white cuboid villas were built to reflect the light or skyscrapers designed to minimise the shadow canyons between them. The pragmatic functional approach has encouraged buildings as variant as Maxwell Fry's Sun House and the Taj Mahal[4] to be built dawn-facing or to maximise exposure to the sun's arc. In Arthur Radebaugh's optimistically-titled comic-strip *Closer Than We Think*, we find the promise of a Follow-The-Sun House (1959): 'Don't be surprised if many of tomorrow's homes are built on turntables. They would slowly pivot all day long to receive maximum benefit from health-giving sun ray and ensure heat in winter.'[5]

Failing this, other measures might be necessary, 'with cities growing constantly larger and sunlight becoming more and more scarce, ultra-violet beds may be called upon to furnish all health rays in the future.'[6]

Such is the abiding allure of the star we orbit that more imaginative and esoteric approaches arise. In Bruno Taut's *Die Stadtkrone*, it is argued that new cities resembled a torso without a head, given they were no longer built around a cathedral. The

3   *Light is the Theme*, Neil Johnson, Pg. 12

4   Its gardens align with the sunrise and sunset during the solstices.

5   *Toronto Star Weekly*, Saturday, May 2, 1959.

6   *Modern Mechanix*, March 1932.

'city as body' model of Vitruvius had been decapitated. Taut sought to create a new 'city crown' 'entirely void of purpose. It reigns above the whole as pure architecture. 'It is a crystal house constructed of glass [. . .] due to its gleaming, transparent, reflective character – it is more than ordinary matter [. . .] The light of the sun penetrates this crystal house, which reigns above the entire city like a sparkling diamond. [. . .] a sign of the highest serenity and peace of mind.'[7]

Taut was seeking, in an act of neo-pagan socialism, to restore the primacy of the sun by placing it in the centre of the city. It would be a city set in stationary orbit.[8]

All great architects paint with light and shadow and the sun has always been central to architecture, whether in attraction or avoidance. Three thousand years before Christ, Gaelic architects built Newgrange burial chamber around a single beam of sunlight on the winter solstice. Less patient and mysterious, the Romans built the Pantheon with the sun bursting through the roof at noon every day (they called the hole 'the oculus' — an unblinking eye). The sun has also been feared. The Moors build their tents initially for the purpose of creating wide shadows as respite from the desert sun while pueblo tribes escaped by creating cave systems in desert mesas and buttes. The channelling of light reverberated through culture: 'the glare of the hot, dry Asian plains, demanding radiation-shielded

7   Taut's *Die Stadtkrone*, 1. Aufl. — Jena: verlegt bei Eugen Diederichs (1919)

8   Taut predicted in *The Earth is a Good Dwelling*, wrongly as it happens with most of the world's population increasingly urban, that cities were a fad and would dissolve.

ventilation-openings rather than windows in the Western sense, encouraged the delicate filigree-piercing of the Indian *jali* and Arab *mashrabiyeh*, while in a very different climate the coloured glass of the medieval cathedral converted the greyer light of northern skies into a kind of celestial blaze, turning its very diffuseness to advantage [by contrast] the Moroccans have tamed the sun's fireworks into noiseless fusillades of sparks, beams, and shafts of light'.[9]

The use of screens to mitigate a potent sun gave rise to shadow puppetry. The boosting of weak northern rays was enabled through coloured stained-glass windows. Both were prototype forms of cinema, conjuring narratives through the manipulation of light.

When Bruno Taut built his wondrous and sadly transient colour-bathed Glass Pavilion he abandoned the bronze-age stories of the Church for stained glass as pure experience[10], with 'no other purpose than to be beautiful'[11]. The story, liberatingly, was the viewer's. Metaphor and parable were flimsy things compared to the thrill of stepping inside a prism in an age when Einstein had shown the speed of light was at the heart of everything.

The sun is power. Ancient Egyptian architects sought to link the Pharaoh's seats of authority decoratively and geographically to the sun, to emphasise his unchallengeable stature as the Sun

9   *Architecture Without Architects: A Short Introduction to Non-Pedigreed Architecture* (1964), Rudoksky, Pg. 210

10   As did the later Haus Feurer by Wolfgang Feyferlik.

11   Pg. 87

God in human form. In Mandeville's entertainingly unreliable travels, he recounts the Egyptian city of Heliopolis built around a temple in which a five-hundred year old phoenix immolates itself upon the altar. All cities, above ground, are canvases for the sun. Impressionism was built intrinsically around sunlight, which transformed the facades of cathedrals and ponds by the hour. So too were the tiled domes of Arabia and Iran, the marine and golden temples of India, the shimmering Sher-Dor Madrasah of Uzbekistan. The machinations of our star continues to inspire in Chetwood's unbuilt Andes House for example, which would bloom during the day and close up to insulate in the desert night, the opposite of a desert flower.

Occasionally the importance of the solar is forgotten. It's easy to overlook that the Egyptian pyramids today are missing their skin. Originally a layer of white polished limestone radiated the sun during the day and glowed at night. This eroded with time and was stolen for later buildings; the rooftops of the Alabaster Mosque in Cairo contain recycled parts of the Great Pyramid of Giza. Just as Ancient Greek buildings are devoid of their original colour and paintwork[12], we have created many classical structures based not on what came before but on modern views of their skeletons.

For the Church, an entire city of the sun was seen as a step too far, back into idolatry and heathenism. Its most notorious advocate was the visionary Tommaso Campanella, whose

---

12   Colour is often neglected in buildings, except in the works of architects like Luis Barragan and cases like Chalfont's unbuilt Fashion Building (1930) and Frank Lloyd Wright's original electric pink Guggenheim.

ideas got him unwisely noticed by the Inquisition. Campanella proposed a return to pre-Christian focus on a health-giving city of open squares, baths and leisure. 'In the City of the Sun,' he wrote, 'while duty and work are distributed among all, it only falls to each one to work for about four hours every day. The remaining hours are spent in learning joyously, in debating, reading, reciting, writing, walking, exercising the mind and body, and with play.'[13] His was a utopia with the dangerous inclusion of free love, elements of communism, astrology ('in the vault of the dome there can be discerned representations of all the stars of heaven . . . to influence terrestrial things') and a pagan focus on nature, 'they hold great festivities when the sun enters the four cardinal points of the heavens.' The city would be surrounded by seven circles of defences; the number of then-known planets, the hills of Athens and the number of providential lumps on Campanella's cranium.

As with all wise revolutionaries, Campanella realised those outside who benefited from the status quo would not permit utopia, so he surrounded it with walls guarded by women in the day and men at night. It was to be a city of contemplation, where every inhabitant could be a philosopher, with 'flights of marble steps' and 'galleries for walking'. There would be historical wall paintings, scientific and technological models, flora and fauna from all over the known world. Pride was to be seen as an 'execrable vice'. Wonder, honour and duty were encouraged. 'They say, moreover, that

13   Pg. 36

grinding poverty renders men worthless, cunning, sulky, thievish, insidious, vagabonds, liars, false witnesses, etc. . . . and that wealth makes them insolent, proud, ignorant, traitors, assumers of what they know not, deceivers, boasters, wanting in affection, slanderers, etc. . . . [Here] they are rich because they want nothing, poor because they possess nothing; and consequently they are not slaves to circumstances, but circumstances serve them.'[14] Just as it was to be a city of inner exploration so too would it reach outwards: 'They navigate for the sake of becoming acquainted with nations and different countries and things.'

For his radical beliefs[15], Campanella was placed under house arrest in a monastery. When he persisted, the church authorities decided to destroy him. They almost succeeded. He escaped execution only by feigning insanity through two weeks of torture, roaring nonsensical phrases like 'Ten white horses!' Finally, he endured two days being hung from 'the wake', tensed all the time above a spike. The ordeal was such that only a mentally ill person was judged to be able to endure it without confessing. Campanella was declared mad and sentenced to life imprisonment. At the moment of his reprieve however, he whispered to his torturer, 'What did you think, that I was a dumbass, that I wanted to talk?'[16].

The City of the Sun is all the more remarkable and tragic because

---

14 Cited in *The Story of Utopias*, Lewis Mumford

15 'If You return to earth, come armed Lord / because enemies are preparing other crosses / — not Turks, not Jews — but those of Your own kingdom'.

16 Introduction to *Selected Philosophical Poems of Tommaso Campanella*, Pg. 8

it was written by a brutalised prisoner in squalid conditions; for four years of a total of twenty six Campanella was shackled in a dungeon. Choosing the protection of meta-fiction and plausible deniability, he attributed his accounts to a Genoese sea-captain. Through his writings, he thought himself out of his cell as if imagination was indeed some form of magic ('I have already told you how I wandered over the whole earth'[17]). The walls could not contain him.

Radicals did not forget Campanella or the city he'd built in his mind. His contemporary Francis Bacon situated his utopian city in New Atlantis, not around a church but around a curious structural contraption called Salomon's House. Though it paid lip-service to God, it was really a surreal laboratory in a city designed at every point to aid experiment. 'We have high towers,' he wrote, 'the highest about half a mile in height; and some of them likewise set upon high mountains [. . .] We use these towers [. . .] for insulation, refrigeration, conservation . . . And upon them . . . are dwellings of hermits, whom we visit sometimes, and instruct what to observe.'[18]

It is a city where discovery is wound into the very fabric of being: 'We have also great and spacious houses where we imitate and demonstrate meteors; as snow, hail, rain, thunders, lightnings; also generations of bodies in air; as frogs, flies . . . We have also parks and enclosures of all sorts of beasts and birds which we use not only for view or rareness, but likewise for

17   Cited Pg. 33, *The Road to Science Fiction: From Gilgamesh to Wells*, edited by James Gunn

18   *Sir Francis Bacon's Journals*, Pg. 525

dissections and trials.'

There is a notable emphasis on the exploration of all the senses, reflecting Bacon the polymath: 'We have also perspective-houses, where we make demonstrations of all lights and radiations; and of all colours . . . sound-houses, where we practise and demonstrate all sounds, and their generation . . . perfume-houses; wherewith we join also practices of taste . . . engine-houses, where are prepared engines and instruments for all sorts of motions . . . a mathematical house, where are represented all instruments, as well of geometry as astronomy, exquisitely made.'

Bacon was building with his imagination not just a city but modern science as we know it. It stood in defiance of dubious revelation: 'We have also houses of deceits of the senses; where we represent all manner of feats of juggling, false apparitions, impostures, and illusions; and their fallacies. And surely you will easily believe that we that have so many things truly natural which induce admiration, could in a world of particulars deceive the senses, if we would disguise those things and labour to make them seem more miraculous.' It is tempting to consider how far we'd have progressed following Bacon's methods, how much wasted time and enforced ignorance could have been dispensed with and whether such a city could ever work unless populated by countless Francis Bacons. Often said to have been the last man to have known everything[19], Bacon was actually dedicated to the fragmentation of monolithic 'truth'. Each building in his

19   *The Territories of Science and Religion*, Pg. 123

city is a science in itself and would expand. Its architect would not live to see this; dying, absurdly but appropriately, having contracted pneumonia whilst experimenting freezing a chicken in the snow.

The sun rises again and pulls its city with it around the globe. We find it in the sketches of Ivan Ilich Léonidov labouring under the inquisition of Stalin's Russia. When the threat of execution or the Gulag subsided relatively in the 1940s and 50s, Léonidov turned to creating his own versions of Campanella's City of the Sun in print. The designer had been an apprentice ikon painter and a Petrograd dockhand before turning his hand to architecture under the free studios initiated by the Revolution. Like so many visionary architects, Léonidov's work remains imaginary, amounting in real life merely to the amphitheatre-style staircase of Ordzonikidze sanatorium in Kislovodsk. Perhaps his failure to build saved him, if not from the show trials and purges then from compromising himself on the neoclassical designs then demanded by the state. 'Do not touch this cloud-dweller'[20] Stalin had written on a death-list next to the name of the writer Boris Pasternak and perhaps this too applied to Léonidov, creating his castles in the sky.

Relegated after a flurry of excitement and notoriety to being a workshop instructor assisting architectural mediocrities, Léonidov was free to design the buildings he wanted because there was little possibility of them being built, from his Lenin Institute thesis to the failed entries for Narkomtiazhprom

20   *Boris Pasternak: A Literary Biography – Volume 2,* Pg. 143

building and the Santo Domingo's Columbus monument. It was our loss. His sketches for his City of the Sun take his early stylings into a strange otherworld, reminiscent at times of hazy Oriental prints or ancient extraterrestrial civilisations. They are no longer in thrall to reason but to mystery, poetry over function. The sun is shackled. Buildings become obelisks. The future and the ancient are indistinguishable. Wherever this is, this is not Stalin's Russia and yet it existed in Léonidov's room, Léonidov's sketchbook, Léonidov's mind. Inside these the sun shone still, outlasting the black sky reign of tyrants.

In the mid to late 1940s, the Hungarian photographer Brassaï ('the eye of Paris' according to Henry Miller) captured a neo-pagan engraving on a Parisian wall, which he named 'The Sun King'. It was part of a cabinet of curiosities he had been assembling from photographs of graffiti around the capital, which began around the time of the Nazis' rise to power. What the carving meant to its creator, no-one knows, though there is the dim possibility they are still alive somewhere. The context however supplied possible meanings; the wild rays flaring from the carving's crown could symbolise both the Occupation and the Liberation of the city, emerging from the darkness. The title was also a nod to the French Emperor Louis XV whose absolute monarchy can be seen both as an age of glory and the beginning of the tilt towards the eventual French Revolution. The monarch had famously claimed 'I am the state', later modified with deathbed wisdom to 'I depart, but the State shall always remain.' He was wrong for even states can fall. Only the sun remains king.

Proteus

Though its glow blocks out the stars, Paris, the grand dynamo of modernism, has not forgotten the cosmos. Its Haussmann-designed boulevards burst from junctions like radiating stars. When the pretender to Haussmann's crown Le Corbusier designed his drastic restructurings of Paris, he did so not just with megalomania but with the sun in mind. In his Ville Contemporaine, 'crystal towers [. . .] soar higher than any pinnacle on earth . . . translucent prisms that seem to float in the air without anchorage to the ground, flashing in summer sunshine, softly gleaming under grey winter skies, magically glittering at nightfall'[21].

For all his style, order and clean lines, Le Corbusier was a remarkably shape-shifting figure, a brilliant social chameleon equally adept at indulging venture capitalists, fascists and Soviet bureaucrats. Should we assume him guilty? If so, of what? Architects want to build and building requires patrons. The Renaissance, as Harry Lime reminds us from a Viennese Ferris wheel[22], was founded upon the questionable activities of the Borgias. Towards Paris, Le Corbusier presented his best Janus profile, appearing both elitist and classless.

Le Corbusier is often accused of somehow being an inhuman vandal. There he is naked, defiling Eileen Gray's sublime E-1027 with his scrawls (the house would vengefully be the last he'd

---

21   Cited Pg. 156, *Emerging Concepts in Urban Space Design*

22   Carol Reed's *The Third Man* (1949)

ever see, as he drowned within sight of it). This criticism often boils down to a distaste with the style of architecture he initiated (he cannot be blamed entirely for the ineptitude of his imitators) and a wilful misreading of his (in)famous assertion that 'A house is a machine for living in.'[23]

Le Corbusier was profoundly concerned with the place of the person within architecture, society and the cosmos. His was, he claimed in relation to his plans for Chandigarh, 'an architecture that fulfils the day-to-day functions but which leads to jubiliation'[24]. It might even be said that Le Corbusier is intrinsically human in terms of his concerns, his conceits and his deceits. With his Plan Voisin (1922-1925), Le Corbusier sought to transform inner Paris to accommodate the burgeoning population as well as opening up the city to become a hub of France and Europe. The plan today looks like an ambitious abomination, crash-landing his Ville Contemporaine where it was neither required nor wanted. There is a naïve tendency that assumes architects regard buildings as sacred when really this only applies to their own buildings. 'The urge to destroy is a creative passion' as the old anarchist Bakunin pointed out[25]

---

23   The full version is a much more complex, rounded and humane assertion
       (*Almanac* Pg. 29): 'The house has two aims. First it's a machine for living in, that
       is, a machine destined to serve as a useful aid for rapidity and precision in our
       work, a tireless and thoughtful machine to satisfy the needs of the body: comfort
       But it is, secondly, a place intended for meditation and thirdly a place where
       beauty exists and brings to the soul that calm which isindispensable.'
       Arguably it is more akin to Taut's — 'dwelling machine' 1921, Pg. 95

24   Pg. 214, Modulor

25   Cited Pg. 14, *Anarchism*, George Woodcock

and architects have proved adept iconoclasts when fires and earthquakes have not complimented their plans. Leonardo Da Vinci's city blueprints come alongside his designs for urbacidal siege engines. Respectability is no guarantee of innocence: 'We hear nothing of [the father of English architecture Inigo Jones] till 1645 when he was involved in the siege and burning of Basing House. "There", says a contemporary news-sheet, "was the famous Surveyor . . . Innico Jones, who was carried away in a blanket, having lost his clothes."'[26]

Yet there is something that redeems Le Corbusier, even beyond his talent. The Czech architect Karel Teige attacked his unbuilt 'wholly idealistic Plan of the Mundaneum . . . [as] an illusion, empty wish-fulfilment, an unrealisable utopia: it is future-music' (the latter said as if a bad thing).

'Your views are typical of the times,' Le Corbusier replied. 'They do not express strength, as you believe, but rather fear. The fear of phantoms, the fear of not being original and even the fear of the instant of pathos . . . I am not so pathetic as to be ashamed of having a heart and I am not so feeble as to dig in behind . . . an artificial frontier; I am not a Malthusian and my instinct is to cross boundaries.'[27]

Here, and in the notes to his blueprints, there is a poetry and hyperbolic narrative arguably missing in Le Corbusier's replicating cruciform skyscrapers. His aim for his future city, at least at this stage, was to abolish the street and the home as

26   Pg. 83, Summerson

27   *Architect of the Century,* Karel Teige, Pg. 166

we know them and his language matched his prophetic fervour in his descriptions: 'The sky is a remote hope far, far above it. The street is no more than a trench, a deep cleft, a narrow passage. And although we have been accustomed to it for more than a thousand years, our hearts are always oppressed by the constriction of its enclosing walls.'[28]

Le Corbusier was acutely, melodramatically aware of the importance of separating the pedestrian from the motorist[29]: 'The street is full of people: one must take care where one goes. For several years now it has been full of rapidly moving vehicles as well: death threatens us at every step between the twin kerb-stones. But we have been trained to face the peril of being crushed between them.' Lucidity vies with melodrama: 'On Sundays, when they are empty, the streets reveal their full horror. But, except during those dismal hours men and women are elbowing their way along them, the shops are ablaze, and every aspect of human life pullulates throughout their length. Those who have eyes in their heads can find plenty to amuse them in this sea of lusts and faces. It is better than the theatre, better than what we read in novels.' He did not envisage that skyscrapers could easily become vertical prisons and the wide open green spaces between them wildernesses. This is the paradox of Le Corbusier, his faith in sociability even though his work was born of monasteries[30], temples and silence. It is a

28   *Warped Space: Art, Architecture, and Anxiety in Modern Culture*, Pg. 60

29   A separation that defined Jellicoe's planned but unbuilt Motopia (1960) outside London.

30   Particularly after visiting the serene Charterhouse of Ema.

paradox which confronts all city-builders.

The world Le Corbusier was railing against is forgotten but worth remembering for he was offering remedies as well as egotism. 'The demiurgic hubris of high modernism is fatefully dramatised by such visions of the towers of the Plan Voisin,' Fredric Jameson wrote 'which stride across a fallen landscape like H.G. Wells's triumphant Martians, or the gigantic symbolic structures of the Unites d'habitation, the Algiers plan, or Chandigarh, which are apocalyptically to sound the knell of the cramped and insalubrious hovels that lie dwarfed beneath their prophetic shadow.'[31]

One dystopia replaces another in space and memory, and we forget the reasons change was originally required. The idea of offering air, space and greenery en masse was revolutionary at a time when urban chaos and squalor existed hand in hand with vast unused country estates owned by the few. 'The materials of city planning are sky, space, trees, steel and cement in that order and in that hierarchy,' Le Corbusier claimed and it was radical to insist these be available to all.

The sun too was always in Le Corbusier's work, no more so than his heliocentric Ville Radieuse with its Y-shaped skyscrapers designed to manipulate the light through angles. He was offering its inhabitants a home in the sky with views of the dawn and the dusk. This he elaborated further with his unbuilt Cartesian Skyscraper (1938), in which he attempted

31   *Architecture Criticism Ideology* ('Architecture and the critique of ideology' essay
          — Fredric Jameson), Pg. 71

to minimise light traps and shadows. It is however the by-products that undermine utopias, even unbuilt ones; the pissed-in dysfunctional lifts, the anti-sociable proximity, the lack of internal space for children. In a sense, what Le Corbusier was designing in his Ville Contemporaine for three million people was not the city but the anti-city. A site where place was abolished, where the street and the walkers who roam it have evaporated (anticipating modern Los Angeles), where the automobile is supreme. 'The well-trodden path of the eternal pedestrian [is] a relic of the centuries, a dislocated organ that can no longer function. The street wears us out. And when all is said and done we have to admit it disgusts us. Then why does it still exist?'[32]

Le Corbusier was the anti-flâneur and his was a world of no chance encounters, no explorations, no side-glances. He bemoaned 'the Balzacian mentality [. . .] content to leave our streets as they are because these murky canyons offer them the fascinating spectacle of human physiognomy!'[33] There is something almost Zen, in the Kamikaze sense, about his plans to redefine the street and the city: 'those hanging gardens of Semiramis, the triple tiers of terraces, are "streets of quietude". Their delicate horizontal lines span the intervals between the huge vertical piles of glass, binding them together with an attenuated web. Look over there! That stupendous colonnade which disappears into the horizon as a vanishing thread is

---

32   Cited in Pg. 56, *CIAM Discourse on Urbanism, 1928-1960*

33   *Pathologies of Modern Space: Empty Space, Urban Anxiety*, Pg. 129

an elevated one-way autostrada on which cars cross Paris at lightning speed . . . In the new business centre office work will be performed, not in the persistent dimness of joyless streets, but in the fullness of daylight and an abundance of fresh air. Do not smile incredulously. Its 400,000 clerks will be able to scan a landscape such as that one looks down on from the lofty crests above the Seine near Rouen and behold a serried mass of trees swaying beneath them. The stillness is absolute . . . When night intervenes the passage of cars along the autostrada traces luminous traces that are like the tails of meteors flashing across the summer heavens.'[34]

It is a city rethought as interplanetary space, but what can live in a vacuum?

34   *Modern Man: The Life of Le Corbusier, Architect of Tomorrow*, Pg. 9

Perfecting the Shipwreck

'The invention of the ship,' Paul Virilio wrote, 'was also the invention of the *shipwreck*.'[35] Everything echoes. Inventing the ship and the shipwreck leads to the invention of lighthouses, judas lights and pirate-plunderers, laws on flotsam and jetsam, the Sirens of Homeric myth, the immrams of Irish verse, Ahab and Prospero. An early human fashioning a makeshift log-boat for the first time sets into motion chains of events that will lead to, amongst innumerable events, the Zong Massacre, the Vikings founding Russia and reaching Baghdad, the USS Indianapolis shark-attacks and the Treasure Voyages of Zheng He.

Even enlightened architects designing spaces in which people can interact and be enriched rather than confined, can fall prey to the law of unforeseen consequences. This can work in reverse. The pollution of Victorian London gave rise to diffused light that attracted Impressionist artists. When you discover gold, you invent the boomtown with pop-up industries from telegraphers to saloon keepers to prostitutes. When you invent the cargo plane, you invent the cargo cult. The future not only has side-effects, it *is* side-effects.

One of the most in-depth, sustained and entertaining explorations of this phenomena is Mega-City One[36] in the comic *2000AD*. From its creation by John Wagner and Carlos Ezquerra, the *Judge Dredd* series has featured not just action with satirical

35   *Open Sky*, Virilio, Pg. 40

36   Architecturally, primarily made up of a mix of bubble architecture with a hint of Ferriss and variations on Erich Mendelsohn's Einstein Tower.

swipes (initially at Thatcherite Britain and the Reaganite US) but also the ripples emanating from developments to come. Most futurologists are content to outline the skylines and inventions of the future but fall short of critical investigation. *Dredd* does not. The inhabitants of the vast city state of Mega-City One, occupying the Eastern sea board of what is now the United States, live in giant block-towers, in varying styles of bubble architecture. Where the series excels is in delving beyond aesthetics to reveal how the future reverberates, reacts and resists, multiplies and escalates, all watched over by the ruling Judges (an echo of Plato's *Republic*). Each self-contained block has its own identity, often named after inane celebrities of the day. Rivalries between the city-blocks and mass claustrophobic neurosis escalated into the Block-Mania wars, fuelled by the neo-Cold War intrigues of East Meg One. A future in which droids replace a human workforce is one of mass unemployment and an epidemic of boredom, which in turn gives rise to a bewildering degree of fads and crazes. These seemed gleefully-ludicrous when they first appeared in the 80s but have proved to be loosely predictive; the illegal sport of Boing predicted Zorbing, the extreme body modification of the uglies is matched today by urban tribes sporting horns or split tongues. The creators of *Judge Dredd* realised what Victorian futurologists had failed to in their portrayals of men in top hats and ladies in evening gowns piloting sky-vehicles. Tastes and fashion inevitably change but human nature doesn't.

'Where there is power,' Foucault wrote 'there is resistance'[37]. Dredd's came not just from undead judges from a dimension where life is a crime or headbutt-fixated cyborgs but from sources we recognise from our age and earlier. The democracy movement chimed with Tiananmen, Prague Spring and the Sixties US Civil Rights movement amongst others. *Judge Cal* directly quoted from Caligula's megalomaniac Rome. *The Cursed Earth* and *Judge Child* sagas had their roots in Homeric episodic voyages. The Call-Me-Kenneth robot uprising had shades of Spartacus and John Brown. In notable cases, the resistance came entwined with the architecture and systems of the city. Dredd's most appealing adversary, Marlon Shakespeare aka Chopper, was first introduced as an illegal sky-surfing graffiti artist, defining his existence as meaningful amidst the human deluge through daring acts of vandalism on the vast cliff-face facades of the city-blocks. The forces Chopper opposed are eternal to urban living; the oppression of un-negotiated space, the faceless mass of the crowd, the conformism of non-conformism. In scrawling his smiley face signature on buildings (later used in *2000AD* alumnus Alan Moore's *Watchmen*), Chopper was trying to speak. In the later *Midnight Surfer*, he was trying to breathe. Inevitably, this put him at odds with the authorities. A giant statue of a Judge towers over the old Statue of Liberty in Mega City One.

Alienation was not so much a side-effect of life in Mega-City One as a direct part of the machinery. In the very first episode of

37   Pg. 95-96 (1978)

Judge Dredd (Prog 2 of *2000AD*), we are introduced to Devil's Island, a traffic-island prison for convicts created as a spin-off from the fact that traffic now came computer-automated and could travel ceaselessly day and night at two hundred miles per hour. It is the urban equivalent of real-life prison islands like Alcatraz, Robben Island and its namesake from the famed accounts of Papillion, where sharks and tides served a similar function. Dredd's opening villain Whitey ends up housed there (rather than in the usual pod-like Iso-cubes) until his ingenious escape in Prog 31. This too makes use of the machinery of the future city. Whitey[38] coerces an engineer-convict to hack into the weather control systems of the metropolis and create a snowstorm that temporarily paralyses the traffic that encircles them. To create a system is to create its potential undoing.

All our innovations come with side-effects, blind spots, unforeseen feedback loops. In Ballard's *Concrete Island*, a middle-aged architect is driving along the Westway in London when he has a traffic accident that propels him unseen into a viaduct and onto the island of the title. There he is trapped, surrounded, with a contrapasso irony that Dante would have relished, by Brutalist[39] modern architecture, a victim like Daedalus of his own creation: 'The sequence of violent events only micro-

---

38   Whitey reappears in a later annual when his brother wages war on the city to get him released, spawning an absurd and prophetic scene; 'Justice H.Q. will never agree! You're crazy!' 'Then I must give you another demonstration! See that old World Trade Centre over there!'

39   It goes without saying there can be a terrible beauty in Brutalism especially at its greatest like Günther Domenig's Steinhaus. Its problem, initially a strength, is that it cannot be modified or evolve. When it is done it is done.

seconds in duration had opened and closed behind him like a vent of hell'.[40] Furthermore, there is something recognisable in his predicament; he has fallen through the cracks of modernity and so too might we, even without realising it.

'Great cities are not like towns, only larger,' Jane Jacobs wrote in *Death and Life*, 'They are not like suburbs, only denser. They differ from towns and suburbs in basic ways, and one of them is that cities are, by definition, full of strangers.'[41] Cities are towns that transcend but also descend.

'A hundred profound solitudes make up the city of Venice,' Nietzsche wrote, 'that is its magic. A symbol for future mankind.'[42]

Just as with the prison-narratives of Polo and Maistre, physical imprisonment does not completely restrain.

'Modern technology,' Ballard wrote, 'offers an endless field day to any deviant strains in our personalities. Marooned . . . on a traffic island, we can tyrannise ourselves, test our strengths and weaknesses, perhaps come to terms with aspects of our characters to which we have always closed our eyes.'[43]

Though we might dream of places impossibly exotic, dreaming is always a process of looking inwards.

40   Pg. 8

41   *The Death and Life of Great American Cities*, Jane Jacobs, Pg. 30

42   *Rites of Spring: The Great War and the Birth of the Modern Age*, Modris Eksteins, Pg. 5

43   Pg. 5, Ballard's Introduction to *Concrete Island*.

The Sublime, Twinned With the Abyss

Space and constriction are key, that daily balancing and evading of agoraphobia and claustrophobia. Rilke was right in suggesting that beauty was the beginning of terror[44] but perhaps the opposite is sometimes true. The Sublime can easily tip into 'that tranquil terror induced by the contemplation of great size, extreme antiquity and decay'[45].

To particular minds like H.P. Lovecraft, contemplating the vastness of space and time is an awe indistinguishable from terror, an abyssal realisation of our insignificance and vulnerability. The universe is as vast and cataclysmic enough to suggest it is nihilist. Lovecraft saw this partially architecturally:

'in a dream of strange cities; and dreams are older than brooding Tyre, or the contemplative Sphinx, or garden-girdled Babylon . . . great Cyclopean cities of titan blocks and sky-flung monoliths . . . instead of describing any definite structure or building, he dwells only on broad impressions of vast angles and stone surfaces — surfaces too great to belong to any thing right or proper for this earth, and impious with horrible images and hieroglyphs. I mention his talk about angles because it suggests something Wilcox had told me of his awful dreams. He had said that the geometry of the dream-place he saw was abnormal, non-Euclidean, and loathsomely

44   First Elegy of Rilke's *Duino Elegies*.

45   *Modern Architecture: A Critical History*, Kenneth Frampton, Pg. 13

redolent of spheres and dimensions apart from ours.'[46]

The open-minded and optimistic might take comfort that other worlds are possible and all things, including tyranny and misery, are transient. By contrast, the cosmos has most often been used in architecture to symbolise and reinforce power, to cast the illusion that it is universal, omnipotent and virtually indestructible. Domes replicate the grandeur of the heavens and the relative insignificance of the viewer; the church hierarchy in the Sistine Chapel roof and the battalions of saints in every church, Islam in the roof of the Ambassador Room in the Alhambra or the Maoist state in the main auditorium of the Great Hall of the People. They are laying claim to a universe in which we are microscopic. When the Maharaja of Jaipur set their base as the Chandra Mahal (the 'moon palace'), they were trying to assert that their authority was as natural and eternal as our satellite. For all these claims, the moon shines down now on its exquisite empty rooms.

Modernity did not abandon cosmological claims. No superpower is complete without the prestige of a space city and vague but stirring promises of future space colonies, the urbanisation of planets and a conquering of the stars. The ceiling of New York's Grand Central Station is adorned by Paul Helleu's astrological mural. The UN Headquarters contains a replica Foucault's Pendulum incorporating the rotation of planetary bodies. For a festival that boasted the brutally functional motto

46   *The Whisperer in Darkness*, H. P. Lovecraft, Pg. 57

'Science Finds, Industry Applies, Man Conforms', the Chicago World's Fair of 1933 was romantically synchronised to begin with the appearance of the star Arcturus; its electricity tripped by light that had been travelling across interstellar space for the forty years since the last Chicago fair. By the time of the construction of the pyramid, sphinx and ziggurats of the Luxor in Las Vegas and its sky beam firing into the stratosphere (the strongest ray of light purportedly on the planet), novelty had slipped into cosmological kitsch. This pagan connection however to the sun, the moon and the stars survives not because it is pagan but because it is real. Unlike the gods, celestial bodies are not conspicuous by their absence[47].

47   The absence of dark matter, for one, adds an intriguing note of doubt to this statement.

Apocalypse Then

During the Renaissance, the concept of an Ideal City emerged from the shadows of Campenalla's dungeon. It developed from the humanistic elements of the City of the Sun, whilst largely abandoning the esoteric. It would be built according to a new faith in reason rather than superstition. Aside from advances in technology, there were two factors which propelled the polymaths who undertook plans of Ideal Cities. One was the development of perspective in drawing, whereby the two-dimensional ikons and Giottos of lore were gradually overtaken by paintings of three dimensional geometric depth. Buildings and indeed cities could be convincingly replicated in paint. They could also be designed from scratch. We owe a great deal to the first unknown artist to discover vanishing points. Artists revelled in the possibilities of vast plazas and colonnades, stretching out to the horizon in gleefully vectored space[48]. Experiments in architecture began to appear in works funded by religious patrons. Fra Carnavale's depictions of biblical scenes (such as *The Birth of the Virgin*) are fascinating not just for the narratives but for the buildings he created in the background. Images of possible (secular) futures were being smuggled into depictions of the ancient religious past.

These backdrop cities amounted to experiments in design and, at times fantasy; both what was and what was not yet

---

48   Leon Battista Alberti, Luciano Laurana and Francesco di Giorgio Martini, for example.

possible. Biblical scenes were placed amidst contemporary architecture[49] ostensibly to flatter clients and engage with local congregations but also to subversively critique the present through juxtaposition. Prophets appear in Lowland cities, Virgin Madonnas amongst Italian piazzas, miracles occur between bell-towers and market-stalls. The differences are implied but dissonant. The viewer would not look upon the real city in quite the same way again.

Specific subjects suited certain architectural ponderings. The Annunciation gave rise to a variety of cloistered walled gardens ('Hortus conclusus') where Mary was kept from the corruption of world; part prison, part sanctuary. The archangel Gabriel would descend into her courtyard like a helicopter in a prison break. The study of St Jerome gave rise to many depictions of cells and libraries, with his trusty lion purring in the corners and corridors. The Temptation of St Anthony encouraged the design of proto-surrealist hermitages. In Perugino's[50] depiction, Christ hands St Peter the keys to heaven in a cityscape that extends off into the distance like a marble *Tron*.

There were secular experiments in architecture of course, from the Limbourg brothers' ornate book of wonders — *Les très riches heures du Duc de Berry* — written before they died of plague, to Francesco Colonna's dream romance *Hypnerotomachia*

---

49   Jean Fouquet's 'The Conquest of Jericho' with Dutch architecture.

50   Perugino's resurrection of the octagonal building (from the Tower of Winds) gave rise to a brief craze for octagonal buildings in the US spearheaded by Orson Squire Fowler whose Fowler's Folly with its pie-chart rooms was eventually blown up.

Poliphili where the architecture resembles the isometric rooms of 8-bit computer games. Religious paintings offered not only funding and protection from criticism but an allegorical Trojan Horse, a method effective right into modern times with James Ensor's *Christ's Entry into Brussels*, Diego Rivera's liberation murals[51] and Woody Guthrie singing of Christ's fate should he suddenly reappear in New York City. Drawn to the imaginary city in the background of Mantegna's *The Agony in the Garden*, Alvar Aalto wrote:

'This is an architect's vision of the landscape, a small hint to our present-day urban planners on how they should approach their task. Moreover, it is a brilliant analysis of the earth's crust . . . for me, "the rising town" has become a religion, a disease, a madness, call it what you will; the city of hills, the curving, living, unpredictable line which runs in dimensions unknown to mathematicians, is for me the incarnation of everything that forms a contrast in the modern world between brutal mechanical-ness and religious beauty in life. It is an everyday yet wonderful form of art, and one that the modern age denies; indeed, the predominant mentality today goes to great lengths to avoid it.'[52]

A belief in the existence of angels was not required to adopt their hovering viewpoint. In the paintings of Brueghel the Elder, we

---

51   Temporarily smuggling Lenin into the Rockefeller Center in his *Man at the Crossroads* fresco.

52   *Aalto in His Own Words*, Pg. 49

witness the simultaneity of the urban[53]. It seems at first, as any mass does, to be chaos but each figure is individual[54]. For all the barbed parables of Brueghel and his descendant Hogarth and the ecstatic scenic contemplations of Hiroshige and Hokusai, there is a sense that the teeming mass so often demonised is actually a collection of worlds, wondrous and terrible. There are no angels except the fallen ones[55]. In Hans Memling's scenes from Christ's life, we have the impossibility of biblical tales taking place in the archways, towers and battlements of a millennium later and a continent away. There is also an impossible simultaneity of events. Time flows and lives unfold through the architecture of a single painting. Yet Memling, wounded and presumed dead, painting for his nursing Knights Hospitaliers, painted no lies. He was including the elements of memory and myth that are found in every city.

The second motor of the Ideal City was the threat and recurrence of plague. For centuries, Europe had been decimated by disease. The Black Death seared its way along trade routes by land and sea. The travelling cities of the Mongols brought the plague from China to the Middle East. Genoese ghost ships brought it to Messina. Pilgrims brought it to Mecca. It seemed like the apocalypse and for many it was. For those who survived, prevention was essential and the superstitious routes of prayers

---

53   A modern Japanes equivalent is the incredibly detailed Yamato-e of Akira Yamaguchi.

54   A surprisingly infrequent observation also found in the collages of Romare Bearden.

55   Hence Brueghel 's *The Fall of the Rebel Angels*.

and bell-ringing to scare the curse away and awaken God were insufficient. Though walling victims up in their homes did occur, the old methods of retreating into walled cities proved ineffective to an illness carried by rat, flea or dying loved one[56]. In an early form of chemical warfare, besieging troops were known to catapult plague-ridden corpses into resisting towns and then simply wait.[57]

What was needed was space; precisely what Boccacio's *Decameron* depicts in its storytelling retreat from the plague or the house of Anabaptists in Johnson's *The Alchemist* or the escaping party in Chaucer's *Canterbury Tales*. It also required hygiene. A genius engineer as well as draughtsman, Leonardo da Vinci's sketches for an Ideal City revolved around perfecting a sewage system before focusing on flamboyant artifice. In fact, the urge for space, cleanliness and order are there in almost all these types of designs from the time, most of which decorate religious paintings when you brush past the archangels and virgins. The artists may not have understood bacteria or viruses but they knew that cramped unclean environs encouraged disease[58]. Every Ideal City was thus the light to real shadow cities. Like all paradises, these places seemed otherworldly and inhuman, places for statues rather than complex individuals. In Fra Carnavale's three-dimensional Ideal Cities there are a few

---

56   Aside from voodoo, one strand of the modern interest in zombies originates here.

57   *The Black Death, 1346-1353: The Complete History*, Ole Jørgen Benedictow, Pg. 53

58   Rajastan's Karni Mata Temple, with its thousands of rats deliberately circumvents this but only could in a modern age of relative sanitation.

straggling two-dimensional figures in unnatural poses. They are designed lifelessly, as if looking back at the ruins of antiquity and perhaps forward to future ruins. Eventually the painter Giorgio de Chirico would inhabit such cities[59] with shadowy threatening figures, at dusk, the hour before dawn, in advance of an eclipse, always a moment away from some terrible act. Those figures were already lurking there in the Ideal Cities. It was a dream superimposed on a nightmare.

59   De Chirico was inspired to paint his imaginary cities by a visit to the actual city of Turin and Nietzsche's writings and breakdown there.

The Urbacides

Military invasion by rivals threatened every prospective Ideal City. Renaissance thinkers turned their attentions both to offence and defence and dreamt up both cities and anti-cities. Leonardo da Vinci put his talents towards the design of siege machines, declaring to the Duke of Sforza: 'In case of a siege, I know how to dry up the water of the moats and how to construct an infinite number of bridges, covered ways, scaling ladders . . . '[60]

Leonardo's tanks, submarines and flying machines followed Archimedes who built legendary war engines, from a giant claw that reached down and crushed warships to a mirror that ignited them with the sun's rays, which helped Syracuse hold out for three years against the Romans. Thousands of besieging troops with their supply lines and need for shelter, food, water and sanitation, were essentially movable nameless cities clashing with stationary ones. They had tents and kitchens, tunnels and structures. The mired siege tower Helepolis was melted down and recycled into the Colossus of Rhodes. When defences were breached through deception, stamina or force, it was one city violently absorbing another. For the idea of Rome to exist, Carthage must be destroyed as Cato the Elder exalted.

As artillery became more powerful, traditional square forts became vulnerable. Castles could still hide behind portcullises, moats and baileys but functioning cities demanded more space than a citadel could offer. Alongside the Ideal City

---

60   *Leonardo: The Artist and the Man,* Pg. 174

rose the Star Fort, both spearheaded by Francesco di Giorgio Martini, designed with cosmological providence in mind but also functionality. The pronounced spikes of the star-shaped battlements meant that any attacker could be assailed by crossfire from two overlapping positions. Any projectile fired at the walls would likely hit at a glancing angle. Though many of the modified versions (stars within stars or patterns overlapping) remained unbuilt, the city design was in cases actualised and the outlines can still be seen today, from the Dutch city of Coevorden to the Venetian Utopian outpost of Palmnova, the Cypriot capital Nicosia Goryōkaku in Hakodate, Japan. A twelve-point star even featured in Michelangelo's design for the piazza on Capitoline Hill in the centre of Rome. This project was vaingloriously finished by Mussolini just as he embarked in the war that would conclude with his corpse dangling from a Milanese garage roof[61].

The success of the Star Fort design waned when shells became explosive and the inability of a medieval walled city to physically swell with population. Yet designs rarely die when they become antiquated and the star fort found its way into leftfield architecture (Tsukuba Science City by Isozaki was an inverted version of Michelangelo's plan), Metabolist pleasure palaces (Yamagata Hawaii Dreamland), garden mazes (Georg Andreas Böckler's Architectura Curiosa Nova), aristocratic follies and cathedral designs such as the Czech Pilgrimage

---

61   Cities fall not only to invasion but corruption from within; Geddes' Parasitopolis and Patholopois passes into cities of the dead.

Church of St John of Nepomuk, which houses the incorruptible tongue of the saint.

Houses of Vice and Virtue

The strangest Ideal City of the era began too with a sacred relic. Having adopted the ironic name Filarete ('lover of virtue') and designed the bronze doors of St Peter's Basilica, the architect Antonio di Pietro Averlino fled Rome after trying to steal the desiccated head of John the Baptist. Denied the city of his predecessors, he built an ideal city from his mind and the questionable memory of what Rome had once been. It was named Sforzinda after his patron and remained tantalisingly unbuilt, if not unbuildable. Its star fort design was populated by a royal palace, cathedral, market, towers and canals, which flowed from an outside river rendering its defensive strength suspect (Paris had found the Seine a blessing and curse, being periodically attacked by Vikings until as late as 886AD). Aware that for all their religious foregrounds, Ideal Cities were a step away from theocracy, Filarete sought to reinstall piety. He did so in the unlikely shape of a ten-storey House of Vice and Virtue. The entrant would have to ascend through the floors learning about the arts, the virtues and the deadly sins. It was a tower of experience, adorned with a beehive-incorporating statue at its pinnacle: 'I represent Virtue as a man wearing armour, his head similar to the Sun, holding a date palm in his right hand and a laurel in his left hand. He stands on a diamond and honeyed water springs from below the diamond. Fame flies above his head'[62]. It was said to aid understanding of sin that a brothel

---

62   Cited in *History of Architectural Theory*, Hanno-Walter Kruft

was installed on the ground floor.

The idea of the Just City, the Heavenly City, the New Jerusalem informed Filarete's plans, as it did all the Ideal Cities, which evolved from and against it. Utopia has always had righteousness at its core and with this comes the temptation of Puritanism, from the Vatican to the Soviet Union to Singapore. This goes further with the drive for perfection and purity, reinforced in books like Anton Francesco Doni's *Worlds* (1552) where the disabled were thrown into wells and criminals poisoned. Filarete may have been inspired by St Augustine but it was in the sense of 'Give me chastity . . . but not yet'[63]. He, at least, admitted that vice was inevitable. The absence of it, along with eternal vigilance and prostration, makes the city of Heaven the likely tyranny it will be. A city free of vice is a city free of humanity like the mythic City of Brass; 'Its pavilions were lofty, and its domes were shining [. . .] it was a city with impenetrable gates, empty, still, without a voice or a cheering inhabitant, but the owl hooting in its quarters, and birds skimming in circles in its areas, and the raven croaking in its districts and its great thoroughfare-streets, and bewailing those who had been in it.'[64]

Even when built in veneration, there is an egotism involved in building from the mind that does not speak of supplication. 'Solomon, I have surpassed you'[65] the emperor Justinian roared at the inauguration of the glorious Hagia Sophia. We might

---

63 Confessions VIII, 7

64 *Arabian Nights*, Pg. 581

65 *Jerusalem*, Simon Goldhill, Pg. 53

substitute Solomon for God. The Babel instinct was alive and well even when masquerading as worship. The writings of the alchemy-dabbling Rosicrucian Johannes Valentinus Andreae combine genuine religious belief with such vanity; 'And so ascending the good ship, Phantasy, I left the port together with many others and exposed my life and person to the thousand dangers that go with desire for knowledge.'[66]

Influenced by Campanella and Dürer, he planned a city called Christianopolis, which stakes its claim in a world of sin by being impregnable, with fortified squares that 'look towards the four quarters of the earth.'[67] For the most part, the city he envisages is a pleasant one ('not extravagant nor unclean') with firebreaks, a well-stocked moat and sectors dedicated to different professions. Amidst such order, and a select population of 400, the only danger would be dying of terminal boredom: 'And next we must take a trip through the city . . . everything is done neatly and with proper appreciation of the gifts of God. Men that have to do the heavy work do not become wild and rough, but remain kindly; the guards are not gluttons, but are temperate, not evil-smelling but cleanly washed. And to conclude, the government is administered in a way so advantageous in all respects, that the people can enjoy all these privileges with a pleasure that is decent and need not be concealed . . . '[68] It was inspired, notably, by Geneva.

66   *Christianopolis: An Ideal of the 17th Century*, Pg. 142

67   Pg. 149

68   Pg. 152

Christianopolis is both saved and damned to ruin by Andreae's prejudices. Having dispensed with money, citizens compete in terms of genius and devoutness. The indisputable joy of working minimal hours is desecrated by Andreae's definition of leisure; listening to interminable lectures (which in a sense is precisely what *Christianopolis* is) raging against 'impostors, jugglers, quacks, tramp musicians, and hair dressers.' This is a city where chess is frowned upon, atheism forbidden and where 'no beggar is known or tolerated.' Its egalitarianism is extended only to those bearing scrotums, with women deemed second-class, 'There is nothing more dangerous than situations where the women rule in secret and the men obey openly . . . No woman is ashamed of her household duties, nor does she tire of attending to the wants of her husband.' It's worth considering how excluding and subjugating half the population could ever lead to anything but a colossal waste. Progress and potentiality are hobbled by exclusivity and so it remains.

Claims of modesty similarly rings alarm bells when approaching Utopia. In Samuel Got's *Nova Solyma: The Ideal City, or, Jerusalem Regained*, we find bold claims of humility. A sign to visitors announces, 'here are no marble giants . . . look not here for a lofty storied mansion gleaming white . . . No gambling nor secret lawless love, no strife nor anger, no long-pent-up revenge crying out for blood can find a place here. Thus it is that no restless spirits of the dead return here to their old abode to wail and fret; neither do the fauns and satyrs raise here their mournful laughter, or batter their deserted homes with vengeful hoof.'

It is a city that does not dare to risk rivalling 'the promised mansions of the father's kingdom'[69], a city of no architecture, with all the formlessness of Paradiso. It is a city that even the ghosts have fled.

69   Pg. 83-84

New Jerusalem, or Nevertown

New Jerusalem is, of course, an impossibility to which old Jerusalem, or rudimentary knowledge of human nature, would have been a resounding hint. Cities exist as melting pots, as eminently corruptible places of disparate attractions and influences. That is their great weakness and their even greater strength. The righteous and the reactionary have long railed against them, from Rastafarians damning Babylon to commuter-belt Conservatives mocking metropolitan elites; 'O Jerusalem, Jerusalem, thou that killest the prophets, and stonest them which are sent unto thee.'[70]

Perhaps because of its unattainability, New Jerusalem has long been dreamt of by those who damned the earthly cities. It is telling that the righteous never quite arrive at this destination despite memorable quests towards it, such as John Bunyan's trek for the Celestial City in *Pilgrim's Progress*, vanquishing worldly foes and demonic end of level bosses. With William Langland's *The Vision of Piers Plowman*, the vision is significantly of a tower, that partial connection to the heavens. Metaphorically or otherwise, church spires have been used as celestial transmitters (just as the vast *Tower of Glass* of Robert Silverberg transmits from the frozen Canadian wastes to far-flung galaxies) whilst mosques broadcast horizontally towards Mecca. This is a desire that predates the discovery of radio-waves by aeons.

Attempts to replicate the heavenly citadel on earth have

---

70   Matthew 23:37

predictably run aground at great human cost. Where the attempts were restricted to a lone figure they could be seen as admirable if misguided. In 18th century London, the gin-soaked and sleep-deprived Samuel 'Poor-Help' Best sought to build New Jerusalem, but had to content himself with calling on rich clients to foretell their fortunes and cure their ailments by licking them and babbling from the gospels. When followers accumulate, there has been a tendency for dark repercussions. Having declared himself the brother of Jesus Christ, the failed civil servant Hong Xiuquan built what he called the Taiping Heavenly Kingdom, centred around Nanjing (renamed, with a vast palace complex, as the heavenly capital Tianjing). Class and private property were abolished, males and females were treated equally but separated in every aspect of life, while vice in the form of alcohol, drugs, prostitution and slavery was punishable by death. Long hair was however encouraged. In the ensuing conflict with the Qing dynasty and their Western allies, twenty million people died, the conflict ending when Hong's remains were finally fired from a cannon for his insolence.

Having attempted to turn Münster into New Jerusalem in 1534[71], Jan Matthys rode out against the superior besieging papal forces, believing God would grant him an army of angels in support. He was instantly (predictably) butchered. Undaunted within the city walls, his follower Jan Bockelson declared himself Messiah, taking over a dozen wives in the process. When the siege broke through, he and his disciples ended

71   *Apocalypse: A History of the End of Time*, John Michael Greer, Pg. 99-101

their days at the hands and red hot pincers of their torturers. Then there was Savonarola, seer of visions, prophet of the weepers, burner of vanities (including a Botticelli or two, having hypnotised the artist), prophet of the weepers, who turned Florence momentarily into a place where vice was channelled into hysteric religious celebration. Having reluctantly promised miracles to a flagging public, he satisfied their curiosity by being hanged and slowly incinerated alive in the Piazza della Signoria (the coffee-drinkers of today separated from the smell of burning flesh by mere time).

These men were martyrs but, it might be asked, to what religion? Perhaps, in the words of Chinese Premier Zhou Enlai regarding the French Revolution, it's too early to tell[72]. We may be in the interim period before such prospective new faiths catch on and the old ones are eclipsed. It has, after all, happened before.

72   *The History of the People's Republic of China, 1949-1976*, Julia Strauss, Pg. 1

Kurtzville

Botched messianic utopias are by no means ancient phenomena. The Icarians repeatedly tried and failed to create settlements based on the writings of the Utopian novelist Étienne Cabet. When Shoko Asahara founded Aum Shinrikyo in a Tokyo bedsit, he cobbled it together not just from religious texts and conspiracy theories but also Isaac Asimov's *Foundation Trilogy*[73]. Unable to replace the real Tokyo with his megalomaniacal version, his followers set to leaving perforated sarin packages on the subway at morning rush-hour; acts of silent horrendous violence against people but so too against the nervous system of the city itself.

Having led his largely African-American flock to Guyana, the faith-healing preacher and American Communist, Jim Jones, sought to build his version of New Jerusalem in South America believing the continent to be a safe haven from the impending nuclear war. In some ways, there was a deranged logic to the paradox of a communist evangelist, given the deep-rooted millenarian aspect to Marxism. Jones' real god was evidenced in the name of the plywood settlement on the edge of the jungle — Jonestown. It would take several months before the site changed from being a promised emancipation from a racist American class system to being an armed proto-Gulag, in which inhabitants were imprisoned, punished in torture holes and screened conspiracy theorist films. When US Congressman

---

[73]   *Evaporating Genres: Essays on Fantastic Literature*, Gary K. Wolfe, Pg. 55

Ryan came to delve into reported abuses and escort dissidents home, he was assassinated at the airstrip with four of his party. Realising the implications, Jones assembled his followers, declared that fascist forces were amassing against them: 'we are sitting here waiting on a powder keg . . . And we had better not have any of our children left when it's over because they'll parachute in here on us . . . if the children are left, we're going to have them butchered'[74].

'Revolutionary suicide' was the only outcome, he claimed. Over 900 men, women and children drank or were forced to drink poisoned Kool-Aid. The tapes were left rolling. Still in preacher mode, Jones is heard encouraging mothers to kill their own children. The cries eventually subside and the organ music continues on automatically, playing to no-one. By morning the utopia had become a necropolis.

Karl Marx had predicted how arcadian communes, opting out of wider society, could easily fall prey to despotism. In *The Communist Manifesto*, he warned against such 'reactionary sects [that] still dream of experimental realisation of their social Utopias, of founding isolated "phalansteres"[75], of establishing "Home Colonies", or setting up a "Little Icaria" [. . .] and to realise all these castles in the air, they are compelled

---

74   *Imagining Religion: From Babylon to Jonestown*, Jonathan Z. Smith, Pg. 127

75   A reference to the teachings of Charles Fourier who believed society would pass
          through various steps — savagery, barbarism, civilisation and finally
          harmony. When the last was achieved there'd be orgies and feasts, the poles
          would melt through comic radiation, the seas would become soda water,
          four moons would orbit the earth. Unsurprisingly, Fournier-inspired communes
          came to ignoble ends almost universally.

to appeal to the feelings and purses of the bourgeois. By degrees, they sink into the category of the reactionary [with] their fanatical and superstitious belief in the miraculous effects of their social science.'

Whilst simultaneously predicting the course of gentrification, Marx had also foreseen that there was a new faith coming, borrowing many of the old traits whilst ostensibly opposing them; he had not foreseen that he would be, for a time, its god.

Fuelled by advances in technology and social sciences, New Jerusalem seemed to be tantalisingly close in the Industrial Age. This proximity made the most unlikely of allies. The production line methods, at once ruthless and aspirational, of the car manufacturer Henry Ford made him an influence on early Soviet Russia, to the extent a US business reporter observed, 'If Lenin was the Russian God, Ford was Saint Peter.'[76]

Each had their secret police and their propagandists. Just as the god failed, so too did the saint. In an ill-advised egotistical scheme, Ford commissioned the building of a rubber-producing settlement, the size of a small US state, called Fordlândia[77] in the Brazilian Amazon. The attempt to create an idyllic mid-west American town in the rainforest was calamitous. Workers were housed in malarial conditions and rioted when given worm-infested food. Wildfires to clear land blazed out of control. Ford had failed in his earlier efforts to build a growable soybean car and an 'industrial arcadia' in the Appalachians but was

76   *The Cultural Life of the Automobile: Roads to Modernity*, Guillermo Giucci, Pg. 7

77   *Fordlandia* by Grag Grandin is a fine account of this ill-fated project.

determined to see Fordlândia through, pouring millions into the project. At every stage, it evaded his distant control. He insisted on prohibition, with waltzes and polkas as alternative entertainment. The town became drunken and hopelessly debauched. He advocated hydroelectricity and quaint gardens. Instead it became an oil-stained cesspit with iron and asbestos-lined houses that baked in the tropical heat. When it was insisted that workers' derisory meals be deducted from their wages, they finally rose up, smashing the factories to pieces. A face-saving facade was kept running, and another anti-semitic utopian, Walt Disney, celebrated it in *The Amazon Awakes* with shots of fire trucks, playgrounds and rounds of golf 'against a beautiful jungle backdrop.' Only once, when it pictures the children of the settlement as 'future conquerors of the Amazon', does the memory of the ephemeral cities of the doomed conquistadors re-emerge, though they were there all along, like phantoms amidst the trees.

The Ancient Modernists

Imagine though that it was possible to sweep away the jungle and extend middle America (hegemony being a defining characteristic of our age). Or go further and imagine that the architect's page is blank after all, an impossible tabula rasa. What would we build given the chance to place our footprints in a field of unspoilt snow? Utopia, of course. Why not? Everyone who builds builds a fragment of utopia even if just a garden shed, even if unintended, even if outwardly malevolent. Utopias are indeed dystopias but the real secret is that all dystopias are utopias, for some inhabitants at least. And *they* tend to pay architects handsomely.

We were condemned, it seems, to build. 'And so, as they kept coming together in greater numbers into one place,' the ballista Vitruvius wrote, 'finding themselves naturally gifted beyond the other animals in not being obliged to walk with faces to the ground, but upright and gazing upon the splendour of the starry firmament, and also in being able to do with ease whatever they chose with their hands and fingers, they began . . . to construct shelters.'[78]

It was our upright view of the horizons that determined it. We were damned to improve and despoil the panoramas; lines and vectors, prospects of elevation and sanctuary but also envy, insults, dominance and submission. Most of all, it contained pride. Architects were the new Prometheans. Humanity had

78   *De Architectura*, Book 2, Chapter 1, Sec. 2, Pg. 39

begun with the opportune shelters of caves (the Puebloan cliff palaces for example): 'Architecture as dwelling place . . . does not start with the hut, but with the hole, by burrowing underground, by caves.'[79]

When our common ancestors ventured out and built on the plains, they began to master their surroundings, to extend dominion rather than to use space solely as a retreat. The age of ego truly began. Even when they built temples, especially when they built temples, architects were celebrating themselves. 'Soli Deo gloria' ('Glory to God alone') may be the words carved but 'Ecce Homo' ('Behold the Man') is the true meaning.

The names of the first cities may be lost or, at least, hidden from us. History is the charting of an ever-changing past but the commonly-held view, at the time of writing, is that the urban was born in Mesopotamia around 4000BC. Small tribes of homo sapiens began to migrate north from Africa 150,000 years ago. Mitochondrial studies show some returned from the Middle East, others ventured slowly into Asia. It might seem an occidental surprise that Europe was reached a mere three thousand years before Australia. The Americas followed with the Far East and Polynesia.

Of all these places, why did the stones rise in the desert? Obligation would appear to be the answer. In a harsh environment, shelter within the collective is the best means of survival. When resources ran low and hunter gathering and foraging gave way to more productive and dependable farming,

79   Gitano, Pg. 20

it made sense to group together, to irrigate the wastes through canal projects, to barter strengths and gain safety in numbers. The latter is one of the paradoxes of urban logic. While the city protects, it also concentrates the attentions of potential attackers. Monks in Ireland and Britain seeking fortification from marauding invaders might run to a round tower to defend themselves. In the Balkans, towers known as kullë were used as sanctuaries from those escaping blood feuds, vendettas which have seen resurgence since the fall of Communism. Gated communities are not simply sanctuaries but also advertisements. We like to tell ourselves that they are gilded prisons for their inhabitants, like Ali Baba's brother Cassim locked inside the treasure chest, having forgotten the password. And we flatter ourselves that we would be different.

The Map is the Real

What were once the largest cities in the world are now Neolithic archaeological sites. Their stories are chilling *memento moris* of flint, bone and erasures. It may strike us as scarcely believable that the bones of an English king can be found beneath a car-park in Leicester but there are entire civilisations beneath the soil; the city of Ji lasted four centuries and is now little more than scrapings beneath a Beijing railway station. What was Ji like? What was it like to inhabit Mureybet or Beidha? In Çatalhöyük, streets had yet to be invented and citizens entered the cellular earthen settlement through skylights. This encouraged mapmakers to sketch the site from a bird's eye view. Had this not fortuitously taken place, we may have struggled for aeons with the clutter of horizontal maps. As it is, there are those today proposing maps that combine the two aspects. BERG's 'horizonless' projection of Manhattan presents a horizontal view of the city streets and buildings and then ingeniously bends the city upwards to look down upon more distant reaches, 'putting the viewer simultaneously above the city and in it'. The effect is at first disconcerting in the way of the Paris-folding dream in Christopher Nolan's *Inception* or Larry Niven's *Ringworld*. Reality warps to fit the map. Art is the telling of lies to reveal the truth. Barbari's incredibly accurate map of Venice added puffing disembodied cloud-faces to demonstrate prevailing winds as well as the protective figures of Mercury and Neptune. Similarly, in the blueprints of Leonidov up to

Leon Krier's 'The Completion of Washington D.C.' (1985), we are reminded, by the inclusion of banking aircraft, of scale and also the pretence of the bird's-eye perspective. To see in maps is to accept the ability to fly.

These imaginings are replicated beneath cities. In archaeology, we attempt to reconstruct ancient three-dimensional cities with the traces of where buildings touched the earth. Architecture is the creation of space and walls are only a means to this end, yet we're forced to treat them as an end in themselves. We know the dimensions of the rooms of Inca citadels, Roman villas, Tikal temples, Siam towers, but can only make educated guesses at what transpired within them, through brickwork and the flotsam that sank into the earth. We might add scraps of descriptive parchment or hieroglyphs[80] if we are lucky but this requires trusting the inevitably unreliable narrators. One of the greatest finds in terms of directly understanding life millennia ago was the graffiti of Herculaneum, preserved not by lofty scribes but written on the walls of brothels and drinking dens, offering instantaneous recognition that they are us and we are they. There are ribald declarations: 'Weep, you girls. My penis has given you up. Now it penetrates men's behinds. Goodbye, wondrous femininity!' There are threats and warnings: 'Theophilus, don't perform oral sex on girls against the city wall like a dog!' There are meta-reflections: 'O walls, you have held

---

80   A remarkable if disputed version of which survives in modern times in the form
        of the chalk symbol language of hobos in North America ('Talk religion get
        food', 'Bad tempered owner', 'Unsafe place', 'Be ready to defend yourself' etc.);
        every sign representing at least one untold story, as all warnings and signs do.

up so much tedious graffiti that I am amazed that you have not already collapsed in ruin.' And there are statements of touching monumental simplicity: 'We two dear men, friends forever, were here. If you want to know our names, they are Gaius and Aulus.'[81]

There is a city called Rome on every continent. Every modern flag of Cambodia, hoisted by warring factions, has featured a silhouette of the abandoned jungle city of Angkor Wat. Authorities seek the appearance of legitimacy and reflected grandeur by claiming descent from past civilisations that never really existed as portrayed. Some are clumsy, like the life-size unruined Parthenon in Nashville[82] ('improving' on the original by recreating the long-lost statue of Athena) or Edinburgh's bankrupt postmodern Parthenon on Calton Hill. Some are ubiquitous, like the use of Greek columns in courts. The awkward fact that ancient Athens at its peak was a relatively sparsely-populated town is ignored, as is the fact that glorious Rome was riven with interminable murder, slavery and lunacy: 'the city of Scipio's and Cicero's dreams vanished even before the sleepers awoke: in fact, it had never existed. Rome's order, Rome's justice, Rome's peace were all built on savage exploitation and suppression.'[83]

Yet the view of infinite ancient glories to be restored remains as seductive as the clockwork birds of Yeats' Byzantium

81   Multiple examples surface in books like *Graffiti and the Literary Landscape in Roman Pompeii* by Kristina Milnor.

82   Built for Tennessee's 1897 Centennial Exposition.

83   Mumford, Pg. 227-228

or Marlowe's 'topless towers of Ilium'[84]. These are dreams, wondrous welcome dreams perhaps, but there are times when to sleep is to court disaster. At such moments, the scrawled obscene, frivolous and profound voices from the walls should rouse us, connecting us to them, and reality, over an expanse of time. The dead have secrets that may just save us.

---

84   *Doctor Faustus*, 13.90-91

Blueprinting Eternity

Official histories come to us woven within tales of dynasties, autocrats, victor's history and loser's retribution. Power struggles are carved into the stone; Rameses the Second airbrushing the monuments of Luxor to usurp his predecessor Amenophis the Third or Constantine transplanting his features onto carvings of Marcus Aurelius. Lessons are underlined like the wedding cake of the Sacré-Cœur rising above Paris in the same blanched white of the bones of the communards it condemns. The supposed permanence of stone was designed to give regimes an immortal quality with pyramids acknowledged as 'houses of eternity'[85]. They were fit to contain gods yet the Great Pyramid at Giza we view today, the last surviving of the Ancient Seven Wonders, is the wreckage of earlier greatness. These are the burial places of gods, not the temples. 'Like the monotonous reiteration of long and formalised prayers for the dead . . . the Egyptian reiteration of architectural units was all part of the same, fearful quest for certainty'[86] but there is little certainty to be found, except that everything gets old and one day dies.

The patrons of monumental masonry projects did so for many reasons but a common consideration was the impossible desire to defeat death. Their inevitable failure gives the buildings the quality of *memento mori*. The architect of one of the first great cities (Uruk), Gilgamesh's quest for immortality, from the

85   *Art and Eternity: The Neferati Wall Painitng Conservation Project 1986-1992*,
        edited by Miguel Angel Corzo, Pg. 22

86   Baldwin Smith, Pg. 246

deserts to the bottom of the sea, was one repeated by other monarchs. The Chinese Emperor Qin Shi Huang dispatched Xu Fu the alchemist and a fleet of a thousand aides out into the unknown oceanic expanses to bring back the elixir of life. None returned. Most dictators indulged themselves by founding or renaming cities in their own honour, which proved unreliable when subject to the tides and cycles of history (even the Red Tsar Stalin had his name stripped from the city that would become Volgograd, formerly Stalingrad, the charnel-house of the Nazi Sixth army). Despite the Bolsheviks' strenuous efforts[87], immortality proved elusive and all the mouldering waxwork of Lenin proves today is that Lenin the man is long extinct. When the original aspirant Gilgamesh died, his followers changed the course of the Euphrates to wash over his burial place. His was a living flowing mausoleum and one that gave a hint of implausible deniability that he'd ever died at all.

Rulers were keen to assert claims of divinity over superstitious followers. In the Eridu Genesis, city building comes god-instructed (recorded obviously in retrospect): 'let the people build many cities so that I can rest in their shade. Let them lay bricks, establish places of divination, organise the sacred rituals and irrigate the earth. Then I will establish well-being there.'[88]

The architectural patrons assumed the status of gods not just for the power, but in the mistaken belief that gods could not die. Pyramids may have become tombs but they also became

87   See John Gray's *The Immortalization Commission.*

88   *Myths of the Near East,* Rachel Storm, Pg. 5

repositories of stories. They are books in stone. If we know of those mentioned in these tales, they *have* in some superficial sense survived their own deaths.

Babel

If the aim of grandiose building was to somehow transcend mortality, it was also an attempt to usurp God, that original benevolent dictator. Buildings erected to venerate the sun eventually conspired to control it, even block it out. Noah's great-grandson Nimrod rebelled against his desert deity by embarking on a programme of city building.

'Now it was Nimrod who excited them to such an affront and contempt of God . . . He said he would be revenged on God, if he should have a mind to drown the world again; for that he would build a tower too high for the waters to reach. And that he would avenge himself on God for destroying their forefathers.'[89]

Until then towers had been built with express or tacit dedication to deities. They may have soared but they did so with apologetic reverence. In Uruk, the ziggurat of E-ana was dedicated to the goddess Inanna. Successive generations sought to rebuild such towers that had been laid waste to by lightning, earthquakes and neglect; each gave dedication to the prevailing god of the time. Each was, in turn, found wanting.

Taking inspiration from Babylonian ziggurats but rejecting their deference, Nimrod's proto-skyscraper would become a lasting symbol for ambition and folly. It would be called Babel: 'It grew very high, sooner than anyone could expect . . . It was built of burnt brick, cemented together with mortar, made of bitumen, that it might not be liable to admit water. When God

89   *Works: The Life of Flavius Josephus*, Pg. 54

saw that they acted so madly, he did not resolve to destroy them utterly, since they were not grown wiser by the destruction of the former sinners; but he caused a tumult among them, by producing in them diverse languages [that] they should not be able to understand one another.'

The Greek Apocalypse of Baruch elaborates: 'And the Lord appeared to them and confused their speech, when they had built the tower to the height of four hundred and sixty-three cubits. And they took a gimlet, and sought to pierce the heavens, saying, Let us see [whether] the heaven is made of clay, or of brass, or of iron. When God saw this He did not permit them, but smote them with blindness and confusion of speech.'[90]

One of the paradoxes of urban life is that these great monuments to singularity are defined by diversity. There is one Paris, for example, and yet innumerable Parises. The New Yorks of Scorcese's *Taxi Driver* and Woody Allen's *Manhattan* are almost contemporaneous. This is reflected in amalgamated Cityspeak, combining words and phrases from various immigrant sources into something distinctly new, an idea underlined by Edward James Olmos in the future L.A. of *Blade Runner* but always evident in the vocal sounds of cities.

The tower is a building both sacred and profane. Herotodus claimed the great ziggurat of Babylon was:

' . . . a tower of solid masonry, a furlong in length and breadth,

90   *The Bible As It Was*, James L. Kugel, Pg. 124

upon which was raised a second tower, and on that a third, and so on up to eight. The ascent to the top tower is on the outside, by a path which winds round all the towers. When one is about half-way up, one finds a resting-place and seats, where persons are wont to sit some time on their way to the summit. On the topmost tower there is a spacious temple, and inside the temple stands a couch of unusual size, richly adorned, with a golden table by its side. There is no statue of any kind set up in the place, nor is the chamber occupied of nights by anyone but a single woman who, as the Chaldeans, the priests of this god, affirm, is chosen for himself by the deity out of all the women of the land. They also declare — but I for my part do not credit it — that the god comes down in person into this chamber, and sleeps upon the couch.'[91]

God still rules this tower, still banishes mortals from its heights but he is evidently in the process of being evicted, his time reduced to nightly accommodation in a single chamber, a love hotel in the sky. The temptation, way beyond the haggling of atheists and theists, is to consider that churches and sacred places represent ways of confining gods rather than celebrating them. Fear is an ingredient of awe and gods are fearful creatures.

It was not the building of the tower necessarily that was the problem; it was the intrusion of the human into the realms of the gods.

'If it had been possible to build the Tower of Babel without

91   Cited in Pg. 264 of *Babylon* by Paul Kriwaczek.

climbing it,' Kafka suggested 'it would have been permitted.'[92] There is virtue in this intrusion. There were no elevators in Babel[93], which was partially the function. The weak-willed remained at the base, like queasy tourists at the Eiffel Tower. Its scale implies and requires a Nietzschean conquering, not simply expending energy but being revitalised by it. The view from the top is Caspar David Friedrich's *Wanderer Above a Sea of Fog*. The sky-lobby musak is Wagner. To qualify as a pilgrim, there has to be a pilgrimage.

It was not for nothing that God, who rarely denied being jealous, laid waste to this tower of pride and insolence. In *Arabian Nights*, an empty city appears of 'lofty palaces laid out in pavilions all built of gold and silver and inlaid with many-coloured jewels and jacinths and chrysolites and pearls; 'Doubtless this is the Paradise promised for the world to come.' Having dared to mimic this divine model, 'Allah sent down . . . a mighty rushing sound from the Heavens of His power, which destroyed them all . . . Moreover, Allah blotted out the road which led to the city, and it stands in its stead unchanged until the Resurrection Day and the Hour of Judgement.[94]'

What would dissuade the survivors, now fired by indignation, to build again?

In Beckford's *The History of Caliph Vathek*, the hubris of aspiring

---

92   *Franz Kafka*, Harold Bloom, Pg. 91

93   Though the proposed Elevated Electric Railroad Tower for the World's Columbian Exposition, Chicago, 1892 and Grant E. Hamilton (*What Are We Coming To*) take extraordinary helter-skelter views.

94   *Arabian Nights*, Pg. 233

cloud-dwellers ends not in nemesis but in epiphany: 'His pride arrived at its height when, having ascended for the first time the eleven thousand stairs of his tower, he cast his eyes below, and beheld men not larger than pismires, mountains than shells, and cities than bee-hives. The idea which such an elevation inspired of his own grandeur completely bewildered him; he was almost ready to adore himself, till, lifting his eyes upward, he saw the stars as high above him as they appeared when he stood on the surface of the earth.' The wisdom is short-lived and soon overcome by ambition: 'He consoled himself, however, for this transient perception of his littleness with the thought of being great in the eyes of others, and flattered himself that the light of his mind would extend beyond the reach of his sight, and transfer to the stars the decrees of his destiny.'[95]

It must be added that the surviving accounts of the Tower of Babel come to us from forces resentful of city-dwellers. 'Judaism, Christianity and Islam all took root among nomads who had recently settled, and all three characterise nomadic traits — the shepherd, the pilgrim, the wanderer in the wilderness — as godly, and the life of the city as degenerate'[96].

In The Bible, this is explicit: 'Woe unto them that join house to house, that lay field to field, till there will be no place.' Even amongst the Roman philosophers, there was some adherence to this. 'Believe me,' Seneca claimed, 'that was a happy age, before

95   *The History of Caliph Vathek*, William Thomas Beckford

96   *No Man's Land*, George Monbiot

the days of architects, before the days of builders.'[97]

In Islam, the possibility of man usurping God resulted in the proscription of all but decorative patterns as graven images (with notable exceptions such as the magnificent tradition of Ottoman miniatures[98]). It was an attempt to banish the unrestrained questioning self in favour of submission to the one and only God and the final binding revelation of the truth as the Koran claims itself. Yet Islam could not entirely banish individuality. It is there in the beauty and Borgesian complexities of the art, in the structures of domes and minarets, from the Selimye Mosque, Edirne to the Blue Mosque of Istanbul. The Green Mosque, Bursa (now robbed of its dazzling emeralds) even has the gate inscription 'this noble place . . . a building such as no nation has been presented with since the sky began to turn . . . a reflection of the Infinite Garden of Delight.'[99]

In virtually all cases, religion is the benefactor of the real source and talent of creation, which is human. When the long view is taken, this may be a temporary state. The glory of Ancient Greek architecture has long out-lasted the gods it was dedicated to. The real reason monotheistic religions feign to loathe the city is the city's inherent polyphony. It has many voices from many angles and they multiply. By its very nature, this is a threat to

---

[97]   Epistle 90

[98]   Nusret Colpan created versions of cities that looked fantastical, based on
        Ottoman miniatures, where Mecca radiated outwards in clouds and waves,
        idealised with no schisms or crusades, an Islamic world utopian caliphate, as
        mythic as it is exquisite.

[99]   *The World of Ottoman Art*, Michael Levey, Pg. 15

any creed that has established itself as the one truth. It is the Babel and not just the tower that is the threat:

'Stephen jerked his thumb towards the window, saying:
— That is God.
Hooray! Ay! Whrrwhee!
— What? Mr Deasy asked.
— A shout in the street, Stephen answered, shrugging his shoulders.'[100]

God is a shout in the street and the street is babel.

100   *Ulysses*, James Joyce, Pg. 40

The Living Ruins

Those who wrote the holy texts went on to claim Nimrod had been insane all along, harbouring an insect in his brain and reaching the apex of his madness after his great Tower had crumbled (gravity being a more formidable foe than any deity), by attempting to invade the floating city of heaven on a bird-drawn chariot. Whilst we might expect a torrential crash as described in the *Book of Jubilees* or the *Sibylline Oracles* or alternatively a gradual decline, it is equally possible it was a combination of the two. A comparable example is the Colossus of Rhodes, the great bronze statue of the Sun God Helios erected in the Greek port by Chares of Lindos. Legend has it that the architect, realising the design was more imperfect or costly than imagined, killed himself before its completion. Felled at the knees by an earthquake, it became a site for tourist visits for eight centuries, a giant toppled verdigris-green man, before being carted off for scrap metal by Arabian merchants.

Ruins have a remarkable capacity for reinvention. In its (after-) life, the Parthenon[101] has been a church, a mosque, a battered hideout against Venetians (who blew its 300 defenders to pieces), the palace of a Duke (complete with a now-lost Frankish tower), a place of execution and target practice for Turks. It has been dedicated and rededicated to, and ransacked by, waves of empires and gods that no longer exist in any meaningful sense.

---

101   As well as modernist inspiration, with Le Corbusier admittiing in *Technika Chronica* (*Architect of the Century,* Pg. 56), 'In everything I have ever done, I have had in mind, in the very pit of my stomach, the Acropolis.'

Too often, we think of sites in stasis, either in the contemporary or in their hey-day when the intervening years of obscurity and change are equally representative. What of all the nights these places have seen, the dusks and the dawns, the bloodshed and the celebrations? What was the Parthenon like under the Rule of the Thirty Tyrants or the pillaging of the Heruli or Byzantine rule or the Crusades, the Catalans, the Ottomans? What of the people who viewed it at each stage? Just like the figures who populate dreams, it is hard to tell whether these are inventions, composites or ghosts from our own pasts.

When we imagine the lifespan of buildings, the evolving time-lapse view is logical though not especially revelatory. There are layers to subjective perception that merge the dubious binaries of truth and fiction, layers we should be less afraid of, given their inevitability.

'Only in this state of sublimity does something deeper become possible,' Werner Herzog rightly attests, 'a kind of truth that is the enemy of the merely factual. Ecstatic truth, I call it.'[102]

When his fellow director Akira Kurosawa filmed the rain-drenched decaying gate in *Rashōmon*, he was channelling his imaginings of the writer Ryūnosuke Akutagawa's imaginings of the actual medieval city of Kyoto, all in order to show things that are perpetually true. The real becomes unreal and the unreal becomes real. Might we imagine a derelict Tower of Babel in pieces serving as a hideout for bandits, an aviary for wild birds, a playground for inquisitive children, a half-believed mirage

102   *A Companion to Contemporary Documentary Film*, Alexandra Juhasz, Pg. 365

or a refuge for travellers in a desert 'full of dragons and great serpents, and . . . diverse venomous beasts all about'[103]?

The folk memory of the first skyscraper remained with us long after the means of building it had been forgotten. Indeed it dwelt in the collective psyche until the first modern wave of skyscrapers began to challenge the gods again. The Tower of Babel was, it is said, unsurpassed in size until the Eiffel Tower, though we might take Giovanni Villani's claim it was 80 miles in diameter[104] as exaggeration. In the days when only churches and castles were permitted to intrude into the heavens, the Tower of Babel rose repeatedly in the work of artists. The myth was endlessly malleable and universal; Babel equivalents have been found in African and South American folklore. It was employed first as metaphor, then, as with Renaissance backdrops, as an experiment in architectural form. Painters could vent contemporary spleen with the authorities or the populace and at the same time depict vertical cities of the imagination. Every age built it again according to their own methods and pulled it down for their own sins.

In Brueghel's version, we have the spiral of the ziggurat and the breadth of Josephus' account adorned with Romanesque engineering, reflecting his time spent in Rome in the 1550s. It is a tower that teems with life, from the bustling medieval docks, bridges and quarries near the base to the strato-climate at its peak. There are pulley systems populated by tiny figures

103   *The Travels of Sir John Mandeville*, Pg. 50-51

104   Cited on Pg. 18, *Lost Buildings: Demolished, Destroyed, Imagined, Reborn*, Jonathan Glancey

covered, in Manichean terms, in white chalk and red-brick dust. Yet there is little to suggest what is transpiring in the depths of the tower, through its darkened archways. Herein lies the narrative genius of the painting, along with the uneven ground and foundations which had already caused portions to collapse. Brueghel is his usual mischievous self, balancing misanthropy with a fascination for the mighty and futile things humans do. There is more than a hint of the medieval symbol of the Ship of Fools to the people constructing this siege engine towards heaven yet Brueghel stills frames them with doomed majesty.

With the Cubists and the Orphists, a temporal aspect was further emphasised[105]. The Tower of Babel was a multidimensional convergence of space and time, as all cities are. The perspectives could be wild and simultaneous like Robert Delauney's eleven Eiffel Towers (with their strange premonitions of war in the colours and soaring aeroplane angles, flitting between ominous and optimistic) or glacially-paced and somehow holy like Andy Warhol's eight hours and five minute footage of the Empire State Building.

In the many glorious depictions of Babel by the van Valkenborch brothers, we see the Netherlands of their day from the Flemish Renaissance-era battlements to the presence of besieging Spanish troops. The raising of the Tower is thus an earthly political act. So too is its razing. Gustave

---

105   Influence is a curious thing with Duchamp's *Nude Descending a Staircase*
        influencing the design of the Gehry Residence, with Gehry making 'models of
        windows that ooked like the ghost of Cubism was trying to crawl out.'
        (*The Architecture of Deconstruction*, Pg. 27)

Doré's later monochrome version reflects the smoke-infested Industrial Revolution of his time and also its orientalist colonial fascinations, appearing as a fusion of Blake's 'dark satanic mills' and the conical Grand Mosque of Samarra. It appears to be emitting sound that could either be the clangour of mechanics or a call to prayer. It was the supposed last roar of the age of faith[106] or the first infant shriek of the age of reason.

The initial unity of Babel was always overstated. It was after all a hierarchical structure. This was defined in generational terms as well as by class. Kafka was mercilessly wise in 'City Coat of Arms' when he wrote how the obligation of building Babel would overtake the romance, 'In this fashion the age of the first generation went past, but none of the succeeding ones showed any difference; except that technical skill increased and with it occasion for conflict. To this must be added that the second or third generation had already recognised the senselessness of building a heaven-reaching tower; but by that time everybody was too deeply involved to leave the city.' Fritz Lang's *Metropolis* predicted the fact that certain classes of people would inhabit the upper reaches of Babel, and that the workers would be excluded into its shadows:

'"We shall build a tower that will reach to the stars!" Having conceived Babel, yet unable to build it themselves, they had thousands to build it for them. But those who toiled knew

---

106 The church of San Ivo Alla Sapienza and Church of Our Saviour, Copenhagen, retain the spiral spire of Babel.

nothing of the dreams of those who planned. And the minds that planned the Tower of Babel cared nothing for the workers who built it. The hymns of praise of the few became the curses of the many — BABEL! BABEL! BABEL! — Between the mind that plans and the hands that build there must be a Mediator, and this must be the heart.'

Lang's visions and fears were not baseless; Lang's father had been an architect and Lang junior had fled home, ending up eventually in New York where his visions of *Metropolis*, viewed from a deck of a ship on the Hudson, had already partly been built[107]. So successful was Lang's reenactment that Hitler, via Goebbels, contacted him to make Nazi films. He wisely into exile without even having time to take money out of the bank[108].

107   It's worth noting that before *Metropolis*, Lang had made another mistaken utopian film (in search of a wonder city from the past) in *The Spiders*.

108   *The Ufa Story: A History of Germany's Greatest Film Company, 1918-1945*, Klaus Kreimeier, Pg. 214

The Return of Mammon

It was not just the theocrats who feared the advance of this version of modernity; the poets did too, realising that much of what was and what could be would be lost in the process. First among them was the London visionary William Blake, a man who had seen angels in the treetops of Peckham Rye and a demon descending his staircase in Lambeth[109]. Blake lamented the atmosphere of the newly urbanised London and recognised crucially, as Plato had, that the city was its people:

'I wander thro' each charter'd street, / Near where the charter'd Thames does flow. / And mark in every face I meet / Marks of weakness, marks of woe.'

He had seen the city of his youth transformed by the arrival of pistons and steam[110] and the soul of his mythic Albion (and its inhabitants) condemned in factories like the Albion Flour Mills. Blake wondered whether the legends of Christ coming to England were true; 'And was Jerusalem builded here / Among these dark Satanic Mills?'

To Blake, there was a clear choice between the former and the latter. A proto-socialist, he pledged himself to the construction or resurrection of the Just City: 'I will not cease from Mental Fight, / Nor shall my Sword sleep in my hand: / Till we have

---

109   *The Ghost of a Flea*

110   'It is not the machines themselves that make work inferior, but our inability to use them properly.' Morris, Pg. 20

built Jerusalem, / In England's green & pleasant Land.'

A typically atypical prophet, his message would be corrupted by those who followed with ulterior motives, and it's hard to look upon his engraving of Flaxman's 75m statue of Britannia on Greenwich Hill with the hopeful radical innocence with which it was once imbued with. Blake was a utopian prophet in an age of priests and, until he was safely dead and able to be exploited, they painted him as a madman.

'Contrary to vulgar illusion . . . ' the aviator surveyor of night cities and deserts Saint-Exupéry wrote, 'the machine does not isolate man from the great problems of nature but plunges him more deeply into them'[111]. The genie had escaped but there were still those who wished to continue redecorating the bottle. It is no coincidence that the Romantics, Sturm und Drang, the Pre-Raphaelites, the Celtic Twilight , William Morris' Arts and Crafts Movement and Art Nouveau's resurgence of nature and myth all took place against the backdrop of the rising Industrial Age. Some tried to humanise what was happening, others to build bulwarks against it. Most failed to grasp that Romanticism was a way of seeing the world rather than a thing observed and was as possible in the city as in the countryside:

'Instead of blaming their inability to control and organise the new world that was being created with the help of the machine, they blamed the machines themselves. They attempted to put

---

111   *Airman's Odyssey*, Antoine de Saint-Exupéry, Pg. 40

the clock back, to return to what they thought of as the more genuine ways of the medieval era . . . They tried to create for themselves a dream world divorced as far as possible from the unpleasant realities they despised.'[112]

Those who offered a future were those who accepted the inevitability of cities. There was always the allure of escape but this was still somewhat defined by the proximity of the urban. Thoreau's transcendental retreat at Walden Pond was a stone's throw from Concord. When Jack Kerouac inspired generations to take to the road[113], he did so simply by charting his efforts to get from one city to another on opposing American coasts. Even those seeking a complete escape from the gravity of cities found its reach extended further than city limits: 'no longer to be poisoned by civilisation he flees, and walks alone upon the land to become lost in the wild,'[114] Christopher McCandless wrote about himself in the bus where he starved to death twenty miles from the George Park Highway. Anyone who has hiked through rainforest or tundra knows that nature is not benevolent. It is without conscience or mercy. There is no more or less soul in a machine than in a pastoral scene. It lies solely with the watcher.

Harry Harrison examined the dangerous mix of arrogance, naïvety and romanticism in *Deathworld*. Deathworld is a planet heightened in cataclysm, torn by the gravity of two moons, where

112   *The Observer's Book of Architecture,* Penoyre and Ryan, Pg. 145

113   Being a continuation of a long Romantic travelling tradition back to the Chinese poets via the German Wandervogel.

114   *The Wonderbox: Curious Histories of How to Live,* Roman Krznaric, Pg. 214

tides pour into volcanoes and nature is carnivorous. Those who live in the midst of nature look with scorn on the city-dwellers and the fatalistic siege mentality they brought with them: 'Well, you know the junkmen, and you've seen where their city is. They managed to put it right in the middle of the most savage spot on this planet. You know they don't care about any living thing except themselves, shoot and kill is their only logic . . . I'm sure my ancestors saw how foolish this was and tried to tell them so. That would be reason enough for a war, wouldn't it?'[115]

On a civilising mission deep in enemy territory, the baffled colonial wonders why they are hated.

City of Angels

The place of organised Western religion today is demonstrated by the skyscrapers dwarfing St Patrick's Church in New York. It would however be a false dichotomy to see the towers of commerce and the towers of faith as opposites given their overlapping dominion over man (there is commerce in faith and faith in commerce). Indeed there have been ill-fated attempts to combine the two. The Woolworth Building for instance marketed itself as a 'cathedral of commerce'[116]. When Washington Heights Methodist church was bulldozed to make way for George Washington Bridge, Reverend Christian Reisner commissioned the 40-floor Broadway Church. It would contain, as deemed essential by scripture, a bowling alley, gymnasium, swimming pool and a rotating illuminated crucifix visible for 100 miles. It would be a 'magnificent advertisement for God's business'[117] but business is by its nature ungodly and spiralling costs saw the plan scrapped in favour of a diminutive version. This was no country for the old gods. Here Mammon had primacy.

By contrast, the Sagrada Família by Antoni Gaudí is a masterpiece in its evolving incompleteness. They have been building its towers for almost a hundred years; Gaudí claimed that God, his patron, was in no hurry. Given that its plans were burned in haste by the Catalan anarchists, it will never be the

116   *Romancing the Cathedral: Gothic Architecture in Fin-de-siecle French Culture*, Elizabeth Emery, Pg. 86

117   *From Abyssinian to Zion: A Guide to Manhattan's Houses of Worship*, David W. Dunlap, Pg. 35

building Gaudí imagined. Yet there is something wonderful in this. It has changed, almost like the magnificent living organism it appears to be, and like the city it adorns. It is a slowly solidifying dream and like a dream it will never quite be tangible or complete. In this, there is inestimable poetry. The roof of the Cistine Chapel has a likewise paradoxical existence. It was designed to subvert the presence of a roof, to go beyond into the heavens, to suggest however grand this is, it is only a window. Yet it is one created by an old man from Caprese. God is reduced to a character, albeit in a leading role, in the drama, reaching out his hand to his co-lead Adam, bracing himself for the hand to be bitten.

Discovering the Diagonal

From the right angle, the real becomes unreal. In M.C. Escher's 1928 woodcut, we have a God's-eye view, resembling impossibly early computer graphics, of the Tower of Babel. In László Moholy-Nagy's *7 a.m. (New Year's Morning). Berlin, circa 1930*, taken from a high window, we see the early morning city as unnatural as it really is. Perspectives, made possible by cranes, increasingly mobile cameras and daring photographers like Moholy-Nagy and Rodchenko, made the familiar look disconcertingly new[118]. Whilst the latter's comrade El Lissitzky was designing his Lenin Tribune, its benefactor was slowly dying, leaving the intended podium an empty unbuilt shell, a crane for a future that was subsequently cancelled.

Traditionalists had sneered at the novelty of the vertical, the satirist Daumier depicting the photographer Nader in a hot air balloon with his camera with the subtitle 'Nadar Raising Photography to the Height of Art' (precisely what he was doing). This was by no means restricted to photographers: 'There is a frightful disease prevalent in "the States," contagious, entirely beyond the skill of the best physicians. It is altitudimania, and its victims, who rarely die of it, but can never be entirely cured, spend half their lives climbing steps.'[119] Babel, for better and worse, offered us an opportunity to gaze back down upon ourselves.

118   The swimming hyper-detail of Andreas Gursky's contemporary large-format
        photographs are even more refocusing.

119   *New York Times*, Sunday, February 19th, 1992, Pg. 4

The Lightning Rod

Towers meant that empty cubits of sky could become real estate. but masonry could sustain its weight only to a relatively modest height (one of the reasons the mud-built skyscrapers of Shibam, Yemen astound[120]). With the development of load-bearing steel, height no longer seemed an obstacle. Inspired by the unbuilt Philadelphia Centennial Tower (with its thousand foot spiral staircase), the Eiffel Tower became an architectural dividing-line. *Le Temps* published a petition[121] condemning it, signed by a host of cultural figures led by Maupassant, who hated it so much he regularly lunched there as it was the only place in Paris he'd be guaranteed not to see it:

'We writers, painters, sculptors and architects, fervent lovers of the beauties of Paris, hitherto unblemished, protest with all our might in the name of slighted French taste against the erection, in the heart of our capital, of the useless and monstrous Eiffel Tower, which public ill-feeling, often inspired by good sense and the spirit of justice, has already christened the Tower of Babel.'[122]

The problem with their complaint was that it actually made the Eiffel Tower appear all the more intriguing:

---

120   C.F. Møller's prospective 34 storey wooden skyscraper in Stockholm has a similar disbelieving impressiveness.

121   *Le Temps*, February 14th, 1887

122   Cited in Pg. 113, *History of Modern Architecture : Volume 1*, Benevolo

'To picture what is in store for us you must for a moment imagine an absurd and dizzy construction towering over Paris, like a dark gigantic factory chimney, dwarfing and humiliating our monuments and our architecture till they vanish under the impact of this astonishing dream.'

Similarly when Paul Verlaine called it a 'belfry skeleton', Bloy a 'tragic street lamp', Huysmans 'a carcass waiting to be fleshed out' or when Charles Gounod anthromorphised it as a gargantuan vestige of its creator, they were adding layers of character. They had not factored in Eiffel's ingenuity at including technological developments such as telegraphic stations that quickly made it indispensable. In Apollinaire's 'Lettre-océan', the tower was communicating with the world in spirals, across the seas, and the world replied, with Mayakovsky beckoning the Eiffel Tower to come to Moscow where its mechanical genius would be appreciated in the dynamic Soviet age[123].

In our age, Paul Rudolph sought to base his Sino Tower, what would have been the tallest in Asia, on the Eiffel Tower, 'to which he gives particular complex geometries and aggressive angularities.'[124] 'Buildings which have been designed but were never built still exist for me, if for no one else,' he wrote sadly but defiantly.

London too was watching in the form of Edward Watkin, a railway baron who wanted to link Britain to the continent by

---

123 *Unreal City: Urban Experience in Modern European Literature and Art,* Edward Timms and David Kelley, Pg. 170

124 *The Sarasota School of Architecture 1941-66,* John Howe, Pg. 143

means of a tunnel dug beneath the English Channel. Frustrated by its failure, he sought to enrol Gustave Eiffel to build another rival tower in an amusement park in Wembley but, for reasons of patriotism, the French architect declined. Undaunted, Watkins threw the project open and received an extraordinary array of designs; enough towers to fill the London skyline with outsider architecture. There were ziggurats, gothic crags, proto-space age and brutalist monoliths, and even one (Albert Brunel's design) that resembles the House of Vice in Sfrozinda. Most however resembled versions of the Eiffel Tower with Romanesque and arabesque fittings; Eiffel Towers mutated enough to avoid outright plagiarism. In the end, Watkin rejected designs that were premonitions of the rocket age for a conservative approximation by Stewart, MacLaren and Dunn of what he'd wanted all along; the Eiffel Tower. It was however a bastardised clone, with the drama and elegance excised and replaced with dance-halls, observatories and a sanatorium for the chronically-ill above the smog. It would be taller but fatally diminished by replication. Watkin's Tower began to sink upon building and ran out of funding having reached only the first level, earning the title Watkin's Folly before being airbrushed from popular history by being blown to smithereens.

Skyscraper Mania

In the 12th Century, the city of Bologna witnessed a craze for tower building. Directly influencing the design of the World Trade Centre, it seems mystifying that the leaning Towers of the Asinelli and Garisenda families have outlived the former, even if the stories behind them have slipped into obscurity. The exact number of structures raised and the reasons for doing so in the city at that time are the matter of conjecture (factional rivalries, a mass Tarantella-esque hysteria for building and a real-estate Dutch Tulip-style bubble have been suggested) but the city would have resembled an impossibly modern metropolis of stone skyscrapers. Most of these would fall through structural faults, lightning strikes, fires and demolition. In the town of San Gimignano, rival tower-building between the Guelph and Ghibelline factions was political violence by other means[125]. Eventually, to prevent chaos, the council forbade any tower taller than its own.

In our present age, competitiveness over tower-building has reintensified. Given skylines and iconic skyscrapers are part of global city-branding, the lust for visibility often overpowers other infrastructural concerns and egalitarian hopes. It is a case of follow the money skyward and the towers' inhabitants (mainly banking and oil magnates) are an immediate guide to where power resides today. Ethics aside, these buildings are not

125   Around the same time, Bolgna fought a war with rival Modena over a stolen
       bucket from a well.

without their character; the twisting Shanghai Tower, the vast clock-faced Abraj Al-Bait Towers which illuminates their peaks at every call to prayer, the earthquake and typhoon-proof Tapei 101 which incorporates traditional Japanese symbolist design comparable to pagoda towers. The current tallest building in the world, Dubai's Burj Khalifa, borrows its climbs from Frank Lloyd Wright's unbuilt mile-high The Illinois, its Y-shape from Le Corbusier and an adaptation of the spiral from traditional regional minarets. They are collectively the perfect setting for slick spy-thrillers and adverts for glossy authoritarianism.

Such skylines have become omnipresent, so too the carefully-manufactured nicknames. Deliberately anthropomorphising structures which are built in the spirit of hard-headed cynicism. In these cases, form disguises function. It also makes these towers difficult to satirise; criticism is deflected from the reality of an imposing exclusive tower to an entity akin to a child's toy or a cherished pet. Hans Hollein's Rolls Royce Grill on Wall Street (1966) pales in postmodern absurdism next to the actually built Johnson and Burgee's AT & T Building (now the Sony Tower). They are brands but what these buildings are advertising is deliberately opaque, as is what they might be hiding. It's as if the buildings simply exist, self-designated icons, man-made natural formations. When we consider the activities of the glass-sharded financial centres and vanity projects of oligarchs, the Ajyad Fortress obliterated to build the Abraj Al-Bait Towers, the people obliterated to build Abu Dhabi, we might reassess how harshly history has judged the likes of mad Prince Ludwig, a man more sinned against than sinful. Where would Maupassant dine now given the few towers he'd be allowed access to would restrict him to a paid appointment of no more than 20 minutes with a high security ID check and body scan?

In von Chamisso's tale, Peter Schlemihl barters a bottomless purse of gold from the devil in exchange for his shadow. He is horrified to find that, despite his immense new-found wealth, he is treated as an outcast and chased from the suburbs. He abandons his cursed wealth and spends the rest of his life in penitential travel, investigating nature. In myths, hubris inevitably meets nemesis. This serves the function of a lesson but it also, like liberal Hollywood films, serves as a pressure valve. There is justice here because in life there is little. The towers shine and glow innocently and dazzlingly from Canary Wharf to Grozny City Clocks. There is certainly condemnation but context is crucial; North Korean architecture is widely mocked as totalitarian and impersonal but outside of the proscribed dictatorships, other silent omniscient ideologies absolve all sins. Repatriate Pyongyang's Mansudae Apartments to Hong Kong or the French Rivera, the Grand People's Study Hall to Japan, give the monstrous Ryugyong Hotel a lick of paint and a glass refit and it would be fit for critical celebration on the former docklands and seafronts of any sparkling metropolis[126]. The spectacle wins at its most spectacular, no matter how many abandoned cars wait at airports or how many dead are buried beneath them.

126   Similarly, The Shard would fit quite well in Pyongyang.

Elevators Through the Stratosphere

Where will the building cease? In the imagination, it is limitless. Space lies beyond the heavens and skyscrapers may converge with the idea of a space elevator posited by the Russian astrophysicist Konstantin Tsiolkovsky, dreaming up interstellar travel in a log cabin in the wilds of Tsarist Russia. Structures may, with geostationary counterweights, escape our atmosphere and a lift could conceivably take us directly into orbital space. In the meantime, the idea of mile-high skyscrapers that soar above the clouds has proved alluring but equally elusive. At such heights the enemy is not a jealous god, high-altitude gremlins[127] or gangs with grappling hooks living on its outside[128] but hurricane-strength winds and an absence of oxygen. Employing aerodynamic ailerons like a stationary plane in the sky, Kuwait's Burj Mubarak al Kabir in the newly created City of Silk aims to reach 1001 metres, in tribute to *One Thousand and One Nights*. In Jumeirah Garden City, the three-pronged 1 Dubai would have had sky-bridges linking each tower while Nakheel Tower in the same state would have been held together with winds rushing through long slots running throughout the building.

To contrast the technocratic sheen, architects have sought to incorporate organic features. Omero Marchetti's Millennium

---

127   Conan Doyle's *Terror of the Heights.*

128   In Jetter's *Farewell Horizontal,* the city of the Cylinder is so large it boasts its own
        orbiting moon, 'Dead Center' wastes in its interior and warring gangs —
        Grievous Amalgam, The Havoc Mass, Razorbacks — battling for territory on
        cables and cybernetic boots on its exterior.

Challenge Tower dispenses with traditional wind-vulnerable moulds for a structure inspired by snowflakes. The Kingdom Tower, according to its creator, 'evokes a bundle of leaves shooting up from the ground [like a] young desert plant.' This, at least, is in the process of being constructed; others remain unbuilt. Some have been postponed or cancelled. Others never had the remotest chance of being erected. The line between imagination and speculation can be a thin one. The line between prospective investment and Ponzi scheme thinner still. The mile-high tower will surely come and we will soon wonder with momentary Sisyphean wonder what the next milestone is and where and how it will end again? The view from the stratosphere will be something to behold, so too will the filling of it with office space and penthouses. The issue then will be how much of a waste we can make of heaven?

Perhaps it's a gut feeling that we should not be so far from terra firma that has architects eager to depict their structures as organic. In some cases, the links between nature and the architect's imaginings are more convincing than others. It is reasonable to compare Lloyd Wright's Mile High Skyscraper or Bofill's Walden 7 to termite mounds, 'the conical shape of the tropical hornet Vespa affinis' to 'the clay house of the Mousgum tribe in Chad'[129]. The German Pavilion at Expo 67, which influenced a thousand stadia, resembles a draped spider's web. Buckminster Fuller's geodesic dome resembles the pupal case of a butterfly. Gaudí's Casa Batllo is a fairytale house of sweets

129   *Animal Architecture*, Pg.11-13

and bones while Candilis, Josic and Woods' Toulouse-le-mirail development resembles branches or blood vessels. When Kisho Kurokawa's structures such as Nakagin Capsule Tower were ridiculed, he corrected his critics, 'they aren't washing machines, they're bird cages, you see in Japan we build concrete-box bird nests with round holes and place them in the trees. I've built these bird nests for itinerant businessmen.'[130]

In Marcus Felson's plans, 'the divergent metropolis becomes part of a Great Metropolitan Reef. Each new piece of suburb fastens onto this 'metro-reef' like coral, building outward and connecting inward.' In the Brussels Atomium, we can move around an enlarged iron crystal. In Kurokawa's Helix City and Helicoidal Towers, we have the possibility of people living in towers based on the structures of their DNA.

130   *The Language of Post Modern Architecture*, Charles Jencks, Pg. 40

The Golem

We've been in the future before. In 1956, Frank Lloyd Wright was commissioned to design a mile-high television antenna in Chicago. Buoyed by new building possibilities and the thought of a structure four times the height of the Empire State Building, he turned it into a skyscraper, 'The Illinois'. It was to be 528 storeys high and contained a-mile-a-minute atomic-powered ride to the top in a glass elevator. An advocate of landscaping and green space in architecture, Lloyd Wright naïvely envisaged it would stand alone and absorb the demand for horizontal building space and parking, for both cars and helicopters. It surpassed even John A. Larkin's megalomaniac Larkin Tower in terms of height, beauty and unbuildability. It would exist only in blueprints, the pages of his book *A Testament* and in the imaginations of those who read them.

Lloyd Wright wished to build but harboured a disdain for actual cities (comparing them to a 'cross-section of a fibrous tumor'). New York to Lloyd Wright was 'Prison towers and modern posters for soap and whiskey'. 'Clear out 800,000 people and preserve [Boston] as a museum piece,' he suggested in *The New York Times*[131]. Of Pittsburgh, he simply shrugged, 'Abandon it.' In 1904, he delivered a lecture to the Daughters of the American Revolution which seems like a prophetic warning

131   November 27th, 1955

of apocalyptic urbanism[132]:

'Go at night-fall to the top of one of the down-town steel giants and you may see how in the image of material man, at once his glory and his menace, is this thing we call a city. There beneath you is the monster, stretching acre upon acre into the far distance . . . the city's flesh outspreads layer upon layer, enmeshed by an intricate network of veins and arteries radiating into the gloom.'[133]

If the problem is that cities sprawl monstrously over the earth's limited habitable surface (as 'demonic stone-desert'[134] according to Spengler) then the key is to restrict it. In 1988, Hans Kollhoff designed Atlanpole, a megastructure in which an entire city, based around a university, is fitted. 'Someone working in a research laboratory or an industrial plant is able to get to his tennis court or home in a few minutes'[135]. In his admirably utopian fervour, Kollhoff (and the likes of Ludwig Hilberseimer's High Rise City) declined to wonder why we keep work and life, and the places they are situated, separate.

132   His regular correspondent, Lewis Mumford, was a fellow reluctant prophet: 'I
       would die happy if I knew that on my tombstone could be written these words,
       "This man was an absolute fool. None of the disastrous things that he
       reluctantly predicted ever came to pass!"'
       — *Lewis Mumford, a Life*, Donald L. Miller, Preface xv

133   'The Art and Craft of the Machine', in *On Architecture: Selected Writings
       (1894-1940)*

134   *Nabokov and His Fiction: New Perspectives*, Julian W. Connolly, Pg. 200

135   *Kollhoff & Timmermann Architects: Hans Kollhoff*, Pg. 122

One invades and erodes the other, and work almost always has the upper hand. A place that has everything risks not having the one thing it surely needs — escape. Here are the blueprints of a gentrified Kowloon Walled City, one you need never leave.

Many of the unbuilt mile-high cities fit the description of vertical cities and their height and hubris far exceed Kollhoff's bulky megalith. Often the emphasis was not just in pushing the city upwards but upwards and outwards, to create horizontal skyscrapers. El Lissitzky was an early proponent, with his sky-hooks resembling cranes, but the idea soon took on all manner of forms. Walter Jonas' Intrapolis proposed a funnel-shaped terraced tornado of a megacity, ensuring a 'high concentration of population and, simultaneously, minimal contact with the ground.' This drive of 'more for less' posed problems as well as solutions (the creation of vast shadows being a recurring issue) but it has proved popular; with the Metabolist's enthusiasm for the horizontal vertical eventually translating into real-life with the likes of the CCTV Tower.

It would take a granite spirit however not to be stirred by the Eiffel Tower-inspired designs of the prospective Dubai City Tower, rising and intertwining like glistening Lovecraftian tentacles from the deep or the fact that it uses essentially a bullet train pointed upwards as a lift. That it might use slave labour, as other projects in the kingdom have, is incidental to some. After all, who recalls the hundreds of workers killed bringing the Great Wall of China, the Panama Canal, the Pacific Railroad, the Qatar World Cup stadium or the Kolyma Highway from idea to reality? Lewis Mumford repeatedly warned against an emphasis on technocracy at the expense of the individual, on technology serving itself or an elite rather than the general population defining. The problem of telling one from the other is a modern riddle of the crossroads. What category would the factory-built 202-storey wind-ignoring Sky City of Changsha, and its 20,000 inhabitants, fall into? Or Bionic City, housing 100,000 people in a tree-like tower floating on a system of roots? These considerations are there each time we build, each time we dream.

Vertical Suburbs

The inclusion of village-style lobbies is an admission that such structures intrinsically alienate. A sense of community must be placed there artificially. Dubai City Tower plans green spaces in its sky plazas. Sky City has farms, gardens and a 10 km walkway from the 1st to the 170th floor. Bionic City 'is made up of twelve vertical neighbourhoods' gathered around gardens and pools. At their most dramatic, these vast tapering towers would resemble mountains shrouded in glass and greenery. At their most mundane, they would be vertical suburbs. These, we are told, will save the countryside.

'Why build a two mile high, one mile wide building?' ask the designers of the Ultima Tower (planning to house one million people). 'To prevent the uncontrolled blight of the natural landscape by rapacious developers and industry. At current rates the surface of the planet will be nearly totally covered with residential, commercial and apartment dwellings within the coming century . . . One must not think in terms of floors but, instead, imagine entire landscaped neighbour-hood districts with 'skies' that are 30 to 50 meters high. Lakes, streams, rivers, hills and ravines comprise the soil landscape on which . . . buildings can be built.' Sunlight will cascade down through the centre of the building via mirrors. Water will be sucked up from a lake and used to create four of the largest, internal, waterfalls on earth.

The design is based not on traditional skyscraper models

but on termite mounds and 'could be thought of as an upward extension of the earth . . . a great expanse of natural land turned upward with ten large forest, lake and stream sanctuaries brought up into the sky.'

It is part pitch, part biblical prophecy: 'And it shall come to pass in the last days, that the mountain of the Lord's house shall be established . . . and all nations shall flow unto it.'[136]

136   Isaiah 2:2

Sanctifying the Secular

The next generation of as-yet unbuildable megastructures have notably Bronze Age characteristics. Shimizu TRY 2004 Mega-City Pyramid imagines a million guests living in smaller pyramids and working in suspended skyscrapers, all floating on Tokyo Bay. Taisei Corporation's X-Seed 4000 would rise too from the sea as the tallest building ever conceived, a skyscraper city in imitation of Mount Fuji, while Takenaka Corporation's Sky City 1000 would consist of stacked sky plateaus. Norman Foster's Crystal Island would have peaked like a glittering diamond fractal in Moscow had the financial crash not stopped it in its tracks. It's arguable whether any of these structures were realistically intended to be built; many were holographic prestige projects designed to drum up publicity and establish reputations. There remains however a sneaking admiration for such nightmarish monomania, most honestly admitted in Ojima's 30 million people-housing, Everest-eclipsing Tokyo Tower of Babel.

We look at such plans with wonder, scepticism and no small degree of righteous ire. Might we admit to having the prophet inside, yearning for these towers to fall? Part of this is down to disgust and exclusion from what and who these towers contain. It is also a sense of what could have been; that these towers, as suggested by Ferriss and others, could have been dedicated to science, philosophy, music[137], culture but instead are continually dedicated to mercantilism. Any criticism is greeted with skittish incredulity incredulity for fear of scaring the self-appointed wealth-creators away like a herd of wild horses. For all the talk of form and function, the truth is that form follows profit. They are glorious terrible manifestations of Capital: 'nothing will hold back [its] thrust towards the glory of the eternal heavens . . . the future is airy and hollow like a distant cloud over the horizon. Capital builds its kingdom amongst these clouds, anchored to the ground by the steel cables of debt. The future is now . . . rejoice, the catastrophe has already happened!' [138]

In 1908, Antoni Gaudí was contacted by two American businessmen to build a prospective Hotel Attraction on what is now the former site of those other biblically-fallen towers of our age, the Twin Towers of Manhattan. No one knows who the commissioners were or why it was dropped and almost entirely vanished from history. Gaudí's papers went up in smoke during the Spanish Civil War leaving only half a dozen sketches from the three years he worked on the plan. The memory of what might have been survives largely through the recollections of his apprentice Juan Matemala i Flotats[139]. The hotel's tiled concrete parabolic towers of galleries, museums and theatres would have shimmered like salmon skin. It would have boasted vast

---

137   As in Fludd & de Bry's Temple of Music from *The Metaphysical, Physical & Technical History of both Major & Minor Worlds*,1624.

138   Kollectiv's Capitalist Manifesto

139   Flotats had created the architect's death mask after he'd been hit and killed by a tram; his body mistaken for a tramp, in the city he had helped to create.

halls, the largest a homage to America and its presidents, and a dining room for every continent. At its peak would be a star, 'the sphere of all space', offering a panorama of the city. The sense of hauntological regret flicking through the sketches of what could have been[140] pales next to footage of what once was; footage from inside the Twin Towers, even holiday videos, has been changed utterly and invested with aura by hindsight. The site returned catastrophically to a state of potentiality, with competing translucent CGI designs that seemed to barely exist. There was even the rejected suggestion of returning to Gaudí's plans. Even the most colossal structures are finite. They will dissipate just as dreamed-of plans will one day be forgotten for the final time.

---

140   To be filed next to W.F.C. Holden's Art Deco Crystal Tower Bridge London, John Russell Pope's Lincoln Memorial and Colonel Trench's Trafalgar Square pyramids, half a dozen Sydney Opera Houses and so on.

Lift Off

Maximising space in the sky and minimising connection with the earth will continue until the next logical step, however improbable; cities breaking free of the ground altogether. This once seemed less absurd than it does now, a view that may well come to pass again. Planes had been dismissed as impossible right up until the Wright Brothers. There were also fragments of the city already in the sky. Replicating the large ocean-going vessels of the time, zeppelins boasted luxury living quarters, restaurants, even ballrooms. With advances in technology, it seemed that these facilities would expand. The Futurist Depero Fortunato breathlessly exalted his Aerial City with its 'squares — aerial parks — station for aeroplanes — flying houses — cafes on immensely tall piles, 100-200-300-1000 metres above the ground'[141].

A flying city would be able to migrate to resources and away from disasters. There would be no risk from earthquakes, tsunamis, or a rise in sea level. There would be endless solar power above the clouds; crop farms might levitate above the seasons for all-year abundance. Steering clear of typhoon and hurricane regions, humanity would no longer be prey to the nihilism of nature. If we could readjust our way of seeing our existence on the planet, there would be health benefits for the city-dwellers according to Hugo Gernsback; 'At the present time we are living at the bottom of a vast sea — the sea of air —

141   *Futurismo*, Pg. 465

our present atmosphere.'[142]

If we were to rise, that pressure would diminish and, temperature and oxygen notwithstanding, we would be empowered. Above the clouds, we would exist in a realm of continual sunshine with few diseases and little bacteria. We need merely consider the proposition not as a beguiling city in the sky with its associations of Cloud Cuckoo Land or Spanish Castles but as huge modified airships; 'Just as we construct leviathans of the sea today, some of them weighing as much as 50,000 tons, we shall construct entire cities weighing billions of tons, which will be held in space not by gas balloons, propellers, or the like antiquated machinery, but by means of gravity-annulling devices.'

To stay afloat in this ocean of atmosphere, the domed cities would fire electromagnetic jets. Individuals would don spacesuits powered by static electricity; deep-sea diving suits to ascend rather than descend. Gernsback estimated we'd have to wait ten thousand years for such developments by which time it's arguable whether there'd be a habitable atmosphere or a human race.

Designs ventured further into the fantastical. There were Wenzel Hablik's[143] ornate spinning top colonies of glass and iron, crystalline floating cities like detached mountain peaks,

142   'Ten Thousand Years From Now', *Ogden Standard-Examiner*, February 12th, 1922

143   Hablik believed filling our rooms with rainbow colours and patterns would
         make us better people, existing versions of which can be seen in Wenzel-Hablik
         Haus, Itzehoe, Germany. Verner Panton's Visiona 2 (1970) continued this idea
         in the form of a plush futuristic cocoon, where the architecture and the
         furnishings were indecipherable.

and settlements on rocky planetoids orbiting the earth. Lazar Khidekel took Malevich's Architecton models and Planit drawings and fired them into space as geometric satellite cities. Kalmykov based his city on Saturn's rings. All were idealists. On the cover of *Frühlicht* (1920), Bruno Taut pictured a semi-mystic house in the sky, radiating like a biblical hallucination. Krutikov's flying apartment blocks may have been more functional but they were no less arresting; a series of atomically-powered towers linked with a ring base, each flat with a balcony and a docking station. Krutikov rejected the idea of a floating palace for an egalitarian view. We would all have the option of living in the sky.

'One of our utopian ideas,' El Lissitsky declared, 'is the desire to overcome the limitations of the substructure, the earthbound . . . [This idea] can be extended even further and calls for the conquest of gravity as such. It demands floating structures.'[144]

When the idea was resurrected in the pulp collage that is *Star Wars*, it was as a Cloud City based around gas production and commerce, run by a gambler; the city, quite accurately as human nature goes, as Machiavellian cherub[145].

As with aviation, the flying city would inevitably be put to malevolent use. Way back in *Gulliver's Travels*, Jonathan Swift had envisaged the levitating metropolis Laputa. It took

---

144   'The Future and Utopia', *Russia: An Architecture for World Revolution*

145   The city bears more than a passing resemblance to Seattle's Googie masterpiece the Space Needle.

a vaguely biblical form[146] but its controls were in the hands of eminently corruptible humans, who positioned the city over neighbouring settlements to block out light to their crops and rain bombs down upon them. Swift used the analogy to skewer Britain's colonial treatment of Ireland. Laputa was in essence a floating London. Centuries before the Sputnik panic and Reagan's prospective Star Wars program, Swift knew that humanity did not and perhaps could not trust itself, even with a glorious recreation of heaven in the skies.

There was always the enticement of escape. If a city could rise, why stop at the exosphere? The energy needed to sustain a city of several million tonnes in flight would be colossal and defies all our current thresholds but if it was achievable, through nuclear fusion for example, then it is not inconceivable it could escape the earth's gravity. In James Blish's *Cities in Flight*, an anti-gravity device called the spindizzy is used to blast cities into outer space. If we are to survive as a race, we are told we must escape a depleted earth and colonise the solar system, moving through the vacuum like Blish's okie[147] cities, towards other planets. The analogy seems always to lie with the sea, from solar wind-powered spaceships to the sailor's *saudade* feeling of melancholy and nostalgia in trying to return to the earth (*Ulysses 31, Red Dwarf* etc.).

---

146   Book of Revelation: 'And I John saw the holy city, new Jerusalem, coming down from God out of heaven, prepared as a bride adorned for her husband.'

147   A reference to Steinbeck's *The Grapes of Wrath*.

It Came From the Depths

The raising of skyscrapers seems like an act of faith, flying in the face of gravity, hubris and decency, to such an extent that even the designers occasionally voiced doubts. The creator of the haunting art deco towers of *The World of Tomorrow* (a crucial influence on Gotham City) Hugh Ferriss questioned the mania for ever taller buildings; 'Do we not begin to apprehend, in this headlong ascent, something ominous? It is not a little disturbingly reminiscent of the Tower of Babel?'[148]

There was something inescapably demonic to urban settings: 'going down into the streets of a modern city must seem — to the newcomer, at least — a little like Dante's descent into Hades . . . a visitor would find, in the dense atmosphere, in the kaleidoscopic sights, the confused noise and the complex physical contacts, something very reminiscent of the lower realms.' Then there were its bad points.

There was something not just godless but inhuman in these constructions, recognised in Christopher Nevinson's *Temples of New York* series which begs the question, who are the temples dedicated to? The poet Allen Ginsberg answered with a bellow of Moloch[149]. To romantically exalt the countryside as free and virtuous is to demonise the mercantile city. 'Cities, architectures, how I loathe you!' Henri Micheaux spits; 'Great surfaces of vaults, vaults cemented into the earth, vaults set out

148   Pg. 62

149   An Ammonite God loathed by the Jews for the practise of child sacrifice, a
       practise still demanded by capitalism in Ginsberg's eyes.

in compartments, forming vaults to eat in, vaults for sex, vaults on the watch, ready to open fire. How sad . . . '[150]

In Georg Heym's expressionist poetry, Berlin[151] appears like some wild nocturnal beast in flames, long before it was so. Steinbeck had something of a prophetic grasp of high finance, to which the towers were then being erected, and how it would, like a golem, break out of control: 'The bank is something else than men. It happens that every man in a bank hates what the bank does, and yet the bank does it. The bank is something more than men, I tell you. It's the monster. Men made it, but they can't control it.'[152]

The monster must fall, and even its inhabitants know it. 'All the legends and songs,' Franz Kafka wrote, 'that came to birth in that city are filled with longing for a prophesied day when the city would be destroyed by five successive blows from a gigantic fist. It is for that reason too that the city has a closed fist on its coat of arms.'

We rehearsed the fall of cities until they actually occurred then we no longer wanted it, like André Breton bashfully confessing, 'We no longer want the end of the world.'[153]

---

150   Ecuador, Pg. 60

151   Heym always threatened escape to China before drowning under the Berlin ice, trying to save a friend.

152   An alternative to the towers of finance is found in Friedrich's St. Florian's Vertical City (1966) which rises above the clouds to offer the occupants of the upper floors (children, the sick and the elderly) extra time in the sunlight. They could be dedicated to any number of things but rapacious greed.

153   Breton had elsewhere urged the firing of a revolver at random into a crowd as a Surrealist act.

It was too late, however, for some. On the morning of August 6th 1945, Japanese telegraph operators ominously noticed there was no longer any contact from the city of Hiroshima. The US atomic bomb Little Boy had detonated above the Shima Hospital obliterating a large radius of the city and tens of thousands of its inhabitants. Nagasaki would follow three days later. Kyoto was spared due to the US Secretary of War Henry L. Stimson having fond memories of honeymooning there. Kokura was saved by low-lying clouds.

The real-life colossus of the mushroom cloud was eventually refashioned into a giant lumbering bogeyman, one it was possible to quantify, understand and perhaps defeat. Godzilla comes, via dragon myths and Gashadokuro[154], from the folk memory of dinosaur bones. Only time and a well-placed meteorite saved the earth from them and for us. Nevertheless, they cast a long shadow. In Victorian Hollow Earth explorer novels, dinosaurs somehow exist still as pterodactyls over the Arctic or tyrannosaurs beneath our feet. These stories overlapped with the time period when it first came possible to deliver mass death from above. We were the pterodactyls. Cities had been ransacked and burned for millennia but it was possible, on paper at least, to defend against incoming forces on the ground. Defending against the sky was far more difficult. With aerial bombardment, the prospect of entire cities being wiped out became a distinct probability in times of war. H.G. Wells took this as a given with

154   Mythic gargantuan skeletons made up from the bones of famine victims, who prey on the living, as depicted in the woodblock prints of Utagawa Kuniyoshi.

his ominously-titled Everytown laid waste to in *The Shape of Things to Come*. This resonated because of the recent memory of baleful German Zeppelins over London, causing mass panic and phantom sightings[155]. At the time of Wells' publication, the Nazis were taking power in Germany and a repeat seemed ominously likely. The contemporary horrors of Guernica (laid waste to by German bombers) and Manchuria (ravaged by the Japanese) demonstrated that civilians were now perceived as legitimate targets and secondly that this was coming to a city near you. A Spanish Republican poster of the time showed a dead child beneath the title 'Madrid' and above the line, 'If you tolerate this, your children will be next.' It was tolerated.

Cities attempted to imagine themselves out of existence and hide at night. Windows were painted black, wardens patrolled for signs of light disrupting the blackout. Japan's wooden cities became tinderboxes for incendiary storms yet it was the nuclear bombs that loomed in memory because of the surprise of their appearance and the lasting radioactive effects. Reality had become a nightmare and an appropriate creature was found from the depths to embody it (in the same way medieval Europeans gave form to intangible plague as the Grim Reaper). It developed from a dream of the American aviator Merian Caldwell Cooper, who would later be involved in the bombing of Tokyo during the Doolittle raids. From a nocturnal vision emerged *King Kong*. Its scale recalled the giants of lore[156], for the simple reason

---

155   His near-namesake Orson Welles managed similar hysteria with his naturalistic approach to his *War of the Worlds* radio broadcast.

156   Goya's Colussus for example.

that air superiority had rendered us ant-size. The vast city-attacking ape can be seen in a variety of ways — a rampaging beast, the freakish 'eighth wonder of the world', a tragic anti-hero or a maverick embodiment of the American Dream. What better symbol do we have of Ayn Rand's philosophies that a hulking gorilla émigré making it in the big city, pursuing the object of his affections, beset by biplanes, ascending the Empire State Building, rising above the bureaucrats and the liberals to command the city?[157] Kong can be seen as the first in a lineage of doomed but spectacular entrepreneurial spirits like Cody Jarrett in *White Heat* and Tony Montana in *Scarface*, with all enjoying blaze-of-glory finales.

Japan borrowed the template of *King Kong* and transformed it according to the trauma of recent history. They placed it in the tradition of the Ōnamazu, a huge mythological catfish[158] that is imprisoned by the god Kashima underground and which, on occasion, thrashes around causing earthquakes. After Edo (now Tokyo) was flattened in the Great Ansei Earthquake, catfish prints became fashionable, serving as explanation of the mindless disaster, cathartic vengeance, pleas for forgiveness and bitter comments towards profiteers supposedly aiding the catfish. The emphasis was now placed on a monster unleashed indirectly by ambition. The cliché is that Kaiju monster films

---

157   Another symbol of Randian philosophy is the small triangle of concrete emblazoned,'Property of the Hess Estate Which Has Never Been Dedicated For Public Purposes', marking David Hess' pyrrhic victory against the demolition of his apartment block.

158   This is still the logo of the Earthquake Early Warning (EEW) in Japan.

were a way of approaching the unapproachable subject of Hiroshima and Nagasaki. Approaching from an oblique angle seems logical in a society where the victims of the bombs were ostracised as unclean 'hibakusha'. Yet the first native Kaiju film, in which a colossal werewolf attacks Edo, was screened before the Second World War. Its reels were incinerated in the bombing campaigns that followed.

One of the earliest examples of an atomic-provoked beast was not Japanese but American in origin — *The Beast from 20,000 Fathoms*. A nuclear detonation in the polar region (the unimaginatively-titled Operation Experiment) awoke a sleeping primeval creature from Lovecraftian deep-sleep ('I feel like I'm leaving a world of untold tomorrows for a world of countless yesterdays'). This adaptation of the old Kraken from the deep mythos came updated for the modern age. The Beast feasted on several lighthouses and Coney Island amusement park before making its way towards the lights and clamour of New York City[159]. There was more than a hint of the prophetic in the melodramatic radio reports: 'New York is like a city besieged . . . All traffic has been halted. And Times Square, the heart of New York, has stopped beating . . . '

The filmmakers had appropriated the tableaux of the beast attacking the lighthouse from a Ray Bradbury short story, 'The

159   *Godzilla* is a reminder that we view cities only in human visuals and scale. We
        might gain something from reimagining what a city resembles to creatures who
        see from different perspectives and on different wavelengths. What is a city to
        a bird, a cat, an insect, a microbe? How strange and new a city looks even just in
        negative, as in Vera Lutter's photos.

Fog Horn'[160]. This, in turn, had been inspired by chancing upon the wreckage of a roller-coaster on a fog-shrouded L.A. beach, wreckage resembling a dinosaur skeleton[161].

The first Japanese appearance of Godzilla eerily echoed the sadly real crew of the Lucky Dragon 5 fishing vessel, poisoned by radioactive fallout in the vicinity of the Castle Bravo H-bomb detonation. From there, the menace comes to the mainland, creating panic and mimicking the demophobia the director Ishirō Honda felt in his years as a soldier and then a prisoner in China. Real terror fed the fiction. Though the Kaiju monsters would differ in appearance, all were fervent architectural critics. Having snapped Tokyo Tower in half, Mothra enveloped the wreckage in a cocoon. Having decided that Paris was too far inland and the audience wouldn't care if Australia was attacked, Gorgo was unleashed upon Elizabeth Tower: 'One of London's oldest landmarks smashed like matchwood! Nothing has stopped this beast so far, nothing! [. . .] Piccadilly. The heart of London . . . There's been nothing like it, not even the worst of the Blitz!'[162]

With time, horror becomes heritage. First as tragedy, then as farce, then as commodity. Before spiralling into remakes and versus battles, the shock of seeing cities destroyed by these creatures had already eased. The real had caught up, then

---

160   'Bradbury's rather touching story of a lonely ocean-dwelling dinosaur who mistakes a lighthouse foghorn for the cry of a long-lost mate.' (*Ray Bradbury*, Harold Bloom, Pg. 10). It was collected in *The Golden Apples of the Sun* (1953).

161   *Death is a Lonely Business*, Pg. 1

162   From Eugène Lourié's 1961 film.

passed by. With the end of the Cold War, Western cities basked in gluttonous safety. They slept as only the unaccountable can. Though critics feigned wonder at *Independence Day*'s obliteration of the White House (a building that had actually been incinerated once before by the British), the film was kitsch gloop, as parodic as it was patriotic. This was the apocalypse in the midst of Francis Fukuyama's musical statues view of history. Only the comedians offered anything of worth, with *Ghostbusters* unleashing the postmodern apocalypse of a rampaging Stay Puft Marshmallow Man on New York[163], where the very architecture is 'a huge super-conductive antenna that was designed and built expressly for the purpose of pulling in and concentrating spiritual turbulence.'

It was on the same urban island that Western history suddenly and violently proved it had not ended. Every channel switched to cover an atrocity that rendered action movies redundant; *The Onion*'s headline after 9/11, 'American Life Turns Into Bad Jerry Bruckheimer Movie', being an fair response. As time passes, we absorb traumatic events through careful editing and symbolic narratives, to the point of self-deception.

163   Though they claimed the building was designed as a demonic portal by a fictional insane architect and dabbler in the dark arts, Ivo Shandor, the skyscraper of *Ghostbusters'* climax is the very real 55 Central Park West building.

The Evaporating Cities

Ill blows the wind that profits no-one. In Katsuhiro Otomo's stunning *Akira*[164], Neo-Tokyo is built from the tabula rasa of a Tokyo obliterated in a nuclear attack; facilitating the ability to drive at high-speed on bikes when the former city was much too pedestrianised and congested. The urge to destroy again is a creative passion. Multiple cities were imagined into being to support the destruction industry and balance out the cities destroyed. Such was the associated prestige, fledgling Mid-Western U.S. communities vied with each other in their claims of being Atomic Towns. By contrast, the sites developing nuclear technology in the U.S. and Russia were kept as closely-guarded secrets due to the danger of leaks and pre-emptive strikes. In the Soviet Union, there were multiple closed cities that appeared on no public map. The monastery town of Sarov, for example, disappeared. When clouds of radioactive debris seared their way across the Urals in 1957, no-one in the outside world knew of the city of its source — Ozyorsk. Hundreds of thousands of people lived in conurbations that had no definitive name. The iron city of Zheleznogorsk, the star city of Zvyozdny Gorodok, the submarines of Sovetsky, the fleet harbour of Gremikha, the chemical warfare base of Shikhany, the nuclear warheads of Seversk, all the buildings and security checks and barbed wire and populations were invisible until Yeltsin declassified them

---

164   Otomo is an undefeated master at creating cities from the psychic and psychotic geography of *Domu: A Child's Dream* and the charming urban scouting of *Tokyo Metro Explorers*.

into existence as if by magic.

Yet they exist still. Mercury, Nevada, for example, is a closed city next to Jackass Flats testing site. It may be a shell of its former self but its population and activities are still restricted. The once-secret 'City Behind the Fence', Oak Ridge, Tennessee, was curiously prophesised by its mystic founder John Hendrix:

'In the woods, as I lay on the ground and looked up into the sky, there came to me a voice as loud and as sharp as thunder [telling] me to sleep with my head on the ground for 40 nights and I would be shown visions of what the future holds for this land . . . And I tell you, Bear Creek Valley someday will be filled with great buildings and factories, and they will help toward winning the greatest war that ever will be. And there will be a city on Black Oak Ridge . . . I've seen it. It's coming.'[165]

Beneath a portrait of Uncle Sam with his sleeves rolled up, three monkeys of the 'see no evil . . . ' variety perch behind the message, 'what you see here / what you do here / what you hear here / when you leave here / let it stay here'. There are presumably many closed cities of which we know nothing. We only learn of the unsuccessful or defunct ones, the ones whose secret escapes. The successful ones do not exist.

'At the moment that we hear the shriek of the melting telephone in Moscow,' announced the president in the novel *Fail-Safe*; 'I will order a SAC squadron which is at this moment

165   *Anderson County, Tennessee*, M. Secrist, Pg. 24

flying over New York City to drop four 20-megaton bombs in precisely the pattern and altitude in which our planes have been ordered to bomb Moscow. They will use the Empire State Building for ground zero.'[166]

In fact, ground zero was planned for Broadway, not far from Tower 270 where the Manhattan Project was born and was baptised. 'By the marble lions of New York's Public Library U.S. technicians test the rubble of the shattered city for radioactivity' ran the acerbically-titled *Life* magazine[167]. On the cover of *Collier's*[168], Chesley Bonestell painted the Manhattan project returning home catastrophically to a New York reimagined as 'Hiroshima, USA'. 'One Bomb vs New York — Now and in the possible future.' You could check maps of obliteration for your home and workplace, where you and your children ate, walked and slept and consider if you'd be an irradiated husk, burnt to a crisp, vaporised or merely a traumatised witness. If the existential threat of a nuclear holocaust got too much for the urbane dwellers of Eastern Seaboard metropolis, they could take a holiday in the organised crime-invented 'Up and Atom City' of Las Vegas, which boasted luxurious viewing points and Dawn Bomb cocktail parties with test detonations boiling in the desert sixty miles beyond. These detonations occurred at least once a month for over a decade. In a 1953 Don English photograph, two-dimensional cartoon cowboys laughing on

166   Pg. 263
167   November 19th, 1945
168   August 5th, 1950

advertising hoardings gesture towards the cap of a mushroom cloud, 'Here it is!' What they referred to was the future.

Except, of course, the future never came. It didn't arrive, at all, for tens of thousands of people in Hiroshima and Nagasaki. It didn't come, thankfully, in this form for the rest of us. Instead, we spent forty years destroying our cities in our imaginations and wondering what we'd do in the four minutes of freedom[169] when the end was coming, how entire lives would be finally lived in those four minutes. Forty years of *Duck and Cover* and Bert the Turtle[170], of the madness of *Doctor Strangelove* and the light relief of *Threads*, of CND marches being spied on and infiltrated by the security services and Mutually Assured Destruction as foreign policy, all those near-misses and dress rehearsals of end of the world. In hindsight, it seems scarcely believable that we forgave the authorities behind it and beneath it in their half-secret never-used underground cities.

What would remain? The speculative books of the time deal with the nightmare of absence and presence, in a world where in a misattributed quote of Khrushchev's 'the living will envy the dead'[171]. The slowly-dying Melbournians in Nevil Shute's *On the Beach* believed there was life in distant Seattle beyond the wind. While not directly atomic, the eerily empty city in *I*

169   This was the period of time between Britain detecting incoming Soviet missiles
        and their detonation, in popular parlance. In reality, there was only three
        minutes.

170   A 1951 civil defense cartoon shown in U.S. schools to instruct on nuclear attack.

171   Though quoted in The Washington Post March 20, 1981, it actually hails from
        Nikolay Chukovsky's translation of 'Them that die'll be the lucky ones' from
        Robert Louis Stevenson's utopian/dystopian *Treasure Island*.

Am Legend reflects the possibility that humanity might suddenly disappear through scientific devilry, or rather revert into mutated barbarism.

The veneer of civilisation which we had taken for stone was thin ice. It is maintained, we are told, by social contracts, contracts underwritten by force and monopoly. There exist a plethora of fake cities across the world used to train riot police and military[172]. The multi-million dollar Asymmetric Warfare Training Center at Fort A.P. Hill in Virginia has fake offices, a subway station, a church, a football stadium, a mosque, all designed as 'kill houses' to be stormed. The British army has Stanford Training Area, once a model Nazi village, now an Afghan settlement manned by tribal immigrants, with authentic scenery and smells pumped in. The inhabitants of the village of Imber on Salisbury Plain were evicted to provide a training ground for the army, recreating the streets of Northern Ireland before real deployment (its listed church holds a solitary annual service before imaginary hostilities resume). The villages of the French army's CENZUB have raised walkways instead of rooftops for instructors and superiors to monitor progress. King Abdullah II Special Operations Training Center in Jordan has a mini airport. In most, mannequins have been largely replaced by actors to mimic human behaviour. Authentic sign posts are used. The Mitteleuropean architecture of Copehill Down gives an indication where the battleground against the Red Army

172   An ominous sign of the times is that private companies have followed, with Pegasus Global Holdings planning a billion-dollar test city called The Center in New Mexico.

would take place[173]. Given the mutual devastation predicted, the church in the village is fittingly dedicated to Saint Jude, the patron saint of lost causes.

Just as humanistic robots induce the uncanny valley sense of unease so too do fake cities primed for the rehearsal of control and violence. The FBI's Hogan's Alley boasts The Dogwood Inn, Honest Jim's Used Cars and the Biograph cinema. Others, like the Orange County Tactical Training Center, are sponsored by real brands. There are banks, coffee shops, fast food outlets, shopping malls, meth labs, schools, all of which change with time and fashion. As with all imaginary cities, they have begun to seep out into the real[174]. They are a mask that begins to wear the face.

---

173   Outlined in unused Soviet plans, 'Seven Days to the River Rhine' (1979)

174   There is rarely a shortage of money to build and maintain these, unlike actual homes for actual people. Likewise, the blurring of real cities and real people as inhabitants of fake militarised cities has had disastrous tyrannical effects.

A Glowing Future

It helped to be a sociopath, not just when living through the nuclear-age anxiety but when creating it. During the Cold War, vast networks of bunkers, subterranean cities in effect, were built to house the establishment, military and the necessary civil servants, while the general population was left on the surface to face the consequences of the political decisions of the great and the good. These plans were accepted unquestioningly at the same time that plans to build inside the earth such as Peter Cook's mountain-hollowing Sponge City (1974) and Raimund Abraham's Glacier City (1964) were met with ridicule. As with Reagan's Star Wars plans and the floating cities of aircraft carriers, military applications have a tendency to make the impossible suddenly suspiciously realisable[175]. There is no limit to what can be achieved in aid of killing each other.

Entering government bunker cities was utilitarian self-preservation indistinguishable from nihilism. In Mordecai Roshwald's Level Seven, the revelation is not, as the author insists, that this subterranean world would be a fear-and guilt-ridden dystopia populated by depressed button-pushing militarists with numbers instead of names but that this would be the culmination of certain lives' works: 'I am the god who pushed the buttons.'[176]

175   A parallel is the sudden ability of the world economies to globally bail out banks
       to the tune of trillions, money we were, and still are, assured does not exist to
       solve poverty, famine, disease etc.

176   Pg. 115

It would be the worst of times, it would be the best of times. 'Above ground, Paris, like most of the world, was uninhabitable, riddled with radioactivity,' prophesised Chris Marker's *La Jetée*: 'The victors stood guard over a kingdom of rats.' They were kings nevertheless.

Part of the problem in facing terrible events and their repercussions is that we cling to deceptions to explain them away. It is all too easy to assume the nuclear nightmare would be universal and therefore somehow a blameless catastrophe afflicting everyone from without. The men who willed this and other horrors, however had not only names and addresses but escape routes. Oppenheimer recalled viewing the results of his work in the first nuclear test: 'We knew the world would not be the same . . . I remembered the line from the Hindu scripture, *The Bhagavad-Gita* . . . "Now I am become Death, the destroyer of worlds."'[177]

This quote is often misattributed as being the words Oppenheimer said whilst facing the blast. His brother revealed these were actually 'It worked!'[178]

Escaping tyranny can lead to new tyrannies. The fabled Emerald City in Oz is a medieval-futurist urban paradise of chlorophyll glass. On closer inspection, it is a fraud. In the book, the city is gloriously emerald through tinted glasses. It is as much spectacle as the Hollywood system that later recreated it. In the film, it glows and beckons on the horizon at the end of the Yellow

177   'The Decision to Drop the Bomb', broadcast by NBC, USA,
         Tuesday January 5th, 1965.

178   *Oppenheimer: The Tragic Intellect,* Charles Thorpe, Pg. 162

Brick Road but even then it appears a two-dimensional facade and one as ominous as it is inviting. To apply a Brechtian eye, where are the emerald mines that supplied such an emerald city? This is to assume that the emeralds are emeralds. In the *Patchwork Girl of Oz*, we encounter a more unsettling possibility: 'We . . . spend all our time digging radium from the mines under this mountain, and we use it to decorate our homes and make them pretty and cosy. It is a medicine, too, and no one can ever be sick who lives near radium.'[179]

Radium was *the* mysterious wonder element of the early twentieth century. It was used in watches, toothpaste, children's toys and cure-all medicines. There was only one small problem; it was highly radioactive. The high-society industrialist Eben Byers drank so much of it, he became riddled with cancers, prompting the *Wall Street Journal* headline, 'The Radium Water Worked Fine until His Jaw Came Off'[180].

An unknown but extensive number of female workers applying 'Undark' radium paints suffered similar horrific fates before it was outlawed. The element's discoverer Marie Curie used to keep radium salts in a vial by her bed. Almost a century later, her papers are still so radioactive they are kept in a lead safe. The radium glowed in the dark, as exquisitely as the Emerald City and as treacherously as the promise of utopia[181].

179   *The Treasury of Oz*, Pg. 378

180   *The Age of Radiance: The Epic Rise and Dramatic Fall of the Atomic Era*, Craig Nelson, Pg. 38

181   Buddy Ebsen who played the Tin Man originally had to drop out of the film as he was poisoned by the aluminium dust they used to paint his skin.

The Great and Terrible Oz is, like all dictators, a facade; admittedly he is more bumbling technocrat than paranoid monomaniac. He is unmasked by an inquisitive dog (a role-model for our age) with the whimper, 'Pay no attention to that man behind the curtain.'

Our cities possess these curtains at every turn.

The Alchemical Cities

Cities Made Without Hands

The Egyptian hieroglyph for city also means 'mother'[1]. This was a rare admission that cities were founded according to nurturing environs. In most cases, the heroism of mythic individuals was enshrined in foundation myths, often to justify dynastic rulers. Yet this is a view that jars with the intrinsically social nature of cities:

'Vitruvius insightfully described an assembly of early humans around a fire initially caused by lightning. He speculated that while learning to keep the fire going, humans learned to speak. This event literally disclosed a clearing in the forest: a political and public space whose main quality was to be a place for

1   *Existence, Space and Architecture*, Christian Noburg-Schulz, Pg. 30

individuals to participate in political and cosmic order larger than themselves. Vitruvius recognised this to be the most original quality of architecture and the making of cities.'[2]

To those weak with superstition, parochialism or power, the city was cast as a means of shrouding man's nakedness and shame. It was built to confine more than expand. Yet even these miserable wretches had pride, and sought to justify the building of settlements by divine preordination. The claim that God instructed them to settle was used to convince nomads that the city was not entirely an unnatural concept. It was also used to justify the invasion of and building on the lands of others. We see this still in the promised lands of today. It also sought to boost the prestige of cities against rivals. A city built by god implies the others are built by man or the devil. Just as god favoured those with the largest regiments so too did he favour the cities with the greatest fortifications.

To convince the casual visitor of divine providence required a monumental rewriting of history. St Petersburg was a planned Europe-facing replica of Amsterdam (with the affected Dutch/ gates of heaven name Sankt Pieter Burkh) on a marsh drained by the efforts of thousands of workers. Peter the Great[3] boasted of it costing the lives of 100,000 serfs[4]. Insult was added to injury,

2   'The Wall and the Stair' by Alberto Perez-Gomez, from *Archipelago* by
        Peter Mackeith, Pg. 17

3   He also designed the Peter and Paul fortress, a notorious prison that once
        housed Dostoevsky.

4   *A History of Future Cities,* Daniel Brook, Pg. 25

when it was then claimed that St Petersburg had been built 'in blue heaven' and lowered onto the earth. The efforts of the dead evaporated.

The Mexican city-state of Tenochtitlan was supposedly located by a wandering tribe who came across the portent of an eagle devouring a snake atop a cactus, an image that now adorns the Mexican flag. The Moses template of leading the chosen people through an exodus to the Promised Land was continually replicated. Having been directed by an angel to a golden Egyptian book buried in woods of New York State, the seer/fraud Joseph Smith gathered followers and set off to create his New Jerusalem of Zion, a city so virtuous it would be lifted, as the apotheosis of St Petersburg, wholesale into heaven. An attempt to set it up in Ohio ended with an unconscious Smith tarred and feathered. An attempt to set it up in Missouri resulted in a bullet-ridden Smith being defenestrated. An impersonator of Smith's (as well as a polygamist racist) Brigham Young successfully led the Church of the Latter Day Saints to found Salt Lake City, Utah, a metropolis that has, somewhat embarrassingly, yet to disappear into the sky. In a wider example, the Moses pose provided the pretext for the United States expansion west and the Manifest Destiny ideology that justified the slaughter and confinement of the natives who already lived there. The 'promised land' narrative often justifies and pre-empts the building of foundations and the crimes therein. It is the construction not just of cities but of pasts.

The remarkable ancient churches of Lalibela, Ethiopia were

carved from rock in an unforgiving climate by tens of thousands of workers. The credit however largely went to angels who supposedly completed the building at night. Bangkok and Los Angeles are both called the city of angels, though traders and immigrants built them. Even Venice, Marco Polo's splendid Republic and testament to man's ingenuity, deemed it necessary to consecrate itself with the bones of St Mark. Such were the benefits of possessing and displaying the relics of saints (pilgrims were the tourists and the church the investment class of the day) that many cities laid claim to dubious ownerships. Protestant reformers and humanists railed against relics with Erasmus noting, 'So they say of the cross of Our Lord, which is shown publicly and privately in so many places, that, if all the fragments were collected together, they would appear to form a fair cargo for a merchant ship.'[5] The tendency continues with the miracle factories of Lourdes and Mecca, where the crowds swirl around the Kaaba cube containing a sacred meteorite the Black Stone, with Muslims the world over praying towards this building. Kairouan, Tunisia was sanctified when a warrior of Uqba ibn Nafi's party recognised a gold chalice in the desert, missing from Mecca, and a spring bubbled up from beneath it, supposedly linked underwater to the Islamic capital two thousand miles away. Kandy, Sri Lanka houses the tooth of Buddha in an ornate shrine while the rival Rosemead, California displays a growing Buddha tooth and a hair from the enlightened one that supposedly moves of its own accord.

5   Cited in Pg. 489-90, *Pietas Mariana Britannica*

'No one in this world, so far as I know . . . ' wrote Mencken, 'has ever lost money by underestimating the intelligence of the great masses of the plain people.'[6]

It's a cynic's view but an admission from one at the heart of the media. Yet even for the godless heathens and recovering Catholics amongst us, there is a certain interest in the stories, however fictive, that gave rise to buildings like Santa Maria dei Miracoli or proto-psychogeographical pilgrimages such as the Way of St. James to Santiago de Compostela.

A recurring theme in architecture is the miraculous nature of building, even if this means erasing the human involvement and ingenuity: 'Silently as a dream the fabric rose; / No sound of hammer or of saw was there' William Cowper wrote in 'The Ice Palace'. This gave rise to acheiropoieta or 'Icons made without hands', manipulated by invisible beings. Some claimed the same for cities. If God did not intervene directly then building was under his surveillance and approval. 'In the elder days of Art / Builders wrought with greatest care' Wadsworth Longfellow claimed, 'Each minute and unseen part; For the gods see everywhere.'[7] Some even took Gaudí at his word when he explained the ornate details on the tops of his La Sagrada Familia towers as being for curious angels to look at[8]. This presumed the heavenly city would still possess angels.

'When God, endlessly disappointed, finally prepared to turn

---

6   Cited in Pg. 18, *American Modernism* (1910-45)

7   *Poems and Other Writings*, Pg. 137

8   *The Invention of Art: A Cultural History*, Larry Shiner

his back on the world forever,' Wim Wenders wrote in the original prologue of *Wings of Desire*, 'it happened that some of his angels disagreed with him and took the side of man, saying he deserved to be given a second chance. Angry at being crossed, God banished them to what was then the most terrible place on earth: Berlin.'[9]

Lineages were constructed, title deeds and family trees. Gods were wound into the fabric of cities and wound within both were the rulers and their progeny. The divine right of kings and the divine providence of cities were inventions but they lasted, by force and by myth. Autocrats of various dubious origins could cement their rule as possessors of sacred genetic code. Those who could prove links to the origin myths could bolster their claims to the throne, especially in times of dynastic feuds and coup d'états. This was carried through to the extent that rulers became city-deities and vice versa. It is telling that engravings of the god Inshushinak feature him with a supernatural tail and cloven hooves but also the crown and beard of an Elamite king, whilst the Aztec leader Ahuizotl took his name from a semi-deified creature. Roman rulers would emphasise their links to Caesar (the Russian title Tsar was a translation of the name) but even earlier they would link to the legendary founder; the wolf-suckling twin Romulus, son of a vestal virgin and a war god. Istanbul was settled by Byzas the Megarian, son of Poseidon. The founder of Memphis Egypt (now ruins due to being abandoned

9   No hell is without redemption if it has Nick Cave and the Bad Seeds as a soundtrack.

by its guardian god Ptah) was Ephaphus, the mocking son of Zeus. Glasgow was founded by the miracle-performing, robin-resuscitating Saint Mungo. The self-immolating Dido founded Carthage. The Holy and Right-Believing King Vakhtang the Wolf-Head established Tbilisi after his falcon chased a pheasant through the woods and into a boiling spring.

City, god and king were constantly merged to create power structures that would appear unassailable. It was to remain a surprisingly resilient template. When Tsar Alexander II was blown up by anarchists along the Griboedov Canal, St Petersburg, his son commissioned the building of the exquisite Church of the Saviour on Spilled Blood (a lavish building reinvented as a mortuary during the Nazi siege of the city). With the collapse of the Soviet Union, the Church of Blood in Honour of All Saints Resplendent in the Russian Land was erected at the former spot of the Ipatiev House, where Alexander's son Tsar Nicholas and his family were killed by the Bolsheviks. They were and are saints in the eyes of some Orthodox Russians[10]. In the cellar where they were shot, bullets ricocheting off diamonds sewn into the children's clothing, an unknown person soon after scrawled a line from a Heinrich Heine poem in German, referencing the biblical king whose doom was foretold by an invisible hand writing on the wall of a feast: 'Balthazar was, in this same night killed by his slaves'[11]. For all our reason and

10   So too, paradoxically, is the Red Tsar Stalin.

11   A line from a Heinrich Heine poem 'Belsatzar' from his collection *Junge Leiden*. Quoted on Pg. 74, *The Many Deaths of Tsar Nicholas II: Relics, Remains and the Romanovs*, Wendy Slater

revolutions, we still think in myths.

As with status and power, great crimes are disguised by belief, narrative and tradition, a process eloquently summarised in Anatole France's *Penguin Island*, in which a colony of mistakenly-baptised penguins begin to build civilisation in time-lapse to the horror and admiration of missionary onlookers:

'"Do you see, my son," he exclaimed, "that madman who with his teeth is biting the nose of the adversary he has overthrown and that other one who is pounding a woman's head with a huge stone?"

"I see them," said Bulloch. "They are creating law; they are founding property; they are establishing the principles of civilization, the basis of society, and the foundations of the State."'[12]

Time, money and status justify all manner of sins in past, present and future. Gold absolves all histories; hence the tempting instant absolutions of gold-rushes. It is not just wealth and new futures prospectors are seeking, but new pasts and identities.

12   Pg. 67

Foundations

The real origins of cities may at times be squalid and mercantile but they can be simultaneously outlandish as Geoffrey of Monmouth's claim that London was formed as New Troy by the giant-slaying Brutus. Some truths seem beyond fiction. The one-eyed gold-obsessed soon-to-be-decapitated conquistador El Adelantado (founder of Santiago de Nueva Extremadura) sent assassins to attack Francisco Pizarro, founder of Lima, who died throat slit, making a cross with his blood and screaming for Christ. On a voyage to search for lost Norse settlers in Greenland, Hans Poulsen Egede sighted a sea monster the size of his ship. Having survived the encounter, he landed and founded the wishfully-named city of Godt-Haab, meaning 'Good Hope' in Danish, where he preached to a scurvy-wracked, weather-scoured congregation.

Romance occasionally played a part in city-founding. Port Elisabeth was founded by Sir Rufane Donkin and named after his departed young love, whose embalmed heart he kept as a prized possession until his suicide. A civil servant for the East India Company, Job Charnock was cited as founding Calcutta, interrupting his work once a year to sacrifice a cockerel at the graveside of his wife Maria. Then there's a mauseoleum masquerading as a monument of love in the Taj Mahal. Sometimes the romance is for the location itself. Leaving the city he founded, General James Abbott of the Bengal Artillery was moved to write MacGonagall-esque verse in tribute: 'Oh

Abbottabad we are leaving you now / To your natural beauty do I bow / Perhaps your winds sound will never reach my ear / My gift for you is a few sad tears'. It's now primarily known globally as the last residence of Osama Bin Laden, a figure not especially known for his romanticism.

For every story of luck and perseverance there is the tale of a city that never succeeded in taking off and whose bright future remains largely imaginary. The French explorer Jean-Baptiste Bénard de la Harpe successfully founded Little Rock Arkansas after being lost in the mountains, attacked by natives and having eaten his horses in desperation, while the lake city of Udaipur, India was founded by Udai Singh II who had survived innumerable assassination attempts. By contrast, Prince Carl of Solms-Braunfels tried and failed to set up New Germany in Texas with considerable backing. Cities inevitably evolve or stagnate and many are the unlikely routes that can transform them from their beginnings. A French fur trapper François Gesseau Chouteau established Kansas City, whilst Donetsk in Ukraine was originally called Hughesovka (and then Stalino) having been founded by a Welsh builder of iron-clad warships.

Often imperial city-building relied on taking what already existed and renaming it and expanding it. Brazzaville was named after the Italian-French explorer who chanced upon it; its original Bateke name Nkuna was disregarded. The aforementioned Calcutta was founded on settlements believed to have been there for over two thousand years. Unrecognised, they essentially evaporated in authoritative histories. Alexander the Great founded, or at least retitled, more than 70 cities, before being felled by a mosquito or bacteria. Both the great man theory of history and the systems theory of history are evident in his reign. His empire rested on the Thracian and Macedonian horsemen veterans he installed in conquered cities yet it depended on his whim and charisma enough to grant him the freedom to name a city (Bucephalia, Pakistan) after his horse.

Slavery, the obscene trade in souls, was a particular urbanising force for ports and trade centres. Cities like Bristol, Bordeaux and Brussels prospered at the expense of their human cargo and must have seemed distant places of intrigue and terror for those stolen from Africa. Other cities were touched by the scourge in indirect ways. The founder of Sydney, Australia, Admiral Arthur Phillip was saved during a South Atlantic storm by the convicts and slaves he was ferrying abroad. Jean Baptiste Point du Sable who founded Chicago was reputedly either an escaped slave or the son of a freed slave and a pirate. The founder of Singapore and anti-slavery activist, Sir Thomas Stamford Raffles was denied a grave in his local church due to a vicar whose family had earned their status from the bartering of lives.

No city, these stories confirm, is natural or inevitable. They are the results of lives and decisions and that which has been imagined into existence can be reimagined.

The Wrath of God

In the lower depths or outer reaches of empire, there were still opportunities for meritocratic or Machiavellian rises. Juan de Tolosa founded the city of Zacatecas on the basis of his talent for finding silver, even if he was incapable of hanging onto wealth. A figure straight out of a Dickens novel, Henry Hopwood was handed a draconian sentence in Van Diemens land for handling stolen silk and turned it to his advantage by founding the bustling river port Echuca where he was enthroned in an iron hotel. Such was the slippery nature of the man, when he died he left two graves.

Just as a system might by intention or omission allow a visionary to found a great city so too did they occasion the committing of great felonies, often simultaneously. Pedro Menéndez de Avilés was the founder of St Augustine, Florida. He was also a murderous psychopath, given to hanging competitors he conveniently labelled heretics. Even honourable or at least conciliatory intentions could run amiss. Pedro Gutiérrez de Valdivia, founder of Santiago, pursued a policy of peace with the native population, undermined by the breakout of a goldrush amongst his colonists. With some irony, Valdivia was said to have been executed by being forced to drink molten gold[13].

The idea of providence, destiny or preordination is a costly

---

13   Other accounts suggest he merely had his roasted arms and still-beating heart eaten in front of him.

one to the unfortunate souls who did not fit into the plans. It was also costly to those who did. In 1561, King Phillip of Spain received a letter from one of his lieutenants 'made lame in [his] service', across the ocean, by the name of Lope de Aguirre. It accused the regent of cruelty, cowardice and oath-breaking to those who had served him in the wilds of Latin America. Aguirre's mood changes curiously throughout the letter from righteous vengeance to mollifying pleading, helpful guide then insulting enemy, deranged then lucid. He mentions they had installed their own king in their new jungle kingdom then he shifts again: 'They tried to kill me, and I hung them all.'

He revealed the remainder of his party had sailed further into the interior; 'I advise you, King and lord, not to attempt nor allow a fleet to be sent to this ill-fated river, because in Christian faith I swear, King and lord, that if a hundred thousand men come none will escape, because the stories are false and in this river there is nothing but despair.'

He then signed off forever, 'I rebel until death against you for your ingratitude. Lope de Aguirre, the Wanderer.' He would add other titles to his name, on his quests scorching native villages and establishing his reign; 'I am the Wrath of God, the Prince of Freedom, Lord of Tierra Firme and the Provinces of Chile.' Centuries after El Loco (another of his titles) was finally cut to pieces, the director Werner Herzog made his own voyage into the wilds with *Aguirre, the Wrath of God*, an inspired tale of megalomania, hubris and madness:

'If I, Aguirre, want the birds to drop dead from the trees ... then the birds will drop dead from the trees. I am the wrath of god. The earth I pass will see me and tremble. But whoever follows me and the river, will win untold riches.'

The lost mythical cities of 'untold riches', the so-called Seven Cities of Gold, exist for two primary reasons. One is that actual lost cities *have* been found. The Inca mountain citadel of Machu Picchu was discovered after centuries of obscurity by the Yale tutor Hiram Bingham III, who ignored a date etched ten years previously in stone by the local trio of Palma, Sánchez and Lizárraga. They had chanced upon it after burning off foliage to reveal a mysterious staircase leading up into the mountains. The Roman outpost of Timgad in the Aures Mountains with its theatre and triumphal arch was found partially buried a metre beneath the Sahara. In Pakistan, a re-discovered city was given the name Mohenjo-daro ('Mound of the dead'), because its actual name goes unrecorded. It is intriguing to think how nature colonised the abandoned buildings, what happened in the sheer ocean of unseen time that engulfed them. It is intriguing too to consider whether they were ever entirely lost or whether like Choquequirao and the fortress of Kuelap in Peru, they were continually found and re-lost, along with relics and the tales of their findings. Did exiles, grave-robbers, deserters inhabit the rooms during these secret histories?

Imagine the thrill of stumbling across the gates of the sun and moon marking out the lost city of Tiwanaku (its original name again unknown) in the Bolivian wilderness or the pyramids of the desert city of Caral or the jungle-shrouded Mayan temples of Palenque[14]. At times the sense of surprise is bolstered when it goes against deep-seated received wisdom and makes us reimagine what once was. In Illinois, there rest the remains of the plazas, terraces and a ten storey earthen structure of a native American city Cahokia, while L'Anse aux Meadows marks the Newfoundland ruins of a lost Viking settlement that proves they were occupying North America ('Vineland') half a millennia before Columbus arrival (though at least 13,000 years after the first settlers). It's no surprise that an explorer from far or near, chancing upon the aureate Minaret of Jam standing alone in the Afghan wilds, would conjure up a lost city of riches to accompany it; perhaps the purported nearby long-lost city of Turquoise Mountain).

Greed and wonder are by no means mutually exclusive entities. Reality seeps into fiction which in turn seeps into reality. The hiding-place of the Ark of the Covenant in *Raiders of the Lost Ark*[15] and the site of the avenue of the Sphinxes, alabaster chambers, bronze baths and temples of black stone in Rider Haggard's *The World's Desire* come from the very real and once-lost Egyptian city of Tanis, a buried metropolis of sacred lakes, golden death-masks of pharaohs and engravings of half-

---

14   A related modern discovery would be the off-course passenger plane that re-
        discovered the giant spider, hummingbird and astronaut of the Nazca Lines
        in the Peruvian desert.

15   A scene within the buried city mischievously features hieroglyphs of C-3P0 and
        R2-D2 (from the producer George Lucas's *Star Wars* series) on the walls behind
        Indiana Jones.

forgotten abdicated gods.

If cities like these existed and went for centuries undisturbed by human contact (or at least the knowledge of cartographers), what other cities are the soil, the jungle and the sands yet concealing? There was also the literary memory of cities of which no trace could be found but which surely existed. There was fabled Troy, the very location of which lay in obscurity and dispute, which spawned not just *The Iliad* and *The Odyssey* but a fashion for furnace-lit depictions of its burning among artists from Schoubroeck to Collantes. There was Willkapampa, the Inca rainforest redoubt destroyed during the Spanish onslaught, the vanished river-bestriding Khazar trading city of Atil-Khazaran, the Biblical Ai destroyed at the Hebrew God's request in the book of Joshua, Akkad the capital of an evaporated Middle-Eastern empire, all in hiding. We know them by reference as if only their shadow impossibly survives, just as we know once-mighty Carthage, destroyed and sown with salt by Rome in a genocidal but ultimately unsuccessful act of *damnatio memoriae*.

The second reason for the appeal of lost mythical cities is a curious retrogressive nostalgia; the seductive deceptive idea that there was a golden age that requires resurrecting (often the purveyor's youth or their time-misted view of it). The problem with the past is that we are still living in its wake yet it is unreachable. We survey it with the torment of Tantalus; it is there but just out of reach. Times which never really existed are elevated, as gilded eras of impossible exacting perfection, often to justify fundamentalisms in the present.

Even conservatives are utopian. To reconstruct a lost world requires an element of fiction, if only in the selective processes of editing or exaggeration (the paintings of Norman Rockwell or the florid phantasias of Louis Jean Desprez for example). The exquisite woodcuts of Katsuyuki Nishijima remove the vestiges of the contemporary world for a Japan nestled in the elements, untouched by modernity. His woodcuts only work as silent empty pristine set designs.

Though they may seem arbitrary, like fairytales, past utopias have functions to serve. The memory of Roman rule in Britain and the loss of technologies when they left (concrete, sewers and aqueducts) evolved into Arthurian legends and 'many-towered Camelot'[16]. This in turn justified chivalric hierarchies and acted as propaganda for the Crusades. Many regimes harked back to sleeping giants and make-believe battalions to aid them but so too did rebels; for every comatose Barbarossa on Kyffhäuser Mountain with his red beard grown through the stone table, there was a usurper like Owen Lawgoch in a deep mine biding his time. In a Viennese classroom where the glory of Ancient Rome was exalted alongside the Hapsburg Empire, a marginalised Jewish boy by the name of Sigmund Freud swore an affinity with Hannibal, marching against Rome on elephants across the Alps[17]. The future may well contain what we put into it, as the May '68 Left Bank graffiti put it, but so too does the past.

16   Tennyson's 'The Lady of Shalott'

17   *The Interpretation of Dreams*, Pg. 148

The Drowned World

It would be dishonest to claim that there is not some romantic attraction to the idea of the lost urban Eden. We might forgive those who listened to the roar of the sea and heard within the tolling of bells, and imagined shoals of jellyfish waltzing through drowned palaces. In legend, the Breton city of Ys was ruled over by Gradlon, whose spoilt and orgiastic daughter Dahut stole the key to the harbour gate one stormy night and gave it to her lover the devil. The gates were opened and the city slipped beneath the waves. Claude Debussy would resurrect the tale for his *La cathédrale engloutie (The Sunken Cathedral)* in which the orchestra mimics the cathedral of Ys rising from the waves, with bells and spectral monks chanting[18]. This was a cinema of sound, a submarine symphony, in the very sheet music on which Debussy included arches of notes as a concealed architecture of sound.[19]

'Know, oh prince, that between the years when the oceans drank Atlantis and the gleaming cities . . . ' wrote Robert E. Howard, 'there was an Age undreamed of, when shining kingdoms lay spread across the world like blue mantles beneath the stars.'[20]

In the *Dialogue of Critias* fragment, Plato referred to this sunken city as the seat of a 'great and wonderful empire [. . .] a

18   As well as Eastern melodic strains the composer picked up at the World
       Exposition.

19   *The Piano Works of Claude Debussy,* E. Robert Schmitz, Pg. 156

20   'The Coming of Conan the Cimmerian', cited in *Robert E. Howard Reader*, Pg. 33

marvel to behold for size and for beauty

. . . [containing] a multitudinous sound of human voices, and din and clatter of all sorts night and day.'[21]

Alas it was doomed: 'human nature got the upper hand, they [grew] full of avarice and unrighteous power' and Zeus accordingly drowned them all. Atlantis was a veiled warning to Athens.

The ocean was another vast blank on the maps and the human mind, like nature, abhors a vacuum. Just as the Arctic had been filled by the illusory continent Hyperborea and the Indian Ocean Lemuria, so too the Atlantic became Atlantis, with the amassed architecture of bygone eras:

'There, before my eyes, ruined, destroyed, overturned, appeared a town, its roofs crushed in, its temples thrown down, its arches disjointed, its columns lying on the ground, with the solid proportions of Tuscan architecture still discernible [. . .] the incrusted base of an Acropolis, and the outlines of a Parthenon ; there, some vestiges of a quay, as if some ancient port had formerly sheltered, on the shores of an extinct ocean, merchant vessels and war galleys; further on still, long lines of ruined walls, wide deserted streets, a second Pompeii buried under the waters.'[22]

Generations of cranks took the drowned city literally, buoyed

21   *Timaeus and Critias,* Pg. 79

22   Pg. 208

by nebulous but deep-rooted folk memories of tsunamis and actual cities crumbling into the sea; in the Netherlands, the city of Saeftinghe never recovered after the devastating All Saints Flood of 1570 and remains to this day 'the Drowned Land'. Atlantis became a canvas onto which was projected all manner of crackpot theories and faiths, often with a heavy dose of retrospective puritanical morality. Ignatius Loyola Donnelly preached Atlantis had been flooded by the gravitational proximity of a comet to the earth and the gods of myth had been its regents[23]. Admittedly in the early Modern age we had little conception of which ideas would gain scientific credence, so bewildering was the range from x-rays to animal magnetism, but there was barely a harebrained belief that Donnelly did not subscribe to. His urge to rewrite ancient history had come from being almost bankrupted by the failure of his utopian river boat city project Nininger in Minnesota; its baseball team, saloons and factories folding with recession, leaving Donnelly alone in his mansion, the sage of nothing but a seaweed-swathed whimsical metropolis of the deep.

Another believer in sunken cities and extraterrestrial civilisations of angels throughout the solar system, the mystic, charlatan and tyrant Thomas Lake Harris attempted to set up religious refuges through the U.S.A ('an outpost in an enemy's country'[24]). Harris hoped for a city with divine escalators to heaven, supported by vineyards (wine for 'medicinal purposes

23   *Atlantis, the Antediluvian World* (1882)

24   *Three Famous Occultists: Dr. John Dee, Franz Anton Mesmer and Thomas Lake Harris*, R.B. Hort, Pg. 131

only'[25]). He claimed to have found the elixir of everlasting life, forcing his disciples to insist he was resting when he'd finally died. The prospective utopia slowly disintegrated when he failed to wake.

The self-declared psychic Edgar Cayce picked up the theme from the cult of Madame Blavatsky, claiming that Atlantis had been an advanced civilisation that had harnessed and then been destroyed by death-ray-emitting power crystals. It was a Platonic if somewhat sci-fi fate that could act as a civilisational warning (Cayce died the year the first atom bomb was dropped). If Atlantis came as a warning, so it also came as a strange comfort. At a time when Allied shipping was prey to German U-boats, Paul Norris and Mort Weisinger invented Aquaman. The comic superhero was effectively an Aryanised young Neptune, telepathically controlling all sea-life and extending the dominion of the Allies to a submarine world they were terrified of in real-life; an opening up of another front against the Nazis. The capital of Aquaman's Atlantis — Poseidonis — was originally encased in an atmospheric bubble which eventually opened to the sea as the inhabitants biologically adapted to marine living. The city boasted a hall of science, a council of worship, parks of prosperity and contemplation, hydrophonic farms, a salt factory, prison and psychiatric hospital. Its architecture was a mixture of Russian onion-domes and Googie. It was geo-thermally powered and could telegraph cities above on dry land. The series occasionally referenced reality (the settlement

25   *Brocton and Portland*, Edward T. Kurtz, Pg. 63

of Sub-Diego for example) but even the creators could not have envisaged that, with global warming bringing the melting of the polar ice caps, increases in sea level would threaten to relocate many of the world's great cities (New Orleans and New York, Dhaka, Shanghai, Bangkok, London etc.) underwater[26].

It was not necessarily always destructive for a city to submerge. Legend has it in the 13th century the Mongol Hordes under Batu Kahn were approaching the Russian town of Kitezh, by Svetloyar Lake, having had its location passed to them by a local in league with the devil. As they approached, they found the inhabitants defenceless but kneeling in prayer to Saint Fevronia. Suddenly the invaders were repelled by a vast thunderous wall of water that engulfed the town behind it. The settlement sank in a golden mist into the lake. Protected by celestial magic, only the righteous can find the submerged city, though hints of holy music, bell-ringing and its gleaming spires are said to fleetingly appear in the depths.

In pursuit of 'ecstatic truth', Werner Herzog filmed *Bells from the Deep* with shots of pilgrims crawling around on the ice trying to catch a glimpse of the lost city, but as there were no pilgrims around I hired two drunks from the next town and put them on the ice. One of them has his face right on the ice and looks like he is in very deep meditation. The accountant's truth: he was completely drunk and fell asleep, and we had to wake him at

26   Callebaut's Lilypad envisages and counters sea rise with a floating and pollution absorbing ecopolis designed to house 50,000 in a lagoon complex with manmade mountains.

the end of the take.'[27] In never letting the truth get in the way of a good story, Herzog was faithful to the myth.

Given this story has appeared in numerous locations and cultures, there is much to suggest it is innate to human interactions with the sea. Just as there was formulated a mythic Super-Sargasso Sea in the sky where all lost things are deposited[28] so too the sea contains the past, from sunken treasures to the bodies of lost sailors. It appears again and again in coastal societies. The city of Vineta lurking beneath the Baltic Sea has been rhapsodised in Slavic and Germanic poetry and song for centuries. So too has Rungholt, Nordfriesland and Lyonesse the city of the romantic hero Tristan. In the past, bell-ringing was used to ward away fevers, plagues and demons but here the bells of such places toll in times of storms, low tides, day-dreaming, melancholy.

These fanciful tales contain echoes of the real. Where one ends and the other begins is characteristically opaque. North of the island of Rueger, 'a diver who brought up medieval guns claims he saw the immense walls of a city.'[29] Birds and wild animals were said to have fled the city of Helike, and strange lights were seen in the skies before a tsunami hit and took the city with it. It was the displeasure of their patron god Poseidon that caused the earthquake it was surmised, when really it was the earthquake that created the wrath of Poseidon. All is

27   *Herzog on Herzog*, edited by Paul Cronin, Pg. 252

28   The Great Atlantic Rubbish Dump is a real-life equivalent of this, pulling plastic from myriad nations into its vortex and drifts.

29   *Northern Advocate*, September 16th 1924, Pg. 5

understood in retrospect and manipulations take place.

'A true report of certaine wonderfull ouerflowings of Waters . . . ' claims a pamphlet printed by Edmund White in 1607, 'destroying many thousands of men, women, and children, overthrowing and bearing downe whole townes and villages, and drowning infinite numbers of sheepe and other Cattle'. The attribution of causes are clear, 'our punishment (is) greater, because our treason against God is more horrible.' The terrified and the craven are quick to claim that it was sin and divine retribution that brought this and therefore the godly city must be built, humanity must be controlled, order restored, sinners punished or cast out. In these senses, the tectonic plates and the insentient surges of the sea are kept placated with sacrifices.

It's worth considering whether the sunken cities might become modernised. Will the sound of bells be joined by phones ringing, car alarms, the glow of neon in the depths? Certainly the surreal juxtapositions, and the mix of wonder and terror facing the immensity of nature remains, however much we now shield ourselves. The sight of ships sailing down Japanese streets during the 2011 Tōhoku tsunami, of buildings moving with them, cities being seemingly pulled into a maelstrom never lose their disturbing power. Beyond the atrocious human cost, there will still be architectural losses to the depths, like the Soviet statue graveyards decaying in algae to Shi Cheng the Lion City slowly dissolving at the bottom of a hydroelectric lake. There will be attempted rescues like Venice against the Adriatic as well as the plans of recovery like the Thracian Seuthopolis from the bottom of Koprinka Reservoir.

In the long run, as with every human endeavour, we are fighting a losing battle against time and the tides. Yet we continue because destruction and defeat are two very different things and the now, at least, is ours. All cities are battling a slow-motion war against ruin by the elements. At the bottom of the sea, this would be accelerated by temperature, pressure, currents and aquatic life. Add to this the complete absence of light on the ocean floor and the illusion of a habitable site dissolves. The underwater city of Caribe in McHugh's *Half the Day is Night* gives an accurately grim reflection of a bitterly-cold badly lit and ventilated submarine city. Within this fourth world utopia, the levels become slums the further down the visitor descends while the abyss of the dark sea outside is interplanetary.

In 2K Boston's *Bioshock*, we find a submarine city in resplendent art deco. A narrator booms over the public address system:

'I am Andrew Ryan, and I'm here to ask you a question. Is a man not entitled to the sweat of his brow? "No!" says the man in Washington, "It belongs to the poor." "No!" says the man in the Vatican, "It belongs to God." "No!" says the man in Moscow, "It belongs to everyone." I rejected those answers; instead, I chose something different. I chose the impossible. I chose . . . Rapture, a city where the artist would not fear the censor, where the scientist would not be bound by petty morality, Where the great would not be constrained by the small! And with the sweat of your brow, Rapture can become your city as well.'[30]

Bioshock is Atlantis, via Manhattan and Fordlândia. It mercilessly satirises the Objectivist philosophy of Ayn Rand (the city's creator Andrew Ryan is a fellow Russian émigré), the right-libertarian godhead. Rand took the liberating aphorisms of Nietzsche and bent them to fit a cult of entrepreneurial individualism, freed from the shackles of responsibility, conscience and empathy. Objectivism turned a blind eye to the fact that much of America's achievements were and remain collective, from FDR's New Deal to Eisenhower's Highways system, from its part in the defeat of the Nazis and Imperial Japan to NASA. As with tax havens and luxury cruise ships, the Objectivist utopia could only exist for a few and in relative isolation and denial[31] — a Swiss or Cayman model of Utopia, that has been nevertheless been applied to financial wealth islands within global cities. Rand's fictional alter-ego Andrew Ryan located his under the sea, his call chiming with John Galt's speech in Rand's *Atlas Shrugged*:

'We will open the gates of our city to those who deserve to enter, a city of smokestacks, pipe lines, orchards, markets and inviolate homes ... With the sign of the dollar as our symbol — the sign of free trade and free minds — we will move to reclaim this country once more from the impotent savages who never

---

30   2K Games, 2007

31   The real life planned Objectivist city Oceania – a floating upmarket holiday
         resort subtitled appropriately 'The Atlantis Project' – failed to find sufficient
         funding.

discovered its nature, its meaning, its splendour. Those who choose to join us, will join us: those who don't, will not have the power to stop us; hoardes of savages have never been an obstacle to men who carried the banner of the mind.'

Minds, however, can be lost. Rapture turns into a nightmare of course, not due to a perversion of ideas (as the old excuse goes) but to the inherent contradictions, naïve limitations and hubris there from the beginning[32]. It is a Babel built with disdain directed not just upwards to God but downwards to those Ryan labels parasites. 'I came to this place to build the impossible' he booms, 'You came to rob what you could never build — a Hun gaping at the gates of Rome . . . God did not plant the seeds of this Arcadia — I did.' Having declared on banners 'No Gods or Kings, only man' Ryan assumes the positions of the God and king and loses his humanity. He shuts down free speech and dissent through the secret gulag of his Persephone penal colony. Rapture decays. Megalomania, though it multi-tasks, is often a monomania. It insists not only in being powerful but in being true even, or especially, in defiance of objective truth; hence Orwell's $2+2=5$[33]. In such a world, both objectivity and subjectivity are heresy. It is the definition of totalitarianism and also the roots of its undoing. Any such ruler or system

32   Its attempts at social engineering ironically parallelling the hated Soviet experiment.

33   This appears in *1984* and has various sources (from Dostoevsky to Göring), though an intriguing Five Year Plan Soviet Poster from 1931 has a similar numeric boast.

will one day collide with facts; whether Catholic cosmology, Puritan sexuality, Stalinist economics, capitalist invisible-hand boom and bust or the hubris of dictators. It is worth recalling the function of the medieval jester as the guarantor of objective truth (through mockery, observation and satire) in courts filled with sycophants. A king who killed the jesters committed a slow suicide. With no one to tell him when he was wrong, he could no longer trust the world he'd created. The neon-lit chambers and lobbies of Rapture are filled with Ryan's booming voice, notably and ominously speaking from the past.

Seasteading

Given the oceans make up 71% of the earth's surface and suitable land is in ever-decline, the desire to build on the surface of the seas is increasingly tempting. Though the idea often meets with ridicule, harking back to Lucian's account of the floating inhabitants of the city of Cork, it is an idea that has been actualised. Oil-rigs, naval sea forts and lighthouses support life in remote oceanic conditions. Armadas were essentially floating cities, as are cruise-ships. There are floating villages in Kampuchea, in the palafitos of Chilote islanders, in the reclaimed cities of the Netherlands, in floating churches on the Delaware, in frost fairs on the frozen Thames and of course there's Venice, that deranged dream city on stilts.

To accept the premise of building directly on the waves (or 'seasteading') requires a reassessment of what we accept as possible. The idea of a floating runway for jet-planes is accepted now without question because military budgets have created aircraft carriers. When we look at Hollein's Aircraft Carrier City in Landscape or Inverted-infrastructure by the Port Of London Authority (the latter with factories and churches on aircraft carriers rather than planes), we see not only how bizarre future plans are but crucially how bizarre the norms we have accepted are. If we can accept floating ships housing hundreds to wage war then surely we can entertain other purposes for them, particularly on a space that has no pre-existing landlords.

Due perhaps to population density, earthquakes and the

fact it is an archipelago, there has been a notable focusing on seasteading in Japan, especially through the radical architecture group the Metabolists. Kenzo Tange's Plan for Tokyo (1960) envisaged the creation of man-made islands on Tokyo Bay with buildings as leaves and bridges as the branches of a fallen tree[34]. Kikutake's Marine City with its surface farms and downward-facing underwater residential towers aimed to sever mankind's reliance on land, and the wars, colonisations and resource depletions that resulted from territorial disputes[35]. It could move around as required and when defunct end its days scuttled as an artificial coral reef. Buckminster Fuller developed his Triton City for Tokyo Bay which for all its daunting scale was essentially a grounded cruise-ship. This paled next to his later oceanic Tetra City of a million inhabitants[36].

Pre-existing modes of seafaring have largely determined the nature of imaginary cities on the sea. Designed for Dogger Bank[37] in the North Sea, Hall Moggridge's Sea City would be a walled harbour sheltering floating marinas. Against the curved wall, it would house, in sixteen storeys, fully-automated flats, schools, a football stadium, a leisureplex and a zoo. Its foundations would

34   *Urban Water in Japan,* edited by Rutger de Graaf. Tange had earlier suggested a Relaxation Island on Tokyo Bay.

35   *Kenzo Tange and the Metabolist Movement: Urban Utopias of Modern Japan,* Zhongije Lin, Pg. 26

36   Lewis Mumford condemned these grandiose projects as 'essentially tombs: they reflect the same impulse to suppress human variety and autonomy.' Cited Pg. 173, *Meanings of Abstract Art: Between Nature and Theory,* Paul Crowther, Isabel Wünsche

37   A former land bridge from continental Europe to Britain, where trawlers still dig up dinosaur bones and traces of primeval forest.

be affixed to the sea-bed like an oil-rig. From the outside, it would resemble a medieval walled city, continually under siege by the sea.

Adopting both a more organic and futuristic approach, Wolf Hilbertz's Autopia Ampere would 'draw up sea minerals over time, creating walls of calcium carbonate' and a coral reef city. Yendo developed this idea with his half-submerged B1-9004 Reef Machine; designed to mechanically encourage a swirling eco-system around what resembles a flooded Giger spacecraft. By contrast Ocean City by Arup Biomimetics seems a bloom of jellyfish, with buoyant spherical structures powered by saline energy siphoned from the sea by dangling tentacles.

Water will determine the existence of cities, next to rising seas, encroaching deserts and, in other regions, colossal rainy seasons. Supermachine Studio's Superbow Project plans to mitigate flooding in Thailand by embedding a city into a hill with a reservoir at its peak. Herman Sörgel's gigantic Atlantropa project in the 1920s would have fundamentally reshaped the Mediterranean region. It involved the construction of gigantic hydroelectric dams, the main one blocking the Strait of Gibraltar. When complete, the sea would fall by 200 metres returning a France-sized area that had been flooded 5 million years ago to ease the rising population burden of Europe. It would be possible to sail deep into a lush Sahara. Venice would be simultaneously saved and ruined by the vanishing of the Adriatic[38]. Europe

38   The comic book maestro Mœbius had anticipated such developments with his levitating gondolas sailing through the air above drained gorges.

would be revitalised by plentiful electricity, crops and land. In an explicit example of how one man's utopia is another's dystopia, Sorel's plans continued with the intention of damning the Congo River and flooding the entire country. The ability to plan and alter landscape and seascape as a city planner would come with immense responsibility and temptation.

'Man will be armed with sufficient power to undertake operations on a cosmic scale,' Earl Birkenhead wrote in *The World in 2030*, 'It will be open to him radically to alter the geography or the climate of the world. By utilizing some 50,000 tons of water, the amount displaced by a large liner, it would be possible to remove Ireland to the deeper portion of the Atlantic Ocean.'

The Seven Invisible Cities of Gold

During the months Christopher Columbus spent in the New World, he mentioned gold in his journals around seventy times. It often came linked with God[39], to the point where the concepts are interchangeable and intrinsically linked; 'Gold is a treasure, and he who possesses it does all he wishes to in this world, and succeeds in helping souls into paradise.'[40]

Money was a route into the utopia of heaven. It greased the palms of the border guards and St Peter head of customs and immigration. The search for the lost cities of gold combined many things; the evocation of a lost age of glory, the search for the Holy Grail and alchemical transmutation, and the discovery of god. Columbus believed paradise would be physically found by following the Orinoco river to Eden, though, according to Genesis, there was still a flaming rotating sword to contend with before the right to enter. All this with the simple but dependable dynamo of human greed attached, adding interest, in every sense, to the intangible.

The search for El Dorado and the lost cities was a falsehood from the start. It developed into a nightmare of eternal recurrence. The reports initially came from Álvar Núñez Cabeza de Vaca, the head of only four survivors of the 600-strong Narváez expedition. The party had trekked through Florida believing they were in the vicinity of Mexico. During the resulting bitter

---

39   Columbus signed himself 'Christo ferrens' meaning 'bearer of Christ'.

40   Cited in Pg. 35, Galbraith, 1987

decade-long odyssey, they would lose men to illness, starvation, storms, drownings and shipwrecks. They were continually harried and eventually enslaved by the arrow-wielding locals. Those who survived did so by posing as shamen. Their downfall had come, initially, in alluring form, after chancing upon coffins filled with relics including gold; 'We inquired of the Indians [by signs] whence they had obtained these things and they gave us to understand that, very far from there, was a province called Apalachen in which there was much gold.'[41]

Throughout the cataclysms to follow, the budding prospectors clung onto this hope until it became a mocking betrayal.

The treasure of the Sierra Madre in the elusive B. Traven's novel is a curse but such is the gravitational attraction that few pay heed to the warnings. Umana and Leyba set off to find city of gold on the Great Plains before turning on each other in a knife-fight. Francisco Vásquez de Coronado's party was led on a wild goose chase through the desert by a mysterious native called the Turk, whom they garrotted when it was unforthcoming, finding only the quaint beehive settlement of Quivira. It was not just gold that led such disastrous expeditions but rich spices in the fabled La Canela, valley of cinnamon. We gaze on such accursed dreamers with scorn whilst searching for the next find.

Such were the dark improbable endings to these quests that another myth came into being; that of the wandering City of the Caesars. As with any faith, lack of evidence is no setback; the golden City of Caesars evades because it constantly moves,

41   *The Narrative of Álvar Núñez Cabeza de Vaca,* Pg. 12

appearing like Kitezh only to the pure of heart, a quality which naturally everyone thinks they exclusively possess. Mentioned by Jesuit missionaries 400 years ago, the lost bejewelled city of Paititi exerts a black hole pull even now. The very impenetrability of the Amazon suggests it is concealing something at its heart to those who anthropomorphise even landscape.

In 1925, Percy Fawcett, accompanied by his son and a friend, entered the jungles of Mato Grosso to find the lost city of Z. They never returned. Though Fawcett hailed from a family of adventurers and cartographers, his early reports from the Amazon were ridiculed, unfairly in the vein of Polo, for the accurate curiosities of enormous snakes and monstrous spiders. The professional lie-tellers were listening however. Such was the reciprocal nature of fact and fiction that Fawcett had been inspired by his friend H. Rider Haggard's tales of exploration and went on to influence the tales of another friend, Arthur Conan Doyle[42]. He was also known to carry Rudyard Kipling's poem 'The Explorer' with him to lift his spirits and stamina.

It was another book however that doomed Fawcett. By chance, he had stumbled across an extraordinary fading manuscript:

'After a long and troublesome peregrination, incited by the insatiable greed of gold, and almost lost for many years in this vast desert, we discovered a chain of mountains so high that they seemed to reach the ethereal regions, and that they served

42   Particularly *The Lost World* which uses Fawcett's accounts of monstrous traces in the Bolivian wilds as an inspiration.

as a throne for the wind or for the stars themselves.'[43]

There the narrators discovered a city, entering tentatively, after scouts had found it uninhabited. They passed through looming archways on which were written indecipherable messages and fought their way through clouds of bats. The sound of their own voices, echoing back through the empty halls, unnerved them. They found the gold and silver by the riverbank: 'I beg of your Excellency to drop these miseries, and to come and utilise these riches.'[44]

Having set up false clues and warnings to pursuers or rivals, Fawcett ventured off into the jungle. He remains there still. Perhaps he found his mythical city Z and lived out his days as the king of a desolate empire. The clues are less encouraging. Fawcett's son and companion were seen by natives in a state of distress without the father. Fawcett's compass would surface with a local tribe. Later, the foolhardy would set off on their trail and dozens met their end in presumably similar but unknown ways in the impenetrable green. In the last letter, to his wife, Fawcett wrote in passing of such compulsions, 'I am not sure how long this will last [. . .] but I had to do this.'[45]

'Over the Mountains / Of the Moon, / Down the Valley of the Shadow, / Ride, boldly ride,' The shade replied— / 'If you seek for Eldorado!'[46] Edgar Allen Poe wrote, through the mouth of a ghost. Poe was keen to bring out the eeriness of such ventures

---

43   *The Highlands of the Brazil - Volume 2*, Richard Burton, Pg. 459

44   Cited from the appendix ibid.

45   *Exploration Fawcett*, Pg. 291

46   Cited on Pg. 128, *The Poet Edgar Allan Poe: Alien Angel*, Jerome McGann

but also to puncture the miasma of greed and wild optimism that fuelled the gold-rushes of his day. The lost cities of gold of South America relocated to North America and became mobile boomtowns[47], the sites not of ancient civilisations but instant pop-ups to exploit metal seams in rock and then the buried liquefied deposits of primeval forests and extinct creatures. The futility of seeking the original lost cities of gold was evident from the beginning to anyone with a keen eye. Many were mistranslations and the result of Chinese whispers with the central idea of the Seven Cities of Gold deriving from the mythic Aztec origin city Aztlán with its seven sacred caves. If the second-hand accounts were suspect so too were the first-hand witnesses from the kidnap stories of Juan Martín de Albujar to Gonzalo Jiménez de Quesada who for all his prospecting skills died as a bankrupt leper.

The most notorious search was for El Dorado, the very name of which hints of the grave error in seeking it. It came from the story of El Hombre Dorado and the glitter-dust king Muisca. Having been given a stay of execution provided he return with a regular supply to gold to his fickle queen, Sir Walter Raleigh memorably described its ritualistic origin, 'When they are anointed all over, certain servants of the emperor, having prepared gold made into fine powder, blow it through hollow canes upon their naked bodies, until they be all shining from the foot to the head[. . .] Upon this sight, and for the abundance

---

47   The dark satanic mills of Blake have just been outsourced. They exist with more
          than a hint of Dante's inferno in the sunken cities scrambling for the heights in
          the Bolivian and Brasilian gold mine photos of Sebastião Salgado.

of gold which he saw in the city, the images of gold in their temples, the plates, armours, and shields of gold which they use in the wars, he called it El Dorado . . . '[48]

There was logic in surmising that a culture with enough gold to waste sprinkling onto bodies as powder and throwing into lakes as votive offerings would be worth conquering but it was still a dramatic leap to equate this with actual cities of gold. It required boundless levels of naïvety and cynicism.

Raleigh was smart enough to know the search was probably madness but voracious or desperate enough to believe it anyway and justified it so: 'But it shall be found a weak policy in me, either to betray myself or my country with imaginations; neither am I so far in love with that lodging, watching, care, peril, diseases, ill savours, bad fare, and many other mischiefs that accompany these voyages, as to woo myself again into any of them, were I not assured that the sun covereth not so much riches in any part of the earth. Captain Whiddon, and our chirurgeon, Nicholas Millechamp, brought me a kind of stones like sapphires; what they may prove I know not.' The former pirate obsesses over gold in his journals. It appears again and again like intimations of mania; in the colour of rocks, houses, soil, in wild and ineffectual grasps, 'But we saw all the hills with stones of the colour of gold and silver'. He implores her majesty to supply him with an army to conquer a city that only really exists in his mind. Raleigh lost his son in a fruitless search and even more fruitless battle with the Spanish over imaginary

48   The Works of Sir Walter Raleigh, Pg. 403

bounty[49]. He returned across the Atlantic in resignation to the axe-man, with his dreaming head (like that other utopian Thomas More, victim of Elizabeth's father) kept for years in a velvet bag by his widow.

In his accounts, Ralegh is still alive and the gold-fever has not left him, writing in *The Discovery of Guinea*, 'I thought good to insert part of the chapter of Lopez in his General History of the Indies, wherein he describeth the court and magnificence of Guayna Capac, ancestor to the emperor of Guiana, whose very words are these: 'All the vessels of his house, table, and kitchen, were of gold and silver . . . He had in his wardrobe hollow statues of gold which seemed giants . . . there was nothing in his country whereof he had not the counterfeit in gold. Yea, and they say, the Ingas had a garden of pleasure in an island near Puna, where . . . they would take the air of the sea, which had all kinds of garden-herbs, flowers, and trees of gold and silver; an invention and magnificence till then never seen.'[50] It remained never seen.

Men died because of semantics; mistranslations of 'realm', 'court', 'gold' and god'. They became raiders of wishing wells, chasers of phantasms, draining lakes for trinkets, dying in tree-filled circles. They placed their invented cities on maps, diagrams that might as well point out the location of the Holy Grail, the Fountain of Youth or the Philosopher's Stone. In their unsuccessful quests, they chanced on other things such as the

---

49   His captain Lawrence Kemys told him the news and, being immediately blamed, stabbed himself in the heart.

50   *The Works of Sir Walter Raleigh*, Pg. 398-399

world's longest river, countless species of animals, new fruits, vegetables, tobacco, cocoa and chocolate. Gold blinded them. A noble explorer by comparison, Alexander von Humbolt encountered many wondrous things by renouncing the cities of gold; electric eels, magnetic storms, a parrot who spoke the last words of a language.

The elusive El Dorado nevertheless remained a canvas onto which was projected every frustrated paradise since Eden. Even the grand humanist Voltaire could not resist in *Candide*:

'The Spaniards have had a confused notion of this country, and have called it *El Dorado*; and an Englishman, whose name was Sir Walter Raleigh, came very near it about a hundred years ago; but being surrounded by inaccessible rocks and precipices, we have hitherto been sheltered from the rapaciousness of European nations, who have an inconceivable passion for the pebbles and dirt of our land, for the sake of which they would murder us to the last man. [. . .] While waiting they were shown the city, and saw the public edifices raised as high as the clouds, the market places ornamented with a thousand columns, the fountains of spring water, those of rose water, those of liqueurs drawn from sugar-cane, incessantly flowing into the great squares . . . Candide asked to see the court of justice, the parliament. They told him they had none, and that they were strangers to lawsuits. He asked if they had any prisons, and they answered no. But what surprised him most and gave him the greatest pleasure was the palace of sciences, where he saw a gallery two thousand feet long, and filled with instruments employed in mathematics and physics.'[51]

Here was a city free and unencumbered by cowering deference to authority, open to enquiry and the advancement of beneficent knowledge, proof that the Just City need not be the City of God but the City for Humanity.

For all the mercantile explorer's losses, the searches exacted a terrible cost on many more natives at the hands of frustrated and sadistic prospectors. Others benefited from aiding these curious strangers. Some tribes experienced both. Returning to *Heart of Darkness*, the gold changes to rubber, ivory and flesh but the language and the drive is the same:

'This devoted band called itself the Eldorado Exploring Expedition, and I believe they were sworn to secrecy. Their talk, however, was the talk of sordid buccaneers: it was reckless without hardihood, greedy without audacity, and cruel without courage; there was not an atom of foresight or of serious intention in the whole batch of them, and they did not seem aware these things are wanted for the work of the world.'[52]

Even here, via the sympathetic if compromised witness, there is the implication that the world is something outside, that this is an unreal vacuum, where terrible acts are kept secret so that civilisation might remain intact and Western capitals appear

51   Pg. 61

52   *Heart of Darkness*, Pg. 58

innocent and glorious despite the obscenities enacted in their name.

True morality is what is done when no one is looking. In a place where all is permitted and nothing seems accountable or even known, man might become a god and a god is a terrible thing to become. We might even call this space utopia, even though it is utopia for one, mimicking the ecstatic dread of the castle utopias of De Sade or Otto Muehl. Whilst his brother was founding the city of Lima, the conquistador and psychopath Gonzalo Pizzaro turned his hand to inflicting barbarisms upon the natives. When the gold they brought him ceased to satisfy, Pizzaro demanded the Inca chief's wife, sparking a mass rebellion. His quests for golden cities brought nothing but the deaths of half his men. Eventually he turned, like Aguirre, against his distant king and ended with his head decorating a spike by the gates of Lima. His trusty assistant Francisco de Carvajal, who joined him there, confessed 'nothing that lies heavy on my conscience, unless it be, indeed, the debt of half a real to a shopkeeper in Seville, which I forgot to pay before leaving the country'. Their great crime, like Raleigh's, was not discovering the lost cities and receiving the absolution of their real god, gold.

Before the vast Inca empire came to an end it had shrunk to the size of the Ransom Room (*El Cuarto del Rescate*), which the emperor Atahualpa filled with bullion in an attempt to persuade the Spanish to spare his life. It earned him only the pleasure of being strangled to death and cremated rather than being burned alive. 'I'll have them fly to India for gold / ransack the ocean for orient pearl . . . ' Marlowe wrote of Faustus' ambitions, to 'wall all Germany with brass . . . fill the public schools with silk'[53] before desperately wishing his soul would turn into rain-drops and fall in the sea to hide. These tales of alchemy, devils and gold, theft, ambition and death, we give the insufficient title, history.

53   *Doctor Faustus*, Pg. 82

The Abiding Desire for No Place

The Thirteenth Hour

The future will be old. It may be bright and shiny, terrible and wonderful but, if we are to be certain of anything, it will be old. It will be built from the reconstructed wreckage of the past and the present and the just-about possible. 'The future is already here' according to William Gibson, 'it's just not very evenly distributed.'[1] You sit amongst fragments of it now.

All prophecies are intrinsically about the now. When George Orwell, slowly coughing himself to death on the wind-scoured island of Jura, wrote *1984* (under the original title 'The Last Man in Europe'), it was a reversal and critique of the year in which he wrote it, 1948. This was the cracked mirror of the present. When he wrote of doublespeak, he was writing not just of the future

---

1   Fresh Air, NPR, August 31st, 1993

and the Soviet Union but of traits he identified and deplored in his fellow journalists, imperial bureaucrats (carving the earth up at Versailles and contemporaneously at Tehran) and the politicians of Britain, the proto-Airstrip One. Orwell took the threads of his day and followed them to their logical and horrendous conclusions[2]. So perceptive was his take, influenced heavily by Zamyatin's exceptional *We*, that it rendered the vast majority of jumpsuit-wearing dystopian literature to follow as somehow naïve. One edge he had was an awareness that things will not entirely work in the future. The architecture of his future London is a transposed version of his contemporary city, yet to recover from the Blitz and mired in widespread poverty; 'Were there always these vistas of rotting nineteenth-century houses . . . their crazy garden walls sagging in all directions? And the bombed sites where the plaster dust swirled in the air?'[3]

In the future, there will be not only flux but pointlessness, frivolity, inefficiencies, all these things that make us human by accident and which we rail against daily.

There are exceptions:

'The Ministry of Truth — Minitrue, in Newspeak — was startlingly different from any other object in sight. It was an enormous pyramidal structure of glittering white concrete, soaring up, terrace after terrace, three hundred meters into

---

2   This technique may lead to absurdist conclusions but it's worth noting how
     often they become true. The future of Verhoeven's *Robocop* would still be
     hilarious if it wasn't actually unfolding in front of our eyes.

3   *1984*, Pg. 2

the air . . . Scattered about London there were just three other buildings of similar appearance and size. So completely did they dwarf the surrounding architecture that from the roof of Victory Mansions you could see all four of them simultaneously.'

They gazed at everything and were blank in response. Orwell knew that totalitarianism would obliterate not just satire but the very meaning from words. Objective truth was illegal if not unknowable. Black was white. The daily torrent of lies was provided and monitored by the Ministry of Truth. Continual war was waged by the Ministry of Peace. Austerity was provided by the Ministry for Plenty; 'The Ministry of Love was the really frightening one. There were no windows in it at all.'

It would be a mistake to see Orwell's vision as an extreme one, unique to the world's obvious tyrannical regimes. Orwell knew that the instincts and interests behind the world of *1984* were evident everywhere. Ideology is faith; irrespective of whether that's in god, dialectical materialism or the invisible hand of the markets. It is faith and in this there is absolution and condemnation. It is this that proves Orwell's warnings so perpetually apposite. The powerful of every conceivable political and corporate variation will employ faith. Questioning and a fidelity to the objective is the only bulwark against it. And yet if and when the worst comes, life will go on, due to humanity's resilience, often when it seems like it shouldn't. We would do well, as Orwell counselled, to see the traces of the dystopian around us, to find the ends of those threads and how far along we are; the most accurate prophecy being that people, and the allure of domination, never really change. We can Copenhagenise our future cities, make them as green and smart as we can, but provided we are still embedded in systems that reward cronyism, exploitation and short-term profiteering, that require poverty and degradation, it will be mere camouflage. Dystopias will have cycle lanes and host World Cups. What may save us is, in Orwell's words, a dedication to 'common decency', and the perpetual knowledge that it need not be like this.

Cockaigne

The future may well fail but the urge for the utopian is a valid one. It emerges from the failures and unsatisfied wants of the present. Inventors identify problems of the present, vacuums to fill and preferable end-results to backcast from. The shadow and dynamo of aspiration is present misery and the utopian impetus contains tragic often-untold real-life stories. It's no accident that Hansel and Gretel find the cottage made of sweets and gingerbread when they are at the point of starvation or that Harry McClintock sang of arcadian joys during the Great Depression[4]. For all its jaunty wide-eyed delinquency 'Big Rock Candy Mountain' is a song of shadows and implications. It speaks, as nursery rhymes do, of pestilence and regicides, of police brutality, starvation, drought and exposure to the elements. Utopia here is simply an escape into a parallel world of fairness, justice and comfort. In medieval times, the popular myth of the land or city of Cockaigne gave vent to these same notes of protest and yearning. 'Work was forbidden, for one thing, and food and drink appeared spontaneously . . . One could even reside in meat, fish, game, fowl and pastry, for another feature of Cockaigne was its edible architecture. The weather was stable and mild — it was always spring — and there was the added bonus of a whole range of amenities: communal possessions, lots of holidays, free sex with ever-willing partners, a fountain of youth, beautiful clothes for everyone and the

---

4   A distant descendant of the utopian English ballad 'An Invitation to Lubberland'.

possibility of earning money while one slept.'[5]

In a version inscribed in an Irish monk's manuscript (circa 1350), Cockaigne was linked to biblical promises of rivers of honey for the righteous but turned subversively against heaven:

'Though paradise be merry and bright,
Cokaygne is yet a fairer sight . . .
There is no thunder, no hail,
There is no vile worm nor snail,
And no storm, rain nor wind.
There no man nor woman is blind . . .
There are rivers great and fine
Of oil, milk, honey and wine.'

The verse then spins off into a ribald account of amorous monks and nuns, as well as a desire to escape the darkness of the buildings of the time:

'When the monks go to Mass
All the windows which are of glass
Turn into bright crystal
To give the monks more light.'[6]

Here is the vacuum speaking; the need for technological solutions (the electric light, mass-manufactured glass etc.) to

5   *Dreaming of Cockaigne: Medieval Fantasies of the Perfect Life,* Herman Pleijl, Pg. 3

6   *Medieval English Literature,* edited by J. B. Trapp

rescue the hours, amounting to years, of darkness spent in stone cells huddled next to reeking candles of animal fat. The absence of this once-common state is an indication that we exist without realising it in what once would have been sought after as an improbable utopia. This is to say nothing of how we can now communicate instantly across the globe, live vastly longer lives, see worlds from the microscopic to the cosmic that we scarcely knew existed, listen to and watch performances by the dead. Despite this, we doubt the existence of progress, partly because we have the luxury of doing so.

The Brothers Grimm speak of Cockaigne with the insightful absurdism of the nursery rhyme: 'There I saw a plough ploughing without horse or cow . . . and I saw two gnats building a bridge . . . ' with the proviso, 'have I not told enough lies?'[7]

Look beyond the nonsense and you can see it is a future of automation they are willing. This is most evident in Pieter Bruegel the Elder's version *Het Luilekkerland* where men condemned as lazy and gluttonous are nevertheless allowed time to sleep or simply stare at the sky, as automated creatures scurry around serving them; an egg with legs, a suicidal roasted pigeon, a suckling pig running around peeling itself. This is a future life of leisure and farmyard robots, granted by the freeing of hours from rudimentary tasks. It is a utopia of time; the ability to waste time as we choose by being freed from the wasted time of obligations. Today, we have never had more labour-saving devices of convenience and yet the blissful life is suspiciously

---

7   *The Complete Grimm's Fairy Tales*, Pg. 501

fleeting and elusive.

'A joke is an epigram on the death of a feeling' Nietzsche wrote in *Human, All Too Human*. Perhaps Cockaigne momentarily eased the pressure of a life lived in struggle and penury. It became, as popular jokes of its kind do, a competitive sport with each teller outdoing the last. In its extravagance, Cockaigne exposed the comparative meanness of reality, where farce and tragedy are intrinsically wedded. Yet there was always the outside possibility, even in the wildest of renditions, that this was a physical place of some description on the face of the earth and escape to it (the realm of the idle rich) might be possible, however remote. The urge for the utopian is strong in the desperately poor, meaning that missionary forces promising better worlds in this life or the next tend to find a ready ear and a base to exploit. It is also proof that utopias were not the sole preserve of indulgent philosophers. By denying the utopian as some kind of failed parlour game, we exclude ourselves from understanding its appeal and the power it still grants those who can offer it. We know Cockaigne does not exist but that doesn't mean we don't believe in it.

The Biological City

The dire shadow of the real puts the promised light of Utopia into perspective. When Leonardo Da Vinci sketched his Ideal City he was not exhibiting his inventiveness but privately trying to work out a city invulnerable to rampaging plague, a city where waste was buried and deposited away as quickly as possible, where the cramped alleyways of old are replaced with plazas, where air and light flowed and health flowed with them. He anticipated the modern drive towards verticality; his plans consisted of raised canals for the gentry and lower ones for the workers. If he did not invent the raised walkway of science fiction and modernist architecture, he certainly propagated its use. In seeing the space and utility of the sky, Da Vinci was not just dreaming of building spires and towers but also of burying that which (or who) was unwanted and superfluous. Having embodied the teachings of Vitruvius in his Vitruvian Man, Da Vinci employed them in his city sketches. A healthy city would require a digestive system. 'With cities, as with people,' Neil Gaiman noted in *Neverwhere*, 'the condition of the bowels is all-important.'[8]

With Vitruvius, a crucially-influential figure for centuries, we have the idea of the city as humanoid. This was an architecture that in Pallasma's words 'mediates between the scale of the human body and the immensity of the world.' The city as a vast Christ figure developed from maps of the world where Christ

8   Pg. 259

would appear at the head with Jerusalem at the heart. This was replicated initially in individual churches, which were generally laid out in a cruciform shape with Christ's brain at the altar. Others like Santa Maria della Salute, Venice represent the Virgin Mary's body or the Holy Trinity as in Longford Castle, England[9]. Cities were, and are still, seen as having organs, from the lungs of parks to the nerves of communications to the blood vessels of roads. This was the city as the very embodiment of god.

But which god and whose? For all the Christian, or even Abrahamic, appearance of these cities of the celestial host, it's worth remembering that Vitruvius himself was a Roman heathen who lived before the birth of Christ and who believed in many gods, in the Greco-Roman tradition. The order he extolled was that of a polytheistic world. Certainly there were binaries and trinities that suited the Christian cities that followed, in Vitruvius' elevation of utility, beauty and strength as the three defining factors of architecture as well as the gendered nature of classical columns[10]. There were even parallels with Jerusalem as the *axis mundi* echoing the Ancient Greek belief that Delphi Omphalos was the navel of the world. Though the Vitruvian superimposing of the symmetry and the proportion of the body onto architecture did take hold, it did so as a translation from a very different culture. The unifying cult of monotheism seems ill-suited to the natural polyphony of cities. What is one giant felled Christ when a city could contain unique gods for every

9   *Architecture in Britain,* Summerson, Pg. 38

10   Doric male, ionic female.

component from bridges to subway stations to streetlights? Or at the very least a two-faced god Janus who looked backwards and forwards into history, god of gateways and meetings?

A singular god who assumed a city shape was also one vulnerable to being demolished outright. The original frontispiece of Thomas Hobbes' *Leviathan* shows a huge regal figure looming over the countryside and the city, his body composed of 300 notables. This is the monarchical hierarchy which came, not to represent God as claimed, but to replace him. The king is the body politic and he casts his dominion over all. For all the triumphalism, there is a revolutionary flaw in concentrating society into the figure of one man; namely what would happen if this one man were to lose his head?

There are subtler means of subversion than the guillotine. In 1843, an enormous map of the world drawn onto goatskin by unknown hands was found in a Saxon nunnery. On it were markings of real places in the form of towers and rivers alongside biblical and mythological scenes[11] including the Tower of Babel, the Garden of Eden, Sodom and Gomorrah beneath the Dead Sea, Alexander the Great consulting the Oracle, sun-gazers and opium eaters smacked out amidst their crops, the giants Gog and Magog, the Golden Fleece, Noah's Ark on Mount Ararat. Between depictions of actual if inaccurate cities and seas appeared centaurs and phoenixes. The face of Jesus levitated disembodied in the deserts of the East with his hands and feet at the remaining cardinal points, strange living monuments

11   Cited Pg. 102, *Mapping Medieval Geographies*, edited by Keith D. Lilley.

of flesh in the wilderness. A walled golden Jerusalem was set at the centre with another homunculus Jesus in its courtyard. Christ was supposedly the world and everything physical and conceptual within it. In his hand is written in Latin 'He holds the earth in his palm'. The Ebstorf map would be incinerated in a bombing raid on Hamburg, at a time when other ideologies were laying claim to the globe.

Beyond ideology, there exists, we hope, the sovereign individual, not alone but enmeshed in interactions, relationships and contexts. There is something mischievous but also something poignant and profound about Grayson Perry's reworking of the Ebstorf map into his *Map of Nowhere*[12]. This is a life exquisitely and satirically mapped with its events, settings and myths, peculiar to the self-deprecating artist (with its celestial ray of light shining from his anus) but possible for each of us, a crucial reminder that the world and the cities within it are endlessly overlaid and interconnecting Cartesian worlds, multiplying with every birth. There are collective mythologies and there are personal mythologies. It is only scale, extravagance, luck, functionality and popularity that elevate one to religion and not the other. All began in the lives and imaginations of individuals. We inhabit our actual cities through these personal mythologies, walking the ghost trajectories of earlier events, of debaucheries, breakups, griefs and glories, sanctuaries and pillories. The city is a memory theatre.

There are a multitude of cities hiding under the white lie

12   The title is a sly nod to the translation of utopia as 'no place'.

of a single name and they articulate themselves in secret significances, unwritten memory maps, daily orbits. In his notes to T.S. Eliot's *The Waste Land*, Ezra Pound noted 'the life of the village is narrative. . . In a city the visual impressions succeed one another, overlap, overcross, they are cinematographic.'[13] This is articulated best in Vertov's *Man with a Movie Camera*, Walter Ruttman's *Berlin: Symphony of a Metropolis*, Hannah Höch's *Cut with the Kitchen Knife through the Beer-Belly of the Weimar Republic*, Grosz's *The Tempo of the Street* and Marianne Brandt's *Our Unnerving City*. Even the great wandering novels of loners (*Hunger, Nausea, Notes from Underground*) are intrinsically concerned with the multiplicity of the city and the characters' alienation from it, searching as they are, in taunted solipsism, for the connections they see fleetingly all around them. The sublime wordless woodcut novels of the modern tragedians Frans Masereel and Lynd Ward find individuals railing against and attempting to transcend assailing forces from all sides in the daemonic metropolis. Before his milestone *A Contract with God and Other Tenement Stories*, Will Eisner created an affectionately-jibbing tribute with 'The Story of Gerhard Shnobble'[14]; 'I'm flyin'! . . . But no one's noticin,' laments the titular schmuck, swooping off a skyscraper towards the pavement. 'But do not weep for Shnobble . . . rather shed a tear for all mankind. . . For not one person in the entire crowd that watched his body being carted away . . . knew or even suspected that on this day

13   *Unreal City: Urban Experience in Modern European Literature and Art,* Pg. 3

14   From September 5th, 1948 episode of *The Spirit.*

Gerhard Shnobble had flown.'

By its very nature, the city atomises its inhabitants. We rail against pod housing proposed by the likes of the Metabolists not simply because it is inhumane, but because it reminds us with a lack of equivocation that most of us are already living in them. We are atoms, yet there is hope in what occurs when atoms link together.

There are other stories which show us what is to be gained from seeing the city in cross-section; Chris Ware's *Building Stories* and Georges Perec's *Life: A User's Manual*. Yet this is by no means an intrinsically good thing as the prying protagonist of Barbusse's *Hell* finds out. There is no guarantee that what is seen or reflected back will be pleasant. Our walls may be oppressive but they protect us from the horrors of proximity. An awareness of other perspectives can however reinstall a certain poetry to urban life that is too often dulled by routine; whether it's the extraordinary history of an apparently mundane corner of a room in Richard McGuire's *Here* or the multiple angles and realities in Hokusai's *Thirty-six Views of Mount Fuji,* Yoshitoshi's *One Hundred Aspects of the Moon* and Hiroshige's *The Fifty-three Stations of the Tōkaidō.*

By the time of the Surrealists, it was clear that one's own conscious view of the city should not be entirely trusted, let alone in comparison to others. Surrealism was a way of seeing the world by giving the dream-worlds of our sleep an equivalence to the waking world and by seeing the significance of irrational juxtapositions. It was often treated as an artistic indulgence when in fact it was an unexplained X-ray of the fears and desires that chart our paths through the everyday. Before starving herself to death, the modern saint Simone Weil castigated the boys' club: 'Men have always been intoxicated by license, which is why, throughout history, towns have been sacked. But there has not always been a literary equivalent for the sacking of towns. Surrealism is such an equivalent.'[15]

Yet Weil was wrong in this case. Theirs was a multitude of views that sought to renew cities through questioning at a time when various competing beliefs were making battlegrounds of them. Memory is our Ebstorf Map, these madmen at play reminded us, and the map is the territory.

For all our contemporary cynicism, having long abandoned the Vitruvian-Christ model, we still have a tendency to still anthropomorphise cities; it's there for example in Niemeyer's emphasis on 'sensual curves' in buildings. Having based his unbuilt Ville Radieuse on an abstracted human shape, Le Corbusier insisted, 'Towns are biological phenomena. They have hearts and organs indispensable to their special functions.'[16] These organs can go wrong and endanger the entirety. 'As the avenues and streets of a city are nothing less than its arteries and veins,' Hugh Ferriss wrote in *The Metropolis of Tomorrow,* 'we may well ask what doctor would venture to promise bodily health if he knew that the blood circulation was steadily

15   Cited on Pg. 97, *Simone Weil: An Apprenticeship in Attention,* Von Der Ruhr

16   *Propos,* Le Corbusier, Pg. 48

growing more congested!'[17] A city robbed of sewers, electricity and people will start to slowly die.

If the body can be applied to architecture, so too can architecture be applied to the body. In 1926, Fritz Kahn created the marvellous and unsettling poster *Man as Industrial Palace*, in which the biological processes inside the body were shown as a factory environment, all pistons and functionaries and symbiotic systems. It is a diagram that inspires both wonder in what occurs naturally within us and a feeling of distinct unease; not simply with a dehumanised human form but the suggestion that this might be all we are, with consciousness as some accidental side-effect. Proof of the duality of the image was confirmed by the Nazis, who burned 70,000 copies of it (Kahn was Jewish) and then saw fit to steal and reprint it under a suitably Aryan pseudonym[18]. In Fritz Lang's *Metropolis*, we have the city as a vast mechanical body. Workers are collectively essential but as individually expendable as blood cells. This is an unholy city and yet there is much of Bronze Age religion with its desert gods and totalities refashioned into steel and concrete. It is Babylon[19] and Moloch, fired by the diabolical magic of electricity like Frankenstein's Monster.

Cities were often cast in human form[20] for propaganda purposes. Taking the hallucinatory Outsider Art of John the Revelator as useful scripture, the Early Church fixated over

---

17   Pg. 18

18   *LIFE*, April 19th, 1943

19   Lang even includes a Tower of Babel.

20   The Greeks had them as gods called 'tyche'.

the embodiment of evil, 'Babylon the Great, the Mother of Prostitutes and Abominations of the Earth.' The Whore of Babylon became a corruption of Hebrew folk-memory of their subjugation in the ancient capital and an indirect criticism of the great Western city of the times, Rome (as well as elevating its antithesis, the motherly Jerusalem). It also became a canvas for all manner of neurotic misogyny, particularly ill-fitting to everything the leftist Christ embodied. At times, the vanquished adapt personas for the city (depictions of Prussian-besieged Paris as an imperilled maiden for example), at other times the vanquisher as in Sherman's promise to 'make Georgia howl.' In terrible times, only the impossible seems fitting:

'While he was shooting the scenes of the massacre on the Odessa steps [the real-life Tsarist massacre reimagined in *Battleship Potemkin*] Eisenstein also photographed three stone lions, one lying, one sitting, one roaring. Edited together in the film they show a single lion coming to life and conveyed the idea of protest – with an emotional meaning something like, "Even the very stones cried out."'[21]

We see ourselves in buildings due to the fact we are pattern-seeking mammals. The face, the gateway to the soul (if we possess such a thing), is transposed or extracted by accident (the Hitler house and a thousand others) or design (from the Lion-faced house in Awash, Ethiopia to PoMo structures like

21   *Film and Reality,* Roy Armes, Pg. 51

Kazumasa Yamashita's Face House, Kyoto). As children we instinctively attribute faces to building facades in drawings; the windows as eyes and so on. This does not leave us. If you have kicked through the charred aftermath of riots or warfare, the building as skull is not an inappropriate metaphor.

The links between architecture and who we are goes beyond childhood scrawls and melodrama. 'You cannot divorce man and space,' Heidegger wrote, 'Space is neither an external object nor an internal experience. We don't have man and space beside.'[22]

The buildings we inhabit become part of who we are. They are the settings for experiences and absences. They are wound into our conceptions of privacy, safety, comfort or the lack thereof. We are conceived in rooms and die in them. We live and dream in them. We begin relationships in raucous bars and clubs and end them in stations and airports. We remember the rooms of childhood and adolescence, the sound of rain like an imitation of infinity on skylight windows, the bedrooms of different lovers. The past is gone forever even though we can see and walk its rooms in our mind's eye. 'One need not be a chamber to be haunted,' Emily Dickinson wrote, 'One need not be a house;/ The brain has corridors surpassing / Material place.'[23]

There are no ghosts in fact. It is the living who are haunted and these hauntings require an architecture, just as dreams do. 'How many people live inside each of us? One on the top floor,

---

22   Bauen Wohnen Denken, 1954

23   *Selected Poems*, Emily Dickinson, Pg. 184

one in the middle, and one in the cellar?'[24]

Experience seeps into setting and setting seeps into experience and both become memory. Rooms inhabit us as we inhabit them. 'I am the product of long corridors' C.S. Lewis wrote, 'empty sunlit rooms, upstair indoor silences, attics explored in solitude, distant noises of gurgling cisterns and pipes, and the noise of wind under the tiles. Also, of endless books.'[25] This juxtaposing of home with books is no coincidence; we can read interiors and the cities beyond them. Rooms are invariably cabinets of curiosity, mimetic armouries, sometimes sacred, sometimes dreaded. In Paddy Jolley's short film *The Drowning Room* all the burdens of upbringing in the Troubles are given physical form in living rooms filled with water, where the inhabitants eat in slow motion and sit in oppressive silence. In Dickens's *Bleak House*, Miss Havisahm, with her mouldering room of stopped clocks, has made peace with stagnation: 'whoever had this house, could want nothing else'[26].

We might disregard the mad woman in the attic at the same time as we daily accept living spaces that treat the inhabitant as a necessary evil and space simply as space. This often occurs through myopia and lethargy rather than outright oppression; Brian Eno got to the crux of the problem when he pointed out the fact that millions were set aside for every aspect of airport design but it was filled, at the last minute, with ill-fitting

24   Reinbeck, Pg. 14, from Pg. 21 Ein kleines Ja und ein grobes nein

25   *Surprised by Joy* (New York: Harvest, 1965), C.S. Lewis, Pg. 10

26   *Great Expectations*, Charles Dickens, Pg. 43

songs from the radio like everywhere else[27]. Architecture had focused much too singularly on the visual when experience and atmosphere depended so much on all the senses: 'everything must be done to avoid monotony, repetition and the wasting of good buildings by failing to provide suitably dramatic and unexpected places for their discovery and contemplation. It is, in short, an 'artistic' approach, not overly concerned with planning criteria such as circulation or land value.'[28]

27   A trait he sought to rectify with his *Ambient 1: Music for Airports*.

28   *Urbanism,* Tim Benton, Pg. 201

Possessed

Given how intimately space is linked to memory, the soullessness of buildings seems anathema to us. So we populated them with souls. Drains were carved into gargoyles (with the added bonus of warding away demons), columns into vase-bearing nymphs, with echoes of Pygmalion and Medusa. To empathise antiquity, establish ambassadors to lost ages and process the horrors of the past into entertainment, we inhabited buildings with ghouls in period outfits and translated murderers and victims obscenely into wedded ghosts. We personalise and in a strange way we depersonalise.

In certain cultures, the lives lived within structures permeate them over time. Certain Zulu Indlu huts and traveller caravans are burnt upon the death of their owner. The houses of Trulli, Italy and the Transvaal Ndebele are personalised with art and graffiti so that no two are quite the same. In fictions, we add a hunchback to a cathedral or a phantom to an opera to mitigate the emptiness of such buildings, just as we nickname skyscrapers from the Gherkin to the Armadillo to the Beehive. The manmade is made to seem somehow soft, approachable, organic when in fact the buildings are anything but.

We transpose morality onto buildings too. Does St Basil's look less beautiful, or more, when we know its architect was blinded after building it? In its life-span, S-21 was a school, a torture chamber and a tourist site; a feeling of palpable dread emanates from it, knowing what took place there. If we did not know the stories however, the buildings might resemble any other from the outside. The stones are neither innocent nor guilty. Smokestacks are unaware whether it is the smoke of firewood, coal or human beings they are funnelling into the sky. Even when we claim hauntings or cursed places where birds do not land, the knowledge of what happened is crucial. Ghosts require memories.

The Jungle

For all the glory of the light-bearing stone-men on Saarinen's Helsinki station, there seems little reason to restrict the living city to human form. Many of Lebbeus Woods's most innovative plans resemble insects with exoskeletons and anthropod legs.[29] Hugo 'Fidus' Höppener designed remarkable neo-pagan temples (dedicated to the likes of still water and Beethoven) that appeared like sleeping dragons. Alvar Aalto developed a plan for the city of Rovaniemi with 'traffic arteries which spread out through the town somewhat in the manner of the branched antlers of a reindeer.'[30] To the Finnish master, building was an inherently natural process: 'The origin of architecture in a way is biodynamic process. One has to build architecture around this process in a manner of sea shell, a shell that has also interior and everything that is necessary.'

This approach was characteristic of but not exclusive to his environment: 'we Finns tend to organise space topographically on the basis of amorphous 'forest geometry' as opposed to the "geometry of town" that guides European thinking.'[31]

Thankfully, the Finns are not alone in seeing that there are many possible geometries and the hints are all around us in the wordless innovations of the natural world; Himeji Castle, for

---

29   'We might argue that the insect metaphor rivals the "machine" metaphor as the
        most obvious avant-garde architectural image'
        — *Subnature: Architecture's Other Environments*, David Gissen, Pg. 173

30   *The Complete Catalogue of Architecture*, Alvar Aalto, Pg. 21

31   *Sensuous Minimalism*, Juhani Pallasma, Pg. 153

example, is built in imitation of white herons rising into flight.

We tend to assume cities have to be monumental or mechanical, but there is every possibility of biomorphic cities being developed in future. Robert Scott Gilson's Quarantena series presents habitations that grow like seeds or organs. Hermann Finsterlin said of his plans, 'inside the new building people will not feel that they are inmates of a fairy-tail crystal gland, but like internal residents of an organism, wandering from organ to organ: the giving and receiving symbiosis of a giant fossil womb.[32]

A city that can grow biologically is nevertheless a city that can grow out of control (perhaps existing cities metastasise without restriction). Organic seems a saccharine idea until you view the 'city as organism' of H.R. Giger[33]. In the Swiss artist's work, the lines between biology, technology and architecture are wilfully opaque. Giger uses methods of poetry to produce inestimable menace. Walls are darkened networks of circuitry interwoven with teeth, claws, gentalia. It is nightmarish and sexual. Can the humanoid figures that are partially absorbed in these cities feel anything? Are they sentient? Is the architecture around them capable of thought, of malevolence, and can they be separated from it? Above all, is it a setting of agony, ecstasy or both? Heaven or hell?[34] The binary differentiation of utopia and dystopia is lost here in a mechanised *petite mort*.

32   *Biomorphic Architecture*, Günther Feuerstein, Pg. 73

33   McCarthy and O'Neill's outer space Inquisition tale *Nemesis the Warlock* is
        another exceptional example of idiosyncratic biomorphic architecture.

34   In his New York series, Giger suggests wherever this is, we're aready here.

We are cursed and redeemed by morality and aesthetics, aspects that set us aside from the animal kingdoms. We view even structures of concrete and steel as benevolent or sinister. To certain utopians, it is not enough that the city is a thing of beauty. It must be good for us, or at least good for some. We find this explicitly in the realm of health and sanitation, where it can be safely said that there has been utopian progress (the average worldwide life expectancy has almost tripled since the Iron Age). There is no assurance however that technological progress equates to moral progress. We may simply have more ways to fail than ever in that regard.

Humanity has been haunted by the idea of a city of health for as long as it has been blighted by the city of plague. There were those who dismissed the writings of Charles Dickens as sentimental socialistic propaganda. He and Victor Hugo were condemned as being 'maudlin sympathisers with crime . . . humanisers of vice'[35]. The London slum engravings of Gustave Doré were dismissed as mythic fabrications. All these accounts tarnished the image of London as the world's shining capital and the Victorian era as a golden age. They were bad for business. The burgeoning popularity of seaside retreats as a health-restoring escape from the pea-soup fog-tarnished capital gave a lie to these dismissals; as did the statistics ('a child born of a labourer in Bethnal Green had a life expectancy of only 16 years'[36]) including Charles Booth's dystopian 1898 Map of the

---

35   *Looking Forward, Or, The Diothas*

36   *East London Record*, No.2 (1979)

London poor.

Perhaps the most chilling images of the era are to be found in newsprint. In *Father Thames Introducing His Offspring to the Fair City of London*[37], the city is personified as the virtuous Lady London, a variant of Britannia bearing a shield and crown. The very thing that raised London to a great city, the trade of its river, is the rot at its core; the polluted Great Stink, the ancient bedraggled Father Thames. The victims are presented in horrifying form with just a hint of typical Victorian ambiguity as to whether they were the victims or the source of the problem (even social reform reeked of class prejudice and eugenics); the emaciated child of Scrofula, the throttled wraith of Diptheria, the feral corpse of Cholera. The rank degenerated Neptune figure of Father Thames recurs in the artist John Leech's other works for *Punch* — he appears as a rustic tramp beckoning an imp into the corpse-laden waters in *The London Bathing Season*[38]. In another, he lures a street urchin like a siren: 'Come, my dear! Come to old Thames, and have a nice bath!' In William Heath's cover for *The Lamentation of Old Father Thames*, he is a poisoned wild-eyed King Lear figure. Elsewhere, he appears in satire responding to the jibes of an MP with the question, 'which of us has the cleaner hands, I wonder?'[39]

There is a departure in The Silent Highway Man, from *Punch*, 1858, where Father Thames appears as the Grim Reaper and

---

37   *Punch, or the London Charivari*, July 3rd, 1858, Pg. 5

38   *Punch*, June 18th, 1859

39   *Punch*, Autumn 1866

the Ferryman of the Styx combined, with all trace of jollity removed. This is echoed in 'death dispensary' of 1830, where he hands out poisoned pump-water to children. In the wishful *How Dirty Old Father Thames was Whitewashed* (1858), he is a reclining Gandalf figure waiting as his abode is cleaned with lime. Eventually, prematurely, he is restored to barrel-chested grandeur as England's most-esteemed wife-killer Henry the Eighth. In his *Discworld* series, Terry Pratchett posits, for laughs, what happened had they not cleaned the Thames; the Ankh River running through the capital being so slow and thick with silt and pollution that chalk outlines could be drawn on it[40]. It was based on the folk-memory of what the Thames had been and other rivers still are. Real gallows humour takes place in the shadow of real gallows.

There were many who benefited from painting the problems of the industrial city as fictive. Like today, it was entirely possible to be inured with wealth against encountering the repercussions of the system upon which that wealth was predicated. The circles of privilege were real of course to their inhabitants — Knightsbridge is as real and unreal as the East End of London — but pan out and its disconnect from the wider reality, and crucially from causation and consequence takes on aspects of wilful delusion. As conditions decline, the need to become physically detached increases through private security, gated communities, tinted windows. This process of islanding finds its most blatant form in tax havens. For all their parasitism,

40   *Turtle Recall: The Discworld Companion . . . So Far*, Pg. 19

these are nevertheless utopias, however selective or morally questionable. *BioShock: Infinite* envisages a dazzling floating city built for the Chicago World's Columbian Exposition (1893) which breaks away from the U.S and takes off, American exceptionalism proving too discerning to even tolerate America.

It's easy to pour scorn and ridicule on the planned casinos, luxury apartments and anti-ageing clinics of the New Utopia by Howard Turney (aka Prince Lazarus Long), a growth hormone-injecting right-wing libertarian, and his self-appointed co-regent HSH Princess Maureen Howard Long. It's easy to laugh but futile given that tax haven utopia increasingly dominates in the age of neo-liberalism. If we look closely, we can see these islands appearing within our cities, unaccountable and unchecked in any meaningful sense. Derision is directed not towards the self-proclaimed wealth-creators burgeoning in austerity, but to powerless subcultures (teenage mothers, disenfranchised workers, urban tribes of scallies, neds, spides, chavs etc.) who don't have the good sense to have their vulgarities sanctified by wealth. Magnates, journalists and politicians were outdone in this daily show-trial by leading theologians such as St. Thomas Aquinas, who argued slavery was inevitable in a world of the fallen and 'produced by human reason for human benefit'[41].

There was once, hidden on Madagascar, an anarchist pirate utopia known as Libertatia[42]. Of all the cities that have claimed the title libertarian, this was perhaps closest, given that it sought

---

41   *The Cambridge Companion to Aquinas*, Norman Kretzmann, Pg. 226

42   *Pirate Utopias: Moorish Corsairs & European Renegadoes*, Peter Lamborn Wilson, Pg. 196-197

to spread liberty, through slave-freeing raids on trade ships. Yet no society can sustain itself solely on bounty, even if it chooses to feed on parasites. Indeed, the chances are the city never existed, except in dreams and nightmares, as mythic as ghost-ships like The Flying Dutchman (whilst accounting for the fact that that legend was based on countless real lost ships)[43].

There were campaigners for social change from above as well as below. Some were utopian. Benjamin Richardson's *Hygeia – A City of Health* is tragic in its optimism. Between the lines of its airy urban arcadia is the ruin of actual human beings. Richardson's vision was halfway between the Ideal City and the emerging Garden City. Space, light, cleanliness, order and greenery were integral:

'The safety of the population of the city is provided for against density by the character of the houses, which ensures an equal distribution of the population. Tall houses overshadowing the streets . . . are nowhere permitted. The streets . . . are thoroughly ventilated, and in the day are filled with sunlight. They are planted on each side of the pathways with trees.'[44]

Though Hygeia is a city built on Reason with Ancient Greek pretensions there is still an incredible emotional resonance to its suggestions, 'The accumulation of mud and dirt in the streets is washed away every day through side openings into

43   Most specifically a lost Dutch ship off the Cape of Good Hope mentioned Pg. 30
        of *A Voyage to Botany Bay* (1795) by George Barrington.

44   Cited on Pg. 84, *Indigenous Modernities: Negotiating Architecture and Urbanism*,
        Jyoti Hosagrahar

the subways, and is conveyed, with the sewage, to a destination apart from the city. Thus the streets everywhere are dry and clean, free alike of holes and open drains. Gutter children are an impossibility in a place where there are no gutters for their innocent delectation. Instead of the gutter, the poorest child has the garden.' All through this text is the shadow of the real city, the crowded squalor depicted in *A Court for King Cholera*[45].

'Happy people never make phantasies, only unsatisfied ones,' Freud wrote. 'Unsatisfied wishes are the driving power behind phantasies; every separate phantasy contains the fulfilment [sic] of a wish, and improves on unsatisfactory reality.'[46] As for people, so too for cities.

The logical deduction from designing the city of health was that cities could create better human beings. It's significant that the first mentioned architect in history, Imhotep, builder of the Pyramid of Zoser[47], was also the patriarch of Ancient Egyptian medicine. This link has proved remarkably durable even in the most cynical of times. If cramped and degraded architecture hampered human development then surely pristine architecture would encourage enlightenment and even transcendence. The obvious impediments to advancement were clear and remain so – poverty, institutional cronyism, inertia, snobbery, mean-spiritedness and stupidity, but instead other ills were highlighted. Sin and breeding were emphasised as a

45   *Punch,* September 25th, 1852

46   'The Relation of the Poet to Day-Dreaming' (1908), Sigmund Freud,
        in *Character and Culture,* edited by Philip Reiff.

47   *Ancient Egypt: Anatomy of a Civilisation,* Barry J. Kemp, Pg. 106

way of maintaining the status quo. Judgements were extracted from architecture and the slightest infraction, from the cracked window theory justifying zero tolerance to the casual assertion that 'too many stairs and back doors make thieves and whores'[48].

Visionary optimists such as Tony Garnier blazed a path out of prudish deadening pessimism. A crucial forerunner of modernism, Garnier made function into a high art. Occupants of his still-stunning Cité Industrielle would be sheltered from ills and served by their surroundings. It would be efficient not in some ruthlessly utilitarian sense but because inefficiency had been the source of misery for so long (this is still the great advantage of Smart Cities). Garnier even naïvely declined to include any buildings for the police or the judiciary because he believed that perfecting architecture would result in the perfection of humanity. So commendably out of sync was he with the times, Garnier would be denied the opportunity to build any of his factories of life and, with colossal waste, saw only his designs for lifeless aircraft hangars and warehouses come to life. The problem with building the mythic city of health was that it encouraged a temptation to conceal or purge the very people afflicted most by the cities of plague. Malthusian horror comes hand-in-hand with a puritanical repulsion towards the wrong kinds of people breeding (namely not 'me and my kind'), from slums to housing estates. This occurs partly because of neurosis and partly because assuming the role of moral arbiter is a power play.

48   Cited on Pg. xi, *The House: A Machine for Living In*, Anthony Bertram

Even the best-intentioned plans can leave room for potential tyrannies. In Jules Verne's *The Begum's Fortune*, the city of Frankville is built around the sanctity of cleanliness. It begins innocently enough but still contains a dangerously malleable fear of germs, railing against 'nests of miasma and laboratories of poison.'[49] There are harebrained but intriguing ideas: 'The smoke, instead of issuing through the roof, is led away by subterranean pipes to special furnaces, established, outside the town.' Gradually rules and exclusivity seep in: 'Any one [sic] wishing to have the right of living in Frankville must give good references . . . An idle life would not be tolerated there.' Power accumulates with he (and it is most often a he) who determines what is a transgression and who has committed it.

At the core of Frankville is an adherence to cleanliness that tips dangerously into purity, 'To clean, clean unceasingly, so as to destroy the miasmas constantly emanating from a large community, such is the principal work of the central government.' Those who transgress, who do not fit, who pollute the purity will be shunned and punished. In almost every genocide, there is an incremental removal of rights and dignity from the targeted peoples but also the equating them with vermin, from Rwandan Tutsis and Twa as incessantly reported on Radio Collines Milnes to Jews in the Third Reich. The victims are presented as bringers of disease, as bacteria, rats, roaches. Killing them is an act of cleansing. For a polis to deceive into believing it is pure, another must be impure. In doing so, the

---

49   *The Short Stories of Jules Verne*, Pg. 95

proponents robbed not only their victims of humanity, but themselves.

The Glass Delusion

The drive towards the city of health ran alongside our belief in progress and the city of the future, forcing us to paint the Nazis and Tutsis as barbarous frauds rather than accept that they merely exploited uncomfortable elements of this drive. Theirs *was* a form of progress, albeit one towards hell. In the West, having shunned healthier ideas of the cyclical or heliocylical nature of history, we are intrinsically bound to the idea of progress. It is a teleological view inherited from the Abrahamic religions. Even those who resist such an inheritance work within its framework, from neoconservativism to Marxist dialectical materialism. In fact this partially comes from the emergence of cities and urban time, when the rural had been tied to cyclical time through life and death connections to the seasons through harvesting. Even if it does exist in the commonly-accepted form, progress is not irreversible. It may be subject to booms and busts, Kondratiev waves and business cycles. Life continues on amidst 'fetish parlors, grog pits, needle alleys, dream salons and Chinese restaurants . . . all we're trying to do is to keep the place someways fucking civilised.'[50] As Benjamin and Klee's Angeguls Novus watches the wreckage pile up, who benefits from progress, and, at what price? are eternally pertinent questions.

Equally open to doubt is our deterministic attraction to the fallacy that things were meant to turn out like this in some

50   From *City of Bohane*, Kevin Barry

preordained scheme. So much of history has, on the contrary, come about through accident, coincidence, oversight, side-effect and lock-in: the would-be assassin of Hitler who traps himself in a toilet cubicle; a wrong turning by Franz Ferdinand's chauffeur leading his convertible directly in front of Gavrilo Princip who is eating a sandwich; Lenin's strokes and Sverdlov's Spanish Flu clearing the way for Stalin; a mosquito, perhaps, felling Alexander at 32. Had Ancient Greek scientists followed up Hero of Alexandria's[51] proto-steam engine the aeolipile, an industrial revolution may have sparked two millennia ago[52] and we might by now have conquered the stars, destroyed our planet or some combination of the two. An infinite number of pasts are possible and, from the view of an alternate universe, our timeline is made of them[53].

If there is a divine plan of progress then it can conceivably be hacked into and its plans revealed. Failing that, it can be railed against. Even the most devoutly secular architects entertained prophetic status; progress is after all a position of faith. Some were messianic. 'I can move mountains,' Theo van Doesberg exalted, 'and know that our ideas will be victorious.'[54]

---

51   Inventor of the first vending machine.

52   James White's *The Silent Stars Go By*.

53   One of the most tragic plans in terms of what could have been and what unfolded was the Plan for Greater Baghdad. It would've featured contributions from arguably the greatest collection of architects ever assembled on a project (Gropius, Le Corbusier, Niemeyer and above all Frank Lloyd Wright). Its opera house, islands and statues of Aladdin and Harun al-Rashid remains a future untaken, even if it was an orientalist fantasy.

54   Theo van Doesberg, Pg. 18

Even when the buildings were humanistic or personal temples, there were still traces of divine preordination. Otto Bartning, heard messages in his head telling him 'build towers, build towers'[55].

This visionary impulse was brilliantly exhibited in the writing of Paul Scheerbart, seer and guide to early Expressionist architects. A glint of light had travelled across the millennia from the deranged revelations of St John the Divine to the German poet, in the words 'the city was pure gold, clear as glass'[56]. Scheerbart would reassert the need to build such architecture to replace the dank mausoleums that had housed humanity for centuries, with translucent light-multiplying buildings of glass. 'Without a glass palace,' he wrote, 'life is a burden'[57]. Scheerbart argued for the abolition of impenetrable buildings:

'We cannot raise our culture except by introducing a glass architecture which will allow the light of the sun, the moon and the stars to penetrate into the rooms, not through a few windows but through the greatest possible number of walls made of glass, using stained glass as well. Through the creation of this new environment, a new culture will come . . . '[58]

Contrary to received opinion, Expressionism, of which Scheerbart was a pioneer, was not simply a vessel of tortured

55   *Expressionist Architecture*, Pg. 18

56   Pg. 87

57   *Century of the Child: Growing by Design 1900-2000*, Pg. 61

58   Paul Scheerbart cited Pg. 55, *Futurismo*.

individuals. Many, particularly members of Der Ring and Arbeitsrat für Kunst, were former sympathisers and compatriots of the butchered Spartakists and sworn enemies of the rising Nazis. 'Art and the people must form an entity,' went a passage in *The Glass Chain* series of letters, 'Art shall no longer be a luxury of the few but should be enjoyed and experienced by the broad masses. The aim is an alliance of the arts under the wing of great architecture.'

There was a degree of play to the designs of the Expressionist: 'let us live then in Utopia, let us fabricate plans, castles in Spain; let us pretend . . . '[59] and the dark angular urbanised Grimm-forest of *Dr Caligari*'s sets was no lie but Expressionism offered much more than this. It could be strikingly optimistic as in the cases of Hans Poelzig's House of Friendship and Wassili Luckhardt's *Ode to Joy*, and defiantly celebrated reason and science in the former's proto-space age Einstein Tower. Pehnt identified[60] the characteristics of Expressionist architecture as the cave and the tower. Cities would be carved as urban landscapes not just from the earth but from the human soul. They would contain and accentuate what they found there, darkness certainly but also as we gather from Poelzig's stalactite-filled Opera House or the Luckhardt brothers' crashing waves of the Berlin Concert Hall, unbridled joy and curiosity too.

Many of Scheerbart's plans, such as his perpetual motion machines, were admirable if deluded but he was right in focusing

59   Hermann Obrist quoted in Pg. 139, Conrad Sperlich

60   *Alpine Architecture*, Pg. 18

on glass and light, two crucial aspects of the cities that followed. Even at the time, his ideas were not as crackpot as they might now seem. Cities were built either to embrace or evade the arc of the sun, but oriental buildings often took into consideration the other celestial bodies[61]. Moon-viewing platforms have featured in Japanese architecture from the Katsura Imperial Villa[62] to the modernist constructions of Itsuko Hasegawa. The esoteric evocations of crystal that appeared in Scheerbart's work were however a breakthrough. The catalyst was Mies van der Rohe's Friedrichstrasse Skyscraper (1921), which used Scheerbart's ideas to show that towers of glass could be built with a frame supported not by space-restricting masonry but by the minimal skeleton of steel. For once, the prophecy came true, though in a very different form from that envisioned by Scheerbart. Encouraged by van der Rohe's unbuilt blueprint, towers of glass would rise in virtually every city, not to open up the world to the moon and the stars but to obscure them with the glow of lights.

Glass was seemingly a miracle invention in solving the long-intractable problem of light versus shelter. Indeed its origin had a note of divine intervention, being first found in fulgates, petrified thunderbolts where lightning had melted sand into glass in the Sahara. For centuries, glass manufacture was elusive and imperfect; fitting only in fragmented stained glass form or

61   Ancient Chinese cities were planned according to a complex ideal chequerboard standard called the Holy Field, based on numerology and cosmology and arranged to gain optimum Qi from the cosmos.

62   An abiding influence on Scheerbart's students - Bruno Taut and Walter Gropius.

treacle-thick in tavern windows. As it became viable as a cheap mass-produced technology, the possibility of crystal palaces arose. With mental illness often acting as a cracked mirror to the zeitgeist, this resulted in the 'Glass Delusion' supposedly originating in Charles VI of France whose schizoid episodes would find him convinced he was made of glass and in danger of being shattered if he moved suddenly.

Other acts of Expressionist prophecy remain as yet unrealised. Inspired by Scheerbart, the architect Bruno Taut advocated sculpting the Alps into a radiant city of glass[63]. In 1912, engineers had created the Jungfrau Railway which snaked up inside the Eiger and which offered a doorway (one of the most extraordinary on earth) halfway up the murder-wall cliff-face. If a train could ascend an alpine peak from the inside, anything seemed possible and Taut's logic was to defy avalanches, blizzards, hypoxia and tectonics to build a city on the peaks. It was conceived whilst the Great War was raging and encapsulated Taut's noble but esoteric belief that he could somehow unite humanity through architecture. This was to be the city as rebirth and catharsis, resembling a cross between a new manmade rising sun and an electrically illuminated Tibetan monastery complex[64]. There would be transparent bridges and godless temples where divergences of languages were banned; a linguistic restoration of Babel in an age where Esperanto

63   The prospect is reminiscent of the mythic lost and glorious kingdom of
        Shambhala in the Himalayas.

64   Chiming with Uriel Birnbaum's illustrations and Hans Scharoun's glowing
        chalice architecture.

seemed to have utopian promise. Eventually the crystalline architecture would grow and colonise the earth and the earth's crust until the planet was a structure to serve man without artificial countries and divisions. It was almost heartbreaking in its marvel and innocence, especially during the First World War: 'Mountains crowned and reworked, valleys improved . . . Airplanes and dirigibles carry happy people . . . Our earth, until now a bad habitat, shall become a good habitat.'

It was, of course, impossible but perhaps it seemed less so in a world where the possible had resulted in several generations being hurled into the threshing machine of war. There would be no purposes because purposes had been used to betray:

'PEOPLES OF EUROPE! CREATE FOR YOURSELF SACRED POSSESSIONS — BUILD! The Monte Rosa and its foothills down to the green plains is to be rebuilt. Yes, impractical and without utility! But have we become happy through utility? Always utility and utility, comfort, convenience — good food, culture — knife, fork, trains, toilets, and yet also cannons, bombs, instruments of murder! To want only the utilitarian and comfortable without higher ideals is boredom. Boredom brings quarrel, strife, and war . . . Preach the social idea.'[65]

The Alps would remain stone and these mountain cities of glass, peace and unity remained unbuilt; so too the cathedrals

65   *Alpine Architektur*, Bruno Taut, Plate 16; Bletter, 1981, cited Pg. 109,
      German Art 1907-1937: Modernism and Modernisation, Martin Ignatius Gaughan.

to humanity and socialism. The explosions of light bursting from the woodcut cathedral ('zukunftskathedrale') by Lyonel Feininger[66] for the Bauhaus manifesto in 1919 would prove to be more reminiscent of artillery shells than fireworks[67]. A mere twenty years later, the war began again.

66   The painter of the most mysterious and enigmatic cities mentioned in this book.
67   Expressionism was not the intriguing dead-end it is often painted as. It exists in
        Günther Domenig's insect carapace Zentralsparkasse Bank, the National
        Theatre, 1963, Singapore, it is there in the disorientations of Daniel Libeskind's
        Jewish Museum and, in one of the world's most iconic and beloved buildings,
        Jørn Utzon's Sydney Opera House (reminiscent as it is of Sternkirche by Otto
        Bartning).

The House of Constructions

The Bauhaus is seen now as an elitist laboratory of style, craft and geometry, all clean lines and function raised to the level of art (or perhaps art raised to the level of function). It was cool and it was cold. It's easy to forget that it had roots in the imaginary and pseudo-mystical; it had after all the Mazdaznan monk Itten, the Der Blaue Reiter veteran Wassily Kandinsky and the Swiss visionary Paul Klee as teachers (the latter creator of many imaginary settlements). Neither was the Bauhaus built on aloof technocratic foundations. Its leader Walter Gropius was a man of action as well as thought, ludicrously so. It seems almost miraculous that Gropius survived the First World War. He had signed up for a Hussar regiment and showed suicidal bravery (and luck) that would earn him two Iron Crosses. He had deliberately galloped through machine gun fire, ending up with bullet holes through his coat, boot heel and hat. He had plummeted to earth in a bullet-riddled plane with the pilot dead at the controls. He was buried alive by shells with the corpses of dead comrades for three days before being pulled out, learning lessons in space and constriction that could not be taught. This was a man who had lived.

Gropius chose Bauhaus as a hark back, via Hermann Muthesius's Deutscher Werkbund, to those who'd built cathedrals in the Middle Ages; before, as he saw it, arts and crafts had been unwisely separated and the artist had been elevated to an isolated ineffectual ivory tower. Gropius wanted to place the Bauhaus within society to change society. He also wanted to break down the artificial barriers between different art-forms. 'The ultimate goal of all art is the building! The ornamentation of the building was once the main purpose of the visual arts ... Let us strive for, conceive and create the new building of the future that will unite every discipline, architecture and sculpture and painting, and which will one day rise heavenwards from the million hands of craftsmen as a clear symbol of a new belief to come.'[68]

Gropius didn't let the small matter of not being able to draw stand in the way of the buildings he designed in his head. Even though it remained unbuilt, one of these buildings, the Chicago Tribune Tower (designed with Adolf Meyer), initiated the modern age of skyscrapers. This would demystify Gropius as a modern functionalist when his real concerns were with bridging the distant past and future — 'all our works are no more than splinters; objects shaped by needs and utility cannot fulfil the longing for a fundamentally new world of beauty, for a rebirth of that spiritual unity which rose to the miracle of the Gothic cathedral. We shall not live to see it. But there is one consolation: the idea, the building-up of a white-hot, bold, far advancing idea which a happier time, bound to come, will realise.'[69]

The Bauhaus was a genuine avant garde, at least initially; the forward-scouting troops of what could be, striving so that everyone could have access to utility and beauty and not just

68   Manifesto of the Staatliches Bauhaus in *Weimar*, April 1919

69   Qouted in Pevsner, Pg. 356

the privileged. The Bauhaus would create beyond the isolated romantic myths of the lone artist that shrivelled version of the great man of history. It would enable people to live within works of art rather than leave culture to the mausoleums of museums. Gropius was a radical rather than a revolutionary, in the sense of returning to the roots. Art had fallen out of real-life and into a separate side-existence and he wished to pull it back.

'With the advent of the age of science, with the discovery of the machine,' Gropius wrote, 'this established form of our society went gradually to pieces. The means outgrew man. The sweeping changes which took place during the last half century of industrial development have achieved a deeper transformation of human life than all of the centuries since Jesus Christ combined. As the great avalanche of progress in science relied on relentlessly, it left the individual bewildered and unhappy, unable to adjust, and lost in the whirlwind of those changes . . . balance must be re-established.'[70]

Before it became institutionalised, the Bauhaus encouraged a spirit of rebellious innovation, 'to emphasise individual freedom of initiative instead of authoritative direction by a boss.'[71] It had a rollicking jazz band. The men grew their hair. The women wore trousers. It was deadly serious and it was fun. Collaboration was encouraged over ego. An exquisite marriage of form and function was sought, even if Georg Muche and Richard Paulick's Metal Prototype House proved they could

70   *Architecture and Design in the Age of Science*

71   *The Synthetic Vision of Walter Gropius*, Gilbert Herbert, Pg. 9

design uninhabitable habitations with the best of them[72]. We need only look at the costumes of Oskar Schlemmer's Triadic Ballet to realise that this was a movement that recognised that life was surreally poised between the microscopic and the cosmic, even if function continually stayed their hand.[73]

For these reasons and more, the Bauhaus had to die in the eyes of the insurgent Nazi Party. It was condemned as degenerate and Bolshevik, with the fascist rag *Anhalter Tageszeitung* declaring their urge to 'tear down the oriental glass palace of the Bauhaus'[74]. The movement had been profoundly influenced by Russian Constructivism and Gropius personally had been influenced greatly by the sublime Ise Shrine, but the wilful ignorance and insinuation of decadence and inferior Asiatic hordes in the threat was characteristic of what was to follow. The Nazis conveniently ignored the fact the Bauhaus had been set up by a German war hero in Gropius, exposing a nihilism that would eventually become all-encompassing and self-consuming.

Many of the Bauhaus alumni would make it into exile, either abroad or internally. Gropius' *Monument to the March Dead* (dedicated to the victims of the proto-Nazi Kapp Putsch), a lightning bolt rendered in concrete, was demolished. The situation is black and white except that, as with Expressionism and many other architectural movements, there was a curious

72   Freezing in the winter, boiling in the summer.

73   Itten and the author of the plot-less *Moon Play*, Lothar Schreyer, were jettisoned along the way.

74   Cited in *The Edifice Complex: The Architecture of Power*, Deyan Sudjic.

awareness of the coming age, part misjudged flirtation, part prophecy.

'In the new society there is no place left for solitary privacy, for cosiness, for special fantasies,' Ilya Ehrenburg wrote[75], 'Architecture has overtaken psychology. Houses to live in? But nowadays people live in factories, banks and cinemas. Once they finally understand that they are not entitled to any different life . . . there will be housing barracks, rooms for sleep cleansed of dreams, for universal washing, for gymnastics and for some procedure which contributes to population increase. We have already known utopias which rested on noble aberrations and hyperbolic love of justice, the paradise of a Francis of Assisi, or the commune of Campanella. But there are – as strange as this may sound – also sober utopias . . . everything is thought through, down to the dustbin which opens and closes automatically. This is awesome and slightly frightening. Matter anticipates wishes.' There is a chilling ambiguity to this as well as admitted self-awareness. It is worth mentioning because it cautions against the convenient distancing myth of evil. This was a question of real complex individuals, of wants and fears and desires, decisions and attractions, just like us. If Bauhaus flirted so might we.

Shortly before the Nazis were invited into power, Oskar Schlemmer drew the Bauhaus stairway. He captures the bustle of ascending figures, dancers and designers but there is a distinct note of the unreal and the uncertain to it; where it leads to is out

75   Ilya Ehrenburg in the *Frankfurter Zeitung*, May 28th, 1927, *Bauhaus*, Pg. 319

of sight, perhaps to another world or a chasm or both. In this respect, it was not inaccurate. Schlemmer remained in Germany as the Nazis took over and was banned from painting with the exception of producing camouflage, in which it might be said cryptic worlds could be hidden. He ended up painting windows looking onto windows, devoid of people.

Books Versus Stone

Just as Gropius was fleeing the end of worlds, other architectural prophets captured the millenarian mood. Frank Lloyd Wright was moved to apocalyptic proclamations by the state of the urban US:

'the carcass of the city is far too old, too far gone. It is too fundamentally wrong for the future we now forsee . . . Hopelessly, helplessly, inorganic it lies there where the great new forces molding modern life are most concerned. Those forces are making concentrations not only useless but deadly, by force of circumstances being driven inward, meantime relentlessly preparing to explode.'[76]

To which Reyner Banham added, 'Wright came from a long line of Welsh preachers, and knew how to say "Vanity, vanity" like old Ecclesiastes himself.'

In contrast to such despondency, Le Corbusier was inspiring yet equally bombastic:

'The only possible road is that of enthusiasm. Postulating the existence of a modern consciousness and awakening that consciousness in all mankind. Solidarity, courage and order. A modern ethic. Already we are hurtling forward into the modern adventure. You think the time is not yet ripe? What terrible

76   Cited Pg. 75, *Scenes in America Deserta*, Reyner Banham

sounds, what rendings, what avalanches must assail your ears then, before they will hear? The thunder now rolling around the world fills the heart of the coward with fear and the hearts of the brave with joy . . . And to you, the idlers, the pleasure seekers and the liars, you in your niches, conservatives and robbers, I say: tomorrow will see the necessary task accomplished . . . on the day when contemporary society, at present so sick, has become properly aware that only architecture and city planning can provide the exact prescription for its ills, then the day will have come for the great machine to be put in motion.'[77]

It is like a speech from *Metropolis*. We might contrast this with the Swiss architect's observation and threat, 'the machinery of society, profoundly out of gear, oscillates between amelioration, of historical importance, and a catastrophe . . . it is a question of building which is at the root of the social unrest of to-day: architecture or revolution.'[78] Perhaps it's wise to ask ourselves when a prophet announces the end times or the coming glory, what exactly is it they're trying to sell? If we indulge ourselves and accept that there is a plan for all creation then we might suppose all architecture to be a constituent of that divine or diabolical blueprint. There are those who believe that God provided perfect measurements for Noah's Ark and ready-made blueprints for Herod's Temple and the Tabernacle of Moses, that Jacob's Ladder was an illuminated escalator and the Temple of

77   *The Radiant City*, Le Corbusier

78   *Towards a New Architecture*, Le Corbusier, Pg. 14

Solomon was commissioned by archangels with sextants and pencils. To the (un)orthodox religious, these designs await rediscovery and rebuilding as parts of an eschatological historical process. The baleful advocate of Manicheanism, original sin and revulsion of the flesh in Christian theology, St Augustine was similarly neurotically ordered towards buildings, asserting that symmetry in architecture was a divinely ordained thing: 'One is shocked at any unnecessary inequality in the parts of fabricated things.'[79]

The development of church architecture would combine spatial awe with an atmosphere conducive to self-recrimination: 'Instead of the cheerful porch of a Greek temple, the Gothic cathedral combines the dark brooding interior which conduces to the spiritual moods of self-examination and exaltation with the infinite up-shooting of its spires and vaults.'[80]

Architecture is not simply the construction of buildings; it is the construction of space, both inner and outer[81]. It is also the enshrining of stories. Cathedrals are 'bibles in stone'[82], designed

---

79   *De Ordine* Book II, Pg. 25

80   *History of Aeesthetics,* Gilbert Kuhn, Pg.

81   It is also power and ideology: 'they need to be impressed by grand spectacles: without these their piety — which rests on unstable, even fragile foundations — will disappear as time passes. However the grandeur of architecture and monuments, which are practically eternal, derives from the fact they serve as testimonies that seem to be constructed by God himself . . . these edifices, then, are the only way to maintain and foster piety, and to preserve it with laudable devotion.' Nicholas V, G. Manetti, *Vita Nicolas V Summi Pontificis, Rerum Italicarum Scriptores* III, 2, Coll. 949-50, cited in Pg. 29 *Interpreting the Renaissance* by Manfredo Tafuri

82   *Set in Stone: The Face in Medieval Sculpture,* Charles T. Little, Pg. 74

to be read by a largely pre-literate society, ideally remaining that way for some in the church. Thankfully, it did not. There is a time travel and clairvoyance aspect to literature, the dead speaking to us over expanses of time and what better material to endure than stone? The stories and lives of the Pharaohs are contained within the stone of pyramid tombs. Ozymandias is remembered for being forgotten. We read in stone the epilogues of former gods. Yet something has come to pass that has overthrown them.

'Architecture is the great book of humanity,' Victor Hugo wrote, 'When the memory of the first races felt itself overloaded, when the mass of reminiscences of the human race became so heavy and so confused that speech naked and flying, ran the risk of losing them on the way, men transcribed them on the soil in a manner which was at once the most visible, most durable, and most natural. They sealed each tradition beneath a monument . . . In the fifteenth century everything changes. Human thought discovers a mode of perpetuating itself, not only more durable and more resisting than architecture, but still more simple and easy. Architecture is dethroned. Gutenberg's letters of lead are about to supersede Orpheus's letters of stone. The invention of printing is the greatest event in history. It is the mother of revolution. It is the mode of expression of humanity which is totally renewed . . . Assuredly, it is a construction which increases and piles up in endless spirals; there is also confusion of tongues, incessant activity, indefatigable labour, eager competition of all humanity, refuge promised to intelligence, a new Flood against an overflow of barbarians. It is the second tower of Babel of the human race.'[83] We are taking part in this building right now as you read these words.

---

83   *The Hunchback of Notre Dame: Or, Our Lady of Paris*, Victor Hugo, Pg. 351

Remembering the Future

The Mechanical Heart

'Life is lived forwards,' wrote Kierkegaard, 'but understood backwards'[1]. To tamper with this formula is to invite trouble. The science, or rather art, of futurology has always had suspect connotations. Court astrologers and druids could gain favour from deciphering portents from the appearance of comets, the flight paths of birds or steam rising from a butchered animal but the threat of execution hung over them for unwelcome or inaccurate predictions. Naturally, the role was suited to the skilled charlatan who can identify trends, needs and apply charisma and cold-reading [2]. So appalled by the practice was Dante that he inhabited a circle of his subterranean city the Inferno with fortune-tellers, who, with poetic justice, had their

1   *Identity: Sociological Perspectives*, Steph Lawler, Pg. 19

2   Barnum statements, shotgunning, blatant flattery.

heads turned backwards to spend all eternity bumping into each other.

Given that vagueness and wideness are key to prediction, only a foolhardy or brave futurologist will provide dates for when their imagined futures will arrive (Orwell's *1984* was simply the year it was written, acerbically switched around). Thankfully there are enough brave fools to have done so who justify an entire study of futures that could have been and in a sense already have been, what Derrida labelled, with reference to the spectre of Marxism, hauntology, and its juvenile fashion-fixated sibling retrofuturism.

Initially writers chose clumsy but effective devices to transmit their predictions. One was adapted from the 'visitor to the island' utopian trope, with another planet[3] or a future city as a substitute. This guided tour approach was only marginally less awkward than the suspended animation route: 'On the night of December 31, 1899 (in popular reckoning, the last day of the century), Brantford took a double dose of his sleeping powder; he lapsed into a coma and slept for 25 years.'[4]

Interstellar tourists were replaced by future-shocked somnambulist Rip van Winkles (originally based on the ancient legend of the Seven Sleepers of Ephesus). The pleasing artifice of the found text simultaneously disguised and drew attention to the inauthenticity involved.

---

3 This is demonstrated in the animation *Forbidden Planet* which places the island of Shakespeare's *The Tempest* into the interstellar sea of outer space.

4 *The World a Department Store: A Story of Life Under a Cooperative System,* Bradford C. Peck

In *The Diothas; or, A Far Look Ahead* by Ismar Thiusen (the Glaswegian John Macnie), the protagonist is transported to a future New York, renamed Nuiore, under a mesmeric spell. 'The New York you knew and dwelt in crumbled into dust almost eighty centuries ago, in the ages that are now regarded as the twilight of history. Its fragments form only the lowermost layer of the five fathoms deep of detritus on which the present city stands, the accumulated remains of a succession of cities, each more magnificent than its predecessor.' His is a reassuringly (for the author) mock-classical version of the future; it is 'rivalled by no edifice now existing, except, perhaps, the pyramids.' There are interesting anomalies. 'Manhattan Island, as might have been expected, had, long ages before, become, so to say, one enormous ware-house' while 'Brooklyn had become a great university city'. There is 'no army, no navy, no expensive hierarchy of public functionaries . . . Psychology had become a real science'.

In this future, glass is as strong as metal. Hammocks magnetically levitate. The sound of orchestras is conveyed down telephones. Machines exist as prototype approximations of 3D printers, televisions and computers. Remote learning was predicted: 'It will readily be perceived how potent a means of education had become the telephone and phonograph. There was no need to gather, far from home influences, crowds of callow youths into assemblages [inclined] to mischief and folly'. Thiusen could see that the future would demand convenience, pre-empting robotics: 'Machines of ingenious construction, demanding little beyond the guidance of mind, performed equally the most laborious and the most complex operations.'

The prejudices of old sadly persisted with the author taking condescending interest in developments in female appearance ('It is their privilege,' said he, 'to be beautiful'). Patriarchal rule has curdled into an Abrahamic cast: 'The almost absolute authority of a father over his offspring was regarded as the main safeguard of the social system. Till their marriage, the father had unquestioned power of life and death over his children'.

There are some undoubted advances to ameliorate the tyranny. Thiusen notes with satisfaction that 'electricity reversed the effect of steam'. Cars can conjoin with the use of electromagnets. Escape from the city is possible on serene gardened rooftops (still forwarded today as an innovative idea), 'like being at once transported from the midst of Broadway at its busiest to the calm of an unfrequented islet in the Southern Ocean.' Citizens work only three or four hours a day ('our work is not drudgery') with the rest of the time for 'mental improvement, and such unproductive pursuits as individual taste may prefer.' Idleness however, even the conducive kind, is stigmatised. The climate has changed with an eerie utopian counter-echo to our own probable dystopian path: 'I may mention, in this connection, that the winter climate of the North-Atlantic region had, from various causes, become greatly ameliorated from its present severity ... on the banks of the Hudson as are now the peach and the vine.'

Further Sleepwalking

The Diothas was hugely indebted to Edward Bellamy's *Looking Backward* which employs many of the same methods of time travel but with a notable political edge. The protagonist, a wealthy young male Bostonian, goes to a quack doctor and 'professor of animal magnetism' to obtain a cure for insomnia. He ends up hallucinating his way into the future. Again this didn't seem as quite as unbelievable at the time when other-worlds and their boundaries (microscopic, the light spectrum etc.) were being discovered. He wakes ('Will you tell me how I came to be indebted to your hospitality?') in the distant translucent year that was 2000:

'At my feet lay a great city . . . Public buildings of a colossal size and an architectural grandeur unparalleled in my day raised their stately piles on every side. Surely I had never seen this city nor one comparable to it before . . . I looked east; Boston harbor stretched before me within its headlands.'[5]

Bellamy's method is beyond idle speculation – he locates himself in the future city so he can, as the title goes, look back and indict the Boston of his day: 'the complete absence of chimneys and their smoke is the detail that first impressed me . . . what impresses me most about the city is the material prosperity on the part of the people which its magnificence implies'.

5   *Looking Backward: From 2000 to 1887*, Edward Bellamy, Pg. 23

In contrast to Thiusen's conservatism, Bellamy's is an egalitarian view: 'What little wealth you had seems almost wholly to have been lavished in private luxury. Nowadays, on the contrary, there is no destination of the surplus wealth so popular as the adornment of the city, which all enjoy in equal degree.'

Looking back now, post 2000, the absence of such developments only heightens a sense of pathos in Bellamy's optimistic account. The meta aspects, the eternal non-recurrence, are heightened: 'when I went into that long sleep . . . I should not have been surprised had I looked down from your house-top today on a heap of charred and moss-grown ruins instead of this glorious city.'[6]

The genius of Bellamy's text is not what changes but what does not change, making it eternally relevant:

'"Human nature itself must have changed very much," I said.

"Not at all," was Dr. Leete's reply, "but the conditions of human life have changed, and with them the motives of human action . . . Let him be as bad an official as you please, he cannot be a corrupt one. There is no motive to be. The social system no longer offers a premium on dishonesty."'

Here is a much-sought paradise of accountability and responsibility. We can smirk at his pneumatic postage tubes[7], his Greek temple conception of a shopping mall and some

6   ibid, Pg. 33

7   From an age when drones are hovering on the horizon for such purposes.

of his more overstated concerns ('it would be considered an extraordinary imbecility to permit the weather to have any effect on the social movements of the people') but there is something very simple and appealing about his idea of justice and opposition to snobbery: '"Do you mean that you permitted people to do things for you which you despised them for doing, or that you accepted services from them which you would have been unwilling to render them? You can't surely mean that, Mr. West?"'

Another aspect Bellamy calls us towards is that all cities change over the space of a life-time. We are all incremental time travellers for better and worse. 'How complete the change had been I first realised now that I walked the streets. The few old landmarks which still remained only intensified this effect, for without them I might have imagined myself in a foreign town.' We realise this only when too late and the haunts of childhood, juvenile delinquency and adolescent attractions are gone. You cannot step in the same city twice. It is not the same and neither are you.

Essentially, *Looking Backwards* is a series of critical essays on Bellamy's society, disguised as a novel, with the necessary distance that a perspective from the future allowed. Inhumanity and inefficiency are intertwined and dispensed with. This was the future as solutions to existing problems and proved immensely influential for future prophets; the architect of the Garden City Ebenezer Howard among them. The tragedy is that it was not influential enough:

'All that about the twentieth century had been a dream. I had but dreamed of that enlightened and care-free race of men and their ingeniously simple institutions, of the glorious new Boston with its domes and pinnacles, its gardens and fountains, and its universal reign of comfort [. . .] had been but figments of a vision.'

A person who inhabits a utopia, even just mentally, is changed. Imagining the future changes the future. Bellamy's greatest strength is, through contrast with what could be, to see the strangeness and obscenity of what is:

'such power had been in that vision of the Boston of the future to make the real Boston strange. The squalor and malodorousness of the town struck me, from the moment I stood upon the street, as facts I had never before observed [. . .] Now . . . the glaring disparities in the dress and condition of the men and women who brushed each other on the sidewalks shocked me at every step, and yet . . . all the while, I knew well that it was I who had changed, and not my contemporaries. I had dreamed of a city whose people fared all alike as children of one family and were one another's keepers in all things . . . '

The narrator's sight has changed. The scales have fallen from his eyes. The merciless city is unveiled, 'The roar and rattle of wheels and hammers resounding from every side was not the hum of a peaceful industry, but the clangor of swords wielded by foemen. These mills and shops were so many forts, each under its own flag.' At its core, a mechanical heart beats an unsteady rhythm still. 'Interesting sight, isn't it, Mr. West,' he said.'Wonderful piece of mechanism; I find it so myself. I like sometimes to stand and look on at it just as you are doing. It's a poem, sir, a poem, that's what I call it. Did you ever think, Mr. West, that the bank is the heart of the business system? From it and to it, in endless flux and reflux, the life blood goes. It is flowing in now. It will flow out again in the morning.'

One of the problems of the Old Testament route to the Just City is that it came with a large dose of Puritanism, ominously laid out with the implicit falsehood that justice and freedom were two mutually exclusive entities. In the future city of Bradford C. Peck's *The World a Department Store*, there are advancements. Humanity has dispensed with 'old-style microbe-breeding currency.' Everyone eats in restaurants. 'In your day the larger cities were filled with stock jobbers. Promoters of windy schemes lived and thrived everywhere. These men laid traps with but one idea, to slaughter their brothers. Gold was their god. They did not exactly use the knife and pistol, as did the pirates of old, yet on every hand could be seen bleeding humanity, which had been robbed through the medium of tricky advertising [. . .] We now need no insurance companies of any description, no stock jobbers, no travelling salesmen, no drug stores.' What begins as a disgust with inequity continues counter-productively into a disgust with the very essence of cities: 'Our vast organization, growing as it did, acquired by purchase real estate properties everywhere; these properties were soon after destroyed. Sometimes whole sections of cities were taken, and every building removed . . . Boston, New York, Philadelphia, and Chicago have been entirely changed. You will not know them, Mr. Brantford. The population of these cities has greatly decreased.'

Prohibition manifested in utopian texts long before its disastrous appearances in reality. In Aleofane in Godfrey Sweven's *Riallaro, the Archipelago of Exiles* (1901), self denial and subjugation of the body is a religion. Pleasure is restricted mainly to nostril-smoking, secret subversion and indoor musical cartwheels, 'these were the select of the marble city including the royal family, turning Catherine wheels round the room in pairs to the sound of quick music [. . .] my thoughts turned to the street arabs of my native land and their cry, 'Stand on my head for a penny.'[8] Puritanism is very often an excuse for, or at least indistinguishable from, sadism. In *Eudaemon* by Gaspar Stiblinus, no free thought or debate is permitted. The tongues of atheists are removed. Abstinence is enforced, with intemperance seen as a grave social ill, unlike slavery and rampant sexism. Ballanches's Expiation City has at least the benefit of brutal honesty, being somewhere between a re-education camp, a rehab centre and the Spanish Inquisition. Each citizen is broken down and rebuilt as a life-negating pleasure-free husk. The city is surrounded, unsurprisingly, with high walls. They are not to keep people out.

Insecurity and a certain self-disgust, even dysmorphia are

8   Pg. 52

at work in the puritan city. These are evident in the squirming body-horror of John Uri Lloyd's *Etidorhpa*:

'The amphitheatre . . . was literally alive with grotesque beings. Imagination could not depict an abnormal human form that did not exhibit itself to my startled gaze . . .

"This is the Drunkards' Den . . . "

"Why are they so distorted?" I asked.

"Because matter is now only partly subservient to will,' he replied ' . . . A drunkard is a monstrosity. On surface earth the mind becomes abnormal; here the body suffers."'[9]

Revellers exhibit exaggerated but pre-existing personality traits and behaviours (in vino veritas). A disgust with such conditions is a disgust for humanity and the position of the humble self-righteous juror is an inherently hypocritical one. Rabelais recognised this when he populated his Chaneph with 'sham saints, spiritual comedians, bead-tumblers, mumblers of ave marias, and such like sorry rogues, who lived on the alms of passengers.'[10] Even if they are genuine and not simply pursuing another form of power, the puritan urge to mould and monitor the lives of others is both futile and dangerous. The goal of cleansing and perfecting the human is not just improbable but undesirable given that our faults are often what makes us human. The perfected human is no human at all and the

9   Pg. 243-244

10   Pantagruel, iv. 63

perfect city would have to be either empty (as the Khmer Rouge attempted) or filled with automatons. In truth, those wishing a puritanical city are pursuing a utopia with only one occupant, the unseeing I.

Of Steam and Clockwork

We see those who created versions of the future in the early modern age in terms of adornments; a steampunk sky scattered with retrofitted airships, Tesla towers and the ornamental addition of goggles and clockwork mechanisms to already largely-fictive Victoriana. It is pantomime fashion and though fun in a tribal sense[11], it pales in comparison to the actual futurism of the time.

In France, the devastating social indictments of Victor Hugo and Émile Zola were joined by images of what could be when — and it seemed inevitable to progressives — the rotten present was replaced. It was a profound critical and appreciative knowledge of the past[12] and present[13], that informed Albert Robida's visions of a future Paris. Far from the mere ornamental, Robida built a vast three-dimensional world in his trilogy *The Twentieth Century* (1883), *War in the Twentieth Century* (1887), and *The Electric Life* (1892). Set in the far-flung 1950s, these are prophetic in terms of the real world and the future of futurology. He envisaged a tunnel under the sea linking France and England. He predicted the creation of manmade continents reclaimed from the sea (à la Atlantropa, the plans to drain the East and Hudson Rivers

---

11   Superior steampunk literature certainly exists, with *Infernal Devices* by K. W. Jeter (1987),*The Difference Engine* by William Gibson and Bruce Sterling (1990) and *The Warlord of the Air* by Michael Moorcock (1971) good places to start. Comics like *The League of Extraordinary Gentlemen* and *The Arctic Marauder* by Jacques Tardi are also fine, if uneven, introductions.

12   As designer of the Old Paris section of the 1900 Exposition Universelle.

13   As co-creator and editor of the satirical magazine *La Caricature*.

in New York and the reclamation of Doggerland by means of a ninety foot high Atlantic dam). He correctly envisaged cities growing skywards, even if the predicted levitating aerocabs, aerobuses, hot air balloons and zeppelins with docking stations on the tops of buildings (Paris's Central Station atop Notre-Dame cathedral) have remained elusive. As too has the ability to manipulate the weather and the mechanics of the solar system.

There were accurate predictions; women are more emancipated though insufficiently so, food is mass-produced, advertisements have colonised public space (in Tony Garnier's Cité Industrielle, instead of ads on facades there were utopian excerpts from Zola's *Travail* and *Saint Simon*). There are approximations of television, telephones, computers and the internet[14]. Robida gets the substance right and the surface wrong. Despite being mid-20th century, his characters are manifestly fin de siècle in appearance; the women are frilly art nouveau ladies, the men top-hat-wearing bearded gentlemen. He forgets that the very definition of fashion is that it changes[15].

Yet this failure is one of the more endearing aspects to Robida's work; it is a charming time-capsule future. At its best, it is a thing of flamboyant splendour; in his romantic vision of a future Paris skyline at night, flying machines with headlights for eyes are piloted, with a ship's wheel, through a fog that

14   Athanasius Kircher was a one man internet for his time (17th century) and
      endlessly worth pursuing.

15   It's entirely possible, of course, that the fashion is postmodern or revivalist,
      much in the way the hyper-stylish *2046* by Wong Kar Wai resembles some
      technologised Godardian past.

seems almost submarine. The rich glide through the moonlight, the police watch over the city by the light of an artificial star. We are crucially high enough above the glittering electric lights of the streets to imagine that all is safe and serene.

Robida was unique but not alone[16]. Across the English Channel, William Heath etched a strange early 19th century view of the future. His 'Society for the Diffusion of Useful Knowledge (SDUK)' lampoons technological advances with an apparatus-filled structure emblazoned 'Acme of Human Invention. Grand Servant Superseding Apparatus for Doing Every Kind of Household Work'. The emerging globalised consumer culture was mocked with the advert, 'Patent Fire: Fresh imported from the interior of Mount Etna.' Technology that emerges after our youth always seems alien. Heath sketches, with incredulity, fantastical satires of his present; a pneumatic tube delivering people directly to Bengal, a bat-winged postal worker, 'the steam horse Velocity', a black mechanical bat taking convicts to New South Wales, a series of castles in the sky labelled sardonically 'march of the intellect'. Heath manages a final sarcastic riposte in the title, though it is the lament of the powerless, Canute staring at a tide of time, 'lord how this world improves as we get older'.

Technology impacts not just directly but as side-effect. In *The Aerial Burglar* by Percival Leigh, people 'were favoured with a peep into futurity' by means of mesmerism. In their visions, mankind had conquered the skies by the year 2000,

16   *Across the Atlantic* by Winsor McCay offered extraordinary dreamlike yet biting urban comics

with floating islands filled with cats and bathed in artificial daylight. Crime had however 'soared into the sky; and theft and robbery contaminated the air.' As a consequence air-police were required with steam-powered vehicles 'in the form of birds or of fishes, others resembled dragons, griffins, and other fabulous animals.' It did not end well for one fleeing thief. A policeman 'drawing an electrical blunderbuss . . . discharged a flash of lightning at his guilty head . . . His hat, singed and blazing, flew to the winds, and his blackened and shattered form fell, with innumerable gyrations to earth.'[17]

As much as the apocalypse industry proves perennially lucrative, sometimes pessimistic predictions are received with hostility. During economic boom, such are the invincible halcyon delusions that questioning voices are treated as treasonous. In 1989, a long-locked Parisian safe was seared open with a blowtorch. A manuscript was found inside, titled *Paris in the Twentieth Century*. It had been placed there over a century earlier. The tale was by Jules Verne. It had been rejected by the publisher Pierre-Jules Hetzel who dissuaded Verne from writing such gloomy improbable visions of the future (the 1960s) in favour of sticking to rip-roaring adventures that were advertisements for the age ('Is *Five Weeks in a Balloon* a reality or is it not?') rather than dissuasions. It will be unbelievable, claimed Hetzel, failing to realise that no-one would believe the actual 1960s either.

Verne's predictions are intriguing for their accuracy and

17   *The Comic Album: A Book for Every Table*, Volume, 1844.

the reasons behind their inaccuracies. Often it seems that his time has not yet come. His hydrogen-powered cars, magnetic and pneumatic trains[18] and synthetic foods seem perpetually imminent even if the latter is not extracted from coal as foretold. The man-made climate change he predicted is underway and his unholy alliance of corporations and the state prevails. Verne's assertion that culture would be controlled under a state bureaucracy seems an accurate reflection of the totalitarian regimes that would follow, while the dumbed-down entertainment-producing committees seem reminiscent of everything from sitcoms to tabloids. The belief that music would become a cacophony was somewhat realised, though harmony has survived. Verne failed to see that art would endure and indeed thrive, due to its role as an ever-inflating investment bubble. His claim that there would be no news seems naïve given we are conversely swamped by it daily, just as we are with the images he imagined would be telegraphically passed around the world. Technology has made the threat of extinction a possibility and also locked adversaries into positions of mutually assured destruction. Verne predicted both. The electric chair he foresaw has come and gone and may well come again. Indeed all surveys of prophecies are incomplete as time refuses to pause.

Verne's most precise prophecies are observations that were just as true in his day. His protagonist is an artist who finds

18   Jules Verne earned a station on the Paris Metro in the port-holed submarine Arts et Métiers, which recalls his *20,000 Leagues Under the Sea*.

himself adrift and ridiculed in a world dictated by commerce and mercilessly-formalist sciences (Verne had been pressured by his father into law and finance against his calling). Poetry is reduced to mechanical treatises, though Verne fails to see the evident appeal in tomes such as *Meditations on Oxygen and Decarbonated Odes*. The protagonist ends up with his tears frozen to the graveside of De Musset. The old writer famously wrote in *L'Orfèvre, Lorenzaccio,* 'Great artists have no country' which was as much a lament of creative exile (as obvious here) as it was an internationalist boast. Verne was voicing the unease of the dandy, who fears beauty will be abolished in the name of function and who defends the sanctity of art as defiantly, exquisitely useless (as Wilde and Ruskin did).

Verne knew the character of his age and how it would pan out. Others focused on the gadgets, the dazzling conveniences and proved Verne's fears of a tyranny of utility to be correct. These accounts, with their shopping lists of inventions, say more than they seem to, by omission and implication; a world where nothing else is needed or required and so real human concerns are silently excised, a world where those reporting unwanted side-effects and consequences are the problem and not the issues themselves. Verne wrote another vision of the future (or purloined one from his son Michel). *In the Year 2889* provides a glimpse of future cities:

'with populations amounting sometimes to 10,000,000 souls; their streets 300 feet wide, their houses 1000 feet in height; with a temperature the same in all seasons; with their lines of aerial locomotion crossing the sky in every direction! [. . .] Think of the railroads of the olden time, and you will be able to appreciate the pneumatic tubes through which to-day one travels at the rate of 1000 miles an hour.'[19]

There is an approximation of atomic power in the far-reaching inventions (the transformer and accumulator) of Joseph Jackson, which extract energy from the sun's rays and convert it to virtually any purpose. As much as nuclear power has been revolutionary (for good and ill), the evasiveness of the cold fusion adds disappointment to Verne's claim that 'They have put into the hands of man a power that is almost infinite' ('almost infinite' being an impossibility especially apt to futurology).

In this vision, Centropolis has usurped Washington D.C. as the political capital of the U.S. Newspapers come in audio form. Advertisements are projected onto clouds. Air is 'nutritive'. Convenience has reached the stage of mechanical servants. 'Why, Doctor, as you well know, everything is done by machinery here. It is not for me to go to the bath; the bath will come to me.' Verne is self-deprecatingly satirical, with his 'hall of the novel-writers, a vast apartment crowned with an enormous transparent cupola. In one corner is a telephone, through which a hundred Earth Chronicle littérateurs in turn recount to the public in daily installments a hundred novels.' Information and its flow are critical; an accurate prophecy of the modern age. Verne pictures an eminent figure in a single day discussing signals of

19   Pg. 1

revolution on Jupiter, changing the borders of Europe, donating money to prospective innovators (one who wishes to engineer a synthetic human, another who is developing a transportable city), inspecting a vast array of accounts, visiting an electricity works at Niagara and undergoing a health-check. Data would set us free, a message we still hear from Smart City and Internet of Things evangelists today, with little acknowledgement that it is what we do with the data that counts, who can access it and for what purpose.

Verne and Robida's visions move us, in part because of what they did not see on the horizon, namely the First World War; the cataclysm of which makes the world of the late 19th century seem almost mythic. Theirs is a world of style, daring and chivalry (however idealised), which they were careful to retain, a world of evening wear and impeccable manners, architecture and machinery with a sensuality of form and florid embellishment. That this world was a largely illusory one accessible only to a privileged few does not matter. Perhaps they envisaged eventually an aristocratic life for all but visions can well be delusions. In *La Caricature*, Robida had ridiculed those modernist city planners pursuing the 'holy straight line', mocking the 'patron saint of the good city, ideal of picturesque beauty, light of the magistrates, star of local councils! Cut, destroy, erase, rake, scrap, trench, align in the name of the very holy straight line and create the modern style, the grand, delicious, superb style of the nineteenth century, or cretinal flamboyant'[20].

Robida was worried that all sense of humanity would be lost in inhuman architecture and technology, not realising that the organic too was artifice. We could not lose what we did not possess to begin with.

One of the most startlingly prescient sets of prophecies was the city of *L'Anno 3000* by Paolo Mantegazza, a cocaine and eugenics-promoting anthropologist who predicted variants on aeroplanes, computers, telephone, cinemas, virtual reality, light-bulbs, X-rays and the EU. His assertion that war would be banned may seem quaint and absurd were it not for the actual Kellogg–Briand Pact of 1928 which unsuccessfully tried to do that. The future would be expedient: 'A simple switch turns the electricity into heat, light, movement, whatever your pleasure.'[21] Destruction would come too at the flick of the bomb-door switch.

We have barely begun to grasp the dimensions of what we lost in the First World War, or the Irish Great Hunger, the Ukrainian Holodomor, the Armenian and Native American genocides and on, endlessly on, let alone the reverberations that followed. Some writers *have* explored alternate histories. In Michael Moorcock's *A Nomad of the Time Streams*, a generation is spared the threshing machine of the Great War. The result is an airship-laden world carved up by empires. The tragedy of the gross avoidability of the war also points out things we might not want to consider; namely that the mass murder was a colossal engine for social

20   *The Rise of Heritage: Preserving the Past in France, Germnay and England,*
      Astrid Swenson, Pg. 100

21   Pg. 3

change, for good and ill. Ward Moore's *Bring the Jubilee* posits a future in which the Confederacy won the American Civil War. It is a society of telegraphs, lynchings, highwaymen, steam cars and the omnipresent airship (the trademark of failed potential). The son of a slave, Sutton E Griggs imagined a black state within America, with Waco, Texas envisaged as its capital[22]. For every historical event, there are innumerable counter-paths untaken. Indeed some have been taken but remain obscured.

Part of the problem of steampunk originated with Robida; namely that it wears only the clothes of 'the great and the good' — the astronomer, doctor, detective, aristocrat, dandy, botanist, explorer and so on. Where are the lark maids, the slaves, the street children, the prostitutes in these recreated cities? They are side-characters down in the rookeries of history, down beneath Robida's sky-bound headlights, down where they will not trouble us. One of the reasons why we find surreal tales of descending into an imaginary underground beneath the city so convincing (like *Neverwhere* and *IQ84*), aside from their metaphor of the subconscious, is that we know histories have been buried.

Such was the popularity and believability of future speculations, given how much societal and technological changes had accelerated, they soon became omnipresent. Failing to envisage a future free of lung cancer, Grey's Cigarettes produced an 'Anticipations' series that combined enlightenment with mercantilism. In #5 of the series ('A Hive of Industry 2500'),

22   *Imperium in Imperio* (1899)

Greys Cigaret Fakrty [sic] occupies a monumental Stalinist palace, served by bridges, monorails and streamlined liners. It is:

'literally a "hive" in that it is a city unto itself . . . radiating from the mammoth superfactory are workers' dwellings and associated institutes . . . architecture governed by the prevailing material — concrete . . . no smoke (other than from tobacco!) . . . no household cooking . . . meals delivered by pneumatic tube from central cookhouse.'

In #2 of the series, we have a closer view of the city (London, specifically Piccadilly) to which this carcinogenic palace belongs. It contains elements of the past with hints of the once-extant Crystal Palace and the unbuilt Great Victorian Way (a glass arcade that would loop ten miles around central London) as well as contemporary masonry and arcade shop fronts ('Mars Express', 'Jaykl & Hyd' etc.). The surrounding infrastructure was innovative:

'Roofed-in under non conductive mica glass . . . moving pathways . . . rubber roadways avenued into 50, 100, 150 and 200 miles per hour [lanes] . . . suspended mono railways . . . motors driven by atomic energy . . . phonetic spelling . . . wireless television . . . lighted by captured solar rays . . . excursions to Mars.'

Notable are the raised bridges and platforms of the layered

city of tomorrow, decorated 'To the heroes of the Martian war', intriguingly unexpanded upon. Grey's Cigarettes would not live to see this brave new world in which they'd place their product so extensively. Many of their customers would similarly have a foreshortened experience of the future.

In Germany several decades earlier, Hildebrand Chocolate had manufactured a similar set of collectible cards showing life in 2000 as imagined in 1899. It too had a distinctly fin de siècle look, displaying a remarkable belief in the tenacity of fashion (unironic top-hats, corsets and waxed moustaches). Aspiring bourgeois families have their own airships for Sunday flights while bachelors and bacholerettes strapped themselves into winged devices. There are zeppelin trips, if not to Mars, then to the polar regions. Cities have giant flat all-encompassing roofs keeping storms out. As with the similar 1949 plans of Professor Archibald Montgomery Low, there's no explanation of how light gets through such vast obstructions. Rainclouds can be conjured, for harvests or war, by cloud-seeding contraptions. Police employ X-ray devices to monitor criminals. Ships can coast up onto harbour rails while automobiles can drive underwater. Balloons and clogs enable social gatherings to take place messiancally on water. Almost by accident, they chance on advances that have come to pass (the rest we eagerly await) such as moving travellators and a proto-cinema projector. The most impressive images typically remain the most ridiculous; above all the sight of a twin-powered steam train hauling half a dozen buildings on a platform, a city literally, absurdly on the move. Jean-Marc Côté and co. produced a similar series of cigarette cards between 1899 and 1910 of the year 2000 with robotic barbers, aero-cabs, bat-winged firemen and aviator-police, divers aboard biomechanical seahorses, fish races, clockwork orchestras, croquet on the ocean floor and a bus strapped to a whale. Opera was still popular though horses were rare enough to display as a curiosity. Though a novelty, the use of speculative ideas in such commercial products marks a notable change in emphasis from solving to selling the future. This in itself would prove prophetic.

The most engaging examples of retrofuturism were those which identified existing or forthcoming societal problems and sought to crack them. Arthur Radebaugh's *Closer Than We Think* syndicated column smuggled this solutions-based future into daily newspapers in the 1950s. Population increases and a relative shortage of teachers would facilitate a 'Push-button Education', where every child was equipped with a computer and an on-screen teacher[23]. Leisure would involve transparent raised swimming pools in giant glorified goblets. Smart-phones seem the logical extension of his Wrist-watch TV — 'sets the size of postage stamps will soon be worn on the wrist, each with a personal dialling number. One man might communicate with another — anywhere in the world'[24] (it's heartening to see his 'Telecast from the moon' even if moon colonies are for the moment abandoned).

23   May 5th, 1958 edition.

24   April 17th, 1960.

Whilst Radebaugh's robot housemaid with 'all-seeing TV eyes' may be missing, thankfully, from general consumption, other design applications seem to have arrived in transformed states; his Electronic Home Library is effectively the internet, his One-World Job Market ('Television will make it possible for an employer in Buenos Aires to interview a job seeker in Philadelphia') is essentially a Skype interview[25]. A truly successful future technology is one that becomes so ubiquitous as to become utterly mundane and barely noticeable.

In a similar light, we might acknowledge that the much-derided[26] idea of suburbia is a utopian one, developed and adapted from Ebenezer Howard's *Garden Cities of To-morrow*. Contrary to popular conception now[27], the idea was a radical one, toyed with by the early Soviet architects, particularly Melnikov and Ginsberg, as a green machine for living[28]. Melnikov envisaged an environmental city with not only gardens and farms but a laboratory called the Sonata of Sleep where workers could rest in scientifically-modified ideal conditions of rest. Ebenezer Howard's Rurisville has children's cottage homes next to cow pastures and artisan wells, fruit farms a stone's throw from a farm for epileptics and sanctuaries for the blind

25   Fritz Kahn's 'doctor of the future consulting his patient in the South Seas' by
      television (1939) is also conceivable today.

26   The San Buenaventura suburban complex of Mexico City, for one, seems
      scarcely believable as real rather than pixellated.

27   'Slums may well be breeding grounds of crime, but middle-class suburbs are
      incubators of apathy and delirium.' *The Unquiet Grave,* Cyril Connolly.

28   Mikhail Okhitovich's contrary disurbanist idea, reminiscent of Broadacre City,
      resulted in him eventually beng shot dead whilst imprisoned in the GULAG.

and deaf. Made for a series of Motorola ads in the '60s, Charles Schridde's glamourous luxury homes of the future, gazing down from canyons on the city's edge, are intrinsically seductive and remain so. The problem with suburbs is not innate, as inverse snobbery dictates, but that it falls so short of what it could have been.

Suburbia was also the by-product of dystopian considerations[29]. Following Le Corbusier's observation[30] that aerial bombardment was inevitable (his isolated skyscrapers were an attempt at a solution), Frank Lloyd Wright's unbuilt Broadacre City spread the metropolis out over a large plush area, one house per acre, that was city and country, 'everywhere and nowhere'[31] by the architect's admission, 'neither so isolated nor so crowded together'.

Attempts to smuggle the countryside into the city were always destined to come up against property prices and the territorial claims of motorists, landlords and business. It has occurred though where these realms have failed, in Paris's Promenade planteé and New York's High Line, rural bridges above the city as fragments of nature; a suggestion taken further

29   The imaginary dystopias of white flight were catered for by the likes of William Levitt and Robert Moses.

30   'The airplane indicts the city . . . By means of the airplane, we now have proof, recorded on the photographic plate, of the rightness of our desire to alter methods of architecture and city planning. With its eagle eye the airplane looks at the city . . . The airplane instills, above all, a new conscience, the modern conscience. Cities, with their misery, must be torn down. They must be largely destroyed and fresh cities rebuilt.'

31   *Frank Lloyd Wright and His Manner of Thought*, Jerome Klinkowitz, Pg. 137

by Raymond Hoods's Hanging Gardens of New York, 'utterly transforming the urban scene by spreading a magic carpet over so much ugliness.'[32] It is easy too to forget that every public park was a utopian idea and their continuing survival remains a utopian struggle; space, green and air being beneath noticing, until they are gone.

'The house shelters daydreaming,' Gaston Bachelard wrote; 'the house protects the dreamer, the house allows one to dream in peace'[33]. Of all the utopias, the most practical is that of maintaining your own sanctuary against outside encroachments. Architects recognised this expressly in the creation of domes in urban settings, within which there might occur exotic fragments of wilderness, jungle, even the primeval past. Haus-Rucker-Co proposed placing their Palmtree Island (Oasis) (1971) atop Manhattan Bridge while their Rooftop Oasis Structures (1971-1973) seemed part-organic urban canopy and part-biomechanical takeover. Unfairly ridiculed in his time as a crank, Buckminster Fuller's domes have proved immensely influential in environmental terms, particularly in ecological parks (like the Eden Project) and in designing colonies in hostile environments such as other planets or deserts of sand or ice.

The mocking of Fuller was particularly unfair as his developments, whilst superficially eccentric, were logical and indeed already existed; Victorian greenhouses had demonstrated the exotic could flourish when hothoused within

32   1931 article in *The New York Times Magazine*.

33   *The Poetics of Space*, Pg. 6

polluted industrial cities.

'The great masonry domes of both the east and the west can ultimately be traced back to the simple arched brick hut or tent,'[34] and the design had appeared everywhere from basilicas to Mousgoum huts. Fuller merely expanded their access to sunlight by replacing stone with glass. Perhaps there were the embers of memory from those dazzled by the Crystal Palace and other 'unnatural glass constructions'. Perhaps it was the feeling that glass domes should remain in science fiction[35], with their suggestion of an oversize bell-jar experiment for some unseen game-playing god. The apparently inevitable solipsism of the domed city is underlined by Diaspar in Clarke's *The City and the Stars*. A billion years into the future on an oceanless earth, the population exists under the artificial light beneath a crystal dome. The Cartesian insularity is even more pronounced given the consciousness of the cities' inhabitants is uploaded onto vast computer memory banks[36] with bodies to be downloaded into when required. Fear and ignorance of the world outside the dome absolves the dystopic interior. The central computer likes it this way.

Hysteria has always been the fear; the idea that confinement

34   *Tents,* Torvald Faegre, Pg. 62

35   In Alphonse Brown's *Une Ville de Verre* (1891), there is the domed Cristallopolis sits ominously near a volcano, powered by geothermal vents.

36   In Philip José Farmer's *Dayworld*, overpopulation is solved by allowing each person to only live in their bodies one day a week, thawing them out from suspended animation; power resides in those who can stay awake longer. In Harlan Ellison's *I Have No Mouth but I must Scream*, the future inhabitants exist within a sadistic computer, a hell from which there is little chance of escape.

with our fellow humans and ourselves, without the pressure valve of possible escape, would inevitably lead to madness. There is also, within this, the fear that respectable civilisation is merely a thin veneer, an artifice disguising while being propped up by base amoral and self-aggrandising appetites. 'Later, as he sat on his balcony eating the dog, Dr Robert Laing reflected on the unusual events that had taken place within this huge apartment building during the previous three months.'[37]

In *The Republic of the Southern Cross* by G. Constable, the polar steel-producing Star City (Zvezdny) houses 2.5 million inhabitants under a vast illuminated dome:

'At their disposal, apart from magnificent accommodation and a recherché cuisine, were various educational institutions and means of amusement: libraries, museums, theatres, concerts, halls for all types of sport, etc.. [. . .] Zvezdny was reckoned one of the gayest cities of the world. For various entrepreneurs and entertainers it was a goldmine.'

Zvezdny was a frozen Weimar. Isolation eventually drove the inhabitants mad, or at least into the grip of an epidemic of 'contradiction' where the normal rules of behaviour became reversed. Lovers insulted one another, police created chaos not order, doctors poisoned patients. There's satire in there but also darkness: 'Two nurses walking in the town gardens were overtaken by "contradiction," and cut the throats of forty-one

---

37   *High Rise*, J.G. Ballard, Pg. 7

children.' Panic sets in, with a mass exodus engulfing the train stations. Thousands froze to death on the tundra outside. The controller of electricity smashed up the power station and the lights went out. Those not afflicted sought refuge in a besieged town hall:

'The gloomy streets, lit up by the glare of bonfires of furniture and books, can be imagined. They obtained fire by striking iron on flint. Crowds of drunkards and madmen danced wildly about the bonfires. Men and women drank together and passed the common cup from lip to lip. The worst scenes of sensuality were witnessed. Some sort of dark atavistic sense enlivened the souls of these townsmen, and half-naked, unwashed, unkempt, they danced the dances of their remote ancestors [. . .] This was the city of the senseless, the gigantic madhouse, the greatest and most disgusting Bedlam which the world has ever seen.'

Such dystopias *are* experiments under bell-jars; when they turn sour the emphasis is on containment and preventing, as in John Carpenter's *The Thing*, the contagion reaching other cities. Here is a realisation that cities and modern transport, our advancements, could be turned into horrendous channels of mass destruction, a latent folk memory of the Black Death. All it might take, as Wells's Martians learned in Woking, are simple microscopic entities and the absence of isolation. Yet again there is a fear of pleasure here, of men and women revelling together, the terror that strikes the prude at the thought of a Dionysian carnivalesque utopia.

We might assume the opposite of the malfunctioning city is the city of absolute functionality but both are extremes. In James Morrow's city of Veritas, the truth is sacrosanct and omnipresent. Everyone is honest, having received the requisite shock therapy. The police are known as the Brutality Squad. The zoo is the Imprisoned Animal Garden, there's a summer Camp Ditch-the-Kids and restaurants serve Murdered Cow Sandwiches. It is hell and would possibly admit to it. The protagonist falls into a terrorist group called the Dissemblers who wish to sow anarchy (that is, freedom) through the beautiful lies of art. They have built the underground city of Satirev where the lie is king. Morrow is, of course, mocking existing hypocrisies and his emphasis that dissent is crucial to a free and functioning society is eternally apt: 'The reasonable man adapts himself to the world; the unreasonable one persists in trying to adapt the world to himself. Therefore all progress depends on the unreasonable man.'[38]

The key then is a delicate balancing of all manner of things; beauty, truth, lies, form, function and so on. An excess in the humors leads to maladies. The nature of the city as either a collage of juxtapositions or monomaniacal plan makes this extremely difficult to achieve and maintain. Often it is a question of mitigating restrictions, from William Morris's radical concept of beauty for everyone to the intricate decorating of Mosques where graven images are forbidden. Both are, in vastly different ways (geometric and floral) attempts to emulate paradise. Frank Lloyd Wright's Broadacre City might appear a perfected city but in many ways it's an attempt to transcend the city or even abolish it. His futurised countryside, with its sleekly phallic sci-fi cruisers and helipods, corresponded more closely than any other form of radical urbanism to the central precepts of the Communist Manifesto of 1848, advocating 'the gradual abolition of the distinction between town and country by a more equable distribution of the population over the land'[39].

This is the suburbs Jim but not as we know it. Lloyd Wright would never abandon the idea and possibilities of countrifying the city. He would add to the Broadacre plans all through life and sketched his last project, a plan for Ellis Island, on the back of a Plaza Hotel napkin. Transformed from the immigration-processing site of old, this would be a pedestrianised island of webbed hotel towers, moving walkways, theatres and marinas, so lush it seemed to have naturally grown from the jungle. Both remain unbuilt.

Antoni Gaudí had marginally better luck with his suburban project Colonia Güell. Strategically positioned on the edge of Barcelona to lure workers away from the booming anarchist movement there, it was designed to be a workers' utopia[40]. When funding was withdrawn, it began a curious afterlife as the Church of the Wonky Columns, semi-ruins that never served their purpose other than demonstrating aesthetic artistry and

---

39   *Modern Architecture: The Disappearing City*, Pg. 187

40   A contemporary trend — Owen and Dale's New Lanark outside Glasgow, for example.

folly[41].

Doom was a powerful catalyst to suburbia. Attempts to mitigate population and building density were well-placed given the death-tolls in the wooden tinderbox cities of Japan and the firestorms of Dresden and beyond (the Nazi Gottfried Feder had urged the building of a suburban Die Neue Stadt in such a model). Parks, cul-de-sacs and lawns would ameliorate the coming apocalypse by spreading out targets and ensuring firebreaks, in works such as Hilberseimer's Decentralised City. It is of some irony then that the US atomic bomb programme built a series of picturesque imaginary suburban areas complete with smiling mannequin families to test the effects of nuclear explosions on civilians.

The suburbs as refuge from the city evolved from the dachas and villeggiatura to which the rich could retreat in times of heat-waves, plagues, baleful comets and moral turpitude: 'Fishman suggests that perhaps the first true suburb was Clapham in London where the evangelicals, led by Wilberforce, sought to protect their families from the evil influence of the city . . . a development of the earlier "dacha" trend.'[42]

Such attitudes might partially explain the disdain with which the lightweights of suburbia are viewed by urban and rural dwellers. The cliché goes that God made the country, man made the city and the devil made the suburbs. The suburbs promised

41   As a side note, anarchists tried to burn his La Sagrada, supported by Orwell in a
        rare lapse of taste but proved unsuccessful as petrol was ineffective against
        concrete.

42   *Building the 21st Century Home*, Rudlin, Pg. 15

much and delivered merely blissful mediocrity. There is a rich seam of literature and film to back up the view of the suburbs as a limbo of deadening conformity and conservatism that stultifies all passions, even negative ones: 'the Revolutionary Hill Estates had not been designed to accommodate a tragedy'[43]. Yet this is precisely what makes them an ideal canvas for dread and curiosity. The insult that the 'silent majority' (traditionally occupants of suburbia) comes from Homer's term for the inhabitants of the underworld still allows for the possibility of being part of a Homeric story. There are stories there — the narrative haunted photographs of Gregory Crewdson; a painted house on fire in the photographs of Ian Strange; the soap opera surrealism of David Lynch or *The Virgin Suicides*. Suburbia was a very different place once. 'Forgers of seals, of bills, of writs, professional pick-purses, sharpers and other thieves, conjurors, wizards and fortune tellers, beggars and harlots found a refuge here.'[44] It might still be a different place.

43   *Revolutionary Road*, Richard Yates, Pg. 323

44   *Bourgeois Utopias: The Rise and Fall of Suburbia*, Robert Fishman, Pg. 7

Micropolis

In *The Shrinking Man*, the protagonist has not just giant cats, insects and arachnids to contend with but also an inadvertently-hilarious existential fear of domestication. 'He moved into the doll house, but doll furniture was not designed for comfort . . . Life in the doll house was not truly life . . . One night he took off his wedding ring.'[45] In Jack Williamson's *Pygmy Planet*, the human character is an omniscient scientific voyeur: 'Larry could not be sure that he had seen correctly . . . but he had a momentary impression of tiny, fantastic buildings, clustered in an elflike city . . . A city of green metal. The buildings were most fantastic — pyramids of green, crowned with enormous, glistening spheres of emerald metal.'[46]

We are fascinated by small worlds from within, from *The Borrowers* to *Issun-bōshi*, and without. Originally titled *Micropolis*, the release of the game *Sim City* was delayed because, like life, it could not be won or lost and was thus predicted to commercially bomb. We play with the God-like view to distract us from the fact that we are those tiny pixellated ants in real life. We view the city from the advantages and limitations of human scale; saved from the horrors of the insect world and prey to the vulnerability of being the pale blue dot in the cosmos.

Sim City was partly inspired by Stanisław Lem's *The Seventh Sally* which depicts a miniscule planet 'with countless signs of

45   Pg. 49

46   *Astounding Stories*, February 1932.

intelligent life. Microscopic bridges, like tiny lines, spanned every rill and rivulet, while the puddles, reflecting the stars, were full of microscopic boats like floating chips . . . The night side of the sphere was dotted with glimmering cities, and on the day side one could make out flourishing metropolises . . . '

The experiment goes wrong but by wrong we usually mean beyond control:

'"I don't understand. It was only a model, after all. A process with a large number of parameters, a simulation, a mock-up for a monarch to practice on, with the necessary feedback, variables, multi-stats . . . " muttered Trurl, dumbfounded.

"Yes. But you made the unforgivable mistake of overperfecting your replica."'

Tomorrow Will Continue Forever

So long as they are profitable for established interests and the cost of change does not yield a profit, the old ways prevail. Radebaugh's solar-powered ('the power of bottled sunshine will propel it') and atom-powered car may be prototyped, the latter in the concept Ford Nucleon, but they still lie some way ahead, especially in a time of cheap oil. We enter, in plumes of diesel smoke, the state of an endlessly-delayed tomorrow. Radebaugh did not quite factor in how much the greater benefit would be gradually absented from the grand schemes. He made the naïve mistake of assuming progress would serve people and that it would not exact a disproportionate price.

Depictions of the future were primarily useful in associating certain products with innovation and tough though stylish reliability. The future was used as one vast as-yet unspoiled advertising space. Futurama was emblazoned with a giant General Motors logo, Progressland with General Electric. Walt Disney obsessed over futurology developing Tomorrowland, the Carousel of Progress, Progress City, even Disneyworld, all sideshows compared to Disney's grand plan for the Experimental Prototype Community of Tomorrow (EPCOT). Inhabitants would move around by monorail or PeopleMovers. The car was to be abandoned. 'Here in Florida we have something special we never enjoyed at Disneyland: the blessing of size. There's enough land here to hold all the ideas and plans we could possibly imagine.' What Disney was creating, between the Reedy Creek and Bonnet Creek swamps, was not just a city but an old island utopia, a Robinsonade cut off from the outside world. 'Well, we're convinced we must start with the public need. And the need is not just for curing the old ills of old cities. We think the need is for starting from scratch on virgin land', away from state. Here, prophetically, the corporation would be a law unto itself.

It was designed, as Disney described it, like a wheel, branching out from a central hub in radial spokes to four secondary hubs (business, apartment blocks, recreation and housing). Disney did not live to see his utopia built and, like many a Caesar, his plans lapsed without the personal neurosis of his genius. Disney and Monsanto's fungus-free, termite-proof hosable House of the Future[47] was also scrapped, though the wrecking balls and axes bounced off it, forcing the demolishers to give up and simply build a Neptune's Grotto around its wreckage. Not for the first time, fantasy usurped reality.

National Oil Seals[48] and Bohn aluminium commissioned Radebaugh for his airbrushed visions of a high-speed streamlined chrome world to come, where almost-liquid vehicles zipped over bridges at record speeds without a pedestrian or guard-rail in sight. His designs for National Oil Seals are a series of wishes − 'when helicopters are mammoth sky cruisers . . . '; 'when atomic machines man the iron mines of Mars . . . '; 'when

---

47   Designed by Marvin Goody and Richard Hamilton.

48   'Engine in rear? Tricycle wheels? Polaroid Plastic top? Atomic power? Just as at home in the water or in the air as on the highway? Whatever the car of the future is like . . . it will . . . be protected with National Oil Seals.'

the speed limit is 200 m.p.h.'

'These are no idle day-dreams of a distant future,' claims a wartime ad for Chase, 'they're realities-in-the-making ... forged in the events of today for the Marco Polos of tomorrow.'

Ad-men of the time were the new men of a million lies. The whiskey-drenched 'Men Who Plan Beyond Tomorrow' in Seagram's series of ads promised much, yet their accuracy was precisely their problem. Their Travelling Kitchens became the distinctly unglamorous takeaway deliveries. Their Skyway Delivery system, parachuting goods from planes, is matched by the planned use of courier drones. Their Private Walkie-Talkie became the mobile telephone[49]. They even invented the unholy creation that is the sports bar. Seagram's overarching vision of the city is spaceport Corbusier, a place of pristine liminality, where legs are excess to requirement; 'High-speed, amphibious motors will whisk along the highways or skin across the waterways with equal ease. Your own car will do a smooth, safe 100 miles per hour on land — and fifty on water. Sky-scrapers will rise from spacious lawns . . . when Health Authorities abolish over-crowding of buildings . . . Fantastic? Not at all!'

Bohn's designs naturally emphasised the metallic; there are vast bridges of aluminium, alloyed housing, tents, fridges, tank trucks, three-storey aircraft, carousels, telephones, airports, ships, fire engines and the monorail, always the monorail, like the ghost at the future banquet.

---

49   Before staring at LCD screens took over the real world, science fiction shows like
       Star Trek were ridiculed for the centrality of their handheld devices.

Not all of the copy-writers of the future were as skilled or entertaining as Radebaugh. Many lapsed into bathos. A gloom-laden figure looms over the city. 'Coming Events cast their shadows before,' reads the title, 'With baleful certainty, the shadow of Time, That Tough Old Tester, falls upon pipe that cannot meet his stern demands'[50]. Tracks pass across the desert towards a pristine metropolis. 'The future just passed!' announced the advertisement for Oliver tractors. Ceiling systems, rubber paint and industrial lubricant (the latter with a spiralling ziggurat of death) were all sold with the dubious promise of fertilising the growth of advanced cities. With so many claimants, from the grandiose to the mundane, it is little wonder the future began to be seen as passé. In another series, the writers railed against possible dystopian futures that America might incur should it pursue 'Socialistic schemes that might lead to Communism', complete with disembodied malevolent hands guiding ship wheels and playing chess, with Uncle Joe lurking behind a mask of peace[51]. If the inducements to come did not keep the populace compliant then fear would.

50   Reading Iron Company

51   In *Is This Tomorrow*, a hysterical comic book issued in 1947 by the Catechetical Guild Educational Society, Communists infiltrate American society ('class conflict and the breakdown of bourgeois morals have been handled very well by our people in Hollywood') and overthrow the government.

Accelerator

Speed was a vital promise in these cities of tomorrow but the very success of innovative automobiles would be their downfall. There was little point in having one of the aerodynamic Norman Bel Geddes' tear-drop cars if the streets were clogged with them (something Bel Geddes had counselled against). The more space required to ease congestion, the more no-go areas there would be for pedestrians. Zünd-Up proposed a novel solution for Vienna in 1969; to lure motorists into a huge pinball machine disguised as an 'Auto-Expander' garage, which would bounce their cars around and pulverise them into wreckage to be buried in gardens.

Layering cities has long promised the solution. What sewers and aqueducts did for waste and water they could also do for human beings and their vehicles. In August 1925, *Popular Science Monthly* ran a cutaway diagram by Corbett showing a functioning tiered city, 'The top level for pedestrians; the next lower level for slow motor traffic; the next for fast motor traffic, and the lowest for electric trains. Great blocks of terraced skyscrapers half a mile high will house offices, schools, homes, and playgrounds in successive levels, while the roofs will be airplane landing fields, according to the architect's plan.' Pollution and lighting problems are not dealt with, though the mind-boggling suggestion of spiral escalators almost forgives this.

To live in the retrofuture metropolis would mean having

either wonder or vertigo-inducing vistas. Radebaugh supplied panoramas from his double-decker buses with maximised glass bubble tops while his trains sped across high arches. It would also require the regulation of the traffic. His highway patrol 'policemen on mechanical pogo platforms'[52] may seem superfluous and injurious to life but Radebaugh's glow in the dark Magic Beam Highway (1961) and his 'autoline' ('a computer-controlled highway in which cars would travel almost bumper to bumper at speeds of 120 miles per hour or more') are desirable and almost within reach. His 'automatic highway, on which drivers can look the other way while electronic controls pilot their cars' is a recurring image of the time. We repeatedly see a family playing a board-game in an unpiloted car as it careens not to their fiery deaths but their destination. This image says nothing of the resistance computer-controlled traffic would face from those who view the roads as a place of escape and freedom, or those among us who doubt if we could trust computers any more than we trust ourselves.

Cities were inevitably rising upwards. The logical conclusion was to join these structures and to link them to transport, to weave railways and walkways[53] through the sky. Henry Pettit's cover for Moses King's *Visions of New York* has a reassuringly classical view with skyscrapers built of stone, framed by statues, bridges and biplanes. King's enigmatic portrayals of

---

52   'Giant, tandem, wheeled vehicles kept upright by gyroscopic action, high
        enough to see across expressway tie-ups, narrow enough to wheel through
        them to any point of trouble' May 4th, 1958

53   *Streets in the Sky*, Van der Vlugt

the city came to an end when he was disgraced in a court case for wrenching the beard off the photographer Arthur G. Massey during a business dispute. R. W. Rummell's *Future New York* (1911) has skyscrapers piling upwards into a quasi-pyramid structure with the suggestion of mirroring slums, a situation that became a reality in the metropolises of South America and South Asia. Frank R. Paul's city from *Amazing Stories* (1928) has the startling sight of railway bridges and walkways travelling through skyscrapers via arches to the extent that the buildings are essentially functioning bridges (ignoring the resulting noise and vibrations). This echoed actual structures that combined bridge and habitation from the Rialto of Venice to the now-demolished Old London Bridge. Given that space is a premium in city centres, there have been attempts to update this idea for living and commercial space over rivers from Raymond Hood's living bridge designs for New York to Glass Age Development Committee's Crystal Span for London[54] to Arnodin's Bosphorus bridge where every pillar is a highly wrought mosque.

Often the old world is stretched to fit a new one. The landscape artist William Robinson Leigh painted his Visionary City (1908) in the hues of a rising sun, a vast stone city of glowing shadows with bridges interconnecting with bridges. Though the promise of the elevated monorails turned out to be a largely empty one (as satirised in The Simpsons) and were sidelined to amusement parks, it was not a complete dead-end. Though the

---

54   These dual purpose bridges surpass the gorgeous but dysfunctional x-shaped
        bridge over the Seine in the July 1910 Popular Mechanics which seems designed
        to encourage crashes.

Meigs Elevated Railway, piloted by bespoke gentlemen, went up in smoke in 1887, the GLC-proposed Regent St monorail went unbuilt and Glasgow's George Bennie Rail Plane was decommissioned ('slowly rotting away near Milngavie'[55] according to Edwin Morgan), there are antecedents to be found in Bangkok's sky-train and Chicago's Loop. Following the law of unintended consequences, bridges over land will offer shelter and cast shadows. What happens in these havens and hideouts is the stuff of further multiplying stories. There is always a shadow, sometimes literally but always symbolically to our advances.

Sometimes the city was stretched out of all sense and proportion. The recent push to move airports into the centre of cities was first anticipated in somewhat impossible style in 1919, even if the writer Carl Dienstbach acknowledged the difficulties: 'Clearly, city streets, flanked by high cliffs of architecture, lend themselves about as well for airplane landing and starting as they do for ice-boating.'[56] Given that planes must reach a requisite speed to lift-off, a dense city is ill-equipped as an airport. The solution posited by the art director of *Popular Science Monthly* H.T. Hanson was a tilted circular runway fitted to the roof of skyscrapers. 'Imagine yourself winging your way in an airplane from your country home eighty miles to your city office [. . .] somewhat to the east of the financial district downtown you see the banked track on top of the building on which you

55   *Beyond Scotland: New Contexts for Twentieth-century Scottish Literature*, Pg. 97

56   *Popular Science*, June 1919

are to alright. You head for it. Spiralling down, you [. . .] run on the landing wheels around and around until at last you come to a very easy stop.' The same publication ran plans in March 1934 to place an airport adjacent to the Houses of Parliament, 'building a monster landing field over the river Thames is now being advocated before officials of the city of London, England, as a means of providing the city with an airport close to its business center. The bridge-like structure . . . would be high enough to clear the tallest masts of ships and would include an upper deck for landing and a lower deck with hangar space for planes.' No doubt it would be a tourist draw to see jumbo jets approaching just above the river though noise pollution and air corridors through a city of skyscrapers are grave considerations. The absurdities of what could have been at least match the absurdities of what came to be, with airports located in no man's lands beyond city limits, bearing city names they were wildernesses away from[57]. The idea of the Aerotropolis has since returned, suggesting it was not as ludicrous as it sounded. Though it would not come to pass in antiquated forms (or those of Le Corbusier and Sant'Elia), it was clear that the future had nevertheless got out and the sound of aeroplanes would be incorporated above our sleeping heads and into our dreams.

[57]   Paris-Beauvais, Glasgow-Prestwick and so on.

Pow

So alluring were the comic books, pulp novels, popular science periodicals and sci-fi films of the 1940s and 50s that for several generations of Americans and Europeans, the future remains located there in the amber of childhood nostalgia. This was not entirely restricted to the Atlantic[58]. In 1930s Japan, the magazine *Shōnen Club* featured images of propeller trains, cars with spheres for wheels, boats that borrowed from aeroplane design, aeroplanes that borrowed from boats. Tekhnika Molodezhi (Technology for the Youth) provided material for young Russian dreamers; painting a future of metallic art deco trams, wingless plane-mobiles and pedestrians in modified pilot-wear on motorised foot-boards. An ability to adapt with the times and social conformity[59] set in, with a cover from 1945 depicting a family in a streamlined car jeering at an old fashioned couple on an antique driving carriage. By 1949, a family beam smiles from gyroscopic helicopters over a Soviet parade marching towards the unbuilt Palace of Soviets[60]. The hope, in the paintings of the likes of Andrei Sokolov, was that Soviet cities would one day grace the moon and beyond, a hope resulting in US alarm. It even became approximate with the Trotskyite Posadists liberating

58   Spain for example had the even earlier tales of Mari Pepa (by Colonel Ignotus), Sevilian innovator and explorer of the cosmos, two centuries hence.

59   Itself a dystopia in Pohl's *Search the Sky*.

60   Only the foundations of the Palace of Soviets were built before the German invasion saw it converted into armaments. Eventually its foundation pit turned into the world's largest swimming pool.

Havana alongside Castro, hoping the Cuban Revolution to be a launch-pad to spread interstellar permanent revolution.

The litany of all these heady plans is astonished disappointment, so universal as to be a cliché. There would be robots, jetpacks, helipads, cities on the moon. 'Helicopters for everybody!' Frank Tinsley predicted in 1951. Within five years, he modified this to 'Flying saucers for everybody!' We would travel by tubes, consume meals in tablet form, perform sports and sex in zero-gravity chambers. Cities would be filled with light and order, curves and parallels; criss-crossed by sky-rails and walkways. Efficiency would be total and leisure optimum. We would gain complete mastery over our own lives and in this sense we *were* lied to.

Suburban housing was still so relatively new then that its future was presumed to require only superficial appendages. The aspirational model of two cars in the garage was complimented by the aforementioned helicopter for each family. In Case Study House No. 4, Greenbelt House by Ralph Rapson, we have one of the earliest examples of this, with the patriarch of the house waving to the archetypal housewife, who is hanging out the washing in a mood of obligatory tranquilisation. In a 1959 advert[61], a mother and daughter take their turn in the vehicle, though bags of groceries give a hint that the purpose was not entirely personal liberty. In Arthur Radebaugh's *Closer Than We Think* of May 11, 1958, we have a much more karmic image of the female members of a family fleeing from suburbia in a

---

61   Independent Electric Light and Power Companies.

bulbous bat-winged contraption, leaving the men-folk to their barbeque and inevitable nervous breakdowns.

Humanity's age-old desire to fly would, the thinking went, enable us to leapfrog the daily traffic-jams and commuter hell that the mass production of automobiles brought. It would be possible, it seemed, to soar over Gale's traffic congestion-blighted depiction of *The Modern Tower of Babel*[62]. What it did not show was that everyone in the cul-de-sac would be thinking the same way and the traffic would be merely elevated into air corridors. Here lay the paradox of the libertarian conformist; longing for the wilds, having insisted that the wilds be tamed.[63]

---

62   *LA Times,* 1923

63   It was not entirely individualist with the cover of *Science and Mechanics* , December 1950 asking, 'Will 'Flying Saucer' Buses Lick Traffic Congestion?'

Sealess Ships, Grounded Spacecraft and the Curse of the Genie

The problem with the future is not simply that it does not come true but that it sometimes does. Fred McNabb's charming 1956 prediction 'This is your future' offers a material utopia that was largely achieved by the middle-classes of the First World. Flat screen 3-D televisions, moving staircases, microwave ovens, glass walls, slide-back roofs and Photo-vision Receivers are there for the purchasing, even if the helipads and ultra-sonic laundry remain elusive. Yet these things seem so tawdry, hollow and duplicitous as to make the title more a threat than a promise. 'Civilisation transforms the object world into an extension of man's mind and body . . . ' Marcuse wrote. 'The people recognise themselves in their commodities; they find their soul in their automobile, hi-fi set, split-level home, kitchen equipment. The very mechanism which ties the individual to his society has changed, and social control is anchored in the new needs which it has produced.'[64] You are what you own.

In Dodd's *The Republic of the Future*, innovations in technology and advances in rights produce an unsatisfied listlessness:

'For a traveller, bent on a pleasure trip, machinery as a substitute for a garrulous landlord, and a score of servants, however bad, is found to be a poor and somewhat monotonous companion. I amuse myself, however, with perpetually testing all the bells

64   *One Dimensional Man*, Herbert Marcuse, Pg. 9

and the electrical apparatus, calling for a hundred things I don't want, to see whether they will come through the ceiling or up the floor.'

The buildings 'are all architecturally tasteless, as utility has been the only feature considered in their construction [. . .] this modern city is the very acme of dreariness. It is the monotony I think, which chiefly depresses me. It is not that the houses do not seem comfortable, clean and orderly, for all these virtues they possess. But fancy seeing miles upon miles of little two-story houses!'

The author is clear about what the problem is: 'Freedom is the ability to live dangerously, inefficiently'. His reasons for this however would be laughable were he not serious; an axis of Irish anarchist dynamiters, Machiavellian Germans and feminists ('there is not even a servant to welcome the master with a smile') brought about this age of pellet food, two hour working days and Ethical Temples[65]. The value of such a hysterical account is that it is just that; it provides a telling indication of contemporary neurosis and who the targets/threats were.

For all the innovations and lateral thinking, it seems remarkably and contemptibly difficult for many to envisage any other future for the female half of our species than ongoing domestic servitude, discrimination and harassment. The 1950s seem a golden age for this combination of Futurism and Neanderthalism. *Better Homes and Gardens* in September 1958

---

65   Notably the actual forces in charge.

boasted 'Six idea homes of the year!' complete with a gleaming cartoon with the byline, 'What does a woman do all day?' It is a question and scene repeated ad nauseam. In Pathé footage from 1939, models wear the supposed fashions of the year 2000, that millennial magnet, including climate-adapting electric belts, removable sleeves, aluminium dresses and 'an electric headlight [to] help her find an honest man' (the latter unintentionally echoing Diogenes of Sinope's unsuccessful quest to ever find such a fanciful creature).

Be careful what you wish for is an eternally prescient warning. Isaac Asimov and Pierre Mion's prediction of a lunar colony as a green bicycle-friendly shopping mall[66] seems hauntingly accurate here and now on Earth, where such spaces reign supreme. Asimov was a particularly accurate prophet, not just because of his reasoning skills but because of his note of scepticism. His electroluminescent walls, robotically-piloted cars, 3D cube televisions and windows that can display any landscape may be coming to fruition but his enthusiasm is tempered with common sense: 'Robots will neither be common nor very good in 2014, but they will be in existence.'

Integration has been a key component of the future in which we live, a situation Asimov envisaged: 'communications will become sight-sound and you will see as well as hear the person you telephone. The screen can be used not only to see the people you call but also for studying documents and photographs and reading passages from books [a fledgling internet]. Synchronous

66   'The Next Frontier?', *Modern Mechanix*, July 1976.

satellites, hovering in space will make it possible for you to direct-dial any spot on earth, including the weather stations in Antarctica.'

No prophet is ever totally vindicated and, though affluenza is said to afflict only a privileged few, the 'society of enforced leisure' and boredom that Asimov predicted (with people rebelling by working) remains conspicuously absent.

So popular however were futuristic conceits to a generation that had lost its youth in the Second World War and wanted just rewards that it gave birth to a stillborn future, forever stylised to that time. It came to be known, in architectural terms, as Googie, Populuxe, Raygun Gothic, the product of an age fascinated with how technology might make our lives quicker, slicker, softer. It was partly a filtering-down of the metallic sensuality of Art Deco, which had been a source of wonder but a distant one, whether the perched metal eagles of the Chrysler Building or the elusive sensual merging of the body and the building in the art of Tamara de Lempicka. Art Deco spoke of impossible aspiration; a remote aristocracy of chrome and capital, yet built by the factory workers of Ford. There was something tantalising about Art Deco that chimed with the age; it contained both excess and ephemerality. A sense of grandeur fading like glowing firework smoke. A sense that if you got close enough to the silver towers to strike them, they'd echo hollow as a bell. The illusion was an attractive one, best reflected much later in the wondrously kitsch paintings of Robert Hoppe where the orchestrated choreographed poses of glamour are somewhere between a Busby Berkeley ensemble and Leni Riefenstahl's footage of the Nuremberg Rallies. It was a heady nightmare and most who saw it wanted access.

Art Deco was democraticised via the tangent of Streamline Moderne, where diners and hotels assumed the forms of ships suddenly landlocked in car parks. This was not as much a novelty as it's been portrayed. Le Corbusier had long been influenced by ships as well as aeroplanes: 'in the twenties, [he] drew a section of an ocean liner which happened to be the Titanic. Later he also drew the deck of the oceanship which was taking him to South America and wrote on his perspective sketch, "for the Algiers building = excellent/find the section drawings of the oceanliner."'[67]

Louis Herman De Koninc transplanted his memories of the Belgian coastline into his buildings, most overtly in the portholes and mock-funnel of his Villa Berteaux. Heinrich Lauterbach's Villa Schmelowský was designed as Schiffsarchitektur ('naval architecture') with the house as an aerodynamic ship letting the urban channel around it. Walter Gropius used the wreckage of a warship when building one of the Bauhaus masterpieces, the Sommerfeld House. Also fitting is the nautical design of the Chabot Museum in Rotterdam, given the artist to whom it's dedicated was renowned for his seascapes and portraits of fishing folk, while José Manuel Aizpurúa's Nautical Club seems to be a ship that somehow moored and then absorbed itself into the docks. Though the styles looked modern, the idea was less

67   Christian Girard, 'The Oceanship Theory' in *Architecture and Philosophy*, Pg. 80

so. Said to be haunted by the coughing cigar-smoking ghost of its former owner (though not reportedly any of the many slaves brutalised there), the San Francisco Plantation resembles an ornate steamboat banked from the nearby Mississippi. Streamline Moderne is what would be left if the sea suddenly drained away leaving the ships adrift on solid ground; a life after the oceans.

The real achievement of this evolution of Art Deco was its raising to greatness things that had been deemed unworthy compared to the penthouses and dining halls of the rich. The streamlined Ibex Building in London remains much-loved, while photos of Angiolo Mazzoni's Stazione di Montecatini Terme-Monsummano have a certain iconic allure for what is essentially a petrol station. The Fiat Tagliero Building in Eritrea is an even more ambitious version of the latter, combining the superstructure of a ship with the wings of a plane. When advised that pillars would be required to support the wings, the architect Pettazzi produced a gun and held it to the head of the doubter until the building stayed true to the original plans. The success and failure of the revolutionary aspect of an 'Art Deco for the people' is exemplified in the Red Banner Textile Factory initially designed and later disowned by a deflated Mendelsohn despite his initial enthusiasm: 'From buildings I deduce history, transition, revolution, synthesis . . . Synthesis: Russia and America — the future of Utopia!'[68] Today it exists as an exquisite shell.

68   *Letters of an Architect,* Pg. 97

The idea that these designs stayed locked within the unbuilt is a false one; we can no more evade our influences than we can our genetic inheritance. They seeped into the actually built and changed the future. Production techniques and materials borrowed from ship-building, which matched durability to tensile strength, and the mass assembly of car manufacturing was the starting point for the visionary pre-fabricated homes of the era. 'Dynamic, maximum, and tension' formed the official name (Dymaxion) for Buckminster Fuller's attempt at a house that could be shipped out en masse anywhere, and exist fully functioning without the need to be wired to existing infrastructure. Fuller's influences were similarly cobbled together from seemingly disparate elements, as all inspiration is; he borrowed from grain silos, automobile chassis, ship rigging and bicycle design. Despite being prototyped and eagerly anticipated, the house never reached mass production, with Fuller vetoing its release, held back by perfectionism or the vertigo of success. It was however adapted into the Wichita House, rounded off into a circular form that looked like it might start spinning and take off at any moment.

The urge to ridicule Fuller's dwelling machine, destined for a ubiquity which never came, is countered by the fact that its central ideas of autonomy and sustainability[69] have only gained more credence with passing years. In the case of Grete Schütte-Lihotzky's Frankfurt Kitchen, we have an idea, inspired by the layout of dining-car kitchens on trains, becoming the archetypal

69   *House in Regensburg,* Thomas Herzog

model of a high proportion of modern urban homes. We do not look upon kitchens as utopian realms but the really successful plans are those which become invisible. If we could not have space, we could at least have function, and Lihotzky gave it to us in our cramped tenements. A left-wing radical from Vienna, she had worked on monumental projects in Soviet Russia and fled Stalin's purges. She had conspired in the resistance against the Nazis and narrowly escaped execution after being seized by the Gestapo, surviving five years in prison before liberation. Hers was a hard-fought and egalitarian radicalism and she passed it on in simple brilliant fashion. Her kitchens made sense. They had order and availability. Knowing that it was disproportionately women constrained to kitchens, she designed one that would, at least, not hamper. In its logic and cleanliness (wipeable surfaces for example), it saved time and arguably lives. It would not be a utopia of liberation but it removed smaller sources of casual misery. 'You will be most revolutionary if you try to be ordinary'[70] is not just a platitude.

70   Denise Scott Brown

Home is Where the Harm Is

Being slowly poisoned or driven mad by our homes doesn't make for exciting literature. When the home goes wrong in print, it does so dramatically. Suburban versions of HAL served and then turned on their owners in a thousand pulp books. A Marxist take might be that the oppressed house had justifiably turned on its master. The psychological view might be that we do not trust the automated house because we do not trust ourselves. In all cases, we project ourselves onto the insentient; 'Yes, sir, you were the best buy I ever made! After all, what can go wrong with a house that loves me?'[71]

There we lie, throttled by electronic hands and swept under the flexicarpet. Lacking ponderous free will and conscience, the machine is as innocent as an animal. 'The child turned over and listened. Listened until the walls. Doors. Breathed in quietness. In the dark. She gave her secret to the house.'[72] It is our fellow humans we have to fear and they us. Ray Bradbury's *There Will Come Soft Rains*[73], with its post-future echoes of Hiroshima, portrays a home that poignantly but blankly serves its long-dead occupants whose shadows have been seared

71   *Starlord*, 1978, 'Good Morning, Sheldon, I Love You!'

72   From Ann Quin's 'Every Cripple Has His Own Way of Walking', *Nova*, December 1966

73   Inspired by the 1920 Sara Teasdale poem:
      'There will come soft rains and the smell of the ground / And swallows circling with their shimmering sound [. . .] Not one would mind, neither bird nor tree, If mankind perished utterly / And Spring herself, when she woke at dawn / Would scarcely know that we were gone.'

onto the gable wall: 'The image of a thrown ball, and opposite [. . .] a girl, hands raised to catch a ball which never came down. The five spots of paint — the man, the woman, the children, the ball — remained. The rest was a thin charcoaled layer.' The daily chores are rendered into a Lacrimosa.

Buildings which anticipate our wishes are buildings which at the very least mimic consciousness. More ambitiously, we might countenance the city as a realm of moods — safety, security and efficiency meet in streets where the lights brighten and the pavements illuminate in tandem with the pedestrian, where buildings instantly alter according to the whims of the occupants or transform without instruction, anticipating, counteracting and accentuating emotions. What was once restricted to Japanese love hotels might be conveyed to other habitations to serve other feelings. Why not change your interiors temporarily, holographically, cerebrally to Isabelline Gothic, Vijayanagara or Shoin-zukuri? The Internet of Things posits that in the near-future appliances will monitor our behaviours and anticipate our wishes. Your bath will be able to tell if you have cancer, your drinks cabinet will refer you to a psychologist. In the further age of nanotechnology, our dwellings will cure us whilst watching everything we do, as we move through a barely-perceptible drag of microscopic monitoring devices. They will drown us in data and good intentions.

If evil exists it is in the superfluous details, the additional quirks that take time and imagination — they are deeds that stray outside of function. We recognise Arendt's banality of evil all too well, perhaps to the extent that we forget it can also be found in the extravagant deeds of men. Would a smart city ever reach sentience? Would that inevitably result in a malevolent city? Arguably the greatest fear is in the singularity, the merging of human consciousness with the city's digital nervous system. The nightmarish cities of lore have all been consequences of mankind's decisions. Gormenghast seems alive because of the throng of life its gothic exoskeleton houses; the New York of *Taxi Driver* seethes and reeks because of political neglect and the troubled mind of its viewer, Sweeney Todd's barbershop is a machine for killing (to invert Le Corbusier) just as H.H. Holmes's real-life hotel was with its rigged death-chambers and disposal chutes. They seem malevolent because they are the setting for man's malevolence:

'In the lone silence of that hoary and deserted city of the dead[74], my mind conceived the most ghastly phantasies and illusions; and the grotesque shrines and monoliths seemed to assume a hideous personality — a half-sentience. Amorphous shadows seemed to lurk in the darker recesses of the weed-choked hollow and to flit as in some blasphemous ceremonial procession past the portals of the mouldering tombs in the hillside; shadows which could not have been cast by that pallid, peering crescent moon.'[75]

74   All cities are, by necessity, cities of the dead. The 94-storey, steam-powered
        Pyramid of the Dead may not adorn Primrose Hill, London as once suggested
        but the London necropolis railway-line was once a going concern.

75   'The Statement of Randolph Carter', H. P. Lovecraft

If a house was perfectly adapted to suit its occupant, to assume his or her personality, what would happen when the occupant is suddenly erased? Would the home continue with a ghost in the machine? How would it react to a new occupant? In Ballard's 'The Thousand Dreams of Stellavista', we have a house haunted by the memories of a previous owner:

'I felt the room shift around me. The ceiling was dilating and contracting in steady pulses. An absurdly exaggerated response to our own respiratory rhythms, but the motions were overlayed by sharp transverse spasms, feed-back from some cardiac ailment. The house was not only frightened of us, it was seriously ill [. . .] The real trouble was that most of Vermilion Sands is composed of early, or primitive-fantastic psychotropic, when the possibilities offered by the new bio-plastic medium rather went to architects' heads . . . The first PT houses had so many senso-cells distributed over them, echoing every shift of mood and position of the occupants, that living in one was like inhabiting someone else's brain.'[76]

There has been progress then, in the sense that Plato's Cave now comes fully-furnished.

With the advances and iconography of the space race, Streamline Moderne (and the remnants of Art Deco) moved from mimicking ships on the ocean to mimicking ships in space. The aliens would land and find they'd already landed.

76   *Vermilion Sands*, J.G. Ballard, Pg. 190

Many architects and particularly architectural critics poured scorn on such designs, but they wielded tremendous and often unacknowledged influence.In the furtive sketches of their notebooks[77], respectable architects had fun with these plans — the curves and jutting thorax of Lloyd Wright's VC Morris House and his unbuilt Gordon Strong Automobile Objective and Planetarium (the apparent model for Ralph McQuarrie's Jabba's Castle in Return of the Jedi), the perched, overgrown long-crash-landed UFOs of his Huntington Hartford Sports Club and Resort designs. The prevailing space age style became known as Googie architecture due to the haughty disdain of the critic Douglas Haskell, who noticed a coffee shop by John Lautner in the style and was affronted to find the architecture of *The Jetsons* and *Amazing Stories* seeping out of his television and comic books into the cityscape.

The problem wasn't simply the offended sensibilities of delicate art hacks. 'We are in pursuit of an idea,'[78] claimed Warren Chalk, 'a new vernacular, something to stand alongside the space capsules, computers and throw-away packages of an atomic-electronic age.'

As with all things space age though, the primary appeal of Googie was to the young, weaned on tales of *Right Stuff* heroism, mail order moon-toy and X-ray spex gimmickry, the Disney shows hosted by the redeemed Nazi and US rocket chief

---

77   *Arts & Architecture*'s twenty year Case Study Houses project was an admirable experimental attempt to stimulate domestic designs from leading architects and translate them into life largely around LA, though many remain unbuilt.

78   'Architecture as Consumer Product', *The Japan Architect* 165, Pg. 37

Wernher von Braun as well as the vast comic book possibilities of the other worlds of space. It became the stuff of roadside buildings, designed to quickly grasp the attention of kids in the back-seat; a sort of impulse architecture. Bowling alleys, cinemas and motels were decorated with orbits, swishes and stars (a last omnipresent vestige of this exists in the arch-Googie of the McDonalds' sign). It thus became synonymous with the infantile and the frivolous, often in their adult form, from revolving sky-restaurants to casinos and bingo halls.

The general assumption has been that Googie died there of terminal kitsch but in fact its influence passed on to unlikely forms; the realm of air traffic control towers and airports, sports stadia and churches.[79] In actual fact, Googie spawned some fine buildings and awaits rehabilitation that's unlikely to come from above given its populism, from Seattle's Space Needle to the television-emitting towers of Berlin's Fernsehturm and Shanghai's Oriental Pearl Radio & TV Tower. The symbiotic relationship of art and life is intricate and recurrent. In the case of *The Jetsons*, we have a cartoon broadcasted by these TV towers that has influenced countless buildings (not just cities balanced precariously on stilts but the domes, slanted roofs and curved glass of shopping malls) and been influenced by real life architecture (the buildings of Eero Saarinen's TWA terminal and John Lautner's Chemosphere[80]). *The Jetsons* went on to inspire the design of the KenAnn Building, built by the drug-smuggling

79   Capilla de Palmira, Mexico, for one.

80   Which in turn inspired the *Charlie's Angels* Pseudosphere.

aviator Ken Burnstine.

In the case of Gerry Anderson's *Thunderbirds* series, the Tracy Island base is not only a model for tropical holiday resorts and billionaire retreats (Tony Stark's residence in *Iron Man* is another fictional equivalent) but also contains obvious nods to existing architecture like Lloyd Wright's stunning Fallingwater[81] and Charles Deaton's Sculptured House[82]. The magnificent rocket-boosted bachelor pads of the aforementioned John Lautner have been the backdrop to the vulgarities of playboys and the skewed ambitions of would-be dictators; the setting for an intolerably psychedelic orgy or being sawed in half by an arch-villain's laser beam (and then there are its bad points). Though the neo-gothic Scott Monument in Edinburgh's resemblance to the rocket Thunderbird 3 seems to have been accidental[83], the various overlaps of inspiration continue. Guðjón Samúelsson's Hallgrímskirkja, Reykjavík resembles not just the volcanic basalt columns of the land or a church organ but a space shuttle about to take off[84].

The capsule returns back to earth in Jan Kaplicky's insectile House for a Helicopter Pilot. Art imitates life imitates art imitates life because we make the pedantic mistake of assuming they

---

81   Also the inspiration behind the Vandamm Residence in Hitchcock's *North by Northwest*.

82   Used as the accommodation of the future in Woody Allen's *Sleeper* (Orgasmatron not included)

83   Though the effect might be the same; 'most people would be disturbed to their depths by a spire which gave the visual illusion of really taking off skywards' — *Architecture: The Appreciation of the Arts*, Sinclair Gauldie, Pg. 21

84   Peder Vilhelm Jensen-Klint's cathedral designs for Odense and Copenhagen.

are separate things. Great architects are particularly attuned to this. 'When in early years,' Lloyd Wright wrote, 'I looked south from the massive stone tower of the Auditorium Building . . . the red glare of the Bessemer steel converters to the south of Chicago would thrill me as pages of the *Arabian Nights* used to with a sense of terror and romance.'[85]

85   'The Nature of Materials', Lloyd Wright, *Architectural Record,* October 1928.

The Cinematic Dystopia of the Everyday

The boundary between 'real life' architectural settings and fiction has been an intriguingly porous one. Fritz Lang had the epiphany that inspired *Metropolis* gazing at the New York skyline from the SS Deutschland and borrowed the Yoshiwara red light district from 17th century Edo/Tokyo. Citroën's collage of the same name, with spliced photos of existing buildings rearranged into an imaginary city, was a major influence:

'Afterwards I tried to explain why *Metropolis* became such a success. Maybe because most collages are somewhat arbitrary. But I planned that, if you would paste pictures of buildings on a large sheet, it should give an impression of the way many cities looked like. It was a view into the future. It was certainly not just a silly idea.'

It worked because the city, as all cities, is a collage. By contrast, *The Cabinet of Dr Caligari* was conceived when one of the creators Hans Janowitz saw a suspicious character darting from a spot on the periphery of a carnival, a spot where a murdered young lady's body was found the next day; reality being far darker than fiction.

When Stanley Kubrick came to create his version of Anthony Burgess's *A Clockwork Orange*, he found the dystopia already existed in fragments around the London of the day. Alex and his droogs roam the Brutalist estate of Thamesmead South. They turn on each other by the banks of Southmere Lake. When Alex is admitted to Ludovico Medical Facility, it is really the lecture centre of Brunel University. Terry Gilliam similarly found a backdrop for his dystopia *Brazil* in the stunning classico-modernism of Les Espaces d'Abraxas, on the outskirts of Paris. It's easy to suggest that the utopian designs of its architect Ricardo Bofil (who aimed to create 'a Versailles for the people' just as Fourier had aimed for with his phalansteries) were destined to turn into a dystopia from the beginning. This is much too facile and aloof an assumption. Nowhere is ever completely utopia or dystopia (just as, for example, the most capitalist system has elements of communism and vice versa) and both locations, for all their neglected ambition, were ultimately chosen because they impress. Yet the stigma, as well as the attraction, of having been the location for dystopia lingers and changes the real, much as the obsession with the ruin porn of Detroit does at the time of writing. A defence of the directors is unnecessary; they make films and the final cut is their only concern. Yet it is notable that the social housing ideal is always shot down with unsuccessful attempts, to damn the inhabitants as well as architects (the Smithsons' 'streets in the sky', Yamasaki's Pruitt–Igoe) whilst ignoring successful examples (the buildings of Álvaro Siza for example).

Cinematic adaptations of real life do lend an air of layered authenticity to speculative fiction, much in the way Orwell's *1984* convinces because it is as grubby and shambolic as the everyday (*Brazil*'s original title was *1984 1/2*).

'The first rule for understanding the human condition is that men live in secondhand worlds,'[86] C Wright Mils wrote. Kubrick used real London pubs for *A Clockwork Orange*'s equivalents with only the names morphing (from *The Old Lather Bottle to The Duke of New York*) while the car the future protagonist of *Brazil* drives is an East German Kabinroller. They remember the valuable lesson that the future will be older than the present. Gilliam, in particular, has an eye for signifiers of futures past. The failure of the Soviet dream finds its way into *Brazil* in the form of a totalitarian poster, reading 'Information the key to Prosperity / Ministry of Information', that shares the same colour scheme, layout and typography as Rodchenko and Mayakovsky's iconic advertisement for pacifiers[87]. The comfort of attributing such messages to overtly totalitarian regimes is countered with the presence of such messages in societies of all descriptions. Much of *Brazil* was filmed in a London still vaguely reminiscent of the one where wartime posters declared 'Careless Talk Costs Lives' and London Underground posters featured vigilant disembodied eyes, from the Department of Records in the CWS Flour Mill, Royal Victoria Dock to the torture chamber in Croydon Power Station[88]. Indeed the name of the film comes from an unlikely source, encapsulating the individual struggling to maintain an independent existence in the face of overwhelming pressure from above.

86   'The Man in the Middle: Design and Human Problems' (1958), cited Pg. 28
       Community and Privacy, Chermayeff.

87   Rezinotrest, 1923

88   Now demolished, though marked with a 'Brazil Close'.

'Port Talbot is a steel town, where everything is covered with gray iron ore dust,' Gilliam recalled, 'Even the beach is completely littered with dust, it's just black. The sun was setting, and it was quite beautiful. The contrast was extraordinary; I had this image of a guy sitting there on this dingy beach with a portable radio, tuning in these strange Latin escapist songs like 'Brazil.' The music transported him somehow and made his world less gray.'[89]

Entire cities have been branded by their cinematic depictions; to the cursory viewer, Vienna is a bootlegger running through a labyrinth of torch-and-moonlit sewers, Tokyo is a view of aircraft warning lights, pedestrian crossings and skyscrapers from the Park Hyatt hotel, Casablanca is a fog-laden airport or a jazz club frequented by various militaries, both murderously reactionary and ambiguously resistant. Myth does not belong solely to the past. The man, and woman, with a thousand faces still walks the earth and always will. Socially-conscious films have often blurred the lines to ground their more speculative qualities and add political bite. Roberto Rossellini's *Rome, Open City* was made so close to the Nazi occupation and liberation that actual German soldiers served as extras. *District 9* filmed ghettoised aliens living in South African slums. They were offered false promises of relocation by the government in the actual slums where people were being treated in the same way. Loosely based on the real-life Vampire of Düsseldorf, Peter Kürten, Fritz Lang's *M* employed criminals and gangsters in the

89   *The Battle of Brazil*, Jack Mathews, VII

court and underground scenes.

Sometimes it's a question of aesthetics, as with the subway scenes in *Total Recall* being filmed on the Mexico City metro, but rarely is the opportunity for satire missed. The heavyweight effectiveness of *Children of Men*'s warnings of a future London comes in the creeping terror of how recognisable it all is, from the bustling barely-functional chaos of metropolitan Fleet Street (pre-bombing) and Hackney Road to the purgatorial Ministry of Power (in New Royal Horticultural Halls), to the sacrosanct elite serenity of the Ark of the Arts (Battersea Power Station on the outside, the turbine room of Tate Modern on the inside). It is real, disarmingly so in recognition, and yet there is something of the last days of Ancient Rome or Egypt to it all.

'It's not about the future,' the director Alfonso Cuarón declared; 'I don't care about the future. The whole intent of the movie was to make an adventure that goes through the state of things, what I consider to be the state of things today.'[90] This is real prophecy, the prophetic awareness of the now and the always.

When John Carpenter came to film *Escape from New York* (inspired partly by Harry Harrison's *Planet of the Damned*), in which the future metropolis has been converted into an enclosed and degenerating lawless prison, he found the perfect set in the streets and factories of East St Louis, a city abandoned and left for dead by the industry and the authorities, who nevertheless were happy to help by shutting down the city

90   Quoted *moviefreak.com* December 25th, 2006, by Sara Michelle Fetters

lights to accentuate the hopeless mood they'd already created. Future utopias too have been developed from the present and notably few have remained utopias for all their gleaming grandeur, partly because perfection is peril-less, lesson-less, unheroic and boring. The eugenics-fixated *Gattaca* and *Logan's Run* both employ existing architecture as their settings; Frank Lloyd Wright's Marin County Civic Center and the Apparel Mart shopping mall in Dallas, Texas respectively. Sometimes the directors go to efforts to remain true to the prophecy. Michael Redford's adaptation of Orwell's *1984* was filmed as the credits boast 'in and around London [from the East End to Battersea Power Station and Beckton Gas Works] during the period April-June 1984, the exact time and setting imagined by the author'.

Sometimes the future confirms predictions in ways that even the prophets couldn't have fully believed, as when the Detroit of the real filed for bankruptcy as predicted in *Robocop* over two decades earlier.

The future nevertheless will be built from fragments of the present rearranged, reconditioned, reimagined. The success of Ridley Scott's *Blade Runner* is significantly down to this; it's a future that looks ancient, a reminder that all cities are built from earlier cities. Different boroughs are essentially the lingering remnants of swallowed villages; 'Our world, like a charnel-house, is strewn with the detritus of dead epochs.'[91] The opening shots, sound-tracked by Vangelis, seem as much the beginning of civilisation as the end of it. The model sets, arcane, hi-tech

91   *The City of Tomorrow and Its Planning*, Pg. 244

and decaying, pay tribute to the unbuilt colossal structures of the Futurist Antonio Sant'Elia but equally they resemble ancient pyramids instilled with electricity[92], fed by the dragon's-breath of refineries. For the city of *Blade Runner* itself, Scott stole from contemporary Hong Kong. The skyscraper-length video billboard advertising birth control pills indicates an intriguing shift in cultural hegemony from West to East. This he merged with the fashion and transport predictions of the futurologist painter Syd Mead via the hyper-modern neoclassic comic books of Jean Giraud (Mœbius), namely *The Long Tomorrow*[93].

One of the iconic aspects of the film, that it is almost always night, was a consequence of the happy accident of budgetary constraints. The dark is there to obscure. *Blade Runner* is nevertheless a future noir where the old Expressionist certainties of shadow and light are even more uncertain, blurred as they are by the rain and the neon. The central character Deckard may be a cynical hardboiled Phillip Marlowe type, but there is little of the stability in a world gone to hell that came with earlier noir. As garnered from the book on which it is based — Philip K. Dick's *Do Androids Dream of Electric Sheep?* — there is little here to suggest that humanity is something worth clinging to. The good, always rare and continually under siege in noir, are

---

92   Echoing Henri Sauvage's monumental modernist projects.

93   There were even nods to William S.Burroughs in the title and to *Batman* in one of the working titles, *Gotham*.

highly questionable[94]. Utopia here is to be healthy, lucky and rich, and to escape off-world, as much an incentivised trap as the gold-seeking conquistadors faced: 'A new life awaits you in the Off-World colonies. The chance to begin again in a golden land of opportunity and adventure!'

The old new world had failed to escape the weight of history, greed and waste, and now it too had to be fled. William Blake saw in *America: A Prophecy* the return of the terrible angels, with the prodigal replicant Roy Batty recounting, 'Fiery the angels fell. Deep thunder rolled around their shoulders . . . burning with the fires of Orc.' Through the chaos that remains on earth, there are fragments of the past, not held as cultural or historical treasures but mouldering as flotsam in an earth abandoned. This is the end of days, as the line from the Noh play booming from the advert says, 'The setting sun sinks down' and yet life does not know when to cease.

Ridley Scott built up a world of layers, an approach that many futurists forget. The future will be not only three but four dimensional, and a composite of junk. On the *Blade Runner* set were written messages that would not show up on the final film, 'WARNING — DANGER! You Can Be Killed By Internal Electrical System If This Meter Is Tampered With', 'Scratch and Sniff Centrespread', 'Driver is Armed; Carries No Cash', 'Multiple Murders — Readers' Own Photos', 'Tit Job Review',

94   Noir's fixation with unreliable identities and shifting loyalties means it very
      often takes place in conflict or post-conflict cities where there are divisions,
      danger, the presence of terrible secrets and the need to rewrite personal
      histories, from Belfast to Berlin to Beirut.

'Death Penalty Snuffs 12 Jurors in Freak Accident', '98 Dead in Spinner Dive', 'Illegal Aliens'. Scott also salvaged the setting from real-life. Frank Lloyd Wright's Ennis Brown House, itself based on the structures of the obliterated Inca civilisation[95], inspired Deckard's apartment, the walls of which were directly moulded from the original and which suggest the wreckage of past glories, and enigmas with their solutions long lost.

Another trace of the now is in the looming presence of the illuminated ghost of the Bradbury Building. Serving as the home of the toymaker J. F. Sebastian, the building is otherwise derelict, inhabited by mannequins and robotic toys; its wrought iron railings, once promising the future at the Chicago World's Fair, are forgotten and lit through its skylight (inspired directly by instructions in Bellamy's *Looking Backward*) by the passing beams of incurious surveillance vehicles and advertising blimps. It is here that Deckard and his adversary Roy Batty face off, battling and climbing towards the rooftop, a setting to remind us when we gaze on the urban wonders of today, we are gazing on future ruins and that time is an enemy, not just for replicants but for us all. The speech Batty delivers before dying, exquisitely improvised by Hauer, makes him a Marco Polo of the stars.

The sanctity of life is the most positive message in Scott's film. A more disconcerting message is revealed in Dick's original book, with references to kipple, the accumulating detritus of existence

95   For all its professed Americanisms, Lloyd Wright's Prairie-style architecture was also influenced by the exotic — namely Japanese prints and Inca/Aztec architecture.

that reproduces and will eventually take over everything:

'"Kipple is useless objects, like junk mail or match folders after you use the last match or gum wrappers or yesterday's homeopape. When nobody's around, kipple reproduces itself [. . .] it always gets more and more [. . .] there is the First Law of Kipple," he said. "kipple drives out nonkipple." [. . .] "No one can win against kipple," he said, "except temporarily and maybe in one spot, like in my apartment I've sort of created a stasis between the pressure of kipple and nonkipple, for the time being."'[96]

This is unsettling because we might number not just waste but all the relics of human achievement amidst this. It is there in language: 'The charmer's name was Gaff, I'd seen him around. Bryant must have upped him to the Blade Runner unit. That gibberish he talked was city speak, gutter talk. A mishmash of Japanese, Spanish, German, what have you. I didn't really need a translator, I knew the lingo, every good cop did. But I wasn't going to make it easier for him.'

Indeed humanity itself exists within this deluge. It is there in the merging of corporate power with what Stalin called 'the engineering of souls'; 'Commerce is our goal here at Tyrell. "More human than human" is our motto.' We are the kipple and our cities are simply containers filled to the brim.

If accusations of exploitation or ruin-tourism can be levelled

96   Pg.57-58

at location directors, claims of megalomania can be directed at those who construct imaginary city sets from scratch (it's no coincidence that Charles Manson established his cult on an abandoned film set). For his film *Playtime*, Jacques Tati bankrupted himself building Tativille on a vacant space near Grenville, France. Employing 100 workers, he built two sleek modern buildings for the startling interior scenes which he intended to sell off at the end (in an act of satire merging into opportunism) but these were demolished after dishonest manoeuvrings by the French government. To capture the sense of a whole city, cars and extra buildings (including the Eiffel Tower and Sacre Coeur seen as reflections in the glass) were created as two dimensional facades or as large scale models that could be used as perspective tricks. Shots of tower blocks being wheeled around and extras talking to cardboard cutouts give some indication of the admirable madness involved. Tati's film was a sustained attack on the soulless modern architecture of steel and glass (echoing Godard's *Alphaville*); on the spread of the liminal from airport lounges, golf courses, industrial estates, doctors' waiting rooms, motorway service stations, the holiday resort, and shopping malls into our workplaces and homes and most of all into our behaviours.

'The possibility of non-place,' as Marc Augé puts it, 'is never absent from any place.' It is a world at the point where real life merges into convention centre or show homes and the two become indistinguishable. It is often where the Spectacle is at its most blatant and thus thinnest, 'at its boundaries the city reveals itself'[97].

Rem Koolhaas[98] labelled it junkspace:

'[it] is overripe and undernourishing at the same time, a colossal security blanket that covers the earth in a stranglehold of seduction . . . Junkspace is like being condemned to a perpetual Jacuzzi with millions of your best friends [a portent of Facebook or whatever its eventual replacements are called] . . . A fuzzy empire of blur, it fuses high and low, public and private, straight and bent, bloated and starved to offer a seamless patchwork of the permanently disjointed . . . [it is] orphaned space; Junkspace is authorless, yet surprisingly authoritarian.'[99]

Born from transport, commerce and homogenising ideologies, it wants and needs to spread and does. It robs the countryside of its wildness and beauty, proving not that 'under the paving stone there lies the beach' but that the beach might be relegated to the world of paving stones, as in Japan's Seagaia Ocean Dome[100]. In the process, it robs cities too of their exoticism, offering everything and nothing. Yet there is a curious beauty in the liminal, as demonstrated by the likes of the photographs of Sze Tsung Leong. Christoph Gielen's photos from helicopters of

97   Cited on Pg. 179, *World Atlas Street Photography*.

98   Koolhaas offered alternative reimagined cities in his seminal book *Delirious New York*.

99   *Content*, Rem Koolhaas, Pg. 163

100   Peter Blake's *God's Own Junkyard: The Planned Deterioration of America's Landscape* is a good start.

convoluted spaghetti junctions and suburban fractals hoped to appal mankind into better planning. The reaction was generally, 'Awesome.' It must also be said there is a comfort in the liminal, for the liminal broaches an undeniable if repellent but addictive comfort. 'A foreigner lost in a country he does not know,' Augé observed, 'can feel at home there only in the anonymity of motorways, service stations, big stores or hotel chains. For him, an oil company logo is a reassuring landmark.'[101] When non-places and their omnipresent brands feel like home, something has gone distinctly wrong with the idea of home.

Tati foresaw it all. Everywhere looks sedately impressive and like nowhere in particular. People are inherently lost. Traffic crawls in barbiturate carousels. The shocking thing watching it back now is not how contrived his sledgehammer and slapstick satire is, but how pertinent. The open plan office floors with their individual cubicles are rife now. The large glass facades, echoing the quiet desolation of Edward Hopper's paintings, are everywhere. This is life as a clean glistening empty waiting room and it is a life we are increasingly forced to live all over the globe.

Deception is not inevitably negative however; it can be merciful. In De Hogeweyk in the Netherlands, there is a village (complete with a supermarket, cafe, hairdresser's etc.) that has seven different artificial environments. Designed by Molenaar, Bol and Van Dillen, each section seeks to replicate the childhood years of its largely aged occupants; there is an

101   *Non-lieux*, Marc Augé, Pg. 106

urban area, an aristocratic area, an area with Dutch East Indies imperial housing, a Christian area and so on. The citizens of this settlement suffer from varying degrees of senility. In contrast to the outside world which can be fearful and uncaring, this is a humane haven of delusion. The music played and the goods exchanged are all comfortingly from their youth, commonly one of the last deep memories to go in dementia-sufferers. Those serving in the village are all medical staff. When an occupant sees through the spectacle, the ruse is admitted to avoid distress. By the following morning, it begins again. It is a lie but a caring one, to which the real cities outside can only appear hard-hearted. Yet it also points out how much a product of our early environment we are and indeed how much of our identities is artificially created to begin with.

The problem with operating elaborate lies in this way is that it is essentially a benevolent dictatorship, a perilous and highly-questionable position to maintain. In almost every case, there is a tipping point, even when 'do no evil' is emblazoned as a rule. For years, the director Khrzhanovsky has been filming *Dau* in an invented city called The Institute, on the edge of Kharkov. Ostensibly a biopic of the physicist Lev Landau, persistent rumours suggest that the line between film and reality, between the Stalinist past it depicts and contemporary Ukrainian society, have been obliterated. The cast, several hundred in number, live in character. They are filmed sometimes in the open, sometimes in secret, sometimes not at all but even then the imaginary film keeps rolling. They work manual jobs. They are spied on.

They live in rooms decorated in 1950s bric-a-brac. Life is an act and the city is a set (and not just here). There are guards, fines, security passes, unique money, rules, transgressions, routines. The unreal through repetition becomes real, just as the real does.

What is the difference between set design and architecture? A script? Differing passages of time? The American visionary Norman Bel Geddes began sculpting fake cathedrals in theatre sets before setting forth his visions[102] of a dynamic 'World of Tomorrow' in the Futurama exhibition at the General Motors pavilion at the 1939 New York World's Fair. Visitors, having gazed at the model of highways and green spacious cities, were given a pin emblazoned 'I HAVE SEEN THE FUTURE'. Earlier[103] he had given various urban prophecies that he predicted would one day be old-fashioned: 'There will be double-deck streets, divided into lanes for slow stop-off traffic and lanes for express traffic; Every roof will be a garden; Whole blocks, in the midst of cities, will be given over to airplane hangars, the roofs of which will form landing fields.'

The Futurist Virgilio Marchi also began designing seemingly impossible buildings, all tangles of shifting angles and crude but imaginative archways and staircases that seemed almost to be caught mid-transformation and mid-motion (the title of his piece 'Seen from a Veering Airplane' captures the spirit of his work). Though intriguing and not without beauty, his scimitar curves, asymmetric cut-outs and crystalline cathedrals to (dis-)order

102   Geddes published *Horizons*.

103   1931, *Ladies Home Journal*

often seem more like neo-baroque outsider art than practical designs. Indeed the improbability of these designs shifted his attentions to an artform in which they could conceivably exist at least through the glorious lie of celluloid and in the inglorious aid of Mussolini's propaganda[104].

---

104   Terragni's empty and unbuilt Danteum is a more fitting legacy.

In Love With Velocity

Between chanting down the modern Jerichos, poets rhapsodised the urban. At first, they imported earlier forms, 'to classicise the machine'[105]. Hart Crane eulogised the skyscrapers and Brooklyn Bridge, Whitman sang to Manhattan, Lola Ridge shone ruby light through the ghetto windows. Joseph Stella's painting, *The Voice of the City 1920-2*, based on O. Henry's writing, 'is a kind of modern altarpiece in which the city appears as a cathedral, with its skyscrapers, bridges, and avenues as so many columns, vaults, and naves.'[106]

In Apollinaire's *Zone*, we have signs of future form and content, of a truly urban artform, desultory and radiant, a polyphony and a disfigurement, spreading across the city's face; advertisements. John Orlando Parry captured the essence early with *A London Street Scene* (1835) in which archaeological layers of posters (marking events to come and half-buried events that have passed) with countless promises and inducements capture the attention whilst a character's pockets are being picked. One repeating message is from a show entitled *The Last Days of Pompeii*.

Futurism took the many voices or at least the many angles of the city and recognised another vital crux where time, simultaneity and motion not only met but defined each other:

---

105   *Art Since 1900*, Pg. 223

106   Pg. 222, ibid

'Space, in fact, is liberty of movement'[107] while motion does not exist without space and the passage of time. These are the essential components of urban life and for a long time they were ignored in favour of the traditional mood of the frozen moment (Cartier Bresson refined an art of finding these in the organised chaos of the city). Brueghel and Bosch challenged this with simultaneity. The Impressionist Monet with the changing of light through the day on his Rouen Cathedrals. Joseph Stella exploded his own classicism into smithereens in Coney Island fireworks of paint.

The way was open for truly urban art. It came on the morning of 20 February 1909. Futurism bragged like the city. It first announced itself to the world in the multifarious voice of the city, the newspaper. And not any newspaper but *Le Figaro* in the city of cities at the time; Paris. The Futurists, particularly their arch-belligerent leader Marinetti, were swaggering students of the Cubists and the Russian Futurists, learning much and paying back little bar nationalistic insults. From Picasso, Braque and the Delauneys, they took the shattering of the traditional view of art as monotheism — a single godly view. They took it further because unlike the sedate and sensual Cubists with their bohemian villages in the metropolis, they were in love with velocity. They aimed to take over with all the insecure yearning of a youthful insecure nation. They damned all that had come before in terms of art, seeking to establish a cult of youth, boundless enthusiasm, daring and ignorance. To the

107   *Architecture of Humanism*, Sinclair Gauldie, Pg. 67

Futurists, all that was old was suffocating and war was a vital purging process. Their art would emphasise vitality instead of stasis. They dreamed up, or cobbled together, an art 'beyond contemporary painting, the way a modern orchestra may outdistance the ancient harpsichord solo.'[108] For a time, until their dreams came true, they were magnificent.

Aptly for the rising age of advertising, the Futurists were masters of hyperbole and manifestly urbanite; 'motor-omnibuses passing and re-passing in the crowded streets, covered with letters, red, green, white, are far more beautiful than the canvases of Leonardo or Titian,'[109] Severini claimed. 'We will sing of the stirring of great crowds — workers, pleasure seekers, rioters — and the confused sea of color and sounds as revolution sweeps through a modern metropolis.'

Marinetti announced, 'We will sing the midnight fervor of arsenals and shipyards blazing with electric moons; insatiable stations swallowing the smoking of the smoke; bridges flashing like knives in the sun, giant gymnasts that leap over river.'

They were as modern and secular as the city ('we no longer feel ourselves to be the men of cathedrals . . . ') and, at first, rejected the ruins of earlier civilisations. 'I have as my ideal not a pyramid architecture (statis state),' Boccioni announced, 'but a spiral architecture (dynamism)'[110].

Again and again, they cited dynamism; speed, vitality, youth

---

108   Russell MacDonald-Wright, quoted Pg. 224 in *Futurism* by Otto.

109   April 11th, 1913, *Daily Express*, cited in *British Prints from the Machine Age*, Pg. 15

110   Cited Pg. 85, *Modern Architecture*, Kenneth Frampton.

and passion, so immoderately it led them at full speed to their destruction. They wholeheartedly welcomed the Great War that claimed the best of them obscenely young. The finest painter and sculptor among them, Boccioni, died absurdly, trampled after falling off his horse whilst training. Their finest architect Sant'Elia died in the battle for Trieste, his last words supposedly the Spartan pomp of, 'Men, tonight we shall sleep either in Trieste or in paradise with the heroes.'[111]

Those who survived the war carried on though in fact they had, ironically, lost vital momentum and talent, allying themselves with the pigeon-chested bluster of Mussolini.

The Futurists systemised a fascination that was taking place across the globe. Speed had been introduced to our lives mechanically in ways previously impossible. Artists were fascinated but they faced the eternal problem of how to translate this quality into mediums that were static or one-dimensional. With a certain jilted ire, the creative dynamo Ezra Pound dismissed the movement and its methods as 'only an accelerated form of impressionism [. . .] Marinetti is a corpse.'[112]

In a letter to James Joyce[113], he castigated 'the young Italians, who seem all tarred with the futuristic taint, i.e., spliced cinematography in painting and diarrhoea in writing.' Pound's barbed criticism highlighted a disdain for the superficial novelty

---

111   *The Work of Antonio Sant'Elia: Retreat Into the Future,* Esther da Costa Meyer, Pg. 197

112   *Ezra Pound and Europe,* Pg. 142 - Pound would meet the ghost of Marinetti in his Italian Cantos.

113   September 1915.

and love of sensation for sensation's sake in Futurism. Crucially, it demonstrated the hint of a fear of unfolding uncontrollable modernity that would lead Pound himself into the service of the Fascists and eventually leave him-broken in a cage under the Pisan sun.

Speed, and the multi-perspective view it brought, spread through the cities of the day. Charles Demuth took the image of a fire-truck speeding past from his friend William Carlos William's poem 'The Great Figure' for his painting *I Saw the Figure 5 in Gold*. Dziga Vertov and his kino-eye comrades clung to the front of trains to capture the symphony of the city, without the artifice of actors or scripts, in *Man with a Movie Camera*.

'I had seen chronophotographs of fencers in action and horses galloping (what we today call stroboscopic photography),' Duchamp explained of the inspiration behind his then-controversial *Nude Descending the Staircase*; 'The whole idea of movement, of speed, was in the air.'[114] This was no mere stylistic fad. People, like cities, exist in motion and stillness, and until now the latter had reigned supreme in art. A reappraisal could bring about a recalibration of how we saw ourselves and our surroundings. 'The world, the real is not an object, it is a process,'[115] claimed John Cage, echoing El Lissitzky's earlier view that 'Every form is the frozen instantaneous picture of a process. Thus a work is a stopping-place on the road of becoming

---

114   Quoted Pg. 48, *The Speed Handbook: Velocity, Pleasure, Modernism*, Enda Duff
115   *For the Birds*, Pg. 80

and not the fixed goal'[116]. This is crucial because, despite the protestations of many, this is how life works.

All architecture is motion. 'In a highly studied and richly expressive building,' wrote Sinclair Gauldie, 'one may find such plays of rhythm-within-rhythm carried down to the smallest detail. The mouldings of the Gothic pier and the fluting of the Greek column are miniature rhythm-plays which can best be appreciated by the finger-tips . . . '[117]

Modern architects have emphasised the flow of people as crucial to the function of cities, with Louis Kahn's unrealised plan for treating the city like a series of rivers, harbours, canals and docks[118] acknowledging the flow of everyday life but also refuges from the resulting storms. The Futurists turned their hands to frozen-motion architecture with Marchi's jittery arches and collapsing expressionist porticos and Chiattone's much sturdier cathedrals for living[119]. None surpassed the designs of Sant'Elia, who had envisaged the city as 'an immense and tumultuous shipyard, active, mobile, and everywhere dynamic.'[120] Sant'Elia was thrillingly lacerating in his assessment of contemporary retrogressive building design; 'Architecture has not existed since the year 700 . . . [damning] carnivalesque decorative encrustations . . . and that stupefying efflorescence of

116   *Fractal Architecture: Organic Design Philosophy in Theory and Practice*, James Harris, Pg. 329

117   Sinclair Gauldie, Pg. 45-46

118   Cited in Pg. 33, *The Pedestrian and the City*

119   *The Architecture of Modern Italy: Visions of Utopia, 1900-Present*, Terry Kirk, Pg. 51

120   Cited Pg. 127, *Theory and Design in the First Machine Age*, Reyner Banham

idiocy and impotence that has taken the name of neo-classicism ... As if we, accumulators and generators of movement, with all our mechanical extensions of ourselves, with all the noise and speed of our lives, could ever live in the same houses and streets constructed to meet the needs of men who lived four, five, or six centuries ago.'[121]

Crucially he backed these condemnations up with dynamic blueprints of 'bold audacity, and simplicity . . . oblique and elliptical lines' that still remain astonishing, creating something approaching a new architectural language. With the monumental waste of his death, the movement descended into farce, and we remain only dimly aware of what we lost.

The problem is the present becomes the past no matter how much we insist it will not. Yet even in the sometimes-knowing buffoonery of their actions (from throwing condemnatory leaflets over Venice[122] to creating noise symphonies to encouraging the making of ball-bearing soup), there is a sense of actions as art and the city as a stage. In the hectic flux of Severini's ballrooms[123] and boulevards, the protagonists cannot be entirely extracted from the environment. We are what we do and where we do it. We are also, however much we reject it, social creatures: 'Marinetti single-handedly discredited the tired cliché of the

121   *Lacerba 2*, № 15, August 1st, 1914

122   Jean Tinguely threw his manifesto out of a plane as they had from the tower, in
        1959. It read: 'For Statics . . . Accept instability . . . Stop painting Time. Stop
        evoking music and gesture. You are movement and gesture. Stop building
        cathedrals and pyramids which are doomed to fall to ruin. Live in the present;
        lives once more in Time and by Time — for a wonderful and absolute reality.'

123   *Dynamic Hieroglyphic of the Bal Tabarin*, for example.

misunderstood artist languishing in his garret and called for the emergence of more robust, dynamic creative spirits, whose works would not only passively reflect the contemporary world, but engage with, influence and shape it.'[124]

We merge into and out of the city, immersed in time like Malevich's *The Knife Grinder*. When we truly see this, even a simple stride can be reimagined as alien and heroic as in Boccioni's *Unique Forms of Continuity in Space* (1912, or train stations seen as places where melancholy accumulates in the ghosts of his *Farewells* triptych. Boccioni's paintings like *The Street Enters the Room* are extra-sensory, demonstrating how the city, that 'moving whirlwind of modernity'[125], enters the mind and the mind gives significance to the city. 'The omnibus rushes into houses which it passes, and in their turn the houses throw themselves upon the omnibus and are blended with it.'[126]

Speed was new from the jolts of Carra's taxi and streetcar confessions to Balla's automobiles accelerated to the point of abstraction. Routine has dulled our minds to these visions but the wonder still exists deep down, waiting.

The city is beyond the straightforward visual. Sound gives extra dimensions to space. It conjures up memories, feelings, even visions in the disharmonic faces of Russolo's painting *Music*, an artist who designed a uniquely urban music in his Art of Noise with instruments like 'howlers, boomers, cracklers,

---

124   *Blasting the Future*, Pg. 10-11

125   'Pittura Scultura Futuriste Milan 1914', cited Pg. 128, *Futurism*, Didier Ottinger

126   *Futurist Painting: Technical Manifesto*

scrapers, exploders, buzzers, gurglers and whistles.'[127] In doing so, he chimed with other orchestral manifestations of the city; Stravinsky's 'The Rite of Spring' with its initially-attacked 'rhythm of engines, whirls and spirals like screws and fly-wheels, grinds and shrieks like laboring metal', Aaron Copeland's soundtrack for Mumford's World's Fair documentary *The City*, Antheil and Leger's *Ballet Mécanique*, where the instruments included an aeroplane propeller.

The metropolis is noise. 'Nothing has changed man's nature so much as the loss of silence,'[128] Max Picard writes but in truth, as John Cage has shown, silence is impossible and approaching it undesirable (soundproofed anechoic chambers, for example, tend to unnerve visitors within short periods, hearing the blood go round their veins in their head). There are always sounds — birds, wind — even in the wilderness but the sound of cities is an ever-changing phenomenon. Peace from it may become, like privacy, a collector's item for those who can afford it. Architecture, being the creation of atmospheres as well as space, will cater for these refuges: 'as an architect I wish to strengthen the silence of the world,' Juhani Pallasma wrote in *Sensuous Minimalism*. At the same time, the tides of sound in the city are part of its innate character.

The Futurists wished for the relative silence to be broken and broken explosively. The ability to fly above cities had enabled us to see them differently as well as escape them.

127   *Futurism,* Jane Rye, Pg. 80

128   Pg. 10

'The aeroplane is a means of getting away from towns and their book-keeping,' the patron-saint of aviation Saint-Exupéry wrote, 'and coming to grips with reality,'[129] comparing the night to a temple 'for the accomplishment of secret rites and absorption in inviolable contemplation.'[130]

The Futurists, in love with motion and danger, had their own breed of aeropoets and in Tullio Crali a frequently-magnificent draftsman of parachutes and loop the loops above the towers and spires.

Yet there was something initially diabolical in the pilot's eye view, like witches above the city during Walpurgisnacht Bulgakov's Margarita, on a broomstick, 'weaving between the cables. Beneath her flowed the roofs of trolley-buses, buses and cars, and rivers of hats surged along the pavements. Little streams diverged from these rivers and trickled into the lighted caves of all-night stores.'[131]

To see people as ants far below might unearth the urge to treat them as such. Crali's paintings change subtly then unsubtly. The pilots, no longer demonstrating their fearless skills to spectators below, turn on the city. In painting after painting (Dottori's *Burning City*, Crali's *Diving on a City*), the pilot bears down on the metropolis; the buildings and their inhabitants no longer intact. The Futurists had raged against cities obsessed with the past; Rome, Florence and especially Venice, proposing to 'fill in

---

129   *Wind, Sand and Stars*, Pg. 227

130   Ibid, Pg. 183

131   *The Master and Margarita*, Pg. 270

its little reeking canals with the shards of its leprous, crumbling palaces'[132] in 800,000 leaflets thrown from its clocktower. There had always been an element of anarchistic fervour to the movement (evidenced in Russolo's *The Revolt* and Carra's *Funeral of the Anarchist Galli*) and claims that 'the new world must be built upon the inevitable ruins of the old'[133], but this went deeper into nihilism.

'To the earthquake / their only ally,' they boasted, 'the Futurists dedicate / this ruin of Rome and of Athens,'[134] while Gabreil Alomar declared the devil to have been the first Futurist. It would be a costly alliance. All cities are accumulations of the past and past dreams, a situation which could not be broached by the more egomaniacal of the artists. In the end, they hated cities because cities are not silent or monotone but rather of the voices of others.

132   'Venise Futuriste', published in *Comoedia* Paris 17th June, 1910, Pg. 3, translated by Flint and Coppotelli.

133   *Futurism,* Bompiani, Pg. 414

134   *Futurismo 1909-1919,* Pg. 10

On the Road

A city of speed needs channels — railway lines, runways, roads.
The escalation into the city as road seems a step into petrol-
fumed dementia, except that it already instinctually occurred
with the settlements of South America and South-East Asia
hugging red roads deep beyond the green gates of the jungle.
Indeed, the Linear City is one of the oldest forms of settlement if
we allow ourselves to consider rivers as roads (and trade routes,
pilgrimage walks, Hiroshige's Frank Lloyd Wright-influencing
Fifty-Three Stations of the Tōkaidō etc.) and note the multitude that
grow up along their banks. This escalation was accelerated by
and intrinsic to modernity:

'As railroad and steam power once tended to centralise and
concentrate urban settlements, so now electricity and motor
vehicles are tending to decentralise them,' Ludwig Hilberseimer
points out, 'Even before the advent of electricity, the tide had
begun to turn. The automobile accelerates this exodus, and
widened its scope . . . electric power is the real force toward
decentralisation. Even the smallest settlement can be supplied
with water, electricity, heat and light.'[135]

When we look at the map of the streetlights at night spreading,
it is not just a sign of civilisation spreading, it is also a cause of it.

Before the Vichy administration had him deported as a 'Trojan

---

135   *The Nature of Cities,* Pg. 114

horse of Bolshevism'[136], Le Corbusier drew up plans to turn Algiers into a linear city with a raised and curved coastal road on top of terraced apartments, a colonial experiment in itself (Le Corbusier spent a great deal of time there sketching naked local girls), provided you count what he intended to do with Paris. Great egos have no country. The strengths (an unencumbered view for all inhabitants) and weaknesses (almost everything else) are obvious in a similar actually built, if unused, site; the three mile-long 10,000-roomed Nazi 'Strength Through Joy' hotel Prora on the Baltic Sea, the world's largest and emptiest, destined for all those summers which never came.

The abiding dream of the Linear City was that it would save the countryside from the city; offering concentrated space rather than sprawl. In Arturo Soria y Mata's pioneering Ciudad Lineal, it was also a question of well-being: 'If you force molecules into a volume smaller than the one they were before you will generate heat. One can verify this same universal law in cities.'[137]

He envisaged, in a still-radical idea (posited at the minute by Malmö and Copenhagen), a transnational city from Barcelona to St Petersburg. One of the problems is exhibited in Boutwell and Mitchell's Continuous City for 1.000.000 Human Beings. Built coast to coast in the US, the 100 metre high city would be a sight to behold and, like all linear cities, a giant wall dividing the country.

This unfortunate side-effect did not deter a wide range of

136   *Le Corbusier and the Concept of Self,* Simon Richards, Pg. 64

137   Cited Pg. 5, *Early Urban Planning,* Volume 1, Richard LeGates

designers. Having personally stormed the Winter Palace and narrowly avoided a Tsarist execution, Nikolay Alexandrovich Milyutin drafted the socialist city of Sotsgorod which stretched industry across the vast steppes and tiaga of Russia; a much more rational prospect than it seems given the distances between inhospitable resource-laden areas in the east and settlements west of the Urals. Edgar Chambless's Roadtown plan combines reason with the pomp and camp of biblical prophecy: 'Read Mr. Chambless, O ye captives of Civilization, and burst your shackles.' He takes a map and a ruler and draws you a straight line from the Atlantic coast . . . What does this line stand for? It stands for the site of the New City'[138]. Roadtown would be a concrete-layered cyclone-proof structure encasing noiseless railways. It would have a promenade for skating and gardens on top and crucially, in a move fatally-overlooked by most planners, it encouraged spaces for other architects to design and build cooperative towers. It was one commanding construction but allowed the plurality of the city to potentially flourish, with 'country air and light on two sides'.

We reel from Linear Cities as if they were alien, but there is logic even a barbed honesty in their design. Given that lives are dominated by the commute, why not just make the very city an inescapable commute? Or the individual home? In the February 1946 issue of *Amazing Stories*, James B. Settles offered the Faustian promise 'Trade Your Trouble for a Bubble', to live in a gyroscopic orb that rolls along a magnetic track. It could

138   *Roadtown*, Pg. 3

also be said that the linear city was simply a toppled Babel. 'The idea occurred to me to lay the modern skyscraper on its side and run the elevators and the pipes and wires horizontally instead of vertically. Such a house would not be limited by the stresses and strains of steel; it could be built not only a hundred stories, but a thousand stories or a thousand miles . . .'[139]

Certainly, there's something dehumanising in Reginald Malcolmson's Metrolinear (1956) and absurd in Justus W. Fry's three-tiered railway of the future with an airport on top. Though intended more as a store of ideas[140] than a grand plan, Richard Neutral's Rush City Reformed (1923-30) is both awe-inspiring and monstrous with its regimented grids around transport terminals, like living on a chessboard while Stanley Tigerman offered drive-through pyramids in his Instant City (circa 1966). It's easy to see how linear structures found more recent manifestations as semi-satirical ways of rethinking, with the divisive gigantism of 'Città Lineare' by Zzigurat collective (1971) and the chrome megastructure Continuous Monument of Superstudio carving up existing cities. Through them, the surreality of reality is emphasised.

The problem with the linear is that in seeking to expand it restricts. Influenced by Sant Elia and Lloyd Wright's unbuilt LA Civic Centre, Paul Rudolph sought to mitigate the evils of the Lower Manhattan Expressway by assembling around it a vast

---

139   *Benjamin in Paris - Capital of the 19th Century:* 'the rail was the first unit of
       construction, the forerunner of the girder.'

140   *Richard Neutra and the Search for Modern Architecture: A Biography and History,*
       Thomas S. Hines, Pg. 61

megastructure. 'The movement of space has velocity,' Rudolph wrote, 'for space flows much in the manner of water from one volume to another.'[141] In such a space, impressive as it is, we might well drown. While Enrico and Luzia Hartsuyker's Biopolis and Koolhaas' Spur Asian City of the Future offered layered linear towns with the pedestrian usurping the driver, most still favoured the motorway model, and motorways as every service station will attest are no place to live. In New Babylon, Constant Nieuwenhuys declared, 'people would be constantly travelling. There would be no need for them to return to their point of departure as this in any case would be transformed.'[142]

This mirrors our increasingly mobile lives. Verve, speed, dynamism and change are virtues up to a point. Continued further they become tyrannies. The option to move becomes an obligation and then a curse. 'If one asks [. . .] why the roads must roll, the answer is to keep 'em rolling.'[143] It is the freedom of the rootless hobo[144].

We can mourn or take solace that these promised futures never came. But perhaps they did, in glimpses. In the US, you

141   Quoted Pg. 52, *Shelter Blues: Sanity and Selfhood Among the Homeless*, Robert R. Desjarlais

142   *Architectural Design*, June 1964, via *Existence, Space and Architecture.*

143   It is asked in *The Heritage of Heinlein: A Critical Reading of the Fiction*, referring to Heinlein's 'The Roads Must Roll'.

144   In the U.S. hobos developed their own complex and fascinating language of signs to be chalked on walls, railroad cars and roads to communicate in tips and warnings wth each other; a cat sketch meant a 'kind-hearted lady', an asterisk was 'police officer lives here', a capital M meant 'Tell a hard luck story here'. Each sign, as signs always do, hinted at an untold story; 'bad water', 'talk religion; get food', 'unsafe place'.

can still drive along unannounced half-intentioned linear cities to visit numerous Googie coffee shops designed by Eldon Davis or the motels and restaurants of Wayne Douglas McAllister or the Las Vegas skyscrapers of Martin Stern Jnr. The orbital space age analogies were ultimately fitting; you pull in off the road on a tangent rather than a real destination. When critics cast aspersions on the superficiality of Googie, they were actually pointing out its main strength. It grabbed the attention of an increasingly portable population with a baby boom in the back-seat, catching the eye with vaults and swoops and starbursts and neon, low-flying UFOs coasting alongside freeways. It had captured the gaze and that's all it ever wanted. We saw it whizz past as we floated in space.

The Crystal Palaces

There is music playing now in the coffee shop, the drive-in, the casino halls with their hidden exits and absence of clocks, strange terrible music. 'There's a Great Big Beautiful Tomorrow' went the anthem of Disney's Progressland. The history of futurology, the stage sets and the dress rehearsals of what's to come, goes further back than Sputnik. With the steam-powered Moloch of the Industrial Revolution rampaging through the world, waves of expos and futuramas arrived to convince us that progress was indeed progress and not something to be entirely terrified of. Organised by Bureau International des Expositions, the World's Fairs manufactured awe to counter the dread of change. Until eclipsed by television (itself first appearing publicly at an exposition), they were the largest mass spectacles of their day attracting millions of visitors and placing their respective cities amongst the guiding lights and benefactors of a new age. In a way, the exhibitions were modern cabinets of curiosities assembled not for the private pleasure of eccentric emperors but by governments buoyed by scientific ingenuity and by wealth extracted, often in the most savage ways, from their colonies. A sense of competitiveness (that would in time descend into all-out war) fuelled the movement . Here we find the city as emerging brand; San Francisco the earthquake survivor, Seattle as the gateway to Alaska, Panama the separator of continents and so on.

The World's Fairs had an ancestor in the dazzling temporary

city erected at the Field of the Cloth of Gold when the English and French aristocracies created fake palaces and towers to out-do one another (a dragon features on the painting marking the occasion for Henry VIII). It was also there in the Triumphal Procession and Arch of Maximilian I, rendered in their full clockpunk glory by Burgkmair, Dürer and others. It began again with a building of seeming impossibility — the 'Great Shalimar' of London's Crystal Palace, a massive structure constructed with the leading new technology of plate glass. This was the largest ever seen. Within this Great Exhibition of the Works of Industry of all Nations (1851), technological innovations (early fax and photographic prototypes, cult revolvers, public toilets) vied with imperial spoils such as the Koh-i-Noor and Daria-i-Noor diamonds and the Tara Brooch. So successful was it in framing London as the capital of the world (the old *axis mundi* position) and laying claims to the future and indeed the past (with the building of the Albertopolis museum section of the city) that Paris felt the need to retaliate by erecting the Palais de l'Industrie at the heart of the Champs-Élysées. Where they had once built monuments to monarchs they now built them to the machine king.

There were soon efforts to oppose and mitigate the alleged soullessness of these grand affairs and their worship of combustion engines, looms, rifles and stolen jewels. Marx railed against the effrontery of the bourgeois exhibitions at a time when inequities had brought workers to the brink of revolution. Analogies were made with earlier fallen civilisations:

'By putting on show the massed resources of modern industry in a small concentrated space, just at a time when modern bourgeois society is being undermined from all sides, it is also displaying materials which have been produced, and are still being produced day after day in these turbulent times, for the construction of a new society. With this exhibition, the bourgeoisie of the world has erected in the modern Rome its Pantheon, where, with self-satisfied pride, it exhibits the gods which it has made for itself.'[145]

Marx was right with the diagnosis but wrong with the prognosis. Revolution would certainly come but the world championed in the exhibitions would not fall. The tragedy would find itself articulated in Calvary architecture; the parched bone-white wedding cake of the Sacre Coeur would rise over Paris as a reminder of the butchered Communards, Franco's Valle de los Caídos would be built on the dead of the Spanish Popular Front.

Even the organisers realised however that technical prowess was not enough to truly sell their takes on the future. They would need to humanise their exhibits. It helped that the displayed locomotive had a suitably Arthurian name — *The Lady of the Lake* — but how they brought soul to the exhibition space was an innovation, acting as a bridge between feudal musical pageantry and the terrible and glorious coming world of lift muzak, film soundtracks and Eno's site-specific ambience. They commissioned an assemblage of safely conservative

145   *Neue Rheinische Zeitung Revue*

European music to inaugurate and fill the space, including a triumphal fanfare by Daniel Auber (who would die in the midst of the Paris Revolution to come), William Sterndale Bennett's imaginatively-titled *Ode Written Expressly for the Opening of the International Exhibition* and an overture march by Giacomo Meyerbeer, with Verdi's choral collage of the future British, French and Italian national anthems championing the spirit of fraternal competition (the paradox underlined by the fact he missed the deadline).

There was no shortage of marvels in the exhibitions that followed. The monumental icons immediately caught the imagination with the Statue of Liberty[146] proving hugely popular; her arm and torch were exhibited at Centennial International Exhibition Philadelphia, 1876, followed by her disembodied head at the Paris Exposition Universelle of 1878[147]. For all the impact, many of the monuments proved to be relative dead-ends with even the mighty Crystal Palace merely providing the template for greenhouses. Catalan Modernisme and the Moorish revivalism of the Neo-Mudéjar style, as celebrated in the exposition of 1888 and the building of the Ciutadella

---

146   A Statue of Responsibility has been mooted on West Coast America, after a suggestion by writer and holocaust survivor Viktor Frankl, to balance and compliment the Statue of Liberty. Designed by Gary Lee Price, it would take the form of two hands vertically clasping, one pulling the other up.

147   W. A. Rogers in *Harper's Weekly* on May 28, 1887 critiqued the industrialisation of New York by having a railway encircle Liberty with her mouth the final destination.

Park, may have offered dazzling routes for Art Nouveau[148] and organic design to enter the forthcoming century but its primary achievement was bringing attention to Barcelona as one of the great cities of the world.

By contrast, the smaller technological prototypes on display profoundly changed all the cities of the future and the lives of the people who inhabited them. They did this mainly by extending our reach, in terms of space and time. The electric light extended our lives into the night after the Place de l'Opéra had first been bathed in arc light and Westinghouse/Tesla had defeated Edison in the War of the Currents by illuminating the White City of the Chicago Columbian Exposition. Jules Verne's fiction was revolutionised immediately by witnessing electricity at the Exposition Universelle. He was one of many. Photographs and phonographs soon meant we could view and listen to the dead as well as distant invisible orchestras. Telephones and telegrams enabled us to communicate across mountain ranges and oceans. The links between cities became discernible if labyrinthine networks. The artists of the Art Nouveau era had pointed this out first with the phenomenal surges of creativity between Glasgow, Barcelona, Vienna and Paris. It was hoped the public and diplomats would follow, though many were too busy watching Annie Oakley performing her sharpshooting skills or admiring the 1,500 pound chocolate Venus de Milo on display.

---

148   Contrary to flowery cliché, the style could be a muscular one as evidenced by
        the more strenuous Rennie Mackintosh designs and Hoffmann's Palais Stoclet.

The expositions gave birth to alternative versions of the cities we now know. These came in the form of buildings which were briefly conjured into life and then just as quickly vanished, existing only in sepia photographs and hand-coloured postcards, the ghosts of which haunt the places where they once stood. There was the vast ornate hangar the Palais des Machines which would contain thousands of machines like a steampunk treasure trove, as well as circuses and a velodrome before it was demolished because it was spoiling a bureaucrat's view. The sculptor (and co-architect of the Cubist House) Raymond Duchamp-Villon recalled the wonder of visiting it as a boy: 'I remember very clearly a hallucinatory passage through the brightness of the nave in a travelling crane, above whirlpools of twisting reptilian belts, creakings, whistles, sirens, and black caverns containing circles, pyramids, and cubes.'[149]

The golden door entrance to Sullivan's long-gone Transportation Building from the 1893 World's Fair became synonymous with the entering of other worlds. Based on a Roman basilica, the polychromic effect was designed to dazzle as if stepping inside not a building but an artwork, 'as regard the colours themselves, they comprise nearly the whole galaxy, there being not less than thirty different shades of colour employed. These, however, are so delicately and softly blended and so nicely balanced against each other that the final effect suggests not so much many colours as a single beautiful painting.'[150]

149   Cited in Pg. 270 of *Space, Time and Architecture: The Growth of a New Tradition*, Sigfried Giedion

150   *The Public Papers*, Louis Sullivan, Pg. 87

In time, they demolished the golden door and with it the galaxy of colour inside. The illuminated Tower of Jewels came down after San Francisco's World's Fair of 1915. The Bastille was re-erected in Paris; it was replaced for over thirty years by the eventually rat-infested Elephant of the Bastille, home to the fictional Gavroche and his kin in Victor Hugo's *Les Misérables*. The Crystal Palace burned down after an inopportune use of wood, as did the three-times-the-size of St Paul's Viennese Rotunda with its caged wild animals and living curiosities on stages[151] and the enormous cathedral of the Sydney Garden Palace. The palatial Moorish-revival Horticultural Hall in Philadelphia was unprepared for the advance of Hurricane Hazel. The only proof we have that they ever existed, now that they are beyond first-hand memory, are traces of silver oxide paper, celluloid or poetry. 'All so completely gone. Alas! 'twould seem / as though the 'Garden Palace' was a dream, / or bright creation by a master hand, / which vanished at the same supreme command.'[152]

They exist little more now than the planned buildings that were never built, like the half a mile-high concrete pleasure lighthouse the Phare du Monde, with a spiralling helter-skelter for automobiles leading to a hotel complex, and views extending all the way across France to Spain and England; 'The project appears far removed from the visionary,' *Modern Mechanix* tried to claim, 'and a new all-time "high" in buildings seems in a fair

---

151   *Barnum & Bailey to Feld,* Ernest Albrecht, Pg. 50

152   *Australian History,* Ian Warden, Pg. 93

way to being achieved.'[153]

It exists only within the pages of that magazine. Though it was built and for a time proved hugely popular, Wyld's Great Globe proved too odd to be included officially in the Great Exhibition. Its creator the mapmaker James Wyld had an addiction to the fictive, dreaming up votes from non-existent voters to reach parliament and providing guides to the underground with non-existent stations. The Monster Globe, as it was nicknamed, was made real for a time, a 60-foot wide sphere with a staircase inside from which could be viewed a three dimensional inside-out representation of the earth's surface, minus Antarctica which he'd dismissed as a fable. Banished from the Crystal Palace as a suspected shyster, he built the Globe in Leicester Square Gardens, at the time 'a "wilderness" or "desert" littered with garbage and haunted by stray cats and ne're-do-well youths.'[154] Though it attracted over a million visitors, the building was doomed due to Wyld's disreputable tendencies. He ended up in court cases with almost every collaborator, invented lectures on fanciful subterranean civilisations, threw away a statue of the former king which had once stood on the spot (its horse and decapitated head were found later) and tried to engineer a robbery to steal counterfeit gold nuggets. The Alhambra-esque touches to the Globe's entrance were complimented by the minareted Royal Panopticon of Science and Art ('western

153   *Modern Mechanix*, July 1933

154   *On Exhibit: Victorians and Their Museums*, Barbara J. Black, Pg. 31

technology in an eastern pleasure dome'[155]) which joined it on the site; 'Wyld's illusion seemed to undo the Copernican revolution: humankind was once again at the center of the universe.'[156]

The illusion appealed to Victorian sensibilities to make a 'temple of geography'[157]; religious, scientific and imperial. It barely mattered that it was a Plaster of Paris artifice and a magnificent fraud; that too was symbolic and fitting. Even more fraudulent was Coney Island Globe Tower designed by Samuel Friede in 1906, with its eleven storeys containing a circus, skating rink, bowling alley and casino, all amounting to a Ponzi scheme. Whether buildings like these were built or not[158], they dissipated in time like a morning dream.

'Oh, where are the snows of yesteryear!'[159] wrote François Villon, the finest poet ever to have killed a priest in a knife-fight, recounting the loss of mythic characters in an age, as he saw it, when genius was left to wrack and ruin. In piques of nostalgia, we might turn our eyes from skyscrapers that seem more CGI than imaginary, now that architects draw with 3D programs, and consider the futures of yesteryear. Where is the Skylon that levitated on cables like a silver slash through the sky, that

155   *The Orient on the Victorian Stage*, Edward Ziterwich, Pg. 119

156   Black quoted in *The Starry Sky Within*, Anna Henchman, Pg. 216

157   *Biopolis: Patrick Geddes and the City of Life* by Volker M. Welter and Iain Boyd Whyt, Pg. 216

158   Another short-lived temple of geography, Elisée Reclus Globe, was built for the 1900 Exposition Universelle by Louis Bonnier.

159   From the poem 'Ballade des dames du temps jadis'.

'glittering riddle of a symbol, like some genie's device in *Arabian Nights*'[160]? Melted down and sold as scrap and souvenirs, the rest propelled into the Thames under Churchill's orders to remove all suggestion of a socialist future. Misha Black's South Bank Exhibition building sadly followed it into oblivion, 'a kind of interplanetary edifice more or less suspended in the sky' [. . .] based around the framework of a spiral ramp from which the buildings would rise in terraces reaching 1,500 feet, topped by a vertical feature that anticipated the Festival's Skylon.'[161]

Skylon itself had been inspired by the Trylon spire built for the New York World's Fair 1939 accompanied by a large Perisphere, which was 'lit at night in a manner to create the optical illusion of clouds . . . racing around its surface. On Halloween, it was transformed into a giant jack-o-lantern.'[162]

Inside the sphere, viewers on moving platforms could gaze upon the miniature Democracity; 'It's attractive and sensible at the same time . . . priest and farmer and miner and housewife . . . men and women of all nations . . . they are marching in triumph . . . they have triumphed over chaos . . . they have built the World of Tomorrow.'

LIFE heralded the city, 'Henry Dreyfuss fills huge hollow ball with a glimpse of the future'; the article informed readers, 'Traffic never intersects. Pedestrians walk at different levels

---

160   JB Priestly quoted in Pg. 59, *The Spiv and the Architect: Unruly Life in Postwar London*, Richard Quentin

161   *The Festival of Britain: A Land and Its People,* Harriet Atkinson, Pg. 8

162   *New York's 1939-1940 World's Fair,* Andrew F. Wood, Pg. 22

from automobiles . . . '[163] In a brief glimpse of the alienation effect, the spell is broken and the real world of the day shone through with reference to the soundtrack 'written for the show by William Grant Still, Negro composer . . . has been providing a busy background for the spectacle of daily life.'

In the real world of tomorrow, Trylon and Perisphere were melted down to use as armaments to be dropped on Nazi Germany. In its comic book afterlife, it became the headquarters of the superhero group All-Star Squadron who were roped in to fight the Axis forces forty years after the event.

Nowhere is the tragedy of the once-built more keenly felt than in those whose fall signalled the cancellation of a surely-certain future. The Glasgow Empire Exhibition of 1938 was attended by 13 million visitors, passing by the constructivistic Tait Tower ('a modest cousin to Vladimir Tatlin's Monument for the Third International'[164]). Such was the incandescent Scotland-shaped Futurism of the building that postcards of it came inscribed 'This is a real photograph'[165]. The postcard is almost all that remains. The building was torn down (though its concrete foundations remain) with the excuse it would be a beacon for German bombers[166], but its demise says more about the authorities' attitude towards Glasgow. Those in power did

163   August 1st, 1938

164   Edwin Morgan in Pg. 97, *Beyond Scotland: New Contexts for Twentieth-century Scottish Literature* , edited by Gerard Carruthers, David Goldie, Alastair Renfrew

165   *Spatialities: The Geographies of Art and Architecture*, edited by Judith Rugg and Craig Martin, Pg. 175

166   *Lost Buildings*, Jonathan Glancey, Pg. 128

not want a future resembling Tatlin's Moscow. In Moscow, sadly, the authorities did not want this either.

Having suffered criminal and financial neglect in his lifetime, the architecture of Glasgow's Charles Rennie Mackintosh has rightly been recognised as both brilliantly idiosyncratic and instrumental in bridging art nouveau to modernism. Yet for all the critical rehabilitation, his finest and most ambitious buildings remain unbuilt; his twin-clock-towered 'cathedral to transport' Railway Terminus and his extraordinary Victorian spaceship Concert Hall, which defies the bounds of its time. There exists in his blueprints an alternative Glasgow, just about evident in the real place in the shape of tea rooms and newspaper offices and ephemera (Mackintosh thought from monumental buildings right down to cutlery in sterling examples of Gesamtkunstwerk). Having submitted his Railway Terminus, the Secretary of the Royal Institute of British Architects replied to him, 'If the design does not look like what it is intended for, you may depend on it that it is wrongly conceived'[167] in which case we might well question all that is rightly conceived. His remarkable School of Art survives, thankfully, after a devastating fire, as a fitting dynamic legacy, sending artists out into the world.

For all their abandoned possibilities, the World's Fairs did have lasting resonance. The inventions displayed escaped into the wider world and the monumental architecture led, in the case of the World's Columbian Exposition of 1893, to the City Beautiful cult, which merged into the Garden City movement

167   *Charles Rennie MacKintosh and the Modern Movement*, Howarth, Pg. 16

and the eco-cities and museum quarters of today. What could our cities have looked like if they'd been allowed to remain or if they'd gone further and built the plans that seemed impossible, like Louis Bonnier's melting biomechanical perfume bottle architecture[168]? Not all of those temporarily built were missed and they live on as curious cul de sacs of history, as in La Porte Monumentale Paris which blends every conceivable orientalist design of the time into a structure that is both alien and alienating. Some dreams are deemed too wild even for ephemeral cities.

There was however a dark side to these shining mirage cities especially when the brutally real seeps in. 'Expositions are the timekeepers of progress,' President William McKinley addressed the Pan-American Exposition, and his future assassin, in Buffalo, New York, 'They record the world's advancements. They stimulate the energy, enterprise, and intellect of the people, and quicken human genius. They go into the home. They broaden and brighten the daily life of the people. They open mighty storehouses of information to the student.'[169]

The next day, the anarchist Leon Czolgosz mortally wounded him as he stood outside the Temple of Music built for the fair ('some Buffaloians believed the city had been cursed ever since'[170]). The grand spectacle could conceal political and social problems and injustices, but it could also become a magnet for

---

168   Exposition Universelle of 1900.

169   *All the World's a Fair: Visions of Empire at American International Expositions,* 1876-1916, Robert W. Rydell, Pg. 4

170   *The Jihad Next Door: The Lackawanna Six and Rough Justice in an Age of Terror,* Dina Temple-Raston, Pg. 12

the dissatisfied. The boast was met with a riposte.

Often the splendour had cancer at its core, with great riches concealing great crimes. The world fairs of Brussels were built on the theft from and torment of Belgium's colonial subjects in the Congo. They erected a Palace of the Colonies and a Hall of Cultures where they exhibited spoils beneath an art nouveau structure built from tropical wood. They also exhibited 'negro villages', human zoos for visitors to gawk at uprooted African families. This would be a recurring theme. What the African villagers thought looking back goes unrecorded, though it's worth recalling the Sioux chief Sitting Bull exhibited in Buffalo Bill's Wild West show cursing the applauding audience in his native language. Within Victor Horta's Temple [though more tomb] of Human Passions built for the 1897 Brussels International Exposition, there is housed Jef Lambeaux' sculpture 'The Human Passions' with its scenes of revelry and death, a writhing mass with an archangel of death at its centre. In its moralist cornucopia of sins, it leaves out the obvious one of its time yet the troubling tone was noted subliminally by the critics who turned against it. It was the guilty conscience leaked and calcified into stone. The building remains locked to the public to this day.

At times, it has been possible to discern the future from these exhibitions, perhaps more so than intended. Before Barbarossa, the Nazis and Soviets faced off architecturally with monumental monstrosities at the Paris Exhibition in 1937. For what little consolation it served, the dying Spanish Republic's pavilion contained the authentic vision to come in Picasso's *Guernica*. The arrival of corporate pavilions at the Barcelona Exposition of 1929 pre-empted the shift in global power we have since witnessed. There were also images of what could have been via what momentarily was; the shades of Philip K. Dick's *The Man in the High Castle* in photographs of the swastika-emblazoned Graf Zeppelin above the skyscrapers of Manhattan for the 1933 Exposition. World's Fairs were finally eclipsed by the world they promised. They had merely displayed the merchandise. Modern commerce offered it, or very often its illusion, up for sale. World's Fairs marked the mutation of the citizen into voyeur and consumer. In his sprawling *Arcades Project*, Walter Benjamin was perceptive:

'World exhibitions are places of pilgrimage to the commodity fetish ... they create a framework in which its use value recedes into the background. They open a phantasmagoria which a person enters in order to be distracted. The entertainment industry makes this easier by elevating the person to the level of the commodity ... the whole of nature is transformed into specialities. He presents them in the same spirit in which the advertisement begins to present its articles. He ends in madness.'[171]

Through the temporary buildings of the exhibitions, we had entered a brave new world. It resembled a crude counterfeit of Ali Baba's cave, in the form of an endless maddening shopping mall. There would be no password to escape.

171   *Arcades Project*, Pg. 7

Plotting the Stars

As the space race altered the cities of the earth, architectural ideas altered the space race. It was assumed that by now we would have colonised the moon, terraformed Mars and be making our way through outer space, leaving American cities on Enceladus, Russian cities on Europa, floating Chinese cities on Titan. These visions gave room for brave pioneering exploration and mercantile dreams of slave-mines on other worlds (the two are not mutually exclusive). Space became a canvas on which to project what had already happened on Earth[172] and it largely remains so in our visualisations of interstellar civilisations, with recyclable tales of smuggling, piracy, new Wild Wests, empires, invasions and insurrections. Speculation was encouraged with the mistranslation of Schiaparelli's 'canals' on Mars and 'The Great Moon Hoax' by the New York newspaper *The Sun* which claimed herds of bison, unicorns and temple-building bat-people had been spotted through new hi-tech telescopes. In *The Island of the Day Before*, Umberto Eco captured such wishful yearning:

'Sometimes I look at the Moon, and I imagine that those darker spots are caverns, cities, islands, and the places that shine are those where the sea catches the light of the sun like the glass of a mirror. I would like to tell the stories of their kings, their wars,

---

172   It fell back to earth in the form of architecture like the space age Bubble House by Pascal Häusermann.

and their revolutions, or of the unhappiness of lovers up there, who in the course of their nights sigh as they look down at our Earth.'[173]

These tales warrant telling and retelling even if they are just composites of earlier earth-bound stories. Created by George Lucas, a student of Joseph Campbell's *The Hero with a Thousand Faces*, the *Star Wars* series ingeniously borrowed from many sources including Kurosawa samurai films, Shakespeare, Arthurian legend, and Buck Rogers. Each of these had borrowed from other sources in turn; culture being an echo chamber. The more we trace influences back the more myriad multiplying branches emerge. The genius of *Star Wars* is that it seems futuristic but it is set long long ago[174] with tales from long long ago; the pauper who becomes prince, the fallen knight, the anti-hero made good. It's easy to be cynical but the collage approach works and such archetypes find their way into unlikely places; Travis Bickle in Scorcese's *Taxi Driver* is the hick naïf struggling in the big smoke, Virgil in The Inferno, the cowboy Shane and Dostoevsky's Underground Man, driving through a city that would for several generations form the backdrops of side-strolling video game beat-em-ups[175] and justify the biblical purging that is Zero Tolerance.

All stories, however contemporary, have already been told

---

173   Pg. 80

174   With hints of Paul Lehr's *Ancient Civilisations of the Future*.

175   Games such as *Renegade, Streets of Rage* and *Final Fight* featured the purging of urban decadence through ultraviolent vigilantism.

long ago and far away. We transpose our own experiences onto other planets as we did islands and exotic capitals before them. The problems are the problems we've faced on terra-firma; hard-working proletarians or maverick individuals versus aloof oligarchs and out of control Machiavellian technocrats for example (from the novels of Ursula Le Guin to *Red Faction* to *Dark Star*). There's always the temptation to categorise, invent tourist planets, mining planets, prison planets, plutocrat planets, slave planets when most likely new worlds, like the old one, will be an ever-changing mix of them all. One of the few certainities we have is that such certainties do not last.

The best ideas in science fiction come from the inventive reprocessing of old tropes; the haunted house in space of *Alien*, the chase and identity noir picaresque *Total Recall*, the medieval monasteries on a wooden planet from the Lebbeus Woods-designed unmade version of *Alien 3*. The relics of the old, the boomtowns and sin cities with the same old desires are dressed up in unfamiliar finery:

'Every fractured strain of humanity was there; a bewildering free-floating riot of colour, like tropical fish in a feeding frenzy. Ultras, Skyjacks, Conjoiners, Demarchists, local traders, intrasystem passengers, freeloaders, mechanics, all following what seemed to be completely random trajectories, but never quite colliding, no matter how perilously close they came. Some — where their bodyplans allowed it — had diaphanous wings sewn under their sleeves, or attached directly to the skin. The less adventurous made do with slim thrust-packs, or allowed themselves to be pulled along by tiny rented tugs. Personal servitors flew through the throng, carrying baggage and folded spacesuits, while liveried, winged capuchin monkeys foraged for litter, tucking what they found into marsupial pouches under their chests. Chinese music tinkled pervasively through the air, sounding to Volyova's untutored ear like windchimes stirred by a breeze with a particular taste for dissonance. Yellowstone, thousands of kilometres below, was an ominous yellow-brown backdrop to all this activity.'[176]

Compare this to Jack London witnessing the Klondike Gold-Rush first-hand in the 1890s: 'Men, groping in the Arctic darkness, had found a yellow metal and because steamship and transportation companies were booming the find, thousands of men were rushing into the Northland.'[177]

We cannot escape the stories we've been telling for millennia. In *Star Trek*, the crew of the Enterprise visit planetary island utopias which inevitably are not as they initially seem; 'This Side of Paradise' (a spore-infested peace and love community reminiscent of Homer's Isle of the Lotus-Eaters), 'Errand of Mercy' (a passive pacifist society, filmed near the Citadelle Laferrière in Haiti) and 'A Taste of Armageddon' (a world of opposing cities where war is conducted in an orderly computer-generated fashion with casualties stepping into disintegration

176   *Revelation Space*, Alastair Reynolds, Pg. 84

177   *The Call of the Wild*, Pg. 1

booths). The crew are emissaries themselves of an earthly Utopia, especially as seen from the turbulent but optimistic 1960s; egalitarian, multicultural, hopeful, technologically-focused and humanist, determined to 'seek out new worlds' to learn from or evangelise to. The message however is superficial and even duplicitous. They are also there to reinforce a colour-coded hegemony and a view that humans are an imperfect but defining synthesis of the impulses that dominate other species, a Goldilocks species from the Goldilocks zone, not as clinically logical as Vulcans, not as barbarously warlike as the Klingons. In reality, we are both, and very often worse.

In the case of *Star Wars*, the locations and characters have distinct precedents: Jabba's Castle hails from several unbuilt Frank Lloyd Wright designs[178], Darth Vader is a knock-off of The Lightning from *The Fighting Devil Dogs*, C-3PO and R2-D2 are peasants from Kurosawa's *The Hidden Fortress* via Lang's *Metropolis*. There are Battle of Britain dogfights and Nazi Stormtroppers, Sergio Leone and *The Searchers*, *Flash Gordon* and a childhood's worth of pulp. It is a scrapyard sculpted to b-movie perfection. The influences were assembled in a spirit at once heartfelt, nostalgic and cynical but in doing so *Star Wars* unintentionally demonstrates how cities work; absorbing the fractured myriad elements to create something that appears new. Even a periodically-exhausted genre like the Western, with its hard-bitten frontiersmen and mercenary drifters, can be

---

178   His Gordon Strong Automobile Objective & Planetarium, Sugarloaf Mountain, Maryland (1925), unbuilt Delano mortuary etc.

resuscitated on a distant planet:

'Smith's errand in Lakkdarol, like most of his errands, is better not spoken of. Man lives as he must, and Smith's living was a perilous affair outside the law and ruled by the ray-gun only ... Lakkdarol roars by night, as Earthmen's camp- towns have a way of doing on every planet where Earth's outposts are, and it was beginning lustily as Smith went down among the awakening lights toward the center of town. His business there does not concern us. He mingled with the crowds where the lights were brightest, and there was the click of ivory counters and the jingle of silver and red segir gurgled invitingly from black Venusian bottles, and much later Smith strolled homeward under the moving moons of Mars, and if the street wavered a little under his feet now and then — why, that is only understandable.'[179]

The sense of noir evident here (and what is darker than space?) re-emerges on the night-side of other planets in works like *Last Days of Shandakor* by Leigh Bracket, 'A new race, an unknown city. And I was drunk.'[180]

Other planets are now perhaps more distant than at any time in the past 50 years. Few saw the US space programme being wound down but it was always conceivable once military advantage was supposedly secured with the Soviet Union's collapse, and immediate profit was accepted as distant. Hope

179   *Shambleau*, CL Moore, Pg.18-19

180   *Startling Stories*, April 1952

lies perhaps with emerging economies though the prospect of it becoming the privatised preserve of billionaires looms. It seems a far cry from the days when Osbourne's popular *Future Cities* could believably propose the Olympics being held on the moon. The always-tenuous future of a democratic space lies evidently in the past. What's clear is that our fascination with space will never ebb so long as the stars are visible. Ilya Kabakov constructed a bedroom covered in posters of Soviet cosmonauts with a gaping hole in the ceiling. It is titled *The Man who Flew into Space*[181]. Whether we burst into the cosmos or fall into it is just a question of perspective.

181   'The man who collects the opinion of others', 'The man who never threw anything away' etc. feature in her *Ten Characters* series.

Flux Us

The Space Age did not completely vanish when run down. It survived as pastiche in fairgrounds and airports but also in visionary or speculative architecture. The need to assemble expanding shelters in hostile environments fuelled the designs of the Metabolists and Buckminster Fuller. The need to continually adapt and recycle materials and space encouraged the likes of Archigram. 'There is no finality in architecture only continuous change'[182] Walter Gropius wrote. However novel and ground-breaking, architecture is almost always out of date by the time it is built. To prevent obsolescence, Archigram made change the essence of their projects. They were not the first or last to do so. As a reflection of the belief in Wabi-sabi (primarily that all things are temporary), the Ise Jingu shrine is burned down and rebuilt every twenty years. In the West, this embracing of impermanence has tended to take a confrontational stance even if it still retained some ceremonial function. John Latham incinerated his Skoob Towers, made of piles of books, outside courts and government offices. The fire brigade saved the building when Jean Tinguely's auto-destructing machine Homage à New York went out of control. To the faint-hearted, it is vandalism. To the likes of the anti-architect Gustav Metzger, witnessing the rise of the Nazis as a German Jew, it was a symbolic affront to power, with the scathing satire evident in his manifesto, 'The artist may collaborate with scientists, engineers. Self-destructive art can

182   *Gropius*, Gilbert Lupfer and Paul Sigel, Pg. 81

be machine produced and factory assembled. Auto-destructive paintings, sculptures and constructions have a life time varying from a few moments to twenty years. When the disintegrative process is complete the work is to be removed from the site and scrapped.'[183]

The destructive-creative dynamic may well be a truism but it's often overplayed, via the reductive use of Bakunin's old maxim. More interesting is the view of architecture that exists for a period of time, an architectural happening that then disappears physically but is retained perfect and vast in myth and memory. This explains the lingering appeal of the World's Fairs and indeed all unbuilt or once-built buildings; they become canvases onto which we project limitless aspirations, which in all but exceptional cases would diminish with their building. The ephemeral somehow weighs more than the permanent.

In letting a wildly democratic impulse overtake the egotistical obsession with posterity that drives and plagues most artists, Cedric Price was remarkable[184]. He railed against architecture that insisted on oppressively enduring and architects who deluded themselves. 'Architects are the biggest whores in town,' Price claimed, 'They talk in platitudes about improving the quality of life, and then get out drawings of the prison they're working on.'[185] Instead he advocated that architecture should exist briefly and brilliantly before clearing a space for the next generation; his

183   First Manifesto of Auto-destructive Art, November 4th, 1959

184   His idea of reviving the starved post-industrial areas Potteries Thinkbelt with essentially pockets of the future is still radical and absurdly necessary.

185   Quoted in *The Telegraph*, August 15th, 2003

'calculated uncertainty' concept led him to theoretically invent the Generator — a structure which, utilising fledgling computer technology, would regularly and dramatically alter. Buildings that outlast their designer and original purpose could become a husk, a mausoleum or a tyranny of space. The Futurists, for all their kamikaze bravado and assertions to the contrary, only feigned to accept their own obliteration when time deemed them redundant; Price encouraged the eventual destruction and reconstruction of his own buildings by others, even heroically joining the National Institute of Demolition Contractors.

'Why *should* cities and buildings stay the same?' seems a reasonable questionable. A more apt question, 'What hubris makes us believe that they would?' Or rather, on what scale of time and influence are we thinking? Everything changes eventually. In the film *Dark City*, buildings grow and contract like living organisms[186]; an idea the director Alex Proyas had from watching sets of scale model cities be moved around on earlier films. The architectural genre of Blobism often looks as if paused mid-metamorphosis; chrysalis buildings frozen in a state of becoming. We are comfortable with this changeability provided it is restricted to simulation, as, for example, in Robert Wilson's neo-expressionist set designs, where, 'he leads the viewer into the dreamland of transitions, ambiguities, and correspondences: a column of smoke may be the image of a continent; trees turn first into Corinthian columns, then columns

---

186   A feature somehow evident in the architectural sketches of Claude Parent.

turn into factory smoke-stacks.'[187]

In Delany's heterotopia Triton[188] settlements, city dwellers can change themselves at a whim while on Le Guin's anti-ego anarchist planet Anarres[189], binaries are evaded and identity spectrums and alterations are embraced as an intrinsic part of life. Might we extend this to our places of living and work and leisure? To inhabit spaces, active rather than passive, that change according to seasons, temperature, wishes, to compliment, contradict and anticipate, to acknowledge the passage of time. This is, of course, as we see from perpetual struggles, a threat to those who benefit from orthodoxies, control and stasis.

We reach for the new and we understand it or explain it through the ancient. 'Swing City is like a coral reef in a tropical sea,' Roger Kemble announced of his 1968 plan for Vancouver, 'constantly growing in one place, dying and diminishing in another, all the time seething with activity, housing life of many colours'. A button is pressed and panels slide, capsules reposition, all maps are rendered temporary and obsolete ('no ego games here'). Its 'capsulated environments' and 'micro-climates' are made optimistically from polycite — 'a figment of the imagination at the moment but if we want it we can do it'. Kemble questions what home is (a seemingly-eternal entity that changes with every country and generation). 'Space is no longer defined as a 30 foot living room,' he claims, 'but as an

187   The Cambridge Introduction to Scenography, Pg. 74

188   Trouble on Triton, Samuel R. Delaney

189   The Dispossessed: An Ambiguous Utopia, Ursula Le Guin

experience'. As with every utopian idea, there are the seeds of dystopia apparent, particularly in the electro-information banks which record everything. The reassurance that it is for our benefit is the perpetual claim of the developing dictator. We must factor into every paradise the desire to be left alone and to opt out. The lack of space to do so is, in itself, a nightmare. Escape from the visions of others and even ourselves must be possible or it is no paradise.

There still persists the much-derided idea that cities can be fun, that they can amuse and delight, serving their inhabitants rather than vice versa, that they might be designed for the enjoyment of the (like Price's unbuilt Pleasure Palace) rather than the profit of a few. Those who put forward such a view are often lampooned as being infantile by those busy monetising space. The mantra that 'it need not be like this' is once again a possible saving grace. The problem is not, as often claimed, that architects have monumental egos (this is no secret or sin) but that the projects are authoritarian. This might seem a political issue but it is one commonly and implicitly felt. Architecture arouses heated emotions because it is an imposition of varying necessity.

Architectural radicals have simultaneously attacked the dictatorial aspects of building and taken it to absurdist lengths. Archigram arrived, in fanzine form, with a shot across the bows. Their creative irreverence and gleeful philistinism ('the pre-packaged frozen lunch is more important than Palladio') was in part a case of pre-emptive retaliation against regressive architectural conservatism but also an attempt to puncture the sanctimonious sides of modernism ('the decaying Bauhaus image which is an insult to functionalism'[190]) and the International Style, whereby buildings were treated as secular cathedrals and architects as a mixture of priest and saint. 'Architecture is probably a hoax,' Warren Chalk wrote in Archigram 7, 'a fantasy world'.

Accepting the premise that architecture is fantasy has the effect of obliterating limitations. Treating architecture as fiction, Raimund Abraham was free to explore narratives in his House without Walls, House for Euclid, House with Two Horizons and so on. Superstudio and Archizoom adapted Marx to suggest that liberation would arrive when architecture had somehow withered away, satirically replaced by semi-naked hippies lounging in bubbles and hangars. In the Endless City, 'the destruction of objects, the elimination of the city, and the disappearance of work are closely connected events.'[191] It is utopia as tongue-in-cheek critique but also a pointed idealisation of aboriginal and peasant cultures[192]. This is an architecture that tries to reverse the evolution of cities back to the beginning or at least recontextualise existing cities by placing over them a vast *tabula rasa* structure, extending across Manhattan and the Cliffs of Moher[193]. 'Approach things,' Oskar Schlemmer wrote,

190   David Greene, *Archigram* Issue 1, 1961

191   *The Situantionist City,* Simon Sadler, Pg. 145

192   *Made in Italy: Rethinking a Century of Italian Design,* Pg. 154

193   *Continuous Monument: An Architectural Model for Total Urbanization,* 1969

'as though the world had only just been created'[194]. Arcadias remain mythic however because they require humans to tend to their artifice and humans inherently despoil them. We destroy Eden and that is our redemption.

The efforts of Reyner Banham and François Dallegret to create the Un-House or Transportable Standard-of-Living Packages was recognised by Charles Jencks as the beginning of a process of transcendence. 'The two ideas behind this,' he wrote, 'are to give everyone a standard of living package containing all the necessities of modern life (shelter, food, energy, television) and to do away with all the permanent structures of building, and men would not be constrained by past settlements.'[195] He compared this move of 'increasing ephemerality' to 'religious mysticism, or a mood controlled environment which is induced entirely in the mind — through drugs, and electrodes implanted on the brain. In this situation, all artifacts would disappear entirely and the only thing left would be a contemplative trance having much the same advantage over tangible things that St. Bernard pointed out over eight centuries ago.'

Though he harked back to monastic hallucinations, Jencks was predicting to a remarkable degree the future city of augmented virtual realities.

Archigram shared this view of the transformative powers of architecture and the ability to live within technology. This would require a profound reassessment of what architecture

194   *Diary*, May 1929, Pg. 89

195   *Architecture 2000*, Jencks

was; not just to the wilder shores of architecture like Taut and Gaudí but Dan Dare and comic books (*Archigram 4* contained a full-blown interstellar comic with Chalk's *Space Probe*).

'It seems I have been over this city for very many miles,' Superman observes flying above Cook's Plug-In City 'yes indeed . . . for it stretches over the channel and beyond . . . into Europe . . . you can see the habitations plugged into the giant network-structure'.

Ron Herron's work in particular (Seaside Bubble for example) blurs the line between comic strip and rendering. This might be seen as devaluing architecture, but in fact represented a revitalising broadening of influence and parameters. 'We are in the cataloguing business,' Peter Cook claimed, 'and our work is that of illuminating and extending and reinventing the catalogue'[196]. They embraced emerging innovations, foretelling the computer's integration into our lives, and also improbable but existing technologies; their recurring cities on stilts came from a tradition that ranged from the tree dwellings of the Korowai Tribe to Ack-Ack Forts on the Thames Estuary. The aim was to advance, using any influence necessary — 'Can the near-reality of the rocket-object and hovercraft-object, which are virtually ceasing to be cartoons, carry the dynamic building with them into life as it is?'[197] It was also to break down the stifling borders set between artforms, a pedantry that had benefited the aristocrats of each medium and held back the

196   *Architectural Design* 1971, Peter Cook, Pg. 486

197   *Architects: The Noted and the Ignored*, Niels Luning Prak, Pg. 190

collisions and combinations that are the dialectics of inspiration. Snobbery was counter-revolutionary. *Gesamtkunstwerk* (or total art) would be the future: 'the separations between art, science, technology, architecture, and everyday life, are beginning to appear as artificial boundaries and hence to disintegrate'[198]. This could have utopian outcomes, as Piet Mondrian noted (his own paintings and those of his fellow De Stijl comrades channelling into the actual living space of the Rietveld Schröder House among others): 'By the unification of architecture, sculpture and painting a new plastic reality will be created.'[199]

Change evades boredom. It promotes, if not freedom, then choice, which is why it seems superficially suited to the consumer age. Whilst deflecting accusations of barbarism ('we shall not bulldoze Westminster Abbey'), Archigram recognised the modern city as a 'living organism — pulsating — expanding and contracting, dividing and multiplying'[200] and not a fossil. If they embodied certain traits of consumerism then they also, like the Pop Artists, critiqued it. 'Change it and dream again,' Peter Cook wrote in illustrations for an Anarchy City, where power is individualised, 'if we value person above object . . . you are in control'.

Looking back, it seems that Archigram predicted the internet, albeit materially in their City Interchange and the various Plug-In concepts (mirrored in Yona Friedman's Spatial City).

198   *Arthropods New Design Futures*, Jim Burns, Pg. 8

199   *Abstract Art*, Anna Moszynska, Pg. 117

200   *City Synthesis*, Dennis Crompton

Furthermore, they envisaged the mix of biological and robotic, in works such as Cook's unbuilt Montreal Tower, which has not yet come to pass.

Wrestling with consumerism bore considerable risks. On the one hand, it promised democracy (for those who could afford it) and an erosion of architectural elitism. 'Does consumer choice of pre-fabricated living units,' Peter Cook wondered in 1967, 'imply that every man might become his own architect?'[201] In doing so, the architect as a keeper of obscurantist knowledge might be abolished and replaced by the owner's imagination or even placing the design of buildings into systems run according to chance[202]. Yet the idea of 'housing as a consumer product', as Chalk put it, would have evident weaknesses in terms of disposability and lack of quality. Warren Chalk designed hip Capsule Homes that seem off-shoots of *2001: A Space Odyssey*. David Greene proposed a Spray Plastic House that would solidify from an aerosol canister and then be burrowed into like a warren. Mike Webb's Cushicle would fit into a backpack while his Suitaloon could be worn — 'if it wasn't for my suitaloon, I would have to buy a house'.

'The house is an appliance for carrying with you,' Greene noted in relation to his Living Pod, '[just as] the city is a machine for plugging into'.

Following Archigram, Ant Farm's *Inflatocookbook* presented autonomous temporary housing in the style of underground

---

201   *Architecture: Action and Plan*, Peter Cook, Pg. 95

202   A contrary argument to this would be that autonomous settlements do exist, in slums and shantytowns.

comix of the time — 'kids make your own bubble easy as 1 2 3'. These may look striking on paper but could we live happily in any of them? Archigram were aware themselves of such doubts — 'Does "home" remain valid when any atmosphere of living can be conjured at a moment's notice — by the press of a switch?' — but they were just as aware that their works were partially thought-experiments to begin with. You begin with the desire to free the occupant and you might well end with the monastic cell. You invent the Plug-In City and you also invent power manifesting in the hands of whoever controls the overarching scaffolding. All city planning requires a continual rebalancing of powers between the individual, the elite and the collective.

For Coop Himmelblau, the future dwelling place was a bubble. Mounted on cranes or the sides of buildings, they let in light and a superlative view. They were 'as buoyant and variable as clouds' and, in crucial differentiation from Le Corbusier's claim, they were 'organism[s] for living . . . The structure is mobile, the space can be modified. The building materials are air and dynamics . . . Architecture is content, not shell.'

They were also completely exposed to the view of the outside world, being ideal only for exhibitionists. When Haus-Rucker-Co installed their bubble for two perched at the side of a Viennese tenement the police arrived[203] after a phonecall presuming a suicide or wanton vandalism was taking place. Though it promised to open up living space to outside society,

203   *Beyond Art: A Third Culture*, edited by Peter Weibe, Pg. 572

there is something atomising about such models, more suited to refuges in places[204] even more inhospitable than the city.

'The Metropolis strives to reach a mythical point,' Rem Koolhaas wrote, 'where the world is completely fabricated by man, so that it absolutely coincides with his desires.'[205] All too often this comes down to the desires of a solitary man. There were efforts to mitigate this that lacked the surreal extravagance of Archigram. In Clifford Harper's poster series *Visions,* a local English neighbourhood is transformed by simply knocking down partitions, enabling communities to have large sustainable gardens and urban farms and autonomous terraces with saunas, libraries, wind turbines, basement workshops, a community media centres and so on. It is one of the contradictions of late capitalism that we have vastly more technologies aiding and connecting us now and yet such suggestions seem to belong to a bygone socialist age, locked away from us. Archigram demonstrated that the city might be refreshed by questioning that which is falsely taken as inevitable and unchangeable.

Other artists have continued examining the city and what it might have been through negative space and X-rays. Rachel Whiteread's cast of a Victorian house, built of solid concrete, could not be inhabited. A shadow of the original dwelling that had once stood there, it was later demolished by the council becoming the ghost of a ghost. Mozuna's AntiDwelling Box might not offer alternative ways of living but it questions what we

204   Ski Haus by Richard Horden, for example.

205   Appendix of *Delirious New York: A Retroactive Manifesto for Manhattan*, Rem Koolhaas

think of as functional and why. Rem Koolhaas and collaborators rethought the idea of the city in his jester-like *Delirious New York*. In his City of the Captive Globe, 'each science or mania has its own plot . . . these bases, ideological laboratories, are equipped to suspend unwelcome laws, undeniable truths, to create non-existent physical conditions to facilitate and provoke speculative activity'[206]. It would be a city with factories in which to think, a city in which to dream of cities.

'All that is solid melts into air,' foretold Marx and perhaps nothing was solid to begin with. We see the shell, the carapace of dwellings and not the systems of power, waste, communication that are functioning in the walls, under the ground, through the sky. In the books of Bruno Schulz and the films of the Brothers Quay, there is a sense that there are unseen worlds and secret mythologies under the floorboards. Might we dispense with the shell altogether when technology permits? Sean Lally has proposed, in his Weathers project, an architecture made of pure energy, providing a protective layer against the elements (a leap from Archigram's wearable homes). Even the wildest visions of future cities tend to be wed to traditional building materials; Lally proposes a glowing swirling architecture without architecture.

'Space is nature's way of preventing everything from happening in the same place'[207]. To understand space is to continually rethink it. We mistake architecture for the

---

206   Koolhaas - *Lotus 11*, open citation Pg. 36, quoted *Late Modern Architecture*,
        Jencks, Pg. 143

207   *Architectural Design — Architecture and Film*, Michael Dear, Pg. 9

aforementioned shell, when it is really the space within. Provided transparency and shelter is catered for, there may be little purpose for the traditional shell at all. Influenced by E.A.T. Pepsi pavilion Expo '70 in Osaka, Elizabeth Diller and Ricardo Scofidio designed the Blur Building, an artificial peninsula, which rather than possessing walls and a roof is covered in a shroud of mist, created from the lake below. While Buckminster Fuller's mile-wide floating geodesic orbs, Cloud Nine, (kept aloft by the difference in air temperature to the outside) and Paisajes Emergente's artificial communications-bearing clouds for remote areas, offer curiosities to ponder, they would be particularly vulnerable to changes in the weather. Wind is the enemy of the Cloud City. More promising is the idea of developing shells that can become tangible and intangible at command, via a mist nanotechnology: 'The wall flickered partially out of existence as he stepped through to the corridor, and its polarised molecules resisted his passage like a feeble wind blowing against his face.'[208]

Even a fixed location for future cities is not a given. Earth's plates are continually shifting. Water, oil and other resources are depleting in areas. Disasters manmade and natural abound. It might even be that the fixed view of a landscape becomes tiring. Nomadism was for millennia the condition of humanity and remains so for many cultures (the Enkang huts of the cattle-grazing Masai, for example). There are many who have suggested a return to the lost advantages of a migratory life,

208   *The City and the Stars,* Pg. 24

beyond the holiday season. Few have been as extravagant as those who suggest moving entire cities en masse, and they are wide-open to mockery — from the Betelgeuse Walking Cities (1944) by Frank R. Paul, which resemble an egg with ostrich legs, to the Very Large Structure of Manuel Domínguez, which posits an oil rig-type city on caterpillar tracks. Yet moving cities *have* existed, from the huge networks, populations and infrastructure involved in the Crusades, the Normandy Landing fleets to the Golden Horde: 'the khan's pavilions themselves were topped with such a quantity of gold that even a visitor from Egypt was startled . . . [fixed] fortifications . . . were regarded as a sign of cowardice.'[209]

To invent the moving city is to invent the destruction it leaves in its wake. It would roll catastrophically across arable land creating dustbowls. Such a city would run the risk of being foiled by mountains, swamps, storms or simply the enormous amount of energy required to fuel it. It would leave behind a trail of waste and encourage pursuing scavengers. Other planets would perhaps be more suitable, or the city could exist invasively as an immense war machine. This raises the possibility of rival moving cities clashing, or simply a solitary one like a huge mechanical beetle scuttling across the face of the planet, consuming resources. Even a malevolent moving city would still be vulnerable. Festooned with cannons and powered by fifty Tatar cyclists, the iron egg of Malacovia in Amedeo Tosetti's *Pedals of the Black Sea* (1884) terrorised the

209   *Red Fortress: The Secret Heart of Russia's History*, Catherine Merridale, Pg. 28

local population and hid by lowering itself into the Danube. It was undone in the end because iron rusts.

Populations move to and from cities in the event of disasters. In Christopher Priest's *Inverted World*, the city itself flees on a self-laying railway track to keep ahead of temporal and gravitational distortions, trying to remain in the eye of a storm. The city is self-contained and the outside world and its perils are kept secret as it inches its way across the landscape. For Archigram, the disaster was the prospect of rural bourgeois life. Having developed a Blow-Out Village that would travel by hovercraft, Peter Cook designed the Instant City, an unfolding airship which would bring metropolitan dynamism and culture to neglected hinterlands. Instead of the circus coming to your local village, a city would arrive. Tentatively inspired, perhaps, by the agitprop trains of early Soviet Russia, which brought cinema and art to peasants and workers in the sticks, the Instant City would have a political purpose, a kind of inoculation against conservatism ('infiltration complete' went one of the instructions). It would spread discernment rather than the terror of the zeppelins of old. Archigram satirised themselves with the 'inevitable next-step' — an Instant Country for the city (complete with hologram horse and instagrow), though another next-step was the Instant City going the way of the Hindenberg at the hands of irate shotgun-weilding farmers.

Change threatens those who have a vested interest in the status quo or those who simply cherish security and familiarity above other considerations. Despite this, people are by no means final or complete. They too, or rather we, are in an evolving state of flux, whether consciously aware or not and the changing city is simply a larger manifestation of this. In his notebooks Leonardo Da Vinci wrote earnestly, 'We ought not to desire the impossible,' [210] at the same time as drawing flying machines, submarines and robotic knights. We ought not to, but we do. It is easy to damn visionary schemes as absurd or unbuildable. In Jonathan Swift's novel Gulliver visits the city of Lagado, which is falling to pieces due to the preoccupation of its leading 'Projectors' with their fanciful schemes: 'the houses very strangely built, and most of them out of repair. The people in the streets walked fast, looked wild, their eyes fixed, and were generally in rags.'[211] Swift's sarcasm is much in evidence towards 'a most ingenious architect, who had contrived a new method for building houses, by beginning at the roof, and working downward to the foundation; which he justified to me, by the like practice of those two prudent insects, the bee and the spider.' Like many innovations that appear ridiculous, this method actually existed; it is thought to have been employed in the construction of the superlative city of Petra and the Temple of Kailasa.

Many of the designs marked as unbuildable paper architecture are simply designs temporarily out of time. They have a tendency to reappear in unlikely places. Cedric Price's Fun Palace directly influenced the Centre Pompidou. The painted designs and

210   Quoted Pg. 8, *Leonardo and the Last Supper*, Ross King

211   *Gulliver's Travels*, Pg. 69

pronouncements ('the straight line is godless and immoral'[212]) of Friedensreich Hundertwasser, were dismissed as Outsider Art, until he constructed his buildings in three dimensions. Indeed the use of outsider artist or outsider architect as a dismissal is a fallacy given *all* are outside until brought inside, through differing routes. These are often blocked for initially justifiable reasons (planning restrictions, lack of academic credentials) that mask more Machiavellian interests (the monopolisation of space twinned with obscurantist or economic control of access to knowledge). There can be wonders when these checkpoints are evaded, and inspiration found amongst the discarded; Ned Chand built his once-secret and illegal rock garden from the wreckage of Le Corbusier's utopian Chandigarh, while the postman Ferdinand Cheval built his Le Palais ideal from flotsam found on his daily routes.

At the very least, outsider architects extend the space of what it is to think laterally, as professionals like Mir, Atelier Olschinsky, Heatherwick and Morphosis (among others) do today. Hundertwasser's assertion that architecture cannot be considered an art until everyone is free to do it chimes with Otto Kohtz's aim of 'architecture for architecture's sake'.

'It is highly possible that later generations will achieve mastery of materials and technique that they will construct a building or a landscape for no other purpose than that of contemplation, simply out of a desire to create in a particular mood, rather in the way that many pieces of music are written today. Just as

212   *Hundertwasser-Bahnhof Uelzen*, Pg. 111

the composer can already, through sound, move thousands to joyful exuberance or to sorrow, so the architect will be able to do the same through form and colour.'[213] Essentially, the only difference between the century-long building of Gaudí's Sagrada Familia and the outsider architecture of Gilles Tréhin or Paul Nobbs is that the former is being built.

If we see architecture as frozen music, as Goethe claimed[214], we might see music as fluid architecture. Steven Holl's Stretto House is designed to suggest the flow of water over dams as well as sections of Béla Bartók's *Music for Strings, Percussion and Celesta*. Xenakis' Philips Pavilion[215] was the soundwaves of Varèse's *Poème électronique* translated into physical form. In Sweven's *Limonora*, structures are made of irelium dust which is conjured into various shapes through the playing of music: 'As we approached [. . .] we could hear the most elaborate and entrancing music, for the design in such cases was labyrinthine.'[216] This is building as the charming of snakes, structures built of petrified melodies.

213   'Gedanken Uber Architektur', Berlin 1919, cited in *Expressionist Architecture*, Pehnt, Pg. 9

214   Quoted Pg. 82, *Cities Built to Music: Aesthetic Theories of the Victorian Gothic Revival*, Michael Bright

215   For Expo '58 in Brussels.

216   Pg. 168

The Megalomania of Cells

The inhabitants of cities change as inevitably as cities do. Just as our cells are replaced (from taste-buds every ten days to the heart every twenty years), the cells of the city replicate, mutate and collapse. The Metabolists embraced this process as inevitable; their very name coming from the Greek word for change and the metabolisms of the body. 'We regard human society as a vital process,' they wrote, 'a continuous development from atom to nebula.'[217] They had witnessed the destruction of their country's cities in the Second World War but also the insistence of people, like cells, to survive. Often portrayed as the builders of intriguing follies or inhuman pod housing, the Metabolists had genuine utopian ideals garnered largely from the natural world. Kikutake's capsule towers, Tange's Cluster City and Isozaki's Clusters in the Air project were designed to replicate trees growing upwards and outwards, as horizontal as well as vertical skyscrapers (inspired by El Lissitszky's Sky Hooks and his Georgian Ministry of Highways[218]).

Philip Drew identified the Metabolists' desire 'to substitute an analogy of architecture with biological processes in place of the orthodox analogy with machinery.'[219] Until then modernist architects had associated buildings with machines, but machines

217   *Kenzo Tange and the Metabolist Movement: Urban Utopias of Modern Japan,*
        Zhongjie Lin, Pg. 24

218   Inspiring in turn the CCTV building Beijing and the Umeda Sky Building,
        Osaka.

219   *The Third Generation,* Philip Drew, Pg. 68

cannot as yet evolve. The organic, even when it looks robotic, can.

Works such as Kurokawa's Takara Beautilion (1970) suggested architecture as crystallisation, with capsules added to a scaffolding matrix; an idea also pursued by Schulze-Fielitz in his infinitely expandable Raumstadt (Space City), and his bridge city, Brückenstadt über den Ärmelkanal, linking England and France. In the City Tower for Philadelphia, Pennsylvania, USA by Anne Tyng and Louis Kahn, the plug-in tetrahedron structure was endlessly expandable in the model of a crystal lattice. It was even more radical because humans would inhabit the inside of the frame: 'In Gothic times, architects built in solid stones. Now we can build with hollow stones. The spaces defined by the members of a structure are as important as the members. These spaces range in scale from the voids of an insulation panel, voids for air, lightning and heat to circulate, to spaces big enough to walk through and live in.'[220] Theirs was 'The desire to express voids positively.'

'The snail lives in its shell; it's a fact.' Le Corbusier wondered, 'Us? From the moment when industrialisation revolutionised society, they have tried to make the snail inhabit, for example, a matchbox. Industrialisation must lead the snail back to his shell. A sensible dream?'[221]

Robert Smithson had shown that crystals were maps which could be endlessly rearranged. Frederick Kiesler had shown

220   *Beyond the Cube: The Architecture of Space Frames and Polyhedra*, J. François Gabriel, Pg. 134

221   *Almanac*, Le Corbusier, Pg. 6

with his Endless House that it could carry on indefinitely until space ran out. Guy Dessauges's Cylinder Houses could be made until recycled materials depleted. Kikutake's Hotel Tokoen, Nakagin Capsule Tower and Habitat 67 even demonstrated that such structures could be physically built and lived in. To counter accusations that such habitations were unnatural, Isozaki compared his designs to kimono weaving: 'a very simple system has produced for centuries an inexhaustible wealth if diversity and beauty'[222]. The problem with replicating cells was whether they were healthy or not. Cancer, after all, replicates. In isolated pockets, they dazzle. Expanding over a city, they would seem an infestation.

---

222   *Pedestrian in the City*, Pg. 180

Revolution! Revolution! Revolution!

As with all historical events, a cursory account of the French Revolution could be told in architecture; the seizure of Les Invalides and the storming of the Bastille (urged by De Sade shouting from his cell window), the womens' march on Versailles, the Tennis Court Oath, the Jacobin Club, Marat's bathroom, the erecting of Madame Guillotine in the Places. It was told in all of Paris. The contemporary chemist Lavoisier had found that mass cannot be created or destroyed, but merely converted. If all of Paris burned, the resulting wreckage and smoke would still be Paris. Lavoisier would lose his head and Paris would burn, in a sense, brilliant and terrible for all the world to see.

Worship of God and King, long-intertwined, was to be replaced with a cult of Reason. Cemetery gates were emblazoned with 'death is a perpetual sleep'. Cathedrals, including Notre Dame, were re-dedicated to philosophy and freedom, before Robespierre attempted a 'Cult of the Supreme Being'. The calendar was reset, with the names of days and months changed from deities to the weather, plants, flowers, trees, soils. Rural worship was inherited from the earlier radical, Rousseau, who nostalgically elevated the 'noble savage' in opposition to the ills of the urban. The reaction of architects to this attempt at a new world was one poised between anxiety and excitement, especially when the blade hung over their necks. Having killed the king and numerous gentry, the new regimes sought legitimacy through neo-classical facades, recalling the Roman and Athenian Republics, but a parallel world already existed in the notebooks of visionary architects.

Chiming with the drive for a celestial humanism or even neo-paganism[223], Étienne-Louis Boullée sought to build a cenotaph for the scientific saint, Isaac Newton. Beyond hagiography, it would be a cathedral to the universe, with not the cross but a glowing sphere hanging in the centre of a concrete sphere, symbolising the sun and, prophetically, the atom. The orb of the building would be punctured with holes to allow the sunlight to shine through in pinpoints of light, like stars, a method Boullée had borrowed from Turkish baths of the era[224]. What was the glory, it asked, of a poor carpenter nailed to a tree, or the visions of a desert trader compared to the cosmos? This building would be a captured universe. Boullée was not a revolutionary, but an aged neoclassical architect, tired of rich miserly clients, who brought proto-Modernism to the fore almost in spite of himself. Yet the Modernism is there, hand in hand with the classical, for example in his D euxième Projet Pour la Bibliothèque du Roi, where the vast arc of space makes the books provide all the ornament, colour and meaning.

The paradox of Modernism being ancient is no real paradox at all if a cyclical or heliocyclical view of history is taken. The links are there in buildings shorn of ornament, in the play of light and shadow, in cubes, curves and columns, in the play

223   The Sol Invictus sun cult of the Romans for one.

224   *Le Corbusier, the Noble Savage: Toward an Archaeology of Modernism*, Adolf Max Vogt, Pg. 63

of styles[225]. To gaze upon the magnificent foreboding faces of the Ziggurat of Ur (or the later Castel del Monte and Lahore Fort) is to see an antique Brutalism; to step inside Daniel Grataloup's Maison d'Anières is to recall the Anchorites' Tufa-pinnacle houses in Cappadocia or the Dogon Ginna housing in Mali. When Charles Delmuth painted mid-Western water silos and named the piece *My Egypt*, he was being truthful. Hassan Fathy's design for New Qurna, now a relative ghost town, was an honest Modernist attempt to bridge back to Ancient Egypt and Nubian vaults. Even Postmodernism has appeared before (without the smirk) in the stretched Aachen Cathedral and the multi-coloured Palácio da Pena. The magnificent Hagia Sophia is perhaps the ultimate existing collage of forms and histories, a plural building.

In revolutionary France, the past was to be abolished, but the past will not lie down in its grave. The architects knew this. Claude-Nicolas Ledoux was a similarly unlikely revolutionary, his works heralding a new age though he manifestly belonged to the old one. Having for decades built for the aristocracy, the architect narrowly avoided the guillotine that claimed his clients. Yet Ledoux had made strenuous efforts to reform architecture, particularly the theatre of Besançon, but running into the conceit and intransigence that soon doomed the nobility. To the revolutionaries, Ledoux was compromised by his past. He was thrown in jail and many of his buildings were demolished, but he survived and continued his work. His utopianism rested

---

225   It is there in Masjid-i-jami mosque.

on urban arcadias, like the remarkable egalitarian plans for the Royal Saltworks at Arc-et-Senans, with its architecture parlante (a 'speaking architecture' where form matches function) providing an on-site brothel designed in the shape of a large erect phallus[226]. Ledoux's River Inspector's House at Loue was similarly literal, with the actual river flowing through it[227]. His spherical House of the Field Watchmen abolished the blind spots of corners and must have looked in its time like a comet gently settled on the earth. Ledoux saw not binaries, but possibilities that would make him loathed by dogmatists: 'for the first time one will see presented on the same scale the magnificence of the tavern and that of the palace . . . '[228]

Had Ledoux built his cock-shaped brothel, the misfit architect Jean-Jacques Lequeu would have been ideal to decorate or indeed inhabit it. Lequeu specialised in proto-Surrealist grotesques as well as erotica. The two were incorporated in the 'highly imaginative erotic rituals for his architecture: a submerged Indian cabinet of delights, surrounded by a pool and lazy fish; a barn in the form of a cow[229]; temples of love inspired by the Hypnerotomachia and analogous to lewd figures; an anthropomorphic gateway, always humid, sited in the Elysian fields; a collage house at Bellevue as a place of encounter for voyeuristic activities.'[230]

---

226   Inspired by a Piranesi Mars design.

227   A distant precursor to Lloyd Wright's glorious Falling Water.

228   *History of Architectural Theory*, Hanno-Walter Kruf, Pg. 164

229   Sunlight would stream into a hay loft through its two eyes.

230   *Built Upon Love*, Alberto Pérez-Gómez, pg. 102

Dismissed as a lunatic, there was a method to Lequeu's madness. His Temple of Silence was a conspiratorial setting for freemasons[231] while he had temples to the earth, equality and the sun. Form reflected function, and anticipated it. His Gate of a Hunting-ground set animal heads atop a series of obelisks. Soon it would be the heads of his aristocratic, then his revolutionary, patrons.

The urge to reset and begin again still remains and occasionally rises when the horrors of existing society have sufficiently piled up. Benjamin's Angel of History flaps her wings from time to time. Other worlds are possible and have briefly existed. The anarchists of Barcelona gave luxury hotel rooms to the homeless. The Bavarian Soviet Republic lasted six days under the rule of poets and playwrights (the Expressionist Ernst Toller, the mysterious B. Traven and the Commissioner of Enlightenment, Gustav Landauer, among them) with the Foreign Minster Dr Lipp filling a room full of red carnations before declaring bloodless war on Switzerland. Having released the details of spies and informers, the judiciary of the Paris Commune issued an arrest warrant for 'one called God who has no permanent residence, and is consequently, contrary to law, living in a perpetual state of vagabondage.'[232] Each had elements of glory and farce. Each was brutally wiped out.

There was another grasp for utopia that would last a little longer, surviving onslaughts from outside, but not from within.

231 *The Architecture of the French Enlightenment*, Allan Braham, Pg. 232

232 *The Rise and Fall of the Paris Commune in 1871*, William Pembroke Fetridge, Pg. 134

Years before receiving an icepick to the brain, Leon Trotsky reflected disapprovingly upon a proposal for a new Soviet Babel to house their Fourth International congress: 'Meetings are not necessarily held in a cylinder and the cylinder does not necessarily have to rotate.' Tatlin's Tower reminded Trotsky of a wooden temple inside a beer bottle that he'd seen as a child — nothing more than a folly. Yet this unbuildable construct set Trotsky's mind spinning, that vital function of the unfunctional:

'There is no doubt that, in the future — and the farther we go, the more true it will be — such monumental tasks as the planning of city gardens, of model houses, of railroads, and of ports, will interest vitally not only engineering architects, participators in competitions, but the large popular masses as well. The imperceptible, ant-like piling up of quarters and streets, brick by brick, from generation to generation, will give way to titanic constructions of city-villages, with map and compass in hand. Around this compass will be formed true peoples' parties, the parties of the future for special technology and construction, which will agitate passionately, hold meetings and vote. In this struggle, architecture will again be filled with the spirit of mass feelings and moods, only on a much higher plane, and mankind will educate itself plastically, it will become accustomed to look at the world as submissive clay for sculpting the most perfect forms of life. The wall between art and industry will come down. The great style of the future will be formative, not ornamental . . . '[233]

233   *Literature and Revolution*, Pg. 203

This would result in humanity transcending itself: 'Man will become immeasurably stronger, wiser and subtler; his body will become more harmonised, his movements more rhythmic, his voice more musical. The forms of life will become dynamically dramatic. The average human type will rise to the heights of an Aristotle, a Goethe, or a Marx. And above this ridge new peaks will rise.'

Trotsky's focus on this imaginary future utopia, with its imaginary future inhabitants, was a way of diverting his attention away from the brilliant and problematic generation of Russian artists — the likes of Rodchenko, Popova, Melnikov, Leonidov, Mayakovsky, Brik, the Vesnin brothers, Malevich, El Lissitzy and Tatlin, who believed that in creating art that engaged with the people on every level, from poetry to graphic design to revolutionary mass festivals, life could be utterly transformed and enriched. They designed theatres, planetariums, cinemas, baths, communal kitchens, working clubs, research stations, youth halls, libraries, laboratories, parks, kindergartens and rest homes. They created a future that was not taken. Most of the plans of the Constructivists remained unbuilt and were sidelined with Stalin's rise to power (the man of steel preferred his buildings neo-classical, and his revolutionaries in the ground), but even then there was a last gasp of stunning, gargantuan ambition in the competition drawings for Elektrobank, the Palace of the Soviets, Lenin's Mausoleum and the Narkomtiazhprom building. An element of theatre seemed always present, even beyond the movie posters of the Stenberg brothers. Vesnin had designed the sets for Tairov's adaptation of *The Man Who Was Thursday*, Popova for Meyerhold's *The Magnanimous Cuckold* and Tatlin for Khlebnikov's *Zangezi*. They took their creations out to the provinces where 'Suprematist confetti scattered along the streets of this bedazzled town.'[234]

If they rejected the archaic folk-art of the rural, it was only in so much as a false series of binaries had been previously set up: 'The machine has not divorced us from nature. We have discovered by means of it a new previously unsuspected nature.'[235]

There was a sense that these artists were living in a play they had written, with the cities of Soviet Russia as their stage. They were doing precisely that. Architecture, design and art always begins as fiction, though we soon forget this. Gaze out of the window at any city and you'll find the skyline is a collection of ideas that emerged from certain minds. Each building contains names, reasons and dreams within it. They *were* in a play, albeit one now we can see with a tragic last act.

What is often forgotten is that the Russian revolutionaries were acutely aware of the past, particularly the failings and crimes of the French Revolution, which the Stalinists would go on to surpass. Boullée's Newton Cenotaph was partly resurrected in Parusnikov's Museum of the Revolution and Leonidov's Lenin Institute. The Gothic, and even German Expressionism, is evident in the designs of Fidman and Istelenov (especially

234   Eisenstein in *Mayakovsky in the Reminiscences of his Contemporaries*, pg. 279-80

235   El Lissitzky, Merz Hanover, April/July 1924 No.8/9

the Temple of Communion Between Nations, 1919) and in the wondrously dark works of Chernikhov. There is the medieval and the Babylonian in Dombrovsky, the Roman in Belogrud, Art Nouveau in Zelenko, the Renaissance in Zholtovsky, and even hints of Bosch in Ladovsky's early works. There is Bauhaus in the Soviet Pavilion of 1925 and Gosolov's Lenin House of the People, 1924. Though the temptation is to make all attempts at utopia an island, as Kim Il-Sung and Pol Pot would brutally try, humans are social creatures and art is but a means of communication[236].

For a time, there was a state of revolutionary creativity. Lamtsov, Korzhev, Komarovam and Petrov all drew blueprints for buildings which could not be easily built to demonstrate mass and weight equations; alien buildings, crystalline bridges, radio towers that morphed into skyscrapers, unfurling skyward like stone bouquets, retracting like armadillo shells, balancing precariously, jutting out from cliff-faces, boulevards absorbed by architecture and vice versa, buildings in a snapshot collision.

'While Le Corbusier's *Towards a New Architecture* ended with this architecture: "architecture or revolution," Rodchenko, true to his Constructivist program, articulated the slogan "architecture as revolution" with every square inch of his Club.'[237]

The past, however, caught up with them. 'Those who found canvas and clay a constraint and went on to create

---

236   Cosmic Communist Architecture features a plethora of amazing futuristic buildings in the soviet republics to suggest that the tendency carried on, informed with various regional styles.

237   *Art since 2000*, Pg. 201

structures,' El Lisstizky wrote, 'found themselves captives in the incantatory ring of an infinite number of bookish teachings, with which solidly established professors crammed them and, slowly but surely, bottled up the whole creative urge of their apprentices. And thus monsters grew up among us, walking encyclopaedias of all bygone centuries . . . '[238]

These monsters were the true figures of the new era of Stalin. The artists were betrayed, if they refused to betray themselves, as the people were.

The death of the fledgling utopia began long before the psychopathic Ossetian's rise. It was over when Trotsky sent his troops across the ice to crush the sailors in Kronstadt Fortress, and when eminent Bolsheviks like Kamenev (Stalin's clock already ticking against him) cast disdain on the artists: 'the worker's government must decisively stop the support which it has given to all kinds of Futurists, Cubists and Imagists — all those contortionists — they are not proletarian artists and their art is not ours. They are the product of bourgeois corruption and bourgeois degeneration.'[239]

Tatlin's unbuilt tower is less our Babel than our Eden, an eternal mythic *could've been*. Tatlin was there from the beginning, poised like Hamlet: '1917. To accept or not to accept the October Revolution, that wasn't a question for me. In an organic fashion I joined active, creative, social and pedagogical life'[240]. He

---

238   *Gazeta 'izo'* 1921, No. 1

239   *A Voice - Russian Architecture*, Pg. 124

240   Quoted January 20th, 2014, *E & T Magazine*

saved enough money to make a pilgrimage to his hero Picasso in Paris by posing as a blind busker, receiving (legend has it) a gold watch from the Kaiser. He had a punch-up with the Suprematist-mystic Malevich over whose idea it was to hang paintings in the corner of the gallery at the 0.10 exhibition. He had lost the hearing in his left ear whilst wrestling in the circus. When George Grosz came to Moscow to visit him, he found Tatlin living in a decaying boarded-up apartment filled with chickens.[241]

'Engineers and bridge-builders, do your calculations and invent a new form,'[242] Tatlin challenged. His tower however did not arise out of thin air, influenced as it was by Shukhov's hyperboloid towers, the frame of the Eiffel Tower and the rigging of Popova's maquette. It was predated by a couple of decades by the leaning corkscrew of Hermann Obrist's Design for a Memorial. It was not completely in isolation either — Melnikov's Leningradskaya Pravda Headquarters resembled a futurist lighthouse. Yet it was, and remains, a startlingly inventive spiral design. It would house the International, designed to spread revolution globally, and in a twist of form and function, it was designed to revolve. It would be double the size of the Empire State Building. Glass chambers would rotate at different speeds, once a year, a month and a day. Messages would be projected onto passing clouds. Loudspeakers and

---

241   Flavell, Pg. 48

242   *Tatlin,* L.A. Zhadova , Plate 177

radios would broadcast information in every language[243]. Tatlin would design individual piloted flying suits called Letatlin to circumnavigate the tower. Due to a shortage of steel, the scale model was made in plywood. The actual tower was never built.

The Soviet Union was on a different course. The innovators of that first wave were generally marginalised, though it was one of the traits of Stalin's paranoid sadistic rule that he continually played cat and mouse with prominent figures. The wisest course of action was not to get noticed, as the Disurbanist Okhitovich did, and end up in the dystopian cities of the Gulag. There was no shortage of vision and talent under Stalin's reign, but it had grown necessarily monstrous. Mordvinov's 1934 entry to the Narkomtiazhprom contest is like a shot from *Metropolis,* while André Gide wrote of Iofan's planned Palace of the Soviets: 'The Russian worker will know why he starves in front of this 415m-high monument crowned by a statue of Lenin in stainless steel, one finger of which is 10m long.'[244]

There are other tendencies of totalitarian cities besides overblown oppressive vanity-architecture. One is the removal of home as a possible place of sanctuary, sovereignty, conscience and free thought. Shostakovich slept in the corridor with a briefcase always packed so his family wouldn't be disturbed when the Black Marias finally came for him, as they had for the

243   A development anticipated in William Bradshaw's *The Goddess of Atvatabar,* with a megaphone emitting maxims like 'Art in nature is the expression of life; in art it is life itself.'

244   Shostakovich worked on unrealised opera called *Orango* about a human-ape partly set in the building.

poets during the so-called Night of the Pencils.

Another tendency of despotic regimes is to reimagine the function of buildings. The Lubyanka with its interrogation chambers was once an insurance building. Mendelssohn's Modernist masterpiece, Columbushaus, would house the offices of Nazi 'euthanisers'. Peter Behrens Building was the headquarters of the poisoners IG Farben. Solovki prison camp was a monastery complex. S21 was a school. Facing the grotesque reinventions of football stadiums under Pinochet, churches in Rwanda, or the silent city of Drancy, it is easy to forget that for a few sadists these *were* utopias. It is again a story told in architecture. VTsIK residential complex was built for leading communists in a metropolitan, vaguely-aristocratic style. It contained, or was supposed to, innovations like an open air cinema on the roof. Except it didn't work and the project ran out of funding. Though it was occupied by party officials, it soon gained a nickname that recognised the fact so many of its occupants had been purged. It was called the House of Ghosts.

Resistance and reality would resurface. Truth was smuggled as underground *samizdat* and disguised as fiction. Alexander Zinoviev's state of Ibansk ('fuck-up land') in *The Yawning Heights* was a veiled study of Soviet society in which the old literary distancing tricks (faux naïvety and the plausible deniability of the found manuscript) proved useful:

'The Ibanskians do not live, but carry out epochmaking experiments. They carry out these experiments even when they know nothing about them and take no part in them, and even when the experiments are not taking place at all . . . The experiment was dreamt up by the Institute for the Prophylaxis of Stupid Intentions, and carried out under the supervision of the Brainwashing Laboratory . . . After historic experiments the village of Ibansk was transformed. The former school building was redesignated The Associate Department of the Institute. The lavatory was rebuilt and clad in steel and glass.'

The effect of the environment on its citizens is mercilessly skewered:

'On the far bank of the river there was a new development of apartment blocks all identical outside, but indistinguishable inside. Chatterer, who by chance had obtained a self-contained unself-contained room in an apartment in this area, used to say that everything there was so much alike that he was never wholly confident that he was in his home or that in fact he was himself and not somebody else. Member took him up on this and argued that this was a sign of progress, challenged only by madmen and enemies.'

Utopia is just around the corner, 'Just you wait' being the recurring double-edged catchphrase.

In the midst of the Soviet experiments, the idea surfaced that not just a new type of city, but a new type of person might be created — *homo urbanus*. The ideal Communist man was posited as a creature of immense productivity, like the miner Stakhanov, or the 'engineer of souls' himself, Joseph Stalin. Capitalist tycoons like Kellogg, Cadbury and Ford had all tried social engineering projects and largely failed. Architects could not resist joining in. 'All these objects of modern life create, in the long run, a modern state of mind,'[245] Le Corbusier claimed. This may well be true but there is no guarantee this is a positive development.

'The metropolitan type develops an organ protecting him against the threatening currents and discrepancies of his external environment,'[246] Simmel noticed. Cities that do not adapt to us will insist we adapt to them. For those who cannot or will not, there is only exile or alienation. In Philip K. Dick's *Clans of the Alphane Moon*, the former route is obligatory for those with mental disorders, who are shipped off to a moon colony. There they are assigned to a city to live with fellow sufferers (schizophrenics to Joan d'Arc, paranoids to Adolfville etc.). This is a pointed and extreme example, but it's worth considering how many of the common phobias are concerned with architecture and our place within it (claustrophobia, agoraphobia, acrophobia). Collective happiness seems desirable until you consider the genetically and technologically manipulated and medicated populace in Huxley's *Brave New World*[247]. We retain our humanity by retaining our flaws.

245   *Towards a New Architecture*, Pg. 276

246   *Mediating Modernity: German Literature and the 'new' Media*, 1895-1930, Stefanie Harris, Pg. 32

247   Its title taken from the island experiment of Shakepeare's *The Tempest*.

There were alternatives. Rodchenko envisaged Workers' Clubs where people could share ideas, reading face to face, inspired by the surroundings. This openness and plurality was the antithesis of what the old seminarian Stalin had planned, or for that matter his adversary Trotsky:

'What is man? He is by no means a finished or harmonious being. No, he is still a highly awkward creature. Man, as an animal, has not evolved by plan but spontaneously, and has accumulated many contradictions. The question of how to educate and regulate, of how to improve and complete the physical and spiritual construction of man, is a colossal problem which can only be conceived on the basis of Socialism. We can construct a railway across the Sahara, we can build the Eiffel Tower and talk directly with New York, but we surely cannot improve man. No, we can! To produce a new, "improved" version of man — that is the future task of Communism. And for that we first have to find out everything about man, his anatomy, his physiology, and that part of his physiology which is called his psychology. Man must look at himself and see himself as a raw material, or at best as a semi-manufactured product, and say: "At last, my dear homo sapiens, I will work on you."'[248]

It is a simultaneously inspiring and chilling desire, calling to mind Bataille's quote, 'Man would seem to represent merely an

248   *A People's Tragedy: The Russian Revolution, 1891-1924*, Orlando Figes, Pg. 447

intermediary stage [. . .] between monkey and building.'[249]

Walter Benjamin cast a cold eye on the emerging Nazis who would eventually chase him to his death on the Spanish border: 'these puppets heavy with sadness that will walk over corpses if necessary. With their rigid body armor, their slowly advancing movements, and the blindness of their actions, they embody the human fusion of insect and tank.'[250]

Epstein's sculpture, *Rock Drill*, evokes such a terrifying creature, even though it is incomplete. The finished version would have drilled through the gallery's floor and escaped.

249   Quoted on Pg. 261 *Architecture, Animal, Human: The Asymmetrical Condition*, Catherine T. Ingraham

250   From Benjamin's essay on Left-Wing Melancholy (Linkc Melancholic. Zu Erich Kastners ncuem Gcdichtbuch), *Die Gesellschaft* 8, no. i

Releasing the Golem

Dystopias arrive as long-needed solutions. We forget what came before. 'Why, though, did we need a Mahoganny?' Brecht asked of his planned city. 'Because this world is a foul one.'[251] Looking around at humanity, ourselves included, transcending the human race might not be a bad idea. Robots began in the modern age with a hint of romance, as with Idelson's marionettes for the Futurist play *The Anguish of the Machines*. In Schlemmer's *Triadisches Ballett* (for the Bauhaus), the humanoids resemble planets and spinning tops, 'pieces on a metaphysical board without personality or virtuosity. Movements resembled fluid geometrics.'[252] The view of robots as derisory functionaries (the word comes from the Czech for 'serf') or uncanny eeriness (from legends of changelings and death-foretelling doppelgängers) disguises the fact that they could be liberating.

Robots have partly evolved from the Jewish idea of the Golem, the animated clay figures (activated by placing the secret name of god in their mouths) who defended the ghetto against pogroms and occasionally rampaged out of control. Even just in terms of saving us time and effort, a release from servitude, they could serve a heroic purpose. The perpetual trope that they would fret over having or not having a soul is to make the dangerous presumption that humans have souls. 'Who needs a soul in times that keep going mechanically?' Raoul Hausmann

---

251   *Rise and Fall of the City of Mahagonny* (1930)

252   *Four Centuries of Ballet: Fifty Masterworks*, Lincoln Kirstei, Pg. 214

wrote about his *Mechanical Head* sculpture. If consciousness is the result of electrical signals sent to the brain then perhaps we are the brain in the vat that the Cartesians suggested. If our behaviours, thoughts and decisions are the result of infinitesimal processes and formulas, biological algorithms, as cybernetics suggests, perhaps we are already advanced robots; perhaps the singularity has already occurred and we are merely waiting for the robots to catch up with us, as Samuel Butler suggested with his AI machines in *Erewhon*. What we really fear is that they will be like us. 'That was the danger Samuel Butler jestingly prophesied in *Erewhon*,' Lewis Mumford pointed out, 'that the human being might become a means whereby the machine perpetuated itself and extended its dominion.'[253] It is not their differences, but their similarities which unnerve.

Perhaps our fear is that we will become the robots, a latent fear and guilt over the centuries when civilisations were founded on slavery, both literal and domestic. It is no accident that the first wave of robot rebellion works coincided with renewed movements for female, workers' and African-American rights, and Third World national liberation movements (in the scathing critique of reality that is *R.U.R.*, the robots are senselessly divided by nationality, a lack of solidarity that curses the underdogs even now). The fear was that they would demand justice for their treatment, a settling of debts. In the cities of the afterlife, perhaps there would be karma. When Gulliver visits Glubbdubdrib he finds 'the governor and his family are served

253   *Technics and Civilisation* (1934), Chapter 6, Section 9.

and attended by domestics of a kind somewhat unusual. By his skill in necromancy he has a power of calling whom he pleases from the dead, and commanding their service for twenty-four hours.'

In Ian McDonald's *Terminal Cafe*, unfortunate returnees are forced to work slavishly in Necroville to pay off resurrection bills, suggesting those being cryogenically-frozen (legend has it Walt Disney among them) are far too trusting of the future.

We might do well to fear the drift towards the robotic, but also to recognise why. To elitists like T.S. Eliot, a disdain for commuter drones, comparable to the purgatorial dead, distinguished *he* as different from *they* (ignoring the diversity of the crowd and even the beauty of regularity in, for example, Cyril Power's transport posters). The robot is always the other[254]. Monsters and grotesques have the same misanthropic origin. The places where they occur are always the places we don't reside; the Brutalist architecture in Chris Cunningham's video for Aphex Twin's 'Come to Daddy' gives birth, with too much order leading to disorder, to horrors, like a landlocked concrete *Island of Dr Moreau*. They are horrific so we, the transfixed voyeurs, are not. Yet there is no they and we.

What we should fear is that the robot is the self, that hell is not other people but ourselves. When Mary Shelley wrote, 'I saw the hideous phantasm of a man stretched out, and then, on the working of some powerful engine, show signs of life, and stir with an uneasy, half vital motion . . . it became a thing such

254   Grosz's Republican Automatons for example.

as even Dante could not have conceived'[255], she was writing essentially of birth. Yet when the upgrade to humanity comes, it will not resemble a nightmare, at least not initially. We will want it. It may only be available to the rich, though there will be hacks, counterfeits and basic editions. In David R. Bunch's *Moderan*, cybernetically-enhanced humans look down on those who had remained flesh as the 'clutter-people'. The post-human will be something to aspire to and, like all Faustian pacts, it will be a gamble, which some will lose. The question is far beyond whether to opt in or out. It is already happening.

255   *Frankenstein*, Pg. 46

The Turk

In the 1780s a curious construction was toured around the courts of Europe — a wooden and ivory cabinet with an Ottoman automaton and a chessboard on its lid. The robot played a succession of challengers, including Empress Maria Theresa of Austria, Benjamin Franklin and Napoleon. Its powers were attributed to scientific invention and devilry alike. It was, in fact, operated by a legless Russian veteran hidden in a covert cabinet behind the clockwork.

Most cities hide their mechanics, tubes and sewers underground or within walls. When a building like the Centre Pompidou dared to show its functioning parts on the outside, it was treated initially as an obscenity, as if it had peeled off its skin. So too cities hide their poor and unwanted (but not unneeded) from business and tourism, pushing slums out to the periphery or downwards into cavernous depths. Anti-homeless grills are fixed to hot air vents, spikes to flat surfaces. With housing bubbles pricing out the young, the result is pristine cities in which those who run the city cannot afford to live there. It is also a highly sought-after model, closer to The Turk than utopia. Slums remain not simply as a curse, but as a dumping ground, in the mode of Toxitown in Ryu Murakami's *Coin Locker Babies*: 'an akusho, an "evil place" designed to siphon off the dangerous contagions of the city: sexuality, criminality, deviance, in a word, dfference.'[1]

The Situationists called the veil pulled over our eyest the Spectacle, but it has had many names and incarnations. It is there partly in Plato's Cave and the miners breaking out of the self-contained cavity in Barrington Bayley's *Me and My Anthronoscope*. It is in the secret room locked by Bluebeard, full of bodies rather than riches. It is the immortal line, 'Pay no attention to the man behind the curtain' in *The Wizard of Oz*. It is the intrepid adventurer in the *Flammarion Engraving* crawling under the veil of the firmament to gaze at what lies beyond. It is there in Marx seeing the mechanics of capitalism, while others later would break through the spectacle of Marxism. To Freud, Derrida, Nietzsche and Debord, we must add Rowdy Roddy Piper, who saw through it all with the help of vision-correcting spectacles in John Carpenter's *They Live*, seeing the truth behind things: 'Consume', 'Conform', 'Submit'. In Frederick Pohl's *The Tunnel Under the World*, a working stiff starts noticing things are amiss in his native Tylertown when the ads start going strange:

1   *Ōe and Beyond: Fiction in Contemporary Japan*, Stephen Snyder, J. Philip Gabriel, Pg. 210

'Feckle, Feckle, Feckle, Feckle, Feckle, Feckle, Feckle, Feckle. Cheap freezers ruin your food. You'll get sick and throw up. You'll get sick and die. Buy a Feckle, Feckle, Feckle, Feckle!'[2]

It is a crack in the ice that spreads until it all begins to sink. '"Poor little Burckhardt," crooned the loudspeaker . . . "It must have been quite a shock for you to find out you were living in a town built on a table top."'

Many are the great cities, both imaginary and real, built on deceptions. In Claire Kenin's *La Mer Mysterieuse*, a fisherman chances upon the fabled submarine city of riches Belesbat, in the storm-lashed Bay of Biscay. Greeted with opulent feasts and palatial splendour, he eventually feigns exhaustion and finds a passageway into a chamber of corpses. The paradise city is predicated on the existence of a boneyard. Ursula K. Le Guin's *The Ones Who Walk Away* examines the price that might be paid to maintain grandeur; where a screaming child sits in a lightless dungeon, covered in excrement, abused and neglected. 'If the child were brought up into the sunlight out of that vile place, if it were cleaned and fed and comforted, that would be a good thing indeed; but if it were done, in that day and hour all the prosperity and beauty and delight of Omelas would wither and be destroyed. Those are the terms.'[3]

We can distance the story as a utilitarian thought experiment or acknowledge that it has been some time since humans were shelved as cargo in the stinking confines of slaveships, except

2   *The Golden Age of Science Fiction*, Kingsley Amis, Pg. 80

3   *The Broadview Anthology of Short Fiction*, Second Edition, Pg. 229

'there is scarcely anything in daily consumption, a child's toy, a garment, a tropical fruit, a piece of jewellery, uncontaminated by the suffering of people whose existence is unknown to us.'[4] We bury it well. Those are the terms and we largely accept them.

The binary absolves us and has done so at least since Aristotle. All sins are hoisted on the Other, a role that requires reappointment periodically. They are the dystopia so we *must* be the utopia. It can be a mutually beneficial relationship for those it benefits. 'Too many corpses strew the paths of individualism and collectivism,' Vannheim writes, 'Two apparently contrary rationalities cloak an identical gangsterism, an identical oppression of the isolated man. The hand which smothered Lautréamont returned to strangle Sergei Esenin; one died in the lodging house of his landlord Jules-Francois Dupuis, the other hanged himself in a nationalised hotel.'[5]

In Roberto Bolaño's *By Night In Chile*, a group of intellectuals are having a cocktail party in a mansion when one of them gets lost and finds his way into a basement where a tortured man is strapped to a metal bed-frame. He looks at the scene then gently closes the door behind him and says nothing. It's a neat parable of the barbarities of the US and UK-backed Pinochet regime and the complicity therein. Except it is no parable at all, but an account of a real event which occurred at the residence of the CIA operative Michael Townley and his wife Mariana Callejas. The real revelation is not that utopias are dystopias as is often

4   *Pauperland: Poverty and the Poor in Britain*, Jeremy Seabrook. Pg. 204

5   *The Revolution of Everyday Life*, Vannheim, Pg. 23

pointed out, but that dystopias are utopias for some. There are profiteers, people with names, addresses and titles.

It is worth considering if the operators and the beneficiaries of the spectacle understand it; whether it is implicit or overt. On rare occasions, the truth will seep through, even rarer still an admission. The socialist millionaire entrepreneur and razor magnate, King Camp Gillette, designed a curious and admirably-deluded Metropolis. Built on the Niagara Falls (in order to harness the hydroelectric potential), it consisted of hexagonal tower-block honeycombs made out of porcelain. In his book *The Human Drift*, Gillette envisaged 'a vast machine', a 'mighty brain', a waterfall-powered 'fairyland', a city of a hundred million rooms:

'Can you imagine the endless beauty of a conception like this — a city with its thirty six thousand buildings each a perfectly distinct and complete design, with a continuous and perfectly finished facade from every point of view, each building and avenue surrounded and bordered by an ever-changing beauty in flowers and foliage? There would be in this city of sixty million souls, fifteen thousand miles of main avenues, every foot of which would be a continuous change of beauty.'[6]

Gillette recognised the danger of imposed uniformity and so he encouraged each block to be artistically independent. Controversially for a successful capitalist, Gillette's shops would

6   *The Human Drift*, Pg. 97

have no prices: 'no system can ever be a perfect system, and free from incentive for crime, until money and all representative value of material is swept from the face of the earth.' Here Gillette lets us glimpse through the veil and incorporates this revelation into his city where transparent pavements would allow inhabitants to see those who were working to their benefit. All citizens would have stocks in the project, giving incentives to make it work. 'Failure means anarchy. Success freedom.'

The Pit and the Pendulum

The control of space and those within it is crucial to dystopias. The manual for tyranny is essentially a guide to the manipulation of architecture. It requires inclusion and exclusion, and the control of physical space. The extent varies dramatically, incorporating ghettos, prisons, dungeons, kettling, exile, prohibited areas, curfews, walls and gates but the intention is the same, to varying degrees. 'The rhythm of masses,' Ilya Golosov wrote, 'that is where compositional innovation in architecture finds its start.'[7] It finds its end in dictatorial control, in the halting and manipulation of the masses, in authority that demands popular respect and fear, and yet is innately anti-social. This is the paradox that makes tyrannies so maddening, and ultimately so vulnerable.

These tendencies are found most explicitly in the Gothic city. Here a conspiratorial, if often-accurate, view of authority is rendered in architecture[8]. With its hidden chambers and passageways, torture chambers and crypts, this is the mechanics of power represented in stone. It reflects our fears of falling victim to the unseen dominant forces, and our fantasies of wielding such powers, to be party or prey to the malevolent forces that know the maps, the passwords, the secret levers

7   Cited in *Pioneers*, Pg. 563

8   The association of houses with power structures, often dynastic, has a long and varied history including *The Fall of the House of Usher*, *Kidnapped*, *Bleak House*'s evisceration of the legal system with its mad woman in the attic, *A Doll's House* and *The Cherry Orchard* as well as the entire Irish sub-genre of the 'Big House' novel.

and passage-concealing bookshelves. We would be different of course, we tell ourselves, such power would not corrupt us. Perhaps we could be benevolent, if moved by guilt, like Mister X in Dean Motter's Radiant City, a speedfreak Le Corbusier with (having designed the city) access all areas. X is an anti-architect come to mend the broken machine for living in, that is further warping the broken human machines within it. The city never sleeps and neither does its builder and patron saint, strung out on amphetamines. X is the guilty conscience of every architect, of all who have the misfortune of watching their dreams come true.

It is no accident that the rise in Gothic literature came with the rise of imperialism and apt that the British Houses of Parliament are matchstick gothic. In Gothic literature, there is a fear and a fascination, sometimes sexual, with the exotic, that acts as a distancing device and also a tacit admission of culpability of what 'civilisation' was doing to the 'savages'. Malevolence is tied up in grandiose buildings, while esteemed lords are revealed as sordid torturers. Even when order is restored or sadism shown to be a perverted aberration, there is still a sense of the backlash that is inevitably coming, that Dracula is relocating to London, that Moriarty is spreading networks through the city, that Fantômas is taking to the rooftops. The Gothic was the troubled subconscious of a civilisation in denial and that knew the game would soon be up.

Though unfashionable, this sense is still found in the modern age. It is there in the castle to which Josef K[9] is denied access yet is obliged to visit. It is there in the squirming fathomless uncertainties of Lovecraft, and it finds its way into the dark surreal films of David Lynch, where other worlds intrude upon the kitsch and the clichéd to suggest that power lies mysteriously and ominously elsewhere. It is also there wherever architecture is actually manipulated to oppress; the use of stress positions against walls, incarceration in tiny rooms where it is impossible to stand or sit, the lightless dungeons replaced by hi-tech super-prisons where the lights never go out.

9   Jan Kaplicky gave Josef K his own bulbous shell of a home to scuttle away from
      the claustrophobia of family, an ambiguous act as his son is called Josef K.

The Gothic Trojan Horse

In a dank alleyway, far beneath the metropolitan skyscrapers, there exists a temporal loop. A rich couple, having taken an ill-advised shortcut from the theatre to reality, are shot dead over and over, each time in slightly different variations but always with the same outcome. Given all that will follow, the perpetrator is a curiously featureless and uncharismatic small-time crook named Joe Chill, but maybe that's the point; he's a cipher and an Everyman. A little boy witnesses his parents' murders and is shocked into a vortex of vengeance and fantasy. The imported stately elegance of Wayne Manor is the ego; the bat-cave beneath is the id. Whatever victories Wayne achieves, he will always start again, in the most famous case of arrested development, as the boy suddenly alone in the alleyway. He is aware of this. He visits his hallucinatory adversaries in an asylum, trying to dispel childhood trauma by re-enacting it, but the past and the dead cannot be resurrected and all exorcisms are temporary. He makes a second home in the shadows, mapping and mastering the blindspots of the city, the empty factories, the unnamed passageways, the spaces behind the official city that hide its functions and its rot. He does all this in order to prevent what has already happened.

Batman's Gotham City, it is often said, should be seen as the dark corrupt side to Superman's squeaky-clean Metropolis. Yet it is arguable that Metropolis is more shrouded and Gotham more naïve, calling for redemption by signalling to a costumed vigilante-billionaire[10]. Metropolis is the way modern dystopias will come; bright and shiny in the daylight, full of promises, wireless and witless. The Just City hides more secrets than the Fallen City. Peel back even the hegemonic figure of Superman[11] and a much more interesting figure emerges, an alien immigrant created as a subversion of the Nazi perversion of the Übermensch by two New York Jews, and one minute away from being an All-Soviet hero of Communism[12].

Ostensibly Gotham *is* New York; more precisely, according to Dennis O'Neil, 'Manhattan below Fourteenth Street at eleven minutes past midnight on the coldest night in November.'[13] Being an arcane nickname for New York, Gotham retains the atmosphere of an earlier incarnation of the real-life metropolis, conjuring up soot, smog, gaslight and stone in an age of steel and glass skyscrapers. Whereas Manhattan was a Dutch colony bought from the native population for a handful of coloured beads, Gotham was a Norwegian outpost. Its architecture is Gothic, both the medieval towers of Prague and the later revivalist versions (with hints of Batman as a protective golem or a marauding demonic spirit like Spring-Heeled Jack) fed through Modernism.

10   The violent, psychologically-damaged pitiable Roscharch in Alan Moore and
        Dave Gibbons' *Watchmen* is much closer to reality, though there is something of
        the 'concealed tyranny' of the De Medici's to the philanthropy of Wayne.

11   The imbecilic light-relief character of Bizarro, an inverted Superman, is
        considerably more endearing while the messianic Silver Surfer is more
        mysterious.

12   Mark Millar's *Red Son*.

13   *Human Geography: A Concise Introduction*, Mark Boyle, Pg. 147

Though Gotham was designed in the comics by the mysterious, long-since vanished, architect Cyrus Pinkney, and it has been the subject to many interpretations[14], the largest influences by far were the sublime monolith cities of Hugh Ferriss, as well as portrayals of New York by artists such as Louis Lozowick, Rudolf Cronau, Howard Cook and Christopher Nevinson. At the time Gotham was conceived, it was finally possible to paint night scenes and indeed light up the exterior of buildings with electric lights. Gotham is thus an extended nocturne of skyscrapers, filled with menacing sleeping giants. The chiaroscuro use of light and shadow radiated through Gotham's gothic vaults, its jagged Expressionist arches, its Art Deco symmetries and polygons[15]. The style of future Gothic was one undertaken contemporaneously in the Soviet Union by the architect Yakfov Chernikhov. Though a degree of satire was permitted in comics like *Krokodil*, such a vision would have been too haunting and perhaps identifiable for the Russian comic book's Tintin-esque characters to inhabit.

For all its man-made sense of doom, there is something oddly organic about Gotham and in the way Batman (and indeed Spiderman in his much more literal New York, albeit with touches of Toronto) moves within it. Its spires, parapets and gargoyles are like mountain crags and overhangs that are

---

14   Christopher Nolan modelled his version on Van der Rohe, the 60s show on the early comics via Pop Art.

15   Basin City in Frank Miller's *Sin City* as well as the New York of *Daredevil* and *The Punisher* are heavily inspired, whilst ramping up the noir and Manichean aspects.

ideal to perch on and survey the canyon-streets far below. Form follows function — a city of glass shards and formalist towers would be problematic and boring, Batman sliding to his death within three frames. This chimes with real-life. 'It seems like a city built on precipices, a perilous city,' Chesterton wrote of Edinburgh, a model for Gotham. 'Great roads rush down-hill like rivers in spate. Great buildings rush up like rockets.'[16]

Georgia O'Keeffe painted the New York streets in the same way, their facades blank, their stature mountainous. This was the city as an inhabited wilderness. When George Bellows painted a New York neighbourhood, he called the occupants and the painting *The Cliff-Dwellers*.

Gotham, we are told, has finite bounds. It is located in present-day New Jersey, a stone's throw from Metropolis ('the Big Apricot') in New York State. There is a paradoxical sense, enveloped in the perpetual space of night, that Gotham is somehow infinite and yet enclosing. There is no escape, even for those breaking out of the sprawling Arkham Asylum, from a city of rooftops that seem to extend forever. The combination of claustrophobia and agoraphobia, the sense of boundless constriction, comes straight from the etchings of Piranesi. Gotham convinces because it allows ancient dark myths, legends, actual events already in our heads (the puritan witch-trials for example), and American folklore, into a modern world. The name Arkham is as significant as Gotham in this sense, being an echo of Lovecraft's city of dread:

16   *Precipitous City*, Trevor Royle, Pg. 175

'What lay behind our joint love of shadows and marvels was, no doubt, the ancient, mouldering, and subtly fearsome town in which we live — witch-cursed, legend-haunted Arkham, whose huddled, sagging gambrel roofs and crumbling Georgian balustrades brood out the centuries beside the darkly muttering Miskatonic.'[17] His 'tall black towers of Dylath-Leen . . . built mostly of basalt' have relocated here.

Batman is a critique of failed urban planning and empathy. Alleyways have dead-ends as traps for the unwary. Abandoned buildings are warrens for criminals. A dark sanctimonious fear of rookeries and today's housing estates, projects and slums as inhuman breeding grounds, prevails. Hints of the occult abound. It is cast in a Faustian light a minute before midnight. The screenplay to Tim Burton's first adaptation introduced Gotham as if 'Hell [had] erupted through the pavement and built a city'[18].

Thomas Nashe claimed the night was filled with demons and Batman faces a cast of them, each with their own particular traits and morals to impart. The Joker may be Satan to the other diabolical saints but it is Doctor Gotham who intrigues historically, a warlock sacrificed in the times of the pilgrims, a collective act of killing for which the city that bears his name has yet to pay penance.

Gotham does however encourage a reimagining of cities. For

---

17   *The Call of Cthulhu and Other Weird Tales*, H. P Lovecraft, Pg. 521

18   Sam Hamm

one thing, Batman reminds us to look up and remember that the city is a sea of rooftops, an entire forgotten level. In Gotham, we find echoes of unbuilt New Yorks; the ghost of Louis Biedermann's wrought-iron futurism ('New York City as it will be in 1999') and Raymond Hood's 'Proposal for Manhattan 1950.'[19] If Piranesi showed us that the industrial age of reason had a nightmare side, Ferriss showed us that even nightmares have reason and style. Ferriss superficially drafted his visions of the city to demonstrate that setbacks would be needed in skyscraper building unless the city was to be bathed in permanent darkness. His stunning renderings of architectural colossi were combined with his writings in *The Metropolis of Tomorrow*, that now read like baleful prophecy: 'Going down into the streets of a modern city must seem — to the newcomer, at least — a little like Dante's descent into Hades. Certainly so unacclimated a visitor would find, in the dense atmosphere, in the kaleidoscopic sights, the confused noise and the complex physical contacts, something very reminiscent of the lower realms.'[20]

A corrupt and venal city, like Gotham, will change those who live there: 'The character of the architectural forms and spaces which all people habitually encounter are powerful agencies in determining the nature of their thoughts, their emotions and their actions, however unconscious of this they may be.'

Ferriss's monochrome, dramatically-lit architecture seems more atmospheric sarcophagi than habitable spaces. He reiterates

19   *The New York World,* December 30th, 1900

20   Pg. 18

the view of the metropolis as an unnatural natural phenomenon in his book's frontispiece where buildings resemble a canyon with a waterfall. The stone buildings came from mountains and may morph back into them one day. This reflects an acute sense of where the city stands in relation to time, but also environment. All it takes is a solar eclipse and Dubai turns full-blown Ferriss. Likewise for New York in sleet or Tokyo in mist. Cities may attempt to exorcise the natural world but it always re-enters.

If there is a tangible devastation to Ferriss's plans, it is his utopian hope that palaces and towers dedicated to art, philosophy and learning would be built has not occurred on the scale he envisaged. The usurping of the humanities and even science by business, and the colonisation of skylines by finance, would have appalled him. 'Are we to imagine that this city is populated by human beings who value emotion and mind equally with the senses, and have therefore disposed their art, science and business centers in such a way that all three would participate equally in the government of the city?'[21] There is little doubt as to which real city Ferriss was projecting his hopes and fears onto. He looks at New York in the morning mist and wonders, 'to an imaginative spectator, it might seem that he is perched in some elevated stage box to witness some gigantic spectacle, some cyclopean drama of forms; and that the curtain has not yet risen . . . And to one who had not been in the audience before — to some visitor from another land or another age — there could not fail to be at least a moment of wonder.

21   Pg. 140

What apocalypse is about to be revealed?'[22]

The new cyclopean scale of modern cities fascinated Ferriss and he became its Ansel Adams. He courted its devilish side — where, after all, are the windows or the populace in his cityscapes? 'Are those tiny specks the actual intelligences of the situation, and this towered mass something which, as it were, those ants have marvellously excreted? Or are these masses of steel and glass the embodiment of some blind and mechanical force that has imposed itself, as though from without, on a helpless humanity?'[23]

For all his grandeur and flirting with autocratic malice, Ferriss is on the side of the ants — 'the human being is the Principal'. He pushed buildings back to allow light and air to reach the depths. He carved a grand arch through a skyscraper as a thoroughfare. For all his love of shadows, he is concerned about those cast by aerial walkways (like Dr. John A. Harriss's New York Skyscraper Highway, 1930). Borrowing from Despradelle's unbuilt Beacon of Progress, he resurrects the pyramid or obelisk to aid the proliferation of light and give a sense of depth, adding ziggurats for restaurants and theatres. On the rooftops he imagines, not crazed chiropteran sentinels in lycra and Kevlar but 'public out-of-door gatherings . . . a masked ball atop some Fine Arts building, companioned by another roof-top carnival across the avenue.' These occur in Gotham, almost always as the prelude to a hijacking or a massacre. Gotham is Ferriss gone wrong, or

22   Pg. 15

23   Pg. 16

perhaps Ferriss gone according to plan. It looms in our minds much stronger than the Metropolis of Superman for the same reason that Dante's Inferno outshines Paradiso. There are times when darkness is stronger than light.

The voyeurism only satisfies when it remains in fiction. The designer Anton Furst incorporated Ferriss's style and atmosphere into his version of Gotham for Tim Burton's film adaptation. 'We imagined what New York City might have become without a planning commission,' Furst told *Time Magazine* in 1989, 'A city run by crime, with a riot of architectural styles. An essay in ugliness. As if hell erupted through the pavement and kept on going.'

Years later, struggling with depression and addiction and waiting to be admitted to hospital, Furst excused himself to friends, made his way to the top of an eighth floor building and stepped off, into the real unknown.

Neo-Neanderthals

If the aim of authority is to conquer territory then the inner space of the human mind poses a challenge. Given that our thoughts (and private lives) are largely secret, attempts to control must either manipulate these thoughts or identify them through observance. In earlier ages, this was done through the primacy of confession. 'Give me six lines written by the most honest man in the world,' Cardinal Richelieu is supposed to have said, 'and I will find enough in them to hang him.'[24] With the thankful erosion of deference, actions as much as words are studied for signs of deviancy. With CCTV and the mass surveillance of internet usage, we are in the true age of the panopticon[25]. Even ignoring the snake-oil mantra of Smart Cities, it is clear that the interaction between cyberspace and actual urban space is going to merge further and further. It will one day be possible to traverse actual cities using augmented realities, to physically live in digitally manipulated cities of our choosing. We will be able to walk down the street with every sight and sound annotated if we wish, with every surface decorated as we wish. Disappointed that Tatlin's Tower or Gaudí's Hotel Attraction was never built? Fear not, it will appear as real as any other on the horizon if you desire. The sky will be an interactive cinema screen. This will not be as vast a leap as it seems but an incremental process and one that gets to the essence that cities

24   *Thunder in the Heavens*, James Lansdale Hodson, Pg. 61

25   Standard farewell for citizens in *The Prisoner* is the prophetic 'Be seeing you'.

are networks of communications into which we are already weaved:

'Cyberspace. A consensual hallucination experienced daily by billions of legitimate operators, in every nation, by children being taught mathematic concepts . . . A graphic representation of data abstracted from the banks of every computer in the human system. Unthinkable complexity. Lines of light ranged in the nonspace of the mind, clusters and constellations of data. Like city lights, receding.'[26]

Whether this is the escape from Plato's Cave or a retreat back into it remains to be seen. The escape from one cave might just lead to another larger one, within an endless sequence. The simulacrum is already in place; cyberspace is just a continuation, sometimes thrilling and expansive, sometimes constrictive. 'The simulacrum is never that which conceals the truth,' Baudrillard asserted, 'it is the truth which conceals that there is none. The simulacrum is true'[27]. The land has become Borges's tattered map and, through augmented reality, nanotechnology, genetic and synthetic modification, we might well join it. It may well always have been like this — 'Animals have no unconscious, because they have a territory. Men have only had an unconscious since they lost a territory'[28] — but just more so now. Debates on

26   *Neuromancer*, William Gibson, Pg. 67
27   *Simulacra and Simulation*, Pg. 166
28   *Simulacra and Simulation*, Pg. 139

what is real are as cyclical as the doubt itself. Philip K. Dick was stuck in such a loop:

'EYE, JOINT, 3 STIGMATA, UBIK & MAZE are the same novel written over and over again. The characters are all out cold and lying around together on the floor, mass hallucinating a world. Why have I written this up at least five times? Because — as I discovered in 3-74 when I experienced anamnesis, remembered I'm really an apostoic xtian, & saw ancient Rome — This is our condition: we're mass-hallucinating this 1970s world.'[29]

Perception *is* a simulacrum and it need not even be anything as extravagant as tripping in the 1970s:

'One walks through the city — whether it is New York, Rome, London or Paris, who cares; one sees lights upstairs, a ceiling shadows, some objects; but as one mentally fills in the rest and imagines a society of unexampled brilliance from which one is fatally excluded, one does not feel exactly deprived. For, in this curious commerce between the visible and the undisclosed, we are well aware that we too can erect our own private proscenium and, by turning on our own lights, augment the general hallucination which, however absurd it may be, is never other than stimulating.'[30]

29   *In Pursuit of Valis: Selections from the Exegesis*, Pg. 177

30   *Collage City*, Colin Rowe and Fred Koetter, Pg. 66

There will be tyrannies in merging the virtual and the real, as predicted by William Gibson, baptist of cyberspace: 'On the Sony, a two-dimensional space war faded behind a forest of mathematically generated ferns, demonstrating the spatial possibilities of logarithmic spirals: cold blue military footage burned through, lab animals wired into test systems, helmets feeding into fire control circuits of tanks and war planes.'[31]

These will come as benefits, like the Internet of Things; everything will be linked, inefficiency reduced, convenience increased, everything watching everything always. With future advances in 3D printing, the virtual and the physical might become indistinguishable: 'The ultimate display would be a room within which the computer can control the existence of matter. A chair displayed in such a room would be good enough to sit in. Handcuffs displayed in such a room would be confining , and a bullet displayed in such a room would be fatal. With appropriate programming such a display could literally be the Wonderland in which Alice walked.'[32]

In a future where humanity has transcended its bounds, for good or for ill, by incorporation with technology, those cryogenically-frozen hopefuls would appear like museum pieces, ancient mummies or circus freaks. Even in such a world, the old battles would likely reign. In Greg Egan's *Permutation City*, minds are uploadable. The rich and powerful can afford

31   William Gibson quoted Pg. 144, *Cyberia: Life in the Trenches of Hyperspace*, Douglas Rushkoff

32   *Proceedings of the International Federation of Information Processing Congress 1965*, Ivan Sutherland, Pg. 506

superior technology and thus superior consciousness. The poor are herded in virtual slums with their consciousness as viable property. In the computer game *Remember Me*, the company Memorise rules over the inhabitants of Neo-Paris by having access to their uploaded memories (a timely warning about the gatekeepers of social networking). The image of the fortress arises not just physically but mentally, as all totalitarianism tries to get inside the mind, even if initially benevolently. Knowledge is power and absolute knowledge corrupts.

Refuges and resistances will always be established, overtly and implicitly in the oversights and inefficiencies. 'They found their paradise, a "pirate's paradise," on the jumbled border of a low-security academic grid,' Gibson wrote, 'At first glance it resembled the kind of graffiti student operators sometimes left at the junctions of grid lines, faint glyphs of colored light that shimmered against the confused outlines of a dozen arts faculties.'[33]

It is, as with all human endeavours, a battlefield for and against ourselves. The question is whether escape will be an option, or if exile will be the last resort: 'Diaspar had been planned as an entity; it was a single mighty machine. Yet though its outward appearance was almost overwhelming in its complexity, it merely hinted at the hidden marvels of technology without which all these great buildings would be lifeless sepulchers. Alvin stared out toward the limits of his world . . . There was nothing beyond them — nothing at all except the aching

33   *Neuromancer*, Pg. 81

emptiness of the desert in which a man would soon go mad. Then why did that emptiness call to him, as it called to no one else whom he had ever met?'[34]

The All-Seeing I

There have long been warnings that a fledgling dystopia of sight would come to pass. Charms to deflect the gaze of the evil eye are found in many cultures, from paintings on Venetian gondolas to nazar amulets hung around the neck in Arabia[35]. In Celtic mythology, one of the chief villains is Balor of the Evil Eye, who is eventually defeated when a stone is slung into his pupil[36]. In Greek mythology, the gaze is not a passive benevolent act, but one loaded with sinister intent, from the man-eating Cyclops to the petrifying stare of Medusa. It is there too in Shakespeare; the eyes and spying and watching in the dystopian prison-city of Elsinore[37]. A student of these tales, J. R.R. Tolkein encapsulated the malevolence of Sauron in a giant flaming eye scouring the land. If its ancient connotations are no accident, neither are its modern ones, with its occasional resemblance to spotlights and watchtowers. It is worth remembering that the book was written in the depths of the war against the Third Reich. Sauron's accomplice Saruman extends his power through the use of gyres, pools that see into far-off places and times. To see is to dominate. This is what caused the towers[38] originally to rise, as defensive positions.

Writers in modern times have expanded upon the

35 In architecture, gargoyles and bell-ringing were used in various times and cultures to ward away the menace of the malevolent gaze.

36 'Lift up my eyelid so that I may see this chatterer' being one of his last words.

37 Based on the real Helsingør.

38 Like Liaodi Pagoda, for example.

superstitious but justified fear of being watched. It is there in Philip K. Dick's *Eye in the Sky* and The Tower of a Thousand Eyes in the *Biggles* story 'The World Menders'. It is there in the blazing red Cyclops eye of HAL. In his remarkable, dystopian *We*, Zamyatin presents a city of glass[39] where privacy has been abolished and with it liberty. 'True literature can only exist when it is created,' Zamyatin warned, 'not by diligent and reliable officials, but by madmen, hermits, heretics, dreamers, rebels and sceptics.'[40]

In an age of officials, state and corporate, certain writing might again become a radical act and its creators are among the men and women to be watched closely. We attribute these concerns to other places. In the race to the dystopian bottom, we reassure ourselves we are fine — there are much worse places of course, there nearly always are. Yet consider the simple but resonating assertion that seeps through our own body-politic and must always be fought against: 'the only means of ridding man of crime is ridding him of freedom.'[41]

Jeremy Bentham developed his Panopticon in the spirit of utilitarianism, not the greatest happiness for the greatest number but the greatest utility towards the greatest number. From a central raised platform, one jailor could potentially watch every prisoner without being seen. Like the raised watchman in the settlement of El-Lahun, Egypt, it would be ostensibly for

39   Taking its lead from the arctic geothermal Crystalopolis in Alphonse Brown's *Une Ville de Verre (A City Of Glass)* (1890-91).

40   From the essay 'I am Afraid' (1921)

41   *We*, Pg. 35

protection but who, as the saying goes, watches the watchmen? Orwell adapted and updated this fearful transparency to the televisual age with his telescreens and memory holes. He encouraged a degree of illusion of privacy whilst maintaining the anxiety-ridden possibility of being watched at any given time. In such a place, individual sovereignty shrinks, in terms of space, to a small alcove accidentally out of sight of the telescreen. The gaze will be intrinsic to how we are supposed to live. It will be refracted and bent like light through a prism. In the past, brute force and schadenfreude was used to control the gaze, to focus it on stocks, gibbets, gallows, lingchi and pikes, the dead strewn on the walls of Gilead. Tomorrow it will be much less crude, but at least as effective.

In Defence of Caliban

Dystopias are partly a lesson in the dangers of getting what we want, even if that is happiness. In a city of enforced glee, the gloomy man is crucial as the only advocate of freedom. 'Community, identity, stability.' All supposedly noble aims. This is the motto of *Brave New World*. Aldous Huxley is a tricky half-blind prophet; an intolerable snob and sometimes visionary because of his elitism. Belonging to a relatively rarefied stratum of society, Huxley followed the threads he saw in Oxford and beyond to their logical and horrendous conclusions. His is an enlightened technocratic hell, where the populace has been pleasured, via the drug Soma, television and meaningless sex, and refined genetically and psychologically into a state of a perfected apathetic banality where no real pleasure can be found[42]. Citizens live amidst a spreading mass of 'vitra-glass' and 'ferroconcrete' skyscrapers, leaving only isolated islands for those who wish to escape the reach of utopia, in a reversal of the traditional method. The choice is a questionable one:

'"All right then," said the savage defiantly, "I'm claiming the right to be unhappy."

"Not to mention the right to grow old and ugly and impotent; the right to have syphilis and cancer; the right to have too little to eat, the right to be lousy; the right to live in constant apprehension of what may happen tomorrow; the right to catch

42   See also James Gunn's *The Joy Makers*.

typhoid; the right to be tortured by unspeakable pains of every kind."

There was a long silence.

"I claim them all," said the Savage at last."'[43]

Huxley borrowed from Zamyatin the colonising zeal of happiness over liberty, the authorities' 'duty to force them to be happy'. In *We*, this involved lobotomisation: 'I told you, we must, everyone's imagination-everyone's imagination must be ... excised. The only answer is surgery, surgery alone ... '[44]

Happiness will come at such a price as to be a form of damnation. '"The gradual extinction of all the emotions — love, jealousy, ambition, rivalry" — Dr. Linister maintained in *The Inner House*, "made life so poor a thing that painless extinction would be the very best thing possible for the whole race. It is useless to point out, to one so prejudiced, the enormous advantage gained in securing constant tranquillity of mind."'[45]

The drug Soma, in its variety of forms, keeps the city compliant. So too does our latent knowledge that we are being watched. If you have nothing to hide, you have nothing to fear. Yet so much, in the past and future, has depended on that which is hidden.

43   Pg. 215

44   Pg. 80

45   Pg. 108

The Gaze

The road to hell is paved with good intentions. 'The conduct of our life,' Descartes asserted, 'depends entirely of our senses, and since sight is the noblest and most comprehensive of the senses, inventions which serve to increase its power are undoubtedly the most useful there can be.'[46]

We can gaze at galaxies colliding and microbes multiplying. We can also watch each other and convince ourselves that our intentions remain honourable. Measures brought in under the guise of protection are used to repress. Whistle-blowers are hounded, prosecuted and ruined for revealing simply what is true. The gaze will not permit being watched itself[47]. Just as military behaviours and hardware seep into the civilian world, so too the Panopticon escaped its prison[48]. Its techniques were adapted from criminals to focus on *potential* criminals; namely everyone but the watchers. The all-seeing-eye only wanted what we all wanted — to see everything. Our mistake was naïvely believing it only wanted to look at others or at us when we wanted it to, but the eye has no capacity to listen[49]. Its dread stare is not even particularly a fear of voyeurism but rather a fear that our thoughts could be seen; that the projection of who

---

46   *Selected Philosophical Writings,* René Descartes, Pg. 87

47   Secret trials, confidentiality agreements, reporting bans, police refusing to wear cameras etc.

48   The effect was reciprocal, with prisons now big business.

49   Andropov's Ears, built in 1983 by O. Kalandarishvili and G. Potskhishvili in Tbilisi, are a notable example of the symbolic panopticon of sound.

we seem, compared to who we know we are, that great lie of existence, would be exposed and exploited.

It began, as nightmares often do, innocently; the hermit's magic pool in C.S. Lewis's Narnia books, Cocteau's mirror in *Beauty and the Beast*. The wonders of transparency and the unveiling of secret things. It might even have begun as rebellion: the telegraph operator prying on 'squanderings and grasping . . . struggles and secrets and love-affairs and lies, she tracked and stored up against them till she had at moments, in private, a triumphant vicious feeling of mastery and ease, a sense of carrying their silly guilty secrets in her pocket, her small retentive brain, and thereby knowing so much more about them than they suspected or would care to think. There were those she would have liked to betray, to trip up, to bring down with words altered and fatal; and all through a personal hostility provoked by the lightest signs, by their accidents of tone and manner, by the particular kind of relation she always happened instantly to feel.'[50]

Soon it became vanity, with the Evil Witch's mirror in *Snow White* evolving into megalomaniacal need for control in the form of the Wicked Witch's crystal ball in the *Wizard of Oz*[51].

'There are eyes everywhere,' Paul Virilo and Louise Wilson discussed. 'No blind spot left. What shall we dream of when everything becomes visible? We'll dream of being blind.'[52]

It is no accident that Zamyatin's City of Glass continually

---

50   *In the Cage*, Henry James

51   The emphasis of the female in these accounts is vastly unrepresentative and telling of the men who created these visions.

52   *Digital Delirium*, Pg. 47

encroaches on our skylines. 'The tricks with mirrors and other real materials,' Jameson writes in *Utopia's Ghost*, 'performed by corporate globalisation produce the illusion that their materiality is illusory, unreal, dematerialised . . . describes what a new stage in commodity fetishism might actually look like: the inability simply to look at something directly, rather than attempt to see through it.'[53]

The glass city certainly sparkles even when it appears wondrously sinister, like Van der Rohe's Friedrichstrasse skyscraper[54], Frank Lloyd Wright's unbuilt St Marks in the Bowery, marked 'All Glass Construction', or Norman Foster's flowering fractal Crystal Island, Moscow, the projected largest building on earth (all unbuilt). The egomania of the ever-rising glass towers is not the problem, nor even is their race towards the stratosphere. It is what the one-way glass conceals.

The inadequacy of the Panopticon as a symbol is becoming increasingly apparent. There will be no central tower and no lone guard. Rather it will be a constellation, not of stars, but of black holes drinking in data like light. What each does with the information will be as mysterious as the intentions and machinations of the judiciary and bureaucracy in Kafka's *The Trial* and *The Castle*[55], but we may learn of the consequences. In the future, of which we are already a part, to be private, among many other things, may be deemed an anti-social radical act.

53   Pg. 462

54   An influence on the actually built inquistaorial Chilehaus by Fritz Höger.

55   Ricardo Bolofil's mischievous version of The Castle, with windows in all directions.

Solitude may become a vice. Privacy may be monetised into being a preserve of the rich and well-connected. We will realise the precious nobility of anonymity when it is gone (perhaps everyone will be private for fifteen minutes, granted brief holidays to do as we pleased). To maintain a position of sovereign free-thinking individual, and, further, to connect with others, will be an active threat. This is at the heart of the dystopias. It is the challenge to our sovereignty over ourselves, buffeted by the domination and vagaries of state and market. We will be both lost in the mass, like De Quincey's Ann of Oxford Street, but also unable to disappear. Robert Browning's lines 'a privacy, an obscure nook for me. / I want to be forgotten even by God'[56] are not an admission of misanthropy but the very definition of free will. In *Electrical Experimenter*[57] May 1919, we find 'The Thought Recorder', a useful tool for psycho-analysis and self-discovery and a nightmarish device in the hands of some. Yet it will not look like a nightmare, at least not until it's too late. It will be undertaken with us in mind. We should remember that free will in *We* is outlawed because it brought unhappiness. We should remember that Big Brother in *1984* wanted to be loved.

The worry in Orwell's writing is that we will not even be able to think of this, or have the language with which to articulate our opposition or deviance. The victory of the Thought Police will be when behaviour is so self-regulating that no Thought Police are required. There is one installed in every mind. The city,

---

56   'Paracelsus' Part V, Robert Browning, 1835, cited *Community and Privacy*, Pg. 78

57   May 1919

both virtual and real, will be the battleground. It will require spaces where freedom is possible, it will require resistance, a maintaining of critical focus to encounter the city not passively but with a degree of Verfremdungseffekt[58]. We will need to rethink and reclaim space, or be claimed by it.

58   Breaking the fourth wall is crucial, not simply in Brechtian theatre, but in life.

474 | *The Turk*

The Blind Watchmakers

Time is the hidden constituent to architecture and the power that is wielded through it. The awe of architecture, the intractable monumental weight, seeks to concretise authority into history forever. There is a nightmarish, fascistic aspect to awe; again it is space that says you, as a sovereign individual, are nothing. Your life-span is insectile in comparison. Here is power that is seemingly immovable, that exists in deep time. You could no more rail against it than you could the mountains or the sea. Yet we do these very things because we must, because so much depends on it. We have seen the ruins. Time moves in mysterious ways.

In Ballard's *Chronopolis*, a dystopian city in which one official form of time overrides all others, the question arises:

'How can you hurt anybody with a clock?'

'Isn't it obvious? You can time him, know exactly how long it takes him to do something.'

'Well?'

'Then you can make him do it faster.'[59]

Sometimes resistance is a question of mere symbolism, except of course that symbols are crucially important (they are often how we think and remember). Take the legend of the French mayor who stopped the clocks of his town hall for the entire

59   Pg. 153

occupation by the Nazis, or the exploited innocent in Conrad's *The Secret Agent* who blows himself to pieces on the way to bomb Greenwich Observatory (the attack being on imperial time itself). In Poe's *Vondervotteimittiss*, a devil steals into the belfry and subverts the chimes, causing chaos in the time-ordered streets below[60]. In Fordlândia, workers rebelled by smashing the clocks that had mapped out their time, while the aforementioned French revolutionaries rewrote the calendar. Power describes itself in dominating buildings. Where today it is the glass towers of finance, yesterday it was church spires that dominated skylines and psyches. Time and people have already changed the unchangeable.

It seems curious to consider that for a vast expanse of human history, we could not accurately determine what time it was. There were people employed as human alarm clocks moving through the cities at dawn. Societies thought in seasons and the arc of the sun and moon. The ingenious time-keeping Alhambra lions were broken by prying Christians trying to find out what devilry made them work. As so often happens, when the tyranny of time arrived, it did so as a liberation from uncertainty. St Florian's idea[61] of spaces that only appear when we need them, such as shops and offices, resonates as an update

---

60   A book like Delany's masterpiece, *Dhalgren*, with its time-warped city of Bellona might make us question the supposedly linear nature of time and see the subjectivity and malleability of it.

61   *Envisioning Architecture: Drawings from The Museum of Modern Art, New York: The Museum of Modern Art*, 2002, edited by Matilda McQuaid, Pg. 154

of the Scottish mirage town of Abaton[62] which only appears once in a blue moon with the sound of a distant harpsichord, or the equally-ephemeral Arabic town of Irem. The measurement of time began as utopian and slipped towards dystopia. 'The clock, not the steam-engine, is the key-machine of the modern industrial age,' Mumford claimed. 'The clock [. . .] is a piece of power-machinery whose "product" is seconds and minutes.'[63]

Where are we, then, at this moment in time? That all depends on where we are located. It is 2015 in the West. It is 1436 in the Islamic calendar. In the Berber calendar, it is the year 2965. In one Chinese calendar, it is 4711. Though it's worth reminding ourselves of this, that is not to say that there are no universal truths or dangers. We have been told that ideology no longer exists, which is itself an ideological assertion. The best are cynical and apathetic or dragged into interminable insignificant battles while the worst are evangelical and strategic. We live, in the West, in the paradox of a Panglossian society ('the best of all possible worlds') but afflicted with Mean World Syndrome whereby, through sensationalist media saturation, the world has never appeared more dangerous. In such a climate, the absence of utopias has become a dystopia (a situation the writers of past dystopian fiction, damning technocrats and bureaucrats, did not foresee, and helped bring about). The widespread cynicism towards politics, however justified, has become a paralysis. The prospect of utopia, however unattainable, is a threat to the

---

62   Sir Thomas Bulfinch's 'My Heart's in the Highlands' (1892)

63   *Technics and Civilisation*, Pg. 14

status quo because it seeks to reform or replace. For all its wide-eyed optimism, it is dissastisfied. That is its greatest strength and our only hope.

Guest List

Inclusion or exclusion. Eden[64] or wilderness. Life does not work in dichotomies, but authority does. The control of city space functions through boundaries. There are systems of gates and walls, sentries and passwords, ways of identifying and shunning the other. Forbidden cities, holy of holies, green zones, gated communities, the purple rooms of Rome, the pleasure palaces, the backstage passes, the palatial halls, first class, no entry.

The levels to which such mechanics are necessary are questionable but there's little doubting the potential for malice and exploitation. In Jules Verne's *The Barsac Mission*, unwitting emigrants are lured to The Factory, where there will be flying machines and retrofuturist contraptions, with the promise of untold riches. They are however immediately seized, blindfolded and forbidden to make contact with the outside world. When the time comes to send them home, they are taken out into desert and killed. This outlandish dystopia is distinctly comparable, in a manner that would have horrified Verne, to the treatment of migrant workers in megacities of today. What price the happiness of the few? Would we want to inhabit a paradise that exacted such a price? Could it still be regarded as a utopia?

'Does the end justify the means? That is possible,' Camus wrote in *The Rebel*. 'But what will justify the end? To that question, which historical thought leaves pending, rebellion

---

64   It is worth noting the crime that banishes them is eating an apple that will result in them assuming powers monopolised by their deity; 'then your eyes shall be opened, and ye shall be as gods, knowing good and evil.'

replies: the means.'[65]

For Rilke, beauty was the beginning of terror. So too is it with cities. In 'A Worker Reads History', Brecht challenges the lone man of history idea, reminding us of the multitudes of individuals who built the glories of antiquity and paid horrendous prices. How many died building Angkor Wat, or the Egyptian pyramids with each Khufu stone weighing fifteen tonnes, places that were tombs not just for the pharaohs? How much misery goes unrecorded, even if it could be conceivably quantifiable? Would aesthetics justify a Gulag? The question is moot; they already have in the man-made wonders of the world. 'O beautiful situation to found a village,' Duarte Coelho Pereira commented on founding Olinda. Did the slaves in its sugarcane industry have time, energy or willingness to contemplate the beauty of the view? What of the dead of today's metropolises, so hidden that even the recording of their deaths becomes a political act?

'Be rejoiced, O Emir; for this is the City of Brass[66],' *One Thousand and One Nights'* account goes ' . . . its wall is of black stones, and it hath two towers of brass of El-Andalus, which the beholder seeth resembling two corresponding fires; and thence it is named the City of Brass. It hath five and twenty gates, and that none of its gates may be opened but from within the city.' What would such a place contain, except riches and corpses?

There is a curious reciprocal aspect to the pharaohs of old

---

65   Pg. 292

66   A childhood favourite, thanks to Edmund Dulac's exquisite Victorian
        illustrations.

and recent dictators. There is the Gilgamesh-like yearning for immortality and when it cannot be granted, the building of stone to contain reality and mortality. Ismail Kadare ridiculed the Albanian dictator Hoxha's megalomaniacal architecture via *La Pyramide*, directly reflecting the pyramid of Tirana that was erected in Hoxha's memory and ended up as disused as his legacy. No matter how thick the walls of the pyramids, no matter how powerful the ruler, death cannot be kept out. Medieval culture is rich with woodcuts of the great leveller slipping into peasant hovels and flamboyant bedchambers alike, to drag away the occupants. It is the fifth regiment in every city. It seeps through the floorboards and the cracks. As Arcimboldo portrayed in his *Allegory of Death*, it steals in the window, disregarding the locked door and the expression on the house's facade like an aghast death-mask. It is our destroyer and our avenger.

'Architecture cannot be dissociated,' Bernard Tschumi claimed, 'from the events that happened to it.'[67] What was glorious Rome to a slave dragged there from his or her homeland? What was the mighty Coliseum to gladiators or Christians but a degenerate pit of mass murder for entertainment? What were the spectacular pyramids of the Incas to a captured youth having his or her throat slit on their peaks? The cities of glory are worth revisiting from angles other than those of the victors. In England, the reign of Elizabeth I is mainly looked upon as a golden age, marking the birth of empire and the country's emergence as a

67   *Architecture of Disjunction*

world power. Yet for all the pomp and glory, Elizabeth's reign was marked with executions and betrayals. The good queen personally enjoyed watching mastiffs attack chained bears. Might it be possible to re-examine the golden city of London of the time through the dream the rebel Robert Wintour told to Guy Fawkes (both of them destined soon to be tortured and brutally executed for treason, a fate celebrated nationally every year), in which he saw 'a scarred city with steeples blown awry and charred disfigured faces.'[68] For whom was this golden age, to what extent was it conjured up by the storytellers, and for what purpose?

We are lucky, if that word can be used, that recent tyrants have lacked taste. We could easily identify them from their gaudy horror-kitsch palaces, their neo-classical pretensions, how they killed or exiled the real artists. This cliché renders us unsuspecting to the tyrants who got wise, who have subtlety and taste, who patronise the arts. The ones who do not close the Bauhaus in future, but commission it. The ones who bring order. 'The lawns are tidy, the façades are gracious, in good repair; they're like the beautiful pictures they used to print in the magazines about homes and gardens and interior decoration. There is the same absence of people, the same air of being asleep. The street is almost like a museum, or a street in a model town constructed to show the way people used to live. As in those pictures, those museums, those model towns, there are no

---

68   *God's Traitors: Terror and Faith in Elizabethan England*, Jessie Childs, Pg. 365

children. This is the heart of Gilead.'[69]

The imaginary city of 'all is well', constructed for investor, tourist and the elite, has a long history. Its most blatant form came with the Potemkin villages built for the Russian empress Catherine the Great. Eager to convince her that she ruled a Russia glorious for all, in the face of the inconvenient facts, her advisor and erstwhile lover, the one-eyed orgiast Prince Grigory Potemkin, constructed a series of fake settlements, populated by actors and the facades of splendid buildings:

'For the delectation of the entourage and the thousands of spectators, Potemkin organised delights and surprises along the route. He installed English gardens on the virgin steppe, complete with mature, transplanted trees. Huge tents, garlanded and pearl-studded, served as dining halls . . . Lanterns shone from trees while bonfires lit up the night sky. Near the city of Kremenchug on the Dnieper River, a magnificent re-creation of Vesuvius rained down fire and brimstone on the peaceful prairie.'

These were 'towns without streets, streets without houses, and houses without roofs, doors, or windows.'[70]

We might regard the Russian gentry of the time as particularly gullible and indulgent, were it not for the fact the Potemkin

69   *The Handmaid's Tale*, Margaret Atwood, Pg. 33

70   *Odessa*, Charles King, Pg. 41

village has been resurrected in our age.[71]

In Western Europe, there's been a notable tendency to spot Potemkin societies abroad (the Ruritania genre of fiction for example, of which Anthony Powell's *Venusberg* is an example) whilst regarding our own pomp, ceremony, hypocrisy and corruption naturally to be nothing of the sort. Chivalry and nobility are theatre, and their environments are inevitably sets in which the audience are compelled to believe. This has continued up to the present in the nation of Latveria in Marvel Comics where a fear-ridden grovelling population bows down to the dictator Doctor Victor von Doom. The setting is unmistakably late medieval Mitteleuropa (taverns, shuttered windows on burgher housing, a dominating gothic castle) with futuristic embellishments. 'Then was Latveria a happy kingdom . . . free of all the strife which so troubles the rest of the world. Under the rule of Doctor Doom each man and woman had all they could desire, and we would call out our thanks as he passed amongst us.' Happiness and freedom are mutually exclusive here: 'the people are happy and content . . . as I commanded they be'. This happens to the East, always the East, over the mountains and far away. Latveria, Ruritania, Donald Duck's Brutopia, Tintin's Borduria and so many dystopias exist, or rather don't exist, to absolve our own. The sins of the near are transplanted to the far, hence the fascination with fantasy oriental terror/pleasure

---

71 When the G20 leaders visited Enniskillen for a security summit in 2013, the British Tory-led government spent millions covering up the effects of their austerity policies by having fake bustling shop-fronts painted onto abandoned buildings.

palaces (from Mirbeau's *Torture Garden* to the machinations of Fu Manchu) when China was being ransacked by empires.

If the East was a chance to relocate dystopia, it was also a chance to build model cities. The curiosity of trying to replicate European capitals in colonial areas was lampooned in *Tarzan and the Lion Man*, where a gorilla Henry VIII rules over a jungle reconstruction of medieval London. It would be a stone heart that would condemn Babar's Celesteville as anything but a benevolent kingdom. Suitably stone-hearted, we can easily see it as a colonialist or even fascistic populist project to civilise the savages, making them French and thus human, bringing order to the jungle with the map of Paris as a stamp. Fake versions of Paris abound, from the sleeping Morphopolis in Maurice Barrère's *La Cité du Sommeil* and Robert-Martin Lesuire's New Paris in Antarctic in the *French Adventurer* to Mœbius's depictions of the future Eiffel Tower dwarfed by surrounding biomorphic, blobist and neo-Art Nouveau buildings, or encaged in the sublime work of Benoît Peeters and François Schuiten[72], which revisit earlier unbuilt versions of cities (like Perret, for one, in Revoir Paris), reimagining the reimaginings. These doppelgängers are not restricted to fiction. In Las Vegas, a city itself dreamt up and developed by mobsters, there is a diminutive replica of Paris with a half-size Eiffel Tower and imitations of the Arc de Triomphe, Opera House, Hôtel de Ville, and the Louvre. An attempt to build a replica of Paris in China, renamed Tianducheng, has largely resulted in a ghost

72   *Les Cités Obscures* is an essential series.

town (much like other ostentatious and deserted cities like New Ordos) with only 2% of the expected populace taking up residence. The garish inauthencity might lead some to dismiss such projects, but there is something disconcertingly fascinating in seeing the Eiffel Tower rise above desert and paddy fields, as if a mirage or some tear in the space/time continuum[73]. Perhaps an uncanny valley effect in reverse, as well as lofty expectations, is the cause of so-called Paris Syndrome, a reported temporary psychological condition that has affected a number of oriental visitors to the real Paris[74], resulting in delusions of varying descriptions. The idea of the city as a state of mind must factor in that minds and cities are by no means stable things.

The crossover between set-designers and architects, in the service of power, is not new. Inigo Jones designed sets for royal masques before designing palaces, and there was little ideological difference between the two. One of the problems of inhabiting imaginary utopias is that the delusion must be enforced or it will crumble. If you choose not to believe, *you* are the problem. This is no doubt a source of considerable alienation: 'One of the things I took from my wartime experiences was that reality was a stage set,' J.G. Ballard acknowledged of his western colonial upbringing in Singapore. 'The comfortable day-to-day life, school, the home where one lives and all the rest of it . . .

73   A fake wooden Paris was built towards the end of the First World War fifteen miles away from the real thing in Maisons-Laffitte, to divert the expected German attack, according to *The Telegraph* November 9th, 2011.

74   Religious mania has given rise to the not dissimilar Jerusalem Syndrome among pilgrims there.

could be dismantled overnight.'[75]

The sense of artifice, that cities have been built as sets in which humans are a secondary or tertiary consideration, is evident all through the paintings of Edward Hopper. Their inhabitants are lost and alone, even when together, on each city-resembling stage. Alienation is portrayed here in terms of space and light, a cityscape of late night bars and out-of-hours offices, but one gleaned from reality, inviting narratives of power dynamics, sublimated sexuality, the romance of the empty room and degrees of human isolation from brief voyeuristic moments[76]. The scenes were 'probably first suggested by many rides on the "L" train in New York City after dark glimpses of office interiors that were so fleeting as to leave fresh and vivid impressions on my mind. My aim was to try to give the sense of an isolated and lonely office interior rather high in the air, with the office furniture which has a very definite meaning for me.'[77]

A related figure is Jeff Jeffries in Hitchcock's *Rear Window*, though Hopper always remained impassively uninvolved with the dramas or anti-dramas he witnessed (it is worth noting however that Hitchcock was clearly a fan, basing the Bates Motel in *Psycho* on Hopper's *House By The Railroad*). The romance and mystery of Baudelaire's candle-lit window is inverted into menace with a cigarette-point of light in an unlit room. Hopper

75   *Hello America*, J.G. Ballard, Pg. 2-3

76   Contemporary examples of such intriguing voyeurism can be found in the photographs of Shizuka Yokomizo and Yasmine Chatila.

77   Attached to letter of 25th August 1948 to Norman Geske, director of Walker Art Center.

captured something essential of the city as a spectre haunted by unfulfilled lives, in the desolate skull-faced buildings of *Approaching a City*. 'There is a certain fear and anxiety, and a great visual interest in the things that one sees coming into a great city'[78] — a sentiment echoed in the similarly ominous *The Soul of the Soulless City* by Christopher R.W. Nevinson.

Our views of the city are often determined by our expectations, and our experiences of earlier cities. 'How quiet the [New York] streets are,' Dickens wrote before going on unintentionally to describe the memory of London: 'By day are there no Punches, Fantoccini, Dancing-dogs, Jugglers, Conjurors, Orchestrinas, or even Barrel-organs?'[79]

Often our expectations are of a purely visual nature, and we are surprised by how our senses of sound, smell and taste are assailed in foreign places.

'I don't think it had ever occurred to me,' John Wyndham writes in his haunting *The Day of the Triffids*, 'that man's supremacy is not primarily due to his brain, as most of the books would have one think. It is due to the brain's capacity to make use of the information conveyed to it by a narrow band of visible light rays. His civilisation, all that he had achieved or might achieve, hung upon his ability to perceive that range of vibrations from red to violet. Without that, he was lost.'[80]

Having their optic nerves burned out by a malevolent comet

---

78   John Morse interview with Hopper, *Art in America*, Vol. 48, No. 2 March 1960, Pg.63

79   *The Monthly Review*, 1842 'Dicken's American Notes.', Pg. 394-395

80   Pg. 113

leaves the inhabitants of London utterly vulnerable, stranded amidst the once-familiar. What is a city when the dominant visual aspect has been erased, what is it to people who are blind? A place of threats, challenges, refuges — a landscape transformed.

Hamlet complains to Rosencrantz, but ultimately to himself, that Denmark is a prison. His friend and spy replies, 'Why then your ambition makes it one. 'Tis too narrow for your mind.' 'Oh God,' the prince replies, 'I could be bounded in a nutshell, and count myself a king of infinite space — were it not that I have bad dreams.'

Cities are states of mind and we live among bad dreams, dreams that morph the very architecture into insults and oppressions.

'My coming to New York had been a mistake,' H.P. Lovecraft admitted, 'for whereas I had looked for poignant wonder and inspiration in the teeming labyrinths of ancient streets that twist endlessly from forgotten courts and squares and waterfronts to courts and squares and waterfronts equally forgotten, and in the Cyclopean modern towers and pinnacles that rise blackly Babylonian under waning moons, I had found instead only a sense of horror and oppression which threatened to master, paralyse, and annihilate me.'[81]

The flâneur delights in wandering[82]. When the delight fades, the wandering remains, like ghosts buried at crossroads to

---

81   'He', August 11th, 1925

82   The badaud, by contrast, enjoys watching the city pass by.

wander between the winds; Nerval's the *Black Sun of Melancholy*, Knut Hamsun's *Hunger*, Dostoevsky and Dazai. There is a corner of the world, where the sublime painting of Munch's is kept, where it is always a tortured evening on Karl Johan Avenue, in what was once Kristiana. The artist wandering the streets of what is now Oslo and the world transforming through the prism of a beleaguered mind. 'Dusk,' Strindberg wrote after seeing it, 'The sun fades, night falls, and dusk transforms mortals into ghosts and corpses . . . '[83]

Night also brings the prospect of glory, abandon and camaraderie to those briefly unburdened by work. Cloaked in dimly-lit anonymity, they might become themselves. Yet it is a fragile glory with the knowledge that every hour eats into sleep and the dread of morning waits. The city nevertheless transforms with the setting of the sun. While commerce and toil have made inroads into the night, there is still something of the sense of lawlessness and liberty to it, to make it a terrible and beautiful temporary metamorphosis. It casts the acceptable horrors of the day into stark light; Michael Wolf's photos of Tokyo commuters vacuum-packed in subway trains for example. There is something heroic about Pinocchio's reaction to the rush-hour in the Land of the Busy Bees where 'even if one were to search with a lantern, not one idle man or one tramp could have been found', 'I understand,' said Pinocchio at once wearily, 'this is no place for me! I was not born for work.'[84]

83   *Revue Blance*, June 1st 1896, Pg. 100, *Symbolism*

84   Quoted Pg. 41, *Pinocchio Goes Postmodern: Perils of a Puppet in the United States*, Richard Wunderlich

If the city is best seen as a collage then perhaps it encourages personalities that are collages. 'My souls (characters) are conglomerations of past and present stages of civilisation,' Strindberg claimed, 'bits from books and newspapers, scraps of humanity, rags and tatters of fine clothing, patched together as is the human soul.'[85]

There have been many tales in which cities warp according to the emotions of the inhabitants. 'In the Moody Land, the sun would shine all night if there were enough joyful people around,' Salman Rushdie wrote, ' . . . and when people were muddled or uncertain . . . the outlines of its buildings and lamp-posts and motor-cars got smudgy, like paintings whose colours had run, and at such times it could be difficult to make out where one thing ended and another began.'[86]

Elsewhere, he tells of a city 'so ruinously sad that it had forgotten its name' containing 'mighty factories in which (so I'm told) sadness was actually manufactured, packaged and sent all over the world, which never seemed to get enough of it. Black smoke poured out of the chimney of the sadness factories and hung over the city like bad news.'[87]

In James Thomson's epic *City of the Dreadful Night*, the poet built an entire Gothic metropolis from his depression — 'The street-lamps burn amid the baleful glooms, / Amidst the soundless solitudes immense / Of ranged mansions dark and

85   Author's foreword to *Miss Julie*, in *Six Plays of Strindberg*, 1955.

86   *Haroun and Luka*, Salman Rushdie, Pg. 33

87   Pg. 1

still as tombs.' It is a city that never sleeps, insomniac and haunted, with charnel houses as machines for dying in. It is silent, sunless, on the shores of a shipless sea, with a River of Suicides running through it. It is a dystopia that anyone might suddenly find they inhabit, no matter which earthly city they live in: 'How he arrives there none can clearly know'. Yet it is not without some glimmer, if not of hope then beauty perhaps: 'I sat forlornly by the river-side / And watched the bridge-lamps glow like golden stars.'

Darkness is rarely total. A chart, any chart through a city will pass those having the times of their lives, others falling to pieces, others somewhere between. And for each of them, the city looks identical and utterly different.

The delusion of structured pleasantness can be perilous. Whilst the incapable Louis XVI took refuge in Versailles, Queen Marie Antoniette spent her days dressing up in rustic fashion in the fake rural village of Hameau de la Reine[88]. The fictionalised hamlet contained a land-locked lighthouse, a barn that doubled as a ballroom, a temple of love on an island, billiard and oriental rooms, boudoirs and harpsichords, a dovecote and a mill with no functioning parts. In a sense, Antoinette was merely acting in the tradition of aristocratic retreats (echoing the menagerie of Pfaueninsel — Peacock Island — in Berlin) and even in the emerging Romantic tradition, which was given to abandoning

---

88   The architect of which Richard Mique was executed along with his son for attempting to rescue Antoinette from the Revolutionary Tribunal.

the industrial-demonic city for idealised rural arcadias[89]. What doomed the regent however was her (and her husband's) dislocation from reality. She could play the role of peasant without any of the actual risks of starvation, destitution or disease that blighted real peasants (and the urban population) under her reign. They had forgotten the function of jesters for earlier regents, namely the preservation of objective truth in courts filled with duplicitous sycophants. Other leaders like Ceaușescu would later follow suit, the Romanian leader in disbelief upon his balcony as the crowd turned against him. 2+2+=5 was for Orwell a sign of the victory of totalitarianism. Truth is what they dictate it is and what everyone feigns to believe. Yet any system which lives by such arithmetic will eventually find itself unravelling. No flaw can be admitted to and no claim believed. 'We had a beautiful dream and that was all . . . '[90] the imprisoned Antoinette confessed, still believing it was anything but a nightmare.

Exclusion and inclusion are key to maintaining and enforcing power and its required delusions. Who is in and who is out. In *Miracles of Life*, Ballard remembered the semi-fictional world of his youth — 'the background music of endless night-clubbing, daredevil air shows and ruthless money-making' — and the otherworld that sustained it: 'Meanwhile, every day, the trucks of the Shanghai Municipal Council roamed the streets collecting

---

89   'After hiking miles into the wilderness and discovering my first real waterfall, I
         immediately began looking for the pumps and conduit that make it work' —
         Fred Tomaselli, interview with Siri Hustvedt, 2007

90   *Lettres*, II, Pg. 433

the hundreds of bodies of destitute Chinese who had starved to death on Shanghai's pavements, the hardest in the world. Partying, cholera and smallpox somehow coexisted with a small English boy's excited trips in the family Buick to the Country Club swimming pool.'[91]

At times divisions manifest in clear definitions of prisoner and protected, at others the interactions are complex and protean. The magnificent 'palace of winds', Hawa Mahal in Jaipur, was built so that female aristocrats could view the outside world without the outside world seeing them. Though he would adapt the architecture to age-old pyramid designs, Orwell initially based 1984's Ministry of Truth on Senate House in London, where the Ministry of Information was located. His Ministry of Love permitted no close-ups: 'Winston had never been inside the Ministry of Love, nor within a half a kilometer of it. It was a place impossible to enter except on official business, and then only by penetrating through a maze of barbed-wire entanglements, steel doors, and hidden machine-gun nests.'[92]

Such division exists psychologically, economically, religiously and politically, which are all ways of saying 'power'; one group rising on the backs of others. Smart PR-savvy regimes try to make themselves amorphous, to locate power everywhere and nowhere, so that protest cannot easily find places to accumulate and when it does, the city creates temporary forms of containment. Zones of exclusion and inclusion are facilitated

91   Pg. 5

92   The most dreaded room of all was Room 101 which housed everyone's worst
        fears, an inversion of the magical treasure room of myth.

subtly but heinously (Robert Moses's racist facilitations for example) or enforced with violence, hence the Israeli commander quote with regards to the Gaza Wall: 'Anything that's mobile, that moves in the zone, even if it's a three-year-old, needs to be killed. Over.'[93]

Where there is power, however, there is resistance and sites of distinct division quickly become the focus of confrontation, both surreptiously and actively, when a tipping point is reached. Buildings are stormed, statues are toppled, walls are demolished, the rubble invested with totemic significance. Icons are defiled and others raised (the line between iconoclast and worshipper is a thin one). We battle in architecture and symbols.[94]

When the Berlin Wall was toppled, Lebbeus Woods perceptively saw that the old division between Communism and Capitalism, West Germany and East would quickly be replaced by new binaries, orthodoxies and tyrannies. Liberation would be undermined by the time those celebrating had woken hung-over. He proposed in the former no-man's land in Berlin a building which would transcend the grand narratives and ulterior motives, a place of no restriction:

'The freespaces are useless and meaningless spaces. The free-zone

93   The Israeli Captain R, after the murder of the thirteen-year-old Palestinian girl Iman al-Hams who had wandered into a designated security zone. Quoted on Pg. 209-210, *Freedom Next Time*, John Pilger.

94   And so it goes. Rivera sneaking Lenin into Rockefeller, Guernica shrouded on announcement of war in the UN etc etc.

is dangerous, subversive, an anarchic event occurring at the very heart of the new Berlin . . . it undermines all carefully laid plans and carefully preserved values. The free-zone is anti-control, anti-deterministic, anti-institutional [...] the spatial forms of free spaces render them unsuitable for conventional types of occupation, and demand instead the invention of new ways of living.'[95]

Woods anticipated that no rules would lead to a vacuum and the subsequent imposition of new rules, so he set out loose criteria: 'use must be invented by those who dare to claim Freespace as their own', 'the faint need not apply', 'absence of discernible order: hierarchy is frustrated; heterarchy is unavoidable.' It was deemed however that space could not be set aside for experiments in living, though it's notable that Berlin's artistic vibrancy came largely through squats in previously-failed architecture (depressingly now being closed). Though it lacks the singular name, freespace already occurs, appearing as fragments of Bohemia or revolution (Free Derry in my hometown kept the occupying army out for two years) to varying degrees in city after city, briefly flourishing before the dread tide of gentrification catches up again and it is forced to reappear elsewhere. It is the weeds in the cracks in the concrete.

These cracks sometimes emanate from bullet-holes. In 1993, Lebbeus Woods stood in the ruins of Sarajevo as his manifesto was read out:

95   'Free Space', *Architectural Design*, Pg. 39

'Architecture and war are not incompatible. Architecture is war. War is architecture. I am at war with my time, with history, with all authority that resides in fixed and frightened forms. I am one of millions who do not fit in, who have no home, no family, no doctrine, no firm place to call my own, no known beginning or end, no 'sacred and primordial site.' I declare war on all icons and finalities, on all histories that would chain me with my own falseness, my own pitiful fears. I know only moments, and lifetimes that are as moments, and forms that appear with infinite strength, then "melt into air". I am an architect, a constructor of worlds, a sensualist who worships the flesh, the melody, a silhouette against the darkening sky. I cannot know your name. Nor you can know mine. Tomorrow, we begin together the construction of a city.'[96]

The architecture of the city which had once hosted the Winter Olympics had been reimagined by the shells of the besieging Serbian forces. What remained was transformed into a treacherous copy of their hometown. The central boulevard Dragon of Bosnia Street became Sniper Alley, which civilians had to traverse by sprinting (1,630 people were not lucky). Inhabitants put up temporary structures to block the targets of the snipers on nearby mountains which added to the feeling of dread, alienation and debasement. Woods wanted to help the city 'to consciously reshape its world, turning ruins and battered remnants into a new kind of architecture, a uniquely

Sarajevan architecture', to turn wreckage and peril into defiant expressions of home. Woods realised that the emphasis, after the war, would be to return the city to what it was or use it as an excuse to sell off to oligarchs[97]. This was a way of burying trauma with the possibility, psychologically, of grave consequences. He proposed using 10% of the architecture again as 'freespaces, for those who did not want to go back, but forward.' Woods knew the oppositions he faced. He also, crucially, knew that the two dimensional and the three dimensional worlds are distinctly different realms: 'architects make drawings that other people build. I make drawings. If someone wants to build from those, that's up to them.' Architecture is after all a form of fiction, and Woods was careful and wise enough to imply that just because something isn't built now doesn't mean it won't be somewhere someday. Nevertheless, Woods's immediate plans for Sarajevo were dismissed in favour of the functional, the traditional and the commercial. The buildings he envisaged with their scars sank deep and ambiguously into the subconscious.

Zones of exclusion and inclusion often emerge in reaction to official delineations of division, encouraged by disenfranchisement, unemployment and racism, from cities remapped with postcode gangs, sharia areas, identity ghettos, sometimes noble and articulate, sometimes self-destructive or themselves authoritarian. Growing up in such a place requires an awareness of silent unofficial maps, the areas to avoid, the shortcuts never to take, the riot interface junctions to bypass or

97   Soldiers in post conflict Beirut, the CPP in Phnom Penh etc.

flirt with. What begins as protective retreat soon becomes a prison. To the besieged, all outside are barbarians, until definitions of what you are and what you are not become indecipherable. This occurs in psychology and architecture. 'Like all walls it was ambiguous, two-faced,' Le Guin writes in *The Dispossessed*, 'What was inside it and what was outside it depended upon which side of it you were on. Looked at from one side, the wall enclosed a barren sixty-acre field called the Port of Anarres [. . .] It was in fact a quarantine. The wall shut in not only the landing field but also the ships that came down out of space, and the men that came on the ships, and the worlds they came from, and the rest of the universe. It enclosed the universe, leaving Anarres outside, free. Looked at from the other side, the wall enclosed Anarres: the whole planet was inside it, a great prison camp, cut off from other worlds and other men, in quarantine.'[98]

Binaries are dangerous not just because they are reductive deceptions or destructive by nature, but because they are useful. They alienate you not only from 'the Other' but, in the process, from yourself, leaving those who wholeheartedly believe in them vulnerable to cynics in power. In China Miéville's *The City and the City*, the schizophrenia is both overt and covert, the latter requiring a collaborating suspension of disbelief. Two cities sit in opposition to one another, merging at points. Each is to be implicitly ignored by the other and yet each is defined by what it is not. To live there requires ignoring what is in clear sight, conspiring in blindness and yet, like Berlin, Belfast, Beirut

98   Pg. 1-2

(indeed every city to varying degrees) becoming obsessed by what it chooses and chooses not to see. It is a tragic farce but with so much invested in it that none can admit this. Citizens are trained to instinctively unsee (noticing or admitting noticing is a crime called 'breach'). Copula Hall overlaps into both, 'a patchwork of architecture defined by the Oversight Committee . . . corridors might start mostly total, Beszel or Ul Qoma, become progressively crosshatched along their length, with rooms in one or other city along them, and numbers also of those strange rooms and areas that were in neither or both cities.'[99]

For all the extravagance of the premise, this has effectively happened. There are distinct hints of East Berlin in the antiquated cop cars, of the Korean DMZ with its fake Potemkin propaganda town (the lights in its empty schools and hospital coming on and off automatically) and indeed of all the liminal processing points that form border controls and customs, those unplaces between countries (and countries are all inventions of varying believability to some extent). The tragedies however are always personal ones of rootless disruption and an absence like a curious nostalgia for what might have been: 'How could one not think of the stories we all grew up on, that surely the Ul Qomans grew up on too? Ul Qoman man and Besz maid, meeting in the middle of Copula Hall, returning to their homes to realise they live, grosstopically, next door to each other, spending their lives faithful and alone, rising at the same time, walking crosshatched streets close like a couple, each in their

99   Pg. 157-158

own city, never breaching, never quite touching, never speaking a word across the border.'[100]

Yet, as always, where there is power, there is resistance; 'There were folktales of renegades who breach and avoid Breach to live between the cities, not exiles but in-siles, evading justice and retribution by consummate ignorability.'

The perceptive and unnerving aspect to Miéville's system is that there must be some level of individual collaboration to the process. 'You did an excellent job. You've seen how we work. Nowhere else works like the cities,' he said. 'It's not just us keeping them apart. It's everyone in Besźel and everyone in Ul Qoma. Every minute, every day. We're only the last ditch: it's everyone in the cities who does most of the work. It works because you don't blink. That's why unseeing and unsensing are so vital.' The terrifying thing is that dystopia, at some level, requires our acceptance.

100   Pg. 160

The Magic Kingdom

There must be barbarians for us to convince ourselves we are the civilised. Baudrillard went further, claiming that Disneyland[101] existed to suggest the rest of America was real. Disneyland was partly based on the fantasies of Prince Ludwig which in turn were based on a legendary medieval Bavarian past. Ludwig's dreams came largely from the operas of Wagner. The music was sublime and perhaps deserved to be frozen into architecture in terms of beauty alone, but they were also nationalistic fictions posing as facts, anthems for the coalescing German nation inventing itself from fragments and stories. The sensitive recluse Ludwig fell prey to phantasms. Wagner had suggested in sound a better world and the prince resolved to build it, commissioning Christian Jank who'd built sets for Wagner's *Lohengrin* to begin work on turning ruins at Burg Falkenstein ('Castle Falcon Stone') into a Wagnerian palace in a mish-mash of architectural styles. He was an outsider artist trapped on the inside, walling himself into his exquisite delusions.

Reality conspired against Ludwig's intentions from the start. The existing ruins had to be dynamited. Then it was discovered that building towers on mountain crags was dangerously impractical. Nevertheless he persisted, exhausting himself and bankrupting his state in the process. The first time Wagner met his patron he noted, 'I fear his life must fade away like a divine

---

101   The subliminal sense of unease towards pleasure parks is evident in the ease
        with which it is turned into dystopia – *Westworld, The Prisoner,* Eurobosch,
        Tommy's Holiday Camp.

dream in this base world . . . You cannot imagine the magic of his regard: if he remains alive it will be a great miracle!' There were to be no miracles. Ludwig's cabinet finally moved against him as he became increasingly erratic. The conspirators who came to seize him were warded off by local police and a baroness armed with an umbrella. Ludwig however hesitated and they moved again. He was put under house arrest at his summer residence. The 'moon king' was found dead there, floating in the shallow waters of Lake Starnberg, alongside the corpse of his doctor.

The Last Laugh

We are real because they are unreal. And we are virtuous because they are evil. We are smart too because they are fools. This is the implication behind the citizens of Chelm, a town which is traditionally the butt of Jewish jokes[102]. The stupidities described in the tales of Chelm were often exercises in skewed and ingenious logic but they were also a way to indirectly protest, to bear witness and to articulate suffering. There was no shortage of this for the Jewish communities of Europe. One joke tells of the depths into which they were thrown. A Christian girl is found murdered in the ghetto. The community gathers panic-stricken, knowing that terrible collective punishment will soon come. Suddenly, a local bursts in and shouts, 'Friends! I have brilliant news! The murdered girl was Jewish!'

To Nietzsche, humour was the epitaph of a feeling, which is the case here, but it's also an emphasis of humanity; we are human because we hurt and we laugh. One day the whole world will be like Chelm, another joke foretells. These were the dim flicker of lights in the ghetto as the darkness closed in, but they were lights nonetheless. The surprise is that Chelm was in fact a real Polish city, from which the Jewish population was deported and slaughtered in extermination camps during the Shoah. A handful survived, descending into an alternative

---

102   There are equivalents in many cultures – Kocourkov in Bohemia, the Wise Men of Gotham, Nottinghamshire, Kampen in Holland.

Chelm underground[103] in medieval chalk tunnels linked to cellars through secret doors. What did they do there? Between necessary silences, they told stories, sang songs and somehow told jokes.

103   As with the Warsaw Ghetto reassembling underground in a desperately brave, hopelessly outgunned last stand against the Nazis.

Waste

Differences are transformed into divisions because this monopolises power. It happens in terms of gender, race, religion, sexuality and class. Though there is latent stigma against the nouveau riche in certain quarters, if you acquire enough money identities are accepted and sins forgiven. The only real crime is the absence of money. Due to the variety of ways wealth is accumulated, myths are required, not least the fabulous mirage of meritocracy. The more you own the more you are, and the more deserving of it you've been. Those who have nothing are nothing and deserve nothing but contempt. It is a morality play so desultory that few medievals would have accepted it yet it plays out every day in tabloids and on television. It finds expression in architecture as the great Other that is the ghetto[104]. These too are plural, from Brazilian favelas to the crazed cube of Kowloon Walled City to the 'pirate utopia' Tower of David in Venezuela. It cannot be admitted that these are the consequence of systems that run on inequity or a failure to provide and maintain dignified social housing. Instead these areas and their inhabitants must be the product of sin, of poor breeding, savagery. It is not enough that they must face odds stacked against them. This must be compounded not just with shame, derision and condescension but with blame; they had done this to themselves. Wealth is virtue and here there is an

---

104   The word, meaning roughly 'waste', originates in Polo's Venice in reference to the Jewish quarter of the city.

absence of both. These are the 'sacrifice zones', mythic cities of sin and their populaces unwillingly performing the traditional ritualisitic role of sineater or scapegoat. In *Riallaro*, Godfrey Sweven contrasts 'marble palaces, margined with gleaming gardens' with 'a reeking human quagmire stretched for miles over the flood-soaked borders of this noble city, like a rich robe of lace that has dragged its train through liquid filth. Groves of trees failed to conceal the squalor and destitution of these low-lying suburbs.'[105] These he suggests are not merely places where people live and struggle to but places of pollution, places and people awaiting cleansing.

Yet the city is defunct without them, a pristine husk. 'The villagers who came to the city do not forget the village,' Suketu Mehta observed, 'They bring village rhythms, trees, roosters, gods with them to the city. The slums of the developing cities are interlocal communities, villages in the city.'[106] They need not even move: 'In many cases rural people no longer have to migrate to the city: it migrates to them.'[107]

Aside from building and servicing essentially everything, workers arrive, changing, reimagining and enriching the city. They revitalise the stagnant and add new influences and antagonisms to creative scenes. Take away the migrants and the workers and you lose virtually all of the musical genres and art movements of the past one hundred years. Given that all urban

---

105   Pg. 24

106   *Reimagining India*, Pg. 361

107   *Planet of Slums*, Pg. 9

inhabitants are immigrants in any extended view, they *are* the city. They are an essential dynamo and they are often despised for it.[108]

Fears of overpopulation from Malthus onwards have been loaded with mistruths, prejudices and ulterior motives. It is not simply a question of there being too many people, but the wrong kind of people. In Béroalde de Verville's imaginary city Lubec[109], the genitals of male proletarians are stored in the town hall and are selectively allocated to respectable citizens on a supervised loan basis. The solution to slums is not to solve poverty because their existence is necessitated by their various beneficiaries; it is to control them, and especially to prevent any signs of radicalism emerging. The cobbled unmapped alleys of old Paris were thus torn down and replaced by long wide boulevards, with the workers pushed out to the red belt. The romantic Paris of today was built expressly to prevent another revolution. Alberti and Palladio had urged renaissance streets to be constructed according to straight regular lines to aid the deployment of the military. Similarly, the broad boulevards of reconstructed Berlin were fitted wide enough for Soviet tanks to roll down, to quell envisaged insurrections; the likelihood of which was simply accepted rather than averted. This mission-creep into the structures of our cities is not restricted to the

108   Acceptance anyway is incidental. They will still come: 'In China the greatest industrial revolution in history is the Archimedean lever shifting a population the size of Europe's from rural villages to smog-choked, sky-climbing cities' — *Planet of Slums*, by Mike Davis, Pg. 11

109   *Le Moyen de Parvenir*

obvious dictatorships; the gridiron plan that defines many cities originated from Roman army camps. This is the silent, almost invisible control that locks us into our cities.

No Man's City

During the First World War, a rumour permeated among soldiers of all sides in their trench cities, a maimed hope in the midst of hell. Those who had vanished into No Man's Land had not been blown to pieces or died tangled in wire or drowned in shell-holes. Instead they were alive and well in a secret city beneath the earth, drinking fine French wine and laughing at the belligerents still fighting above. Those lucky enough to return from the trenches carried such impossible thoughts back, along with their injuries, addictions and maladies, with them to cities that were eager to forget, except for the solemn insult of Remembrance Day once a year. Otto Dix and George Grosz did not forget these men mutilated in body, mind and spirit by the orders of their superiors, the latter a cavalcade of hypocrites, profiteers and death-worshippers spat at in painted parades, brothels and feasts. For many of the survivors, the war never ended and the dead never ceased laughing and carousing. One such survivor was a failed postcard painter called Adolf Hitler, temporarily blinded by mustard gas, hysterical and subject to visions. Had he been alone, we would not even know his name.

Years later, as the Red Army closed in, Hitler pored over architectural models in his Führerbunker. 'If ever a building can be considered the symbol of a situation,' his favoured architect Albert Speer noted 'this bunker was it. From the outside it looked like an ancient Egyptian tomb. It was actually nothing but a great windowless block of concrete . . . It seemed as if the concrete walls sixteen and a half feet thick that surrounded Hitler separated him from the outside world in a figurative as well as literal sense, and locked him up inside his delusion.'[110]

Speer had designed an immense world capital named Germania at Hitler's request, a vast metropolis that would never be built but which Hitler fixated on. As he did so, Berlin was being reconstructed as a corpse-strewn obliterated wilderness above them: 'I sensed rather than saw the architecture. There was an almost ghostly quiet about everything, like a night in the mountains. The noise of a great city, which in early years had penetrated to here even during the night, had totally ceased. At rather long intervals I heard the detonations of Russian shells.'[111]

We barely notice clouds forming high above us, fragments of the levitating sea, shadowing the earth. It is different when they fall to earth, recreating the streets in mist. The Dutch artist Berndnaut Smilde manufactures low-altitude clouds through the careful manipulation of interior microclimates and a smoke-like substance called aerogel. In his Nimbus series, clouds swirl through deserted churches, galleries, castles. It is the stuff of charming minor miracle, far from the days when witches were burned for allegedly conjuring sea-storms against kings or dispensing gales from bags. Smilde's clouds exist fleetingly but the camera proves they did. No cameras captured the clouds of the Volkshalle, Hitler's and Speer's grand hall, a building so gargantuan (the dome was to be sixteen times the volume

110   Pg. 391

111   *Inside the Third Reich*, Pg. 485

of St Paul's) and populous (housing almost 200,000 people), that clouds would gather inside its upper reaches. It was a technical flaw that became a boasting point but also a sign of the megalomania of its patron. All sense of human scale would be lost bar an optical illusion of shadowing which would resemble a silhouette of Hitler's face. He was enraptured contemplating his Germania[112], playing like a child with a train-set: 'Even though Hitler developed his plans with a serious, even solemn, expression, I did not think an adult was talking to me. For a split second, I imagined as if it were a magnificent play with little building blocks.'

Even the sense of awe can be a curse when pushed into absolutism. 'The best chains our feelings and imagination,' the poet Goethe wrote, '[it] robs us of our will power, for we cannot do what we please with the perfect we are compelled to surrender to it in order to receive ourselves again, raised and ennobled.'[113]

Goethe's beloved oak tree came to symbolise the romantic fate of Germany. The Nazis, defilers of history but debased romantics nonetheless, constructed the city known as Buchenwald Concentration Camp around it and hanged prisoners from its branches.

The Nazis claimed their Reich would last a thousand years (it lasted twelve) but it was never really meant to. It was a state obsessed with death to the extent its destruction was intentionally

---

112   Which resembled Franklin Smith's vast plans for Washington, itself a pastiche
        of Ancient Athens and Rome.

113   'Trust and Submission', *On Art*, Gage, Pg. 11

in-built; a death-cult extolling war and extermination. This was implicit in its monumental architectural projects like Kreis's Berlin tomb the Hall of Soldiers, and his Totenburgen, castles for the dead, which were planned to litter the conquered lands from Scandinavia to the Egyptian desert. Their concern for their living volk was demonstrated by their efforts to protect the bones of Frederick the Great, ferrying them to bunkers and mines whilst the German people faced the onslaught brought upon them.

The architecture matched the regime, 'autocratic, axial, symmetrical and hierarchical.'[114] Germania seems a city that required emptiness, a city never designed for people to inhabit[115], unless they were ghosts of some fictitious Aryan Sparta. Ceremonial military buildings are almost always follies; triumphal arches that are not gates, halls that do not house, and Nazi militarism would have seen them colonise the entire living space of a city. Eclecticism would be dispensed with ('It is as though one had to tune a violin,' Gauldie wrote in a common complaint towards modernity, 'in the middle of a railway accident'[116]) with Nazism now giving us a wise aversion to any attempt at a singular vision of the future.

Part of Hitler and Speer's plan was to base Germania on the Eternal City of Rome and usurp the Italian city's title in the process. His allies in Mussolini's Fascist party had put

114   *Third Reich,* Pg. 134 Politics of Order

115   Reflected in the Berlin Holocaust Memorial.

116   Gauldie quoted from *Architecture of Humanism,* Pg. 130

great emphasis on resurrecting the Roman model[117] whilst desecrating any sense of grace in the capital. Mario Palanti was assigned to build the world's largest skyscraper, a tower of white marble called Mole Littoria, 'to eternalise their work.' It would contain a compliant parliament, a large hotel and a lighthouse, and would eventually be cancelled with the outbreak of war. Palanti returned to life as an architect in South America. When Le Corbusier viewed his Palacio Salvio there, he began looking around for 'where to put the cannon'. 'The purpose of architecture is to move us,'[118] Le Corbusier had noted elsewhere; he did not insist that it was necessarily in a good way. Palanti's sole work on the Italian peninsula was a tomb in Milan that was later used to intern victims of the Holocaust. Another vanity project, Mussolini's unlivable facade of the White City, was fittingly reinvented as a house of the dead in Aldo Rossi's San Cataldo Cemetery. There are glimpses in this and many Fascist failed attempts at a new city of the eerie paintings of De Chirico, the empty porticos, the menace of shadows bathed in the light of an eclipse as Cocteau put it. Fascism was this eclipse; a black sun extinguished at noon[119]. It is best summed up in the unintended gallow's humour of the Fascist Headquarters in Palachhio Veccio, emblazoned with Mussolini's cosmetically-chiselled mask and the repeated order of 'Si, Si, Si . . .' in a relentless affirmation of negation.

---

117   Their very name was from the Roman symbol of strength - the fasces or bundled sticks.

118   Quoted on Pg. 39, *Modernism and the Spirit of the City*, Iain Boyd Whyte

119   The Greek god of reason Apollo was also the sun god.

Hitler had always intended destruction, especially of his own dream-cities. He was an inept architect of sorts, sketching autobahns in Landsberg prison; painting palatial Vienna on postcards whilst living in dosshouses between wars. As occupying ruler, he came to Paris to steal from Hausmann. His own sketch of a triumphal arch over Brandenberg Gate (1924) shows a competent draftsman with no discernible architectural charm or grace and a sense of gigantism in the lumbering monolith of stone[120]. None of his plans were meant to last (nor were the cities he visited, with Von Choltitz ignoring his order to incinerate Paris). Hitler urged Speer to encapsulate ruin-value in his monuments. His were cities designed to die and leave grandiose millenial corpses; his passion for posterity being proportional to his nihilism towards the present. When historians gratify his Wagnerian pomposity by continually comparing his end, and Nazi Berlin's, to Götterdämmerung, it is worth remembering another analogy in the callous funeral pyre of the Assyrian King Sardanapalus, where possessions and innocents burned with the regent. And yet neither Wagner nor cruel Sardanapalus ever sent children with rifles to face tanks while they cowered underground.

Some saw this attraction in Hitler and his movement early on. While many smirked at the Beerhall Putsch and Chaplin's lampooning *The Great Dictator*, there was little amusement, bar the sadistic, in Max Beckmann's foreboding home invasion

---

120   The postmodern classical pastiches of Venture, Scott Brown & Rauch from
          the ironic column to basilica-influenced National Football Hall of Fame appear
          noble in comparison.

triptych *Night*. George Nelson deciphered in the immediate aftermath of their assumption of power that the Nazi 'classicising architecture, which made others believe in the thousand-year future of the Third Reich, in fact signified an unconscious fortification against self destruction.'[121]

Sylviane Agacinski draws attention to the deathly monumentality of Nazi architecture, noting 'it is worth recalling the word monumentus in the Latin sense of the term, which contains the idea of perpetuating a memory, of commemoration, of building an epitaph or funereal monument.'[122] 'As world capital, Berlin will only be comparable with Ancient Egypt, Babylon, and Rome!' he boasted, 'What is London, what is Paris compared to that!'[123]

What did survive is enlightening. It was not the Volkshalle or Hitler's transformed local city of Linz, which he planned to turn into the stolen art capital of the world and, as Führerstadt, his own burial-place (in a crypt in an enormous clocktower). It was not even the suddenly orderly cities[124] with their many conspicuous and unmentioned absences. Speer lamented that his ethereal cathedrals of light at the Nuremberg rally would be their legacy, 'the most successful architectural creation of my life

121   Juhani Pallasmaa, Pg. 183

122   *Sylviane Agacinski, Space and Work, Philosophy and Architecture,* Andrew Benjamin, Pg. 77

123   Werner Jochmann: Adolf Hitler. Monologe im Führerhauptquartier 1941–1944, Pg. 318

124   Meccania, a jingoist indictment of Germany, predicted the mix of mundane order with underlying unspoken repressive horror; 'You see, then, that our police are not idle.'

is a chimera, an immaterial phenomena.'[125] The architect was being much too modest. There were always the sub-Modernist proto-Brutalisms of the Atlantic Wall[126] (inadvertently beautifully-built with oblique angles and curves to mitigate incoming barrages), stretching from the Arctic Ocean to the Bay of Biscay. There was the wall-city of the Siegfried Line, which was as much a failure ultimately, though formidable initially, as the French equivalent, the Maginot Line, a city with its underground railways, telephone bureaus and hospitals, cinemas and Moroccan cafes. There were, or rather are, the flak towers, some built in neo-romantic medievalist styles (Dietel Tower) or even castles (the Holg Ghost bunker, Hamburg), disguised as country houses, with shades of Futurism in the rocket of the Winkeltürme or straight-forward monstrosities like the Hochbunkers. Though they remain indestructible titans of concrete to this day as reverse *memento moris*, they are strangely unfinished. 'The architect realised that [the flak tower in Augarten, Vienna] would be impossible to remove after the war, and planned to finish it in the style of the medieval Hohenstaufen castles with tiles and French marble.'[127] All were monuments to failure.

The Nazis did succeed in building a new kind of city, in the woods and marshes of the East, cities that were never supposed to be named or remembered, cities for the purpose

---

125   Speer quoted in *Berlin: The Politics of Order*, Pg. 80

126   Resurrected as a place of worship in Claude Parent's St Bernadette du Banlay.

127   Wojciech Luczak

of slavery and murder. They had gateways, railway lines, huts, crematoria and miles of electrified barbed wire in common but they made room for individual personal touches; Mauthausen had a staircase where inmates were worked to death, Treblinka was disguised as a transit camp Majdan with timetables, ticket kiosks for non-existent trains bound for imaginary destinations, when the only exit was through the smokestacks. Some required reinvention; the murder camp of Sajmište was placed in an old fairground, Jewish Parisians were housed in a velodrome and Drancy, the silent city, a modernist complex before being exported to Auschwitz and the afterlife. The Nazis even hastily designed cities without architecture. Millions of captured Soviet soldiers were assembled in vast open fields marked Stalag, with no sanitation, shelter or food. Some clawed holes in the ground with their bare hands. Some turned to cannibalism. Such was the completeness of the death-toll, itself uncountable but in the millions, that the full story will never be truly known. If they have a legacy, it is of disownment. 'I played in the bricks of ruined buildings around me and with which I built houses,' Anselm Keifer recalled, 'But I believe above all that I wanted to build the palace of my memory, because my memory is my only homeland.'[128] Of that which survives, the death camps with their piles of hair, watches, shoes, we have a warped version of Wren's epitaph, 'If you seek his monument, look around you.'[129]

Before he fled, George Grosz had forseen it, in fragments all

128   Interview with Philippe Dagen, *Le Monde*, August 4th 2005.

129   The inscription in Latin on Wren's tomb in St Paul's Cathedral.

around him (which he channelled in paint as *The Parade*):

'I could see examples of heroism, but they seemed to me to be blind. What I saw more clearly was misery, want, stupidity, hunger, cowardice and horror. It was then that I painted a large picture that today hangs in the museum in Wiesbaden. In a gloomy street at night — for where were the stars then? — a diabolical procession of dehumanised figures roll by: they have half-animal, half-human grotesque faces, marked by alcohol, syphilis and plague. One figure is blowing a trumpet. Hurray, brother! Someone calls out, parroting it like a madman, and he hears no echoing cry. Over the top of these masses Death is riding, seated on a black coffin, as a direct symbol. A skeletal figure. This painting was related to the works of my medieval predecessors Bosch and Bruegel, who also lived in the dusky half-light of a new epoch and found forms to express it. I painted this work as a protest against a mankind which had turned insane.'[130]

He was right, and yet there was a logic, there were beneficiaries; this hell, again, was utopia for some.

The effect of the horrors of the past is that it renders speculative fiction, indeed all fiction, relatively redundant (which does not exempt it from being enjoyable). The dilemmas faced are contrived; 'what if people were permanently retired at 30?' — in *Logan's Run* for example (with its domed city as a cross between

---

130   *Notes for My Trial*, December 1930, Pg. 314

exposition site, beach resort, futurist nail salon, Tange Kenzo and Niemyer's Brasilia). Literary fiction is arguably more inept in the obvious thought experiment stakes. The only fictional dystopias that really haunt are the ones that tread on reality; *1984* used not as a warning but as an instruction manual, the confessionals of *Darkness at Noon* which mirror Bakunin's futile begging letters to Stalin, the underground occupied Paris of *La Jetée*, the shades of the CIA's MK-Ultra experiments in Camp Archimedes in Thomas M. Dischs's *Camp Concentration*. Kafka's penal colony is fictional but it seeps out of its storytelling bounds[131] with the fate of his sisters in Auschwitz (had Kafka survived TB, he would likely have died at the hands of the Nazis) and notably because Kafka recognised the very real sense of shame felt by victims that other fiction tends to forget. The repulsion of the human origin of the food Soylent Green in Harry Harrison's *Make Room, Make Room* pales next to Swift's 'A Modest Proposal' and the culpable Irish Famine that followed. Communications in Fritz Leiber's *The Wanderer* had 'chiefly provided people and nations with the means of frightening to death and simultaneously boring to extinction themselves and each other.'[132] This is no longer restricted to fiction.

---

131   Hugh Despenser the Younger suffered a very real fate comparable to that of the machine in The Penal Colony, with biblical verses carved into his skin.

132   Pg. 158

Conquest

The city wants to grow. Science fiction portrayals tend to show the end-game as a mechanised motherboard planet extending across the entire surface and into the core of the Earth. Resources to support the population, food for example, must come from other rural planets. In *Star Wars*, the most important city in the galaxy is the planet-sized Coruscant, which is made up of over five thousand different levels. Traditionally, cities have built upon the two dimensions of the planet's surface. Coruscant builds not just up but down. To conquer the globe, the city must consume it.

The fear is that homogenisation comes too. It is voiced wearily by the protagonist of *Ringworld*:

'It occurred to him then that every city in the world had slidewalks, and that they all moved at ten miles per hour. The thought was intolerable. Not new; just intolerable. Louis Wu saw how thoroughly Munich resembled Cairo and Resht . . . and San Francisco and Topeka and London and Amsterdam. The stores along the slidewalks sold the same products in all the cities of the world [. . .] Pessimistic thinking, for a man's two hundredth birthday. But the blending of the cities was real. Louis had watched it happen. All the irrationalities of place and time and custom, blending into one big rationality of City, worldwide, like a dull gray paste. Did anyone today speak Deutsche, English, Francais, Español? Everyone spoke

Interworld.' When Viktor Shklovskii visited Weimar Berlin, he remarked 'there are many streetcars, but it's hardly worth using them to ride through the city, because the city looks the same everywhere. Palaces made out of the business of prefabricated palaces. Every monument — a service. We don't go anywhere; we live in the crowds in the middle of the Germans like a sea between its coasts.'[133]

Whether this feeling of being landlocked in déjà vu is the fault of the city or the observer is a matter of unlikely debate.

There is a danger that the all-consuming city will consume humanity. Having coined the word Ecumenopolis or planet-city (as well as designing modern Islamabad), C.A. Doxiadis has counselled that we must be prepared for this coming state ('as inevitable as the village after the agricultural revolution'[134]). We must be conscious, he declares, 'Ecumenopolis is under way, but we lack the overall concept and the courage to guide [it] rather than just letting it happen by chance and necessity . . . If we have the most perfect neighborhoods without proper connections between them we do not have a city, but nomadic life in a jungle.'[135] To invent the ship is to invent the shipwreck and to invent the Ecumenopolis is to invent an inescapable concrete jungle. '

'The brilliant superstructure, the crazy verticality will have disappeared,' Baudrillard predicted, 'New York is the final

---

133   *Berlin,* Pg. 97

134   *Building Entopia,* Pg. 19

135   Pg. 240

fling of this baroque verticality, this centrifugal eccentricity, before the horizontal dismantling arrives, and the subterranean implosion that will follow.'[136] Except it is not an either/or situation. Cities can and will grow upwards and downwards until where the earth's surface once stood will be indecipherable In the case of Coruscant, a crime-ridden labyrinthine Undercity is formed in the sunless realms near the core, though typically there is pleasure and freedom in the lawlessness, particularly around the Uscru Entertainment District. In the case of Asimov's Trantor (from which *Star Wars* borrowed the idea), its reliance on other planets for agriculture and imports made it critically exposed to being besieged[137]. A city that is planet-wide might well be impressive but it is, in essence, a walled medieval city floating in space.

A global urban singularity coincides with concerns about computational singularity. Might we envisage a sentient planet, one, if it's anything like its creators, which will lack the benevolent spirituality of Tarkovsky's *Solaris*? In all likelihood the human race will continue to expand but the complete colonising of the earth would seem a failure rather than an achievement. Though it taunts us, we need the open spaces, and we would likely be surprised by what else was lost with them. With the vast cube and sphere city-spaceships of the Borg in *Star Trek*, all trace of individuality is obliterated, through genetics and cybernetics, to unthinking obedience to the collective. It is a

136   *America*, Pg. 22

137   It was as much a densely populated nightmare for the agoraphobic Asimov as a
        wonder.

hive-mind reflected in a decentralised architecture of layers and cells, mobile through the universe assimilating living creatures and resources with the mantra 'resistance is futile'. The Borg is essentially a hyper-advanced but soulless biomechanical city that, like a shark (or more accurately the plunder economies of old like the Vikings), must keep moving and keep feeding to survive. It is, in some warped sense and perhaps the end point of all dystopias, perfection.

The further down, the darker it gets. On Coruscant, each level descending into the depths reveals new revulsions but also new truths. Here we have gone beyond the spectacle. Beneath the paving stones, the horror. It is where the mechanics and robotics of the glorious city of the rich above are located, where the junk falls and the vermin supposedly breeds. It is the consequence of the Just City above with its Jedi Temple and its Grand Senate. It is the guilty subconscious. Those exiled to this belly of the mechanical beast are the fearful result not the cause. The rot, consisting of theocratic cults, aristocratic upheavals, militarism, colonialism and trade deals, is high above them.

Of Wealth and Taste

On the Kola Peninsula in northwest Russia, scientists drilled a borehole over seven miles deep into the earth's crust. When the site was shut down in the 1990s, it was rumoured they'd inadvertently accessed the infernal city of hell. Recording equipment had reportedly picked up an avalanche of high-pitched sound deciphered as the screams of countless former people. A giant bat-shaped figure was seen escaping into the sky. This was of course the product of local over-active imaginations but it proved the durability of diabolical visions in a relatively secular age. It joined a plethora of modern myths, many centred around supposedly demythologised urban spaces. We cannot escape our stories. As psychogeographers point out, the cities we live in are saturated with layers of history, most of it lying unstirred, but cities are also saturated in fictions. There are alligators in the sewers of New York, the ghost of a Silver Arrow train in the Stockholm metro, the Aka Manto and Hanako-san ghouls who haunt Japanese toilets, the white lady who haunts the Bölchentunnel, the bridge-collapse augury of the Mothman. There is even, in the case of Rudolph Fentz, a figure who escaped from 1876 into 1950 in the manner of old utopian books and, dazed by the sensory overload of Times Square, was run over by a taxi[138].

Often the myth is intrinsically linked to place, with stories

---

138   Fentz had in fact escaped from a short story by Jack Finney into the realm of hearsay and unsubstantiated newspaper reports.

that appeal to the parochial and the universal from headless horseman-haunted highways to cry-baby bridges, chimera houses to lovers' lane murders. These travel in a childhood oral tradition that is remarkably global (especially before the internet) or else the myths emerge from some innate aspect of human nature. Sometimes the myths define a specific area such as the satanically-charged Helltown of Boston, Ohio, or involve the conjuring of entire cities such as the Swedish neo-Amazon city of 25,000 lesbians Chako Paul City that the Chinese press and several million Chinese men titillated themselves with in 2009. Often urban myths serve a warning function. The bogeyman haunts the alleys and waste-grounds of cities in almost every civilisation, often depicted with a sack designed to abduct children. The lesson is not to trust strangers. This was updated in the mechanised age with the Black Volga myth, where cars served the same fearful purpose. River-haunting phantoms, like Jenny Greenteeth in Britain, caution children away from waterways.

Pandemonium

The ultimate scapegoat Satan, of course, makes an appearance amidst the architecture. He is there as an explanation for mysterious natural bridges in Germany. He is there as conspiracy theory in the 666 glass panels in the Louvre pyramid. He is there as our excuse for genius and damnation, lurking at the crossroads[139] or in university cloisters to negotiate Faustian bargains. He is hiding in the gateways of mirrors in variations of the Bloody Mary myth and conceals himself in Demon Alleys for unwary urban explorers. He makes an infernal appearance as Spring-Heeled Jack breathing blue fire and bounding over the fog-bound rooftops of Victorian London or terrorising New Delhi in the form of the Monkey Man. As Milton expertly demonstrated, Satan is the model for the crucial figure of the anti-hero. He is there in Perak, the Spring Man of Prague defending its inhabitants, in another update of the Golem, against their oppressors. He is the rebel, the angel who rose against god, the architect, if you will, of Babel.

Traditionally the devil has been assigned his own city in the afterlife. 'Hell, which at the beginning was but an obscure village,' Thomas Nashe wrote, 'is now become a huge city, whereunto all countries are tributary.'[140] In Johann Weyer's *Pseudomonarchia Daemonum*, there are hierarchies of orders and councils in a hell comprised of 40 million demons plus inmates.

139   Traditionally the place where criminals were buried so their ghosts would be perpetually lost.

140   From the pamphlet *Pierce Penniless, His Supplication to the Divell* (1592).

Hell even appoints ambassadors to countries back here in the land of the living. In Dante's *Inferno*, hell is constructed like a vast upturned ziggurat, intentionally, given it's God's revenge, an upside-down conical subterranean Babel. Each layer is populated by prisoners whose crimes and tortures increase in severity as Dante descends with his psychopomp guide Virgil promising, 'Through me you go to the grief-wracked city.'[141] Hell is a place, if god-made, that poses many questions and paradoxes; are the instigators of torment prisoners or wardens themselves? Are they doing the supposedly benevolent work of God? Where are the masochists put? How are sinners judged equally when there is no level playing field in this life (what need do the rich have to steal for example)? Is Satan, locked in ice at the core, sentient and culpable? There is at least one question for every inhabitant of a multitude. Similarly questionable are the boundaries of this infernal city. It is a place of many entrances and few exits. It spills out onto the earth and the earth into it. In Memling's *Last Judgment Triptych* (1467-71)[142], hell is a tumbling chasm of fiery rocks[143] while the heaven resembles a hallucinatory Romanesque and Gothic cathedral with a crystal staircase, a glimpsed marble interior, carved angelic figures coming to life playing instruments, celestial muzak to drown out the cries of sinners.

'I thought within myself,' Amos Tutuola writes in *The Palm-*

---

141   Robin Kirkpatrick translation.

142   Seized by pirates in transit, it has been housed in Poland ever since.

143   Ideally placed for geo-thermal power.

wine Drunkard, 'that old people were saying that the whole people who had died in this world, did not go to heaven directly.'[144] Given the quantities entering the celestial and diabolical cities (particularly during natural disasters and massacres), a transit system would surely be required for Donne's 'numberless infinities / of souls'[145], and a bureaucracy to keep it in order. The waiting room of Beetlejuice would prove woefully inadequate, with the demand being more reminiscent of a refugee crisis. Perhaps the paintings of George Tooker with their watchful cubicles, their replicated faces and sense of menace and resignation might be necessitated. The truth, if there is one, is that there are innumerable possibilities regarding the afterlife and the traditional ones, with their neoclassical cloud castles often seem the unlikeliest. Heaven could be an Aztec city-complex or a Japanese megacity, a city built of elements that do not appear on the Periodic Table, shimmering in colours never before seen. Perhaps the skies above the cities swarm with every insect that has ever lived and dinosaurs roam between the towers. Perhaps it, like the real cities, is different for every inhabitant. Perhaps each case needs to be heard in a heavenly court with an endless limbo of appeals.

Such was the appeal of Dante's version of the diabolical city that for many years it was taken verbatim. To some, this place existed. Ever-inquisitive, Galileo examined Dante's text from both an architectural view and in relation to what would

---

144   Quoted Pg. 105 *Pre-Colonial Africa in Colonial African Narratives,* Dr. Donald R Wehrs

145   'At the round earth's imagined corners' (Holy Sonnet 7)

eventually be called physics. Though enthused, he found there were many elements that didn't add up. Consulting Archimedes, the measurements Dante gives for various circles and bouncing angles off the sun, Jerusalem and the earth's core, Galileo found that Dante's Inferno could not possibly have the dimensions it claimed to have (centuries later Aalto would claim that the worst thing about the Inferno is the stairs have the wrong proportion[146]). Similarly, he calculated that Satan could not be the size Dante claimed[147]. Neither would the structure be able to support itself, collapsing inwards. It had been built only in the vastness of Dante's mind. Inferno is of course, as all hells are, man-made. It was a poet's creation, a shadow city to the Florence he was exiled from, populated by those who had crossed him (to the extent his enemies were to be found there even before they'd died). It spoke of Dante's heartbreak, vengeance and impotence. Denied the possibility of home, he designed the worst of all possible homes for his enemies.

In Milton's *Paradise Lost*, the infernal city housing the demons is called Pandemonium. It was designed by the fallen architect-archangel Mulciber, who had helped build the 'Chrystal Battlements' of Heaven from which he was eventually hurled for his insolence. In hell, he built a capital of arches, porches, golden seats and halls, which the giant devils nevertheless had to shrink down into to enter (Milton cannot disguise a sneaking admiration, seeing himself perhaps as one of the damned elect).

146   *Aalto in His Own Words*, Pg. 205

147   'To me his face appeared as long and full / As the bronze pinecone of St. Peters' at Rome / With all his other bones proportional,' *Inferno* XXXI, Pg. 58-60

In John Martin's depictions of Pandemonium, there are signs that the city of Hell is reflective of the cities on the earth's surface. His 1825 painting is an infernal reimagining of London with a gothic thinly-disguised Houses of Parliament and a lava-choked Thames[148]. The composer Berlioz slipped into this metropolis, in a dream after a choir recital:

'I saw St. Paul's spinning around me; I was again inside it and saw it now weirdly transformed into a pandemonium; the scene was that of Martin's famous painting. Instead of the Archbishop in his pulpit, I saw Satan on his throne; of the thousands of worshippers and children grouped around him, hosts of demons and damned souls darted their fiery glances from the bosom of a visible darkness; and the iron amphitheatre in which these million sat vibrated as one mass in a terrible fashion, emitting hideous harmonies.'[149]

In Martin's *Satan Presiding at the Infernal Council*, we have the devil as the would-be ruler of the globe he bestrides, a structure he is in effect locked within[150]. All structures of power ultimately have their limits, even God, and for that reason there is perpetual hope even amongst the fallen.

---

148   By contrast, Joseph Gandy's version, *Pandemonium, or Part of the High Capital of Satan and His Peers* (1805) is almost an ideal airy classical city of golden colonnades and domes with only a slight hint of brimstone.

149   *Buildings for Music*, Michael Forsyth, Pg.132

150   It seems no accident it resembles the proto-modern humanist architecture of Ledoux and Boulee etc.

We expect hell in the hereafter but maybe it is already here. In Félicien Rops's heliogravure *Satan Sowing Tares,* a colossal long-haired skeletal Satan scatters, not weeds, but seductresses onto a sleeping Paris. His foot rests on Notre Dame Cathedral. This ambiguous mix of puritanism and hedonism reflects the obsession people still have with the idea of a city of sin. Repulsion and compulsion are two sides of the same coin. We need not seek or blame the devil; we invented him and we answer, when we answer, to ourselves alone. In Will Self's *How the Dead Live* those without prospects in the afterlife, the old and the infirm, get shuffled off to two of the more purgatorial, yet affordable, areas of London. The question implied is, as the graffiti in Ballymurphy once asked, 'Is there life before death?'[151]

'Crossing the continental United States by night, by day, on the train,' Bradbury wrote in 'The Town Where No One Got Off', 'you flash past town after wilderness town where nobody ever gets off.'[152] It is one form of damnation; so too is stepping off, and finding yourself in one of the plains cities, a Sodom or a Gomorrah. They don't exist anymore, if they ever did, except for every night in every city, when through the alchemy of the sun setting, every city is reimagined. We become devils in miniature sin cities like the damned and lost night-shades of Kirchner and the huddled nocturnal damned of Jakob Steinhardt[153]. It is our curse[154] and salvation. 'Indoors were hung these anaemic,

151   Quoted in 'Whatever You Say, Say Nothing' from Seamus Heaney's *North.*

152   A *Medicine for Melancholy*, Ray Bradbury, Pg. 56

153   *The City*, 1913

154   *Death of the Poet Walter Rheiner* (1925), Conrad Felixmüller

bloodless, lifeless studio daubs,' Kirchner wrote, 'Outside was life, noisy and colourful, pulsating.'[155] It reminds us of our place in life and in the universe.

'Once you get out in the night,' Woody Allen reflected, 'there is a sense that civilisation is gone. All the stores are closed, everything is dark and it's a different feeling. You start to realise that the city is just a superimposed man-made convention and that the real thing that you're living on is a planet. It's a wild thing in nature. All the civilisation that protects you and enables you to lie to yourself about life is all man-made and superimposed.'[156]

As night is a ramshackle bridgehead of liberty in the city, it is despised and feared by puritans. 'Worldly cities wither away from day to day under the weakness of wickedness' accuses Andreae in *Christianopolis* before launching a tirade against sodomistic night-dwellers: 'They do not allow the night to be dark, but brighten it up with lighted lanterns, the object being to provide for the safety of the city and to put a stop to useless wandering about, but also to render the night watches less unpleasant. They would strive in this way to resist the dark kingdom of Satan and his questionable pastimes; and they wish to remind themselves of the everlasting light.'[157] Yet the light seen furthest, through the sea fogs of sailortowns, was the red light. In Lucien's tales, the voyager visits Lamptown populated

155   Quoted in *Modern Architecture and Expressionism*, Dennis Sharp, Pg. 17

156   *Woody Allen on Woody Allen*, edited by Stig Björkman, Pg. 242

157   Pg. 172

by living lanterns who are put under trial and executed by being extinguished, yet the light does not know what scene it illuminates.

The night is the time of carnival, a time feared by some not simply because of neurosis or insecurities of the flesh but also because it is a social leveller. The strictures of the day are suspended, the class system momentarily shaken off, or so the illusion appears until dawn. The dead return in Mexico. The city is purified in Lupercalia. There is catharsis and reenergising. In Venice, masks and costumes might still denote status but anonymity allowed all kinds of otherwise forbidden connections. 'All were considered equal during carnival,' Bakhtin wrote, 'Here, in the town square, a special form of free and familiar contact reigned among people who were usually divided by the barriers of caste, property, profession, and age.'[158] It is the revolution realised, if only while the moon is out.

For these reasons, the night, and the decadence it permits, must be conquered in certain minds. 'O Rome, / in such a sewer sunk, in such a sleep,' Petronius writes in *The Satyricon*, 'What surgery could cure, what skill could waken into life, / but war, the rage of war, the passion of the steel?'[159]

Here we have a recurring life-negating tendency; that pleasure is a greater sin than violence, sex less preferable than death. The honest thoughtful reactionary would at least admit a dualism. The Russian heretical sect the Khylsty believed that

---

158   *Rabelais and His World*, Pg. 10

159   Pg. 132

only by sinning and then repenting could they feel the full glory of God's forgiveness; the bigger the sin, orgies mainly, the bigger the forgiveness. It is rumoured that the inadvertent catalyst of a new Russia, Rasputin, was a secret member.

'"Explain it," Hamilton muttered."This place — this bar. Why doesn't God erase it? If this world operates by moral laws — "

"This bar is necessary to the moral order. This is a sinkpit of corruption and vice, a fleshpot of iniquity. You think salvation can function without damnation? You think virtue can exist without sin? That's the trouble with you atheists; you don't grasp the mechanics of evil. Get on the inside and enjoy life, man. If you're one of the Faithful, you've got nothing to worry about.'"[160]

Few hedonists could dream up scenes like the prurient zealot can; disgust being somehow conducive to the imagination. In the irradiated Venice, Los Angeles of Tim Powers' *Dinner at Deviant Palace*, a degenerate funhouse that contains as many quivering orgasmic terrors as your imagination can fill it with, 'In his years in Venice Rivas had prided himself on being a particularly wild, nothing-to-lose young man, boating by moonlight down canals sane people shunned even at noon and participating in several foolish duels, he had taken care never to venture within blocks of Deviant's Palace. But the stories he'd heard about the place still colored his nightmares: stories of fantastic towers and spires that threw dark stains on the sky, so that

160   *Eye in the Sky*, Pg. 66

even at noon stars could be seen twinkling around the warped rib-cage architecture of its upper levels; of nonhuman forms glimpsed weeping in its remoter windows; of what creatures were sometimes found dying in the canals that entered the place through high arches, and what things these creatures sometimes said; of wooden gargoyles writhing in splintery agony on rainy nights and crying out in voices recognised by passersby as those of departed friends.' In William Temple's *Fleshpots of Sansato*, everything is for sale while in De Sade's castles the totality of the ruling caste's freedom necessitates the absolute subjugation of their victims. These are however escapist fantasies as absurd as the yearning for a pleasure-dome on a Martian moon ('Ah Xanadu. Why had he ever left that distant sanctuary?'[161]). It is often forgotten that when Coleridge floated off in an opium-daze to a medieval Chinese pleasure-dome, he was trying to escape 18th century England. For New Jerusalem to exist, there must be a cursed Sodom. For New Jerusalem to be endured, there must equally be Sodom.

The truth is that leisure, at its best, is a spell in utopia, a glimpse how our lives could be. Cedric Price's Fun Palace was designed to expand this gateway. Formulated at an 'alcohol-inspired brain-storming session off Times Square in 1962', the instructions of the rearrangeable playpen-shipyard were naïve and charming:

'Choose what you want to do — or watch someone else doing

it. Learn how to handle tools, paint, babies, machinery, or just listen to your favourite tune. Dance, talk or be lifted up to where you can see how other people make things work. Sit out over space with a drink and tune in to what's happening elsewhere in the city. Try starting a riot or beginning a painting — or just lie back and stare at the sky.'[162]

Leisure was opposed by religious institutions, councils and conservative citizen groups. 'Puritanism,' as Mencken defined is, 'the haunting fear that someone, somewhere, may be happy.'[163]

Like all 'Others', it is Sodom's curse to bear the neurosis of the virtuous. It must be burned and drowned again and again for them. 'And also, the cities there were lost because of sin,' Mandeville recounted on his travels, 'And there beside grow trees that bear full fair apples, and fair of colour to behold; but whoso breaketh them or cutteth them in two, he shall find within them coals and cinders, in token that by wrath of God the cities and the land were burnt and sunken into hell . . . And into [the] sea sunk the five cities by wrath of God; that is to say, Sodom, Gomorrah, Aldama, Zeboim, and Zoar, for the abominable sin of sodomy that reigned in them. But Zoar, by the prayer of Lot, was saved.'[164] Sodom, of course, is always destroyed in hindsight; God's wrath promised after the fact. It has been used to celebrate the bursting of levees in New Orleans, the

162   *Non-Plan: Essays on Freedom, Participation and Change in Modern Architecture*, Pg. 23

163   *H.L. Mencken*, Vincent Fitzpatrick, Pg. 37

164   Pg. 68

earthquakes of San Francisco, countless famines. Just as the ruins and survivors are exploited materially by arch-cynics[165], so too are they by fundamentalists, keen to elevate themselves above the unworthy victims. The incinerated occupants of Sodom are so damned that even sympathising with them is to be punished; the Nuremberg Chronicle by Hartmann Schedel depicts Lot's wife being transformed into a pillar of salt for looking back at the massacre. As Sodom is destroyed completely, she is turned into architecture and left there as a reminder, punished for the inquisitiveness and empathy that has taken us from the caves to the cities[166].

In real life, Rome's arch-rival Carthage was destroyed and the very land sown with salt. It was to be damned from memory (*Damnatio memoriae*), except that it survived through literature; in a twist on Victor Hugo's assertion that the printing press would usurp architecture, the book saves the memory of what was once built[167]. The problem with censorship, for the censors, is that it inadvertently points out where our attentions should go; the banned book is the one we wish to read most, the veiled Black Doge Marin Faliero in the Venetian Palace is the one, above all others, to which we are drawn. There is much to learn from following the heroics of Lot's wife.

---

165   The Shock Doctrine, as Klein has defined it, proves 'ill blows the wind that profits no-one'.

166   It is traditional to punish mortals for positive humanist traits, see Sysphus, Tantalus, Prometheus, Adam and Eve, Pandora etc. Theirs are jealous Gods.

167   In Normon Juster's *The Phantom Tollbooth* the cities of Dictionopolis and Digitopolis create words and numbers respectively.

'My brother once forced me to spend a day wandering through Tokyo looking at the victims of the Great Kanto earthquake of 1923,' Akira Kurosawa recalled, 'Corpses piled on bridges, corpses blocking off a whole street at the intersection, corpses displaying every manner of death possible to human beings. When I involuntarily looked away, my brother scolded me, "Akira, look carefully now." When that night I asked my brother why he made me look at those terrible sights, he replied: "If you shut your eyes to a frightening sight, you end up being frightened. If you look at everything straight on, there is nothing to be afraid of."[168] With my camera, like Dostoyevsky with his prose, I have tried to force the audience — which is often unwilling — to look carefully *now*.' It is fear we are afraid of and it makes slaves of us.

The righteous City of God will be indestructible we are told; from Nicholas Roerich's pristine dragon-beset 'Fairest City' (1914) to the cathedrals of glass built on Californian faultlines as a sign of faith (and perhaps a hubristic challenge[169]). God has continually taken the form of disaster; the fire of the burning bush, the lightning on Mount Sinai, the comet hanging in the sky for twelve days above Herman Gall's Nuremberg woodcut of a ruined Constantinople. These are riddles to unravel and the answer too often has not been tectonics or weather but morality,

---

168 *Akira Kurosawa: Interviews*, Pg. 184

169 Architects have begun to outwit the god of natural disasters with buildings that bend, have shock-absorbers or, like Kengo Kuma, focus on weak architecture that doesn't try to compete with the earthquake for strength but facilitates its movements.

simply because the urge to control and punish is too tempting. The earthquakes and the seas rise because men have sex with men just as witches caused shipwrecks and Jews poisoned wells. The senselessness of mass destruction and death might make the sober question the existence of a benevolent god, so distractions are in order, not with the pleasures of sex or libation but with more death.

'After the earthquake, which had destroyed three-fourths of the city of Lisbon,' Voltaire writes only semi-fictionally in *Candide*, 'the sages of that country could think of no means more effectual to preserve the kingdom from utter ruin than to entertain the people with an auto-da-fe, it having been decided by the University of Coimbra, that the burning of a few people alive by a slow fire, and with great ceremony, is an infallible preventive of earthquakes . . . The same day there was another earthquake, which made most dreadful havoc.'[170]

There is of course pleasure at work here, namely that it is happening to someone else. In Conan Doyle's *Maracot of the Deep* the destruction of Atlantis is watched on a proto-video screen: 'And doom came . . . but thousands dashed up to the Citadel, which stood upon higher ground, and the battlement walls were black with people. Then suddenly the Castle began to sink. Everything began to sink . . . The roofs looked for a while like successive reefs of rock forming lines of spouting breakers until they, too, went under.'[171]

170   Pg. 18

171   *The Strand Magazine*, Volume 75, Pg. 12

Destruction need not even be total. The avenging angels might fly over marked and unmarked homes or cleanse the streets as lone vigilantes. *Punch* depicted one such knife-wielding phantom placing the blame on the surroundings: 'Dank roofs, dark entries, closely-clustered walls / Murder-inviting nooks, death-reeking gutters / A boding voice from your foul chaos calls / When will men heed the warning that it utters?'[172]

The source of endless fiction and gleeful guided tours, Jack the Ripper was not a decrepit coward preying on vulnerable women but a moralistic obsession of a sick society. One of the problems in identifying him was that hundreds of people wrote to the police and newspapers claiming to be him, creating a vast network of false leads. Of the authenticated letters, there is only one mythical sending address: 'From hell.'

172   *Punch*, September 29th, 1888

Nothing Ever Happens

The one unquestionable difference between heaven and hell is that in hell we will not be bored. 'The secret source of Humour itself is not joy but sorrow,' Mark Twain wrote, 'There is no humour in heaven.'[173] A utopia without humour, and the requisite pain, is no utopia at all. We might add to this debauchery, though schadenfreude might well be included, with a viewing platform provided to gloat upon the miserable wretches in hell. Our architectural conception of heaven is largely a Western European construct; an acropolis, with gates more fitting to the mansion of a 19th century robber baron or newspaper magnate. Hell, by contrast, is dark, murky and crucially interesting. Many read *Inferno*, much less bother with *Paradiso* or *Purgatorio*. In the early film *Just Imagine* (1930), a magnificent construction of a future metropolis is let down by a knockabout love story. Drama is conflict and very often tragedy, and the absence of this is deadening. It is very easy to imagine an architecture of misery. An architecture of perfection seems to fade into nothingness.

The afterlife is different elsewhere. The entrance tunnel of white light that is often seen in near-death experiences is not uncommon to disassociative hallucinations, suggesting it is the product of biochemical reactions in the brain. What is found therein is reflective of the culture from which the visitor has come and the religious figures and environments they've grow

---

173   *More Tramps Abroad*, Pg. 70

up with. Cross-cultural experiences are sadly few; Hindus for example rarely find themselves entering the feasting halls, via rainbow bridges, of Valhalla. Cultures remain curiously segregated in an afterlife suspiciously close to our own world. Heaven is rarely updated with the passage of time, though the heaven of *A Matter of Life and Death* has installed an escalator and modernist circular perforations to view the earth from. Such conventions seem to denigrate the infinite potential we were promised, 'colossal aerial buildings, with neither foundations nor roof-tops,' as Gustave Moreau wrote, 'covered with teeming, quivering vegetation, this sacred flora standing out against the dark blues of the starry vaults and the deserts of the sky.'[174]

To remain infinite an idea must never be realised.

174   Gustave Moreau commenting on his *Jupiter and Semele* notebooks, 10th October 1897.

Flotsam and Jetsam

All buildings contain their own ruins, just as Michelangelo's Prisoners are locked in marble. Ultimately all cities, as well as their inhabitants, will lose the battle with time. The most forward-thinking futurologists could see this; Gandy envisaging *Soane's Bank of England as a Ruin* (1830), Hubert Robert's *Imaginary view of the Gallery of the Louvre as a Ruin*, Salon of 1796, the Roma Interrotta competition entries which placed modernism in the midst of the wreckage of the past. 'The tides of centuries have passed and left behind on the sand the relics of remote shipwrecks'[1].

It is a brave and humble architect who imagines his or her own life's work in ruins. There is an attraction to the essence of things, the skull beneath the skin. 'I like ruins,' Tadao Ando admitted, 'because what remains is not the total design, but the

---

1   Guilio Carlo Argan (1978), cited in *Studio One*, October 18th, 2008

clarity of thought, the naked structure, the spirit of the thing.'[2]

To Mies Van Der Rohe 'skyscrapers reveal their powerful structure during construction; only then is the gigantic steel truly expressive. When the panel walls are in position, the structural system at the basis of the composition is hidden behind a chaos of insignificant and trivial forms.'[3]

There is something seductive about the destruction that time wreaks and also the idea that we would survive to bear witness. It is the unlikely victory of the human David over the architectural Goliath. The atmosphere of ruins cannot be underestimated from the hypnotic flotsam of Tarkovsky's long tracking shot of flooded former rooms in *Stalker* to Leigh Brackett's *The Last Days of Shandakor*:

'the lights of many colors that had burned there were burning still but they were old and dim, cold embers without radiance. The towers of jade and turquoise rose up against the little moons and they were broken and cracked with time and there was no glory in them. They were desolate and very sad. The night lay clotted around their feet. The streets, the plazas and the market-squares were empty, their marble paving blank and bare. The soldiers had gone from the walls of Shandakor, with their banners and their bright mail, and there was no longer any movement anywhere within the gates . . . suddenly from the darkness of the valley and the slopes beyond there rose a thin

---

2   From *Seven Interviews with Tadao Ando*

3   *Poetica Dell'Architecttura Neo-Plastica*, Mies van der Rohe, B Zevi , Pg. 123

fierce howling as of wolves.'[4]

These have been such real places in the past, in a million unwritten unpainted nights across the planet, from Fatehpur Sikri to Pripyat to Hashima Island, and they will occur again, in the seemingly-immortal metropolises of ours.

Our cities are built on the ruins of earlier incarnations. The soil conceals and reveals a layer of burned ash from when Boudicca burned an earlier London to the ground[5]. In *Riddley Walker*, there is a sense that our descendants are haunted by this buried time and a sense, if not a knowledge, of all that was lost and could have been (Hoban got the idea from viewing the fresco of St Eustace at Canterbury Cathedral, itself surviving from an earlier world). It is a land, post-Britain and post-England, where language has evolved[6] and the facts of nuclear holocaust have been swallowed up in folklore that retains the message but has lost the details. What is left of the cities of now are the barest ruins, shrouded in myths that read like the accounts of medieval voyages: 'There ben the dead towns all them years. Ram out poasts in 1 part of them and dogs hoalt up in other parts. And all them years you heard storys of dog peopl. Peopl with dogs heads and dogs with peopls heads.'[7] We are back in the map-making days.

4   From *Prize Science Fiction*, Donald A. Wollheim (1953), Pg. 124

5   *The Great Fire of London: In That Apocalyptic Year, 1666,* Neil Hanson, Pg. 34

6   Denis Johnson's *Fiskadoro* is another fascinating, though very different, book on this theme.

7   Pg. 14

'I will tell you only that this living, speaking ruins filled my spirit with images,'[8] the artist and architect Piranesi wrote of the surviving remnants of Ancient Rome which had inspired his visions. Piranesi's etchings seem to extend into infinity, despite their claustrophobia, essentially because he was sketching the rooms of his imagination.

'In one set of etchings after another,' Kenneth Frampton wrote, 'he represented the dark side of that sensation already classified by Edmund Burke in 1757 as the Sublime, that tranquil terror induced by contemplation of great size, extreme antiquity and decay.'[9]

The invention of architectural scenes — *capriccios* — was almost a competitive sport in Italian art, with the likes of Canaletto resassembling or adding to existing cities. Piranesi went furthest in bringing the dungeons, slave quarters and infernal engines (the mechanics of empire[10]) to the fore, extending staircases to impossible heights, expanding the labyrinth. The scenes that look ancient and apocalyptic, with past and future joining in a circle, reflect his state of mind: 'I need to produce great ideas, and I believe that if I were commissioned to design a new universe, I would be mad enough to undertake it.'[11]

The fall of Rome, or what they wished Rome had been, haunted generations. It cast a *memento mori* shadow onto

8   *The Sphere and the Labyrinth*, Pg. 28

9   *Modern Architecture*, Kenneth Frampton, Pg. 13

10   Emily Allchurch's series *Urban Chiaroscuro* constructs these as photographs
       interwound with elements from Fascist and contemporary architecture.

11   *A History of Western Architecture*, David Watkin, Pg. 372

all achievements. The fall could, and would, happen again. Piranesi industrialised these ruins. In this nightmare of wheels and staircases, there lurked an unlikely stouthearted romantic and explorer[12]:

'Many years ago, when I was looking over Piranesi's *Antiquities of Rome*, Mr. Coleridge, who was standing by, described to me a set of plates by that artist, called his Dreams, and which record the scenery of his own visions during the delirium of a fever. Some of them (I describe only from memory of Mr. Coleridge's account) represented vast Gothic halls: on the floor of which stood all sorts of engines and machinery, wheels, cables, pulleys, levers, catapults, &c.&c. expressive of enormous power put forth and resistance overcome. Creeping his way upwards, was Piranesi himself: follow the stairs a little further, and you perceive it come to a sudden abrupt termination, without any balustrade, and allowing no step onwards to him who had reached the extremity, except into the depths below. Whatever is to become of poor Piranesi, you suppose, at least, that his labours must in some way terminate here. But raise your eyes, and behold a second flight of stairs still higher: on which again Piranesi is perceived, by this time standing on the very brink of the abyss. Again elevate your eye, and a still more aerial flight of stairs is beheld: and again is poor Piranesi busy on his aspiring labours: and so on, until the unfinished stairs and

12   Piranesi's endless staircases and platforms seem a blueprint for the computer games centuries later.

Piranesi both are lost in the upper gloom of the hall — With the same power of endless growth and self-reproduction did my architecture proceed in dreams. In the early stage of my malady, the splendours of my dreams were indeed chiefly architectural: and I beheld such pomp of cities and palaces as was never yet beheld by the waking eye, unless in the clouds.'[13]

13   *Confessions of an English Opium-eater: And, Suspiria de Profundis,*
        Thomas De Quincey, Pg. 115

The Fall

'All happy families are alike,' Tolstoy claimed, 'every unhappy family is unhappy in its own way.'[14] So too is it with cities. They take off much in the same way and fail in a myriad. They can be built via gold-fever and the ethnic cleansing of the native population (the Trail of Tears for example) and shrivel when the goldrush dissipates or rumours arrive of easier money elsewhere. They can slip into gentrified self-parody and become stage sets or doppelgängers of themselves like parts of Montmartre or Tombstone. The markets can abandon them and the deserts can swallow them like the diamond-town of Kolmanskop, Namibia, with its living-dead rooms filling with sand. The land can slide from beneath their feet as in the hill town of Craco, its shell gazing down on the hanging Judas in *The Passion of the Christ*. They can drown under water or earth or radiation. They can be deserted when the occupants realise they are harvesting death as in the asbestos mine-town of Wittenoom or when they accidentally ignite a coal seam that will burn for centuries beneath them as in Centralia. They become spectres and attract visitors to what amounts to a Grand Tour of how not to live. There are even those that vanish altogether like the Roanoke Colony, leaving a cryptic message 'Croatoan' carved onto a wooden post[15]. The multiple ways of failing still invite

---

14   *Anna Karenina*, Pg. 1

15   The child Virginia Dare, first to be born there, vanished with them but returned in a curious afterlife as the vivacious adult she did not live to become in Victorian ads for tobacco and alcohol.

singular moralistic explanations, proving we have never quite escaped the desire to appease gods with sacrifices.

Written in a fever-dream by Joachim, a disciple hiding on the Greek island of Patmos, the Book of Revelation focuses in on binary cities of good and evil. One city named Babylon, but suspiciously like the superpower Rome of the day, would try to dominant mankind through an urbane Antichrist and would, after a period of ascendancy, be punished by cataclysms culminating in a visitation by the Four Horsemen of the Apocalypse. It would eventually fall in a battle at Armageddon, vanquished by the jewelled City of the Just. It was a revenge tale written by a runaway in an obscure outpost and it was vague, destructive and malleable enough for every generation since to find relevance in it. They've been creating Antichrists ever since. The reassuring dichotomy of the tale gained particular currency during the Cold War with the American Christian Right and its supposed antithesis the godless 'Evil Empire' of the Soviets. In dozens of posters, publications and sermons, it was asserted again and again that the Atomic bomb was not just God's gift to America, it was 'the spirit of God'[16]. Few but the incurably credulous actually believed this but it proved valuable to televisual preachers up to and including President Reagan, who restored America's faith in itself, having been shaken by the hard cold realities of Viet Nam, JFK and Watergate, by telling the nation pleasant Manichean bedtime stories. They are Babylon so we are the Just City. They are the damned, we are

16   Psychiana ad, 1946.

the chosen. For the first time it was conceivable for humanity to bring about the apocalypse through technology. Despite not a single mention of an atom in *Revelation*, it seemed certain the Rapture predicted there was coming. Embarrassingly, it failed, as it has done for each generation, to arrive (we remain blissfully unmelted at our workplaces and unburnt in our beds[17], other nations have not been so fortunate) but it will not be long before the Just and Damned Cities require rebuilding again.

The end of the world will come eventually, until then the end of the world prophecy industry will remain a busy one. Every generation, once safely out of its youth, sees the end of days beginning in younger generations:

'Whence shall come the new barbarians? Go through the squalid quarters of great cities, and you may see, even now, their gathering hordes. How shall learning perish? Men will cease to read, and books will kindle fires and be turned into cartridges! It is startling to think how slight the traces that would be left of our civilisation did it pass through the throes that have accompanied the decline of every previous civilisation. Paper will not last like parchment, nor are our most massive buildings and monuments to be compared in solidity with the rock-hewn temples and titanic edifices of old civilisations. And invention has given us not merely the steam engine and the printing press,

---

17   Medardo Rosso's Omnibus sculpture resembles calcified forms, as if the
         commuters were suddenly struck by a nuclear detonation or a pyroclastic flow.

but petroleum, nitro-glycerine and dynamite.'[18]

Despite this nostalgic myopia, such is the incremental nature of disaster and humanity's capacity to deny and to cling, that catastrophe is often easy to ignore: 'when the vandals were hammering at the gates of Hippo, Augustine's city, the groans of the dying defenders on the wall mingled with the roar of the spectators in the circus, more concerned with their day's enjoyment than with even their ultimate personal safety.'[19]

The reassuring thing is the barbarians are always here for we are they, endlessly rehearsing the end of the world, just as we have always done.

'Architecture aims at Eternity'[20] Wren pointed out, and architecture fails. There are constant reminders of this, not just in the monstrous vines creeping over Angkor Wat, or the sudden cataclysmic appearance of a waterfall in New York City in Tsunehisa Kimura's photomontage, but in the continual need to repaint the Eiffel Tower, to dig Old Skagen Church out of the sand, to replaster the Djenne Mosque. All cities are slowly eroding, with gravity and the conspiratorial elements conspiring, and we fight a largely-unseen war of attrition just to stand still. Unless innovations are found, a host of metropolises will relocate underwater, others will be absorbed into swamps, forests, tundra. The African continent will continue pushing

18   *A Menace and a Promise*, Henry George [1897] 'whence shall come the new barbarians?'

19   Mumford, Pg. 230

20   Christopher Wren, 'Of Architecture', *Parentalia; or Memoirs of the Family of the Wrens*, comp. by his son Christopher (1750, reprinted 1965), Appendix, Pg. 351.

north until the Mediterranean is squeezed out of existence and a range of mountains larger than the Himalayas rises from Paris to Istanbul. Should humanity simply die out before then like Wells's Martians laid low by microscopic creatures. The skyscrapers will all collapse. Unmaintained, the glass facades will fall away, leaves and detritus will ignite with lightning and sunlight. Modern buildings will be the first to go[21], leaving the solid stone Victorian banks, the Gothic cathedrals, last of all the buildings already surviving from antiquity, the pyramids and ziggurats.

If there are survivors, they will visit the wreckage of our civilisations just as people visited the ruins of the Wonders of the World. In Mitchell's *The Last American*, travelling Persians sail into the ruins of New York City, which for eleven centuries has 'decayed in solitude'. It is a setting which the writer cannot help recount in barbed satire:

'Historians are astounded that a nation of an hundred million beings should vanish from the earth like a mist, and leave so little behind. But to those familiar with their lives and character surprise is impossible. There was nothing to leave. The Mehrikans possessed neither literature, art, nor music of their own. Everything was borrowed . . . They were a sharp, restless, quick-witted, greedy race, given body and soul to the gathering of riches. Their chiefest passion was to buy and sell.'

21   Stanley Tigerman's sinking of Mies van der Rohe's Crown Hall in *The Titanic* (1978) may be wilfully absurd but it is not inaccurate in terms of what might go first.

Even when damned by the self-righteous as a fallen decadent civilisation, there is still a pervading sense of sadness: 'while in this park we came to a high tower, standing by itself, and climbed to the top, where we enjoyed a wide-spreading view. The extent of the city is astounding . . . All about us in every direction as far as sight can reach were ruins, and ruins, and ruins. Never was a more melancholy sight. The blue sky, the bright sunshine, the sweet-scented air with the gay flowers and singing birds only made it sadder. They seemed a mockery.'[22]

A lone figure in a canoe surveys what was once the capital of England in *After London, or Wild England*[23] by Richard Jeffries. The only traces of the metropolis are found in the poisons that corrupt a marsh, polluting the wildlife that has otherwise recolonised the area. It is an ominous setting with half-buried memories of Dante:

'Ghastly beings haunted the site of so many crimes, shapeless monsters, hovering by night, and weaving a fearful dance. Frequently they caught fire, as it seemed, and burned as they flew or floated in the air . . . The earth on which he walked, the black earth, leaving phosphoric footmarks behind him, was composed of the mouldered bodies of millions of men who had passed away in the centuries during which the city existed . . . He looked around, supposing that he might see the gleaming head and shoulders of the half-buried giant, of which he recollected

---

22   Pg. 79

23   Ballard's *The Drowned World* is a future echo.

he had been told. The giant was punished for some crime by being buried to the chest in the earth; fire incessantly consumed his head and played about it, yet it was not destroyed.'[24]

The sense that the ruined cities were the cause and not the consequence of diabolical crimes gives credence to anti-cosmopolitan forces, like those who make the thirtieth amendment to the U.S. Constitution in the epigraph of Leigh Brackett's *The Long Tomorrow*; 'No city, no town, no community of more than one thousand people or two hundred buildings to the square mile, shall be built or permitted to exist anywhere in the United States of America.'

The feeling of lost greatness or lost futures is a curious one, combining the sense of the transitory in the Japanese term *mono no aware* and the feeling of yearning Portugese sailors call *Saudade*. It is home-sickness, melancholy and (self-) betrayal. Even now we have it when we consider the buildings that have been lost to us, the Telschow House, the masterpieces of Victor Horta, the Singer Building, the Garrick Theatre, Penn Station but above all the hauntological sense of what could have been and was not permitted. It is the sum of what we have ruined compared to what we could've been. The accounting is not finished.

In the moments when we fluctuate between strength and weakness, we might well wish to reimagine our cities into ruins. '"I hope from my soul that I may live to see the day when that damned city will be a desolate wilderness,' wrote the architect

24   Pg. 380

Ralph Adams Cram in an urge that is as natural as toying with self-destruction; 'when those chimneys shall rise smokeless; when those streets shall be stony valleys between grisly ridges of fallen brick; when Nature itself shall shrink from repairing the evil that man has wrought; when the wild birds shall sweep widely around that desolation that they may not pass above; when only rats and small snakes shall crawl though the ruin of that thriving commercial and manufacturing metropolis; when the very name it bore in the days of its dirty glory shall have become a synonym for horror and despair!" Having thus relieved himself he laughed softly, and felt better.'[25]

25   *Walled Towns*, Pg. 11

The Wounds of Possibility

Meaning will be lost from the ruined cities of the future and new meanings will be attached: 'By AD 302 when the future emperor Constantine the Great passed by [the ancient city of Memphis], the place had already become a deserted tumble of ruins. The old gods and their worshippers had fled; the ibises were just birds and the cats just cats.'[26]

Our gods and our heroes will be curios, as hieroglyph figures are to us now. Cities will become warrens, caverns for bats, coral reef. Sacred buildings will be ransacked and recycled for stone just as the Coliseum was and the Great Wall of China is today. Future Raphaels and Piranesis will sketch and learn from the ruins. Between then and now, destructions will be witnessed and normalised. Abandoned cities will encourage artful ruin-porn. Politicians will host summits on preventing catastrophe whilst at the same time exhibiting the same approach as Pliny the Elder bathing as Vesuvius erupted around him or the Mayor of London commenting upon viewing the Great Fire that 'A woman could piss it out'[27], then returning to his bed. Money will ensure change is paralysed or tokenistic and when catastrophe occurs, catastrophe industries will emerge. Life will struggle on.

Nature will prove even more resilient, as it has proved even where nuclear catastrophe has occurred. While Isozaki considered building new structures on the *Re-Ruined Hiroshima*,

---

26   *Cities of the Classical Age,* Pg. 205

27   *John Milton: A Biography,* Neil Forsyth, Pg. 162

nature got there first. The unwanted apocalyptic experiment of Chernobyl resulted not only in irradiated forever-downed helicopters, abandoned classrooms and fairgrounds, and a deathly sarcophagus tomb, but also a burned red forest thriving with wildlife that is now protected from human interference. In *The Garbage World* by Charles Platt, pleasure cities dump their rubbish onto the asteroid Kopra. Citizens there live by scavenging in miles-deep layers of trash (echoing existing shanty-towns now like those at Olususun landfill or and the Super-Sargasso vortexes in the ocean where our city waste has accumulated). Even if society has been largely lost[28], even if our languages have been forgotten and our cities utterly destroyed, if there are survivors they will sift through the wreckage, look upon the landscape and be drawn to placing stone upon stone once again[29].

---

28   *Dark Age Ahead*, Jane Jacobs - 'Writing, printing, and the Internet give a false sense of security about the permanence of culture.' Pg. 5

29   Yves Tanguy's *Multiplication of the Arcs* (1954) anticipates such a scene while the post-human architecture of Kay Sage seems the next step. The haunted Marc Antoine Laugier frontispiece for 'Essai sur l'architecture' with a cherub and goddess examining a primitive structure is not prehistory but post-history and suggests the fundamentals of architecture are intrinsic.

Terraforms

To survive might require escape but also to take portions of the Earth with us. Cities floating in space will require vegetation to provide food and oxygen. The biodomes we see in films like *Silent Running* were dreamt up by the aged Konstantin Tsiolkovsky in his shack in Russia. NASA imagined their own version by commissioning O'Neill and Davis's *The High Frontier*. This thought experiment is written in the old-fashioned conceit of a letter, albeit one from space: 'All the habitats are variations of basic sphere, cylinder or ring shapes. We live in Bernal Alpha [where] the land forms a big curving valley.' The effect is essentially the suburbs of the planet, 'mainly in the form of low-rise, terraced apartments, shopping walkways, and small parks. Many services, light industries, and shops are located underground or in a central low-gravity sphere, or are steeply terraced, because we like to preserve most of our land area for grass and parks.'

Being above weather, the cities have their optional climates with Bernal Alpha opting for mid-morning on Hawaii most of the time. Like all suburbs, occupants are relatively select (the cities house 10,000) and tastes are middle-brow, from low-gravity ballet to waterless swimming baths. Teenagers are conscripted into maintenance crews for a year rather than dying in foreign wars. 'You asked whether we feel isolated. Some of us do get 'island fever' to some degree, probably because we're really first-generation immigrants; it never seems to bother the kids who were born here.'[30]

Given the colossal effort required to reach escape velocity and the amount of resources needed to be transported to space cities, Tsiolkovsky's idea of a space elevator has been resurrected. With an orbiting anchor in space, a structure of incredibly strong polycarbons could ferry cargos and people to and fro. Energy will naturally be crucial to any space city with the most dramatic and potentially economic model being a vast orb called a Dyson Sphere which will encompass a star, harnessing the energy emitted with little waste. Rotation might well provide artificial gravity so that a city-system like *Ringworld* could come to exist; a strange linear city that arcs overhead.

We might even return to the ultra-resilient stone cities of the past, particularly in inhospitable environments like Mars. On more distant planets, we may well find they already exist or once did. The Martian palaces of *John Carter* bear a striking resemblances to the very real Great Kyz Kala in Turkmenistan, the Tomb of Askia or Jaisalmer Fort in Rajasthan. When a face was spotted, through pareidolia on the surface of Cydonia, the assumption was that it was a structure akin to the Sphinx[31]. The transplantation of Egyptian tombology to other worlds is not uncommon: 'I have seen the hoary, sky-confronting walls of Macchu Pichu amid the desolate Andes, and the teocallis that are buried in the Mexican jungles. And I have seen the frozen, giant-builded battlements of Uogam on the glacial tundras of

30   Quoted Pg. 57, *The Kids' Whole Future Catalog*, Paula Taylor

31   The World of Tiers in Philip Farmer's *The Maker of Universes* resembles a
        Babylonian ziggurat in space.

the nightward hemisphere of Venus.'[32] The mistranslations that Mars had canals might well be corrected with actual canals filled with melted polar ice being used to terraform the planet. The reclamation of the desert posited in fantastic tales like *Electropolis* by Otfrid von Vanstein or Arrakis in *Dune* is after all now undertaken on earth in the oil-rich but water-depleted Gulf States[33].

Venus and Mars are warnings of where the Earth may be heading. Life would cling on, for the most part greatly diminished and precariously. In P Schuyler Miller's *The Titan*, a race of degenerating Martians retreat from the onslaught of cold by digging and building deeper and deeper into the core where there is warmth. Even if the sun suddenly disappeared, the red eye of the caves permanently dimmed, cities might build around geothermal vents for energy[34]. In *The Night Land* by William Hope Hodgson, populations build up around fissures and volcanoes in a newly-Vulcanised earth before retreating to pyramid Redoubts, metal mountain cities 'with the lowest half-mile sealed' as defence and a Tower of Observation at the peak, fed by Underground Fields and powered by Earth-current. A curious gentleman who'd run off to sea to escape from a cruel religious father (from whom he regularly hid in treetops), Hodgson kept elaborate journals charting the marine world, saved a ship-mate from sharks, returned and tried to establish

---

32   *The Narrative of Rodney Severn*, Clark Ashton Smith

33   Jinns have regrettably not yet been tapped for nuclear energy as once posited.

34   The city of Rapture in *BioShock* is powered from submarine volcanic vents.

a doomed proto-gym which he advertised by careering down stairs on a bicycle and was ruined trying to sabotage Houdini's act. He was eventually blown to smithereens by a German shell in the war, leaving only his helmet. When he was still alive, he would stay up all night writing, gazing out to the almost lightless sea: 'To me, in this last time of my visions, of which I would tell, it was not as if I dreamed; but, as it were, that I waked there into the dark, in the future of this world. And the sun had died . . . '[35]

The tombs of nuclear shelters and pharaohs will remain as funerary remnants of our existence. Within them might survive our writings, these messages from the past, words that serve as time travel and clairvoyance. The city is the repository of information, how long it will all last and whether digital will dissipate as the Library of Alexandria did, is debatable. Even this is an age-old concern: 'In Agharti the learned Panditas write on tablets of stone all the science of our planet and of the other worlds. The Chinese learned Buddhists know this. Their science is the highest and purest. Every century one hundred sages of China collect in a secret place on the shores of the sea, where from its depths come out one hundred eternally-living tortoises. On their shells the Chinese write all the developments of the divine science of the century.'[36]

We live and build our cities on the skin of the planet. To ensure we can speak to the future, we must descend into the protection of the Earth. Just as the contents of the National

35   *The Night Land*, Pg. 23

36   *Beasts, Men and Gods*, Ferdinand Ossendowski, Pg. 316

Gallery were housed through the Second World War in a Welsh slate mine, so too are data and seed banks. To dissuade prospective adventurers from opening deadly sealed bunkers filled with nuclear waste, scientists working on Onkalo in Finland debated various approaches[37]. Obstacles would only encourage prospective treasure-hunters. Linguistic warnings might well outlast the languages they are written in. One symbol proposed was an engraving of Munch's *The Scream*, one last portrait for posterity.

Humans might well join their treasures and their waste underground. Verne's coal town of New Aberfoyle in Scotland is lit by artificial electromagnetically-powered suns and stars. At a time of suffocating industrial smog, life as a trogolydte was portrayed as preferable, 'What wonder then, that excursionists from Stirling came in considerable numbers to enjoy the calm fresh air in the recesses of the mine? The electric discs shed a brilliancy of light which the British sun, oftener obscured by fogs than it ought to be, might well envy.'[38] The problem with refuges is that they often become prisons. In the article Depthscrapers Defy Earthquakes[39], a tiered 35 storey well is built downwards, protected by a treacherous Earth. Sunlight is refracted in through a rotating system of mirrors and air is pumped in. The blueprints, as with perhaps the mood, resembles the ever-recurring Inferno.

---

37   This features in the 2010 documentary *Into Eternity* by Michael Madsen.

38   *The Underground City*, Pg. 75

39   *Everyday Science and Mechanics,* November, 1931

Before obliteration comes solitude. Someone will be the last human and somewhere will be the last metropolis. Most children entertain the idea of being alone in a city (some adults indulge themselves in the gloriously desolate streets around dawn) and the devilry that could be indulged in. 'At eighty-nine miles an hour, he shot down the lifeless, empty boulevard, one roaring sound in the great stillness.'[40]

Very soon the solipsism of such a wish would give rise to fear — 'Imagine all human beings swept off the face of the earth, excepting one man. Imagine this man in some vast city, New York or London. Imagine him on the third or fourth day of his solitude sitting in a house and hearing a ring at the door-bell!'[41]

In Wyndham's *The Day of the Triffids*, the feeling is palpable[42]: 'Moreover, I was beginning to experience something new — the fear of being alone. I had not been alone since I walked from the hospital along Piccadilly, and then there had been bewildering novelty in all I saw. Now, for the first time I began to feel the horror that real loneliness holds for a species that is by nature gregarious. I felt naked, exposed to all the fears that prowled . . . '

Nevertheless liberated from work and want, time might become expansive and filled with possibilities, though a person would need to remain lucky with no professional help to hand, hence Henry Bernis, in *The Twilight Zone*, on all fours with his smashed glasses and his stacks of books,

40   Pg. 24

41   *Ponkapog Papers*, 1904

42   Borrowed for countless films such as Danny Boyle's *28 Days Later*.

saying 'That's not fair. That's not fair at all. There was time now. There was all the time I wanted . . . ! That's not fair!'

After The Fall, cities may be shunned as the source of ruin, like the glowing cities of *The Chrysalids*, the feared realms of *Riddley Walker* and the banned territories in *The Long Tomorrow*. Time capsule knowledge of what once was will sleep in the soil but also in books as it did in the so-called Dark Ages[43]. In *A Canticle for Leibowitz*, bootlegging monks maintain the knowledge of our world, before the nuclear holocaust: 'We are the centuries . . . We have your eoliths and your mesoliths and your neoliths. We have your Babylons and your Pompeiis.'[44]

The first death is the physical death. The second is when you're forgotten about completely and, to all intents and purposes, cease to ever have existed at all. If Bishop Berkeley's logic of 'to be is to be perceived' is accurate, what happens when there is no-one around to bear witness? If the lights of the last city finally go out and no-one is around to see it, did it happen? Does the universe preserve some form of memory when all the relevant material is obliterated? It is our role to bear witness, to defeat the second death for as long as possible because we cannot halt the first? The photographer Roman Vishniac took 16,000 photos of Jews in Central and Eastern Europe, a now largely lost Ashkenazi world. He had them hidden (paralleling some of their real-life subjects) under floorboards in occupied Europe and sewn inside his clothes when he escaped to the US. It

---

43   *The Swerve* by Stephen Greenblatt, posits that forgotten manuscripts found in a German monastery from Ancient Greece kickstarted the Renaissance.

44   Pg. 200

is a miniscule consolation but the butchers who sought to totally erase these individuals have somehow not won completely.

In the long run, it may all be for nought. With the sun swelling to engulf the Earth and beyond that the universe fading towards heat death, all that we've known will evaporate. Jesus, Napoleon, Sappho, Mao, Picasso, Hitler, Joan of Arc, Alexander, Einstein, Homer and the Jolly Green Giant will all vanish[45]. Lyotard reiterates this: 'While we talk, the sun is getting older. It will explode in 4.5 billion years . . . In 4.5 billion years there will arrive the demise of your phenomenology and your utopian politics, and there'll be no one there to toll the death knell or hear it. It will be too late to understand that your passionate, endless questioning always depended on a "life of the mind" . . . With the disappearance of the earth, thought will have stopped — leaving that disappearance absolutely unthought of . . . if there's death, then there's no thought.'[46]

All true of course but what such views casually dismiss is that this takes place in the future, and we only ever occupy the present.

In the meantime, we are a resilient species[47] and even the grimmest apocalyptic literature assumes that some of us have survived and some semblance of progress, illusory or otherwise, is being crawled towards. From the ruins of Berlin, there emerged rubble literature ('Trümmerliteratur'). From

---

45   Along with everyone, including less western-centric choices.

46   Pg. 286-289

47   See the post-war photography of Jo Ractliffe.

Auschwitz, contrary to platitudes, there emerged the poetry of Celan and others. The servant, huddled from the rain under a crumbling Rashomon gate, does what he can to survive but survive he does, however inglorious. Humanity will leave traces of its cities not simply where they stand but as junk, orbiting the earth, littering the moon, spinning off into interstellar space as a record of songs (Blind Willie Johnson, Mozart, Aboriginal morning song) made of solid gold.

We will have as many endings as can be found. The young Expressionists of pre-war Berlin flirted gloriously with grand finales in their cabarets; the monstrous city-devouring forms of Georg Heym (who would die young trying to save a friend who had slipped beneath the ice on the frozen Havel) and the newsprint apocalypses of Jakob van Hoddis (who would lose his mind and eventually vanish into the death-camps). The end of the world does arrive, albeit selectively. Their friend Ludwig Meidner joined them with his paintings, bursting with colour and motion, barely contained by the picture-frames, premonitions of aerial attacks on cities. Their little movement would be consumed first by the Great War then the darkness which followed in Germany. In the early 1960s, a posthumous retrospective of Meidner's work took place at a gallery in the Ruhr. As it was being introduced, a small voice at the back piped up, 'It's me, Meidner! I'm not dead.'[48] Endings have a tendency towards impermanence.

The idea of cities will exist so long as there is a mind left to

48   *Art of the Twentieth Century*, Pg. 63

imagine them. The two are intricately linked: 'it is all dispersed within me,' Rilke wrote, 'the rooms, the staircases that descend with such elaborate ceremony, and other tight, spiral stairs where one passed through the dark as the blood passes through the veins; the rooms in the towers, the balconies hung on high, the unexpected galleries on to which one was thrust by a little door — all of these things are still with me, and will never cease to be in me.'[49]

The memories of what he'd seen and what he'd imagined never left Marco Polo. When Il Millione, the man of a million lies, was lying on his deathbed, a priest approached him and offered him absolution if he admitted his falsehoods. 'I did not tell half of what I saw, for I knew I would not be believed,'[50] he replied, and he took these secrets with him.

---

49   *The Notebooks of Malte Laurids Brigge*, Rainer Maria Rilke.

50   Cited Pg. 238, *Orientalism Revisited: Art, Land and Voyage*, Ian Richard Netton

For further material, full bibliography, acknowledgements and
recommended further reading, please visit:

www.imaginarycitiesbook.com

@Oniropolis

About the Author

Darran Anderson is a writer from Derry. He is former contributing editor to *3:AM Magazine* and *Dogmatika*. He has written the 33 1/3 study of Serge Gainsbourg's *Histoire de Melody Nelson* (Bloomsbury, 2013) as well as the forthcoming *Jack Kerouac − Critical Lives* (Reaktion Books) and *A Hubristic Flea* (3:AM Press, 2014). He has also written several collections of poetry including *Tesla's Ghost* (Blackheath Books, 2009). He regularly writes on art, literature and music for the likes of *Studio International*, *3:AM* and *The Quietus*.

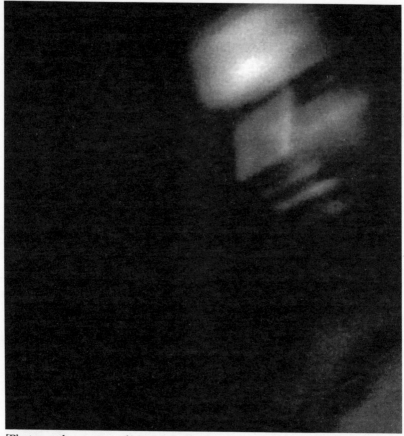

[Photograph courtesy of Nic McGuffog]

Influx Press is an independent publisher specialising in writing about place.

We publish challenging, controversial and alternative work written in order to dissect and analyse our immediate surroundings, to blur genres and to produce site-specific fiction, poetry and creative non-fiction.

www.influxpress.com

@influxpress